Shakespeare and His Contemporaries

Shakespeare and His Contemporaries

Jonathan Hart

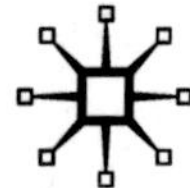

SHAKESPEARE AND HIS CONTEMPORARIES
Copyright © Jonathan Locke Hart, 2011.

First published in 2011 by PALGRAVE MACMILLAN® in the United States—a division of St. Martin's Press LLC, 175 Fifth Avenue, New York, NY 10010.

Where this book is distributed in the UK, Europe and the rest of the world, this is by Palgrave Macmillan, a division of Macmillan Publishers Limited, registered in England, company number 785998, of Houndmills, Basingstoke, Hampshire RG21 6XS.

Palgrave Macmillan is the global academic imprint of the above companies and has companies and representatives throughout the world.

Palgrave® and Macmillan® are registered trademarks in the United States, the United Kingdom, Europe and other countries.

ISBN: 978-0-230-10509-6

Library of Congress Cataloging-in-Publication Data
Hart, Jonathan Locke, 1956–
Shakespeare and his contemporaries / Jonathan Hart.
      p. cm.
   ISBN 0-230-10509-2
   1. Shakespeare, William, 1564–1616—Criticism and interpretation. I. Title.
PR2976.H363 2010
822.3'3–dc22   2010031397

A catalogue record of the book is available from the British Library.

Design by Scribe Inc.

First edition: March 2011

10 9 8 7 6 5 4 3 2 1

Printed in the United States of America.

Transferred to Digital Printing in 2011

For R. B. Parker

Contents

Preface and Acknowledgments

This book, like my other works, is meant for general readers, students, and scholars in the field. I have tried to make the writing accessible while attending to detail. Like its companion volume, *Shakespeare: Poetry, History, and Culture*, the book was written on and off over the course of thirty or so years perhaps something of a work of letters as well as scholarship. The newer scientific paradigm of literary criticism and theory can involve hastening into print to stake a claim. Here, I have revised some work and brought it together with unpublished work, much of it first written some time ago, sometimes given as a lecture, sometimes not. The chapter on dramatic history and parts in the middle of the book on Shakespeare's Second Tetralogy or major history plays are the origins of the book, then the chapter on Shakespeare's romance and Marlowe followed, and after the one on Greene's romance. The part on narrative and drama came after all this, and finally, a number of years later, the material on empire. On the whole, then, I left much of the material for well over a decade to see whether it should be brought into a book, which is the matter of letters and accessibility. Ultimately, I crafted a beginning, middle, and end and examined matters of beginnings and endings, history and story, showing and telling, past and present, narrative and drama, rhetoric and poetics, writing and reading, audience and reception. In bringing this together as a book, I have tried to add some notes to allow the reader to see some relevant work done in the field after the writing. In all this, I have attempted to pay attention to text and context, language and history, concerns I have had for a long time now. Earlier parts of some of the book have appeared in journals and volumes in Europe, India, Canada, and the United States, but some parts, for example the one about Greene's romance, appear here in print for the first time even if they were first created some time ago. Evidence is still a basis for my work, and I have decided to let this method stand, working from the text while looking outward when the work suggests that. As texts in this period are matters of editorial controversy themselves, with variants in spelling, lines, and scenes in places, I have not tried to standardize any of these, but have gone with the editions I used at the time.

Shakespeare and his contemporaries drew on a rich tradition, and they innovated. I have brought in the classical and medieval past as well as subsequent ages to try to illuminate these writers of the sixteenth and seventeenth centuries. Their use of language, genre, story, and history in dramatic and nondramatic works is full of innovation. Rabelais, Guarini, Shakespeare, Marlowe, Greene, Calderón, Cervantes, Molière, and others all work in a western European milieu and are rough contemporaries, and this is the spirit of my book. To make the greatness of Shakespeare and the expansion of England something seen in context, not to detract from them but to find a different focus, is one of the aims of this study. Here is my point of view to be shared with readers with many different views. As I said in *Shakespeare*, I am a reader reading or a viewer watching, a member of the audience being overheard. There are many admirable scholars to whom I owe a debt and without whom this book could not be written.

This book I dedicate with thanks to R. B. Parker, who taught me Shakespeare and American drama and was a guide and teacher who helped to inspire me to take up Shakespeare and write about him and especially his history plays. Brian Parker is a person of great talent and good humor.

As has often been said, the faults in a book are the author's. It is certain that I could not have written this or any other work without the kindness and support of many others. I have been fortunate in my teachers and mentors from an early age. In other Prefaces and Acknowledgments, I have thanked many, and here I express my gratitude to all those and others in particular and will focus more particularly on the Renaissance and criticism and theory. At the University of Toronto, I thank John Baird, Anne Lancashire, Jill Levenson, and Michael Sidnell and remember with thanks Ronald Bryden, Northrop Frye, David Galloway, John Margeson, Marshall McLuhan, and Sheldon Zitner. At the University of Alberta, I thank Linda Woodbridge, former department chair who hired me twice, and am grateful to Robert Rawdon Wilson and remember Milan Dimić, both of whom were responsible for encouraging my work on narrative and drama in the Renaissance. I also thank Nicole Mallet and remember John Orrell, for welcoming me to Alberta, and the many capable scholars in the Renaissance and express my gratitude to Ronald Ayling, for selecting me for the University of Calgary Exchange Lecture in 1985. Thanks also to Kerri Calvert, Gillian Edwards, Anne MacKenzie, Jennifer Thorn, and others at Alberta in the Research Office. At Calgary, I thank my hosts, especially James Black, Ronald Bond and Pamela McCallum. At Trent, I thank my colleagues, particularly Michael Peterman, and remember with fondness Michael Treadwell.

At Harvard, I thank Daniel Aaron, James Engell, Marjorie Garber, and James Simpson and remember with thanks Gwynne Evans, Barbara Johnson, and Harry Levin. More recently, my thanks to the chairs and colleagues in English and in Comparative Literature for welcoming me on a number of visits, including on two Fulbrights. At Fulbright, I thank many over the years including Victor Conrad, Alma Ford, Michael Hawes, Brad Hector, and Denise Yap. Kirkland House has welcoming me since I was a tutor there in the mid 1980s. I would like to thank the acting masters Hugh McKay and Elizabeth Gray as well as the masters, Donald and Cathleen Pfister and the current masters Tom and Verena Conley. The Conleys provided me with a community to go to Houghton to finish what I had worked on there decades ago. At Kirkland House, there are too many people to thank, but among the many are Diane Barrios, Stacey Dell Orto, Scott Haywood, and Linda Matarazzo. In English, my particular thanks to my host Gordon Teskey, for the most recent Fulbright visit this year. This book started in Toronto and migrated to Alberta and back to Toronto and Peterborough and to the universities at Cambridge, Princeton, Paris, and elsewhere. This study was punctuated by four term or year visits to Harvard from 1986 into 2010. The librarians at Houghton, Widener, and elsewhere at Harvard have been wonderful to me over the years, and I thank them all and in particular Susan Halpert. To the School of Criticism and Theory, then at Dartmouth College, my thanks, and there I remember with thanks Thomas Greene and Edward Said. At Cambridge, I have many people to thank, but here I also express my particular gratitude to Anne Barton, Philip Ford, Anthony Pagden, and Andrew Taylor. At Princeton, there are also too many to thank, but here I say thank you to Jeremy Adelman, Sandra Bermann, Anthony Grafton, Dale Miller, Kenneth Mills, and Nigel Smith. At the Sorbonne Nouvelle (Paris III), my particular thanks to Jean Bessière, Philippe Daros, Stéphane Michaud, and Alexandre Stroev.

Institutions, scholars, librarians, and other friends have been important to my work generally. Thanks, at various times of my tenure, to the provost and fellows of Trinity College, Toronto; the master and fellows of Massey College, Toronto; the president and fellows of Victoria University in the University of Toronto; the director of the Centre for Reformation and Renaissance Studies (Toronto); the master and fellows of Lady Eaton College, Trent; the co-masters of Kirkland House, Harvard; the provost and dean of arts at Alberta, the president and fellows of Clare Hall, Cambridge; the master and fellows of Wilson College, Princeton; the master and fellows of Churchill College, Cambridge; the president and professors of the Sorbonne Nouvelle. To the academic vice presidents and provosts of the University of Alberta, Peter Meekison, Douglas Owram, and Carl Amrhein, my thanks to them and our colleagues for their support of my teaching and research during the more than 25 years that I have been at Alberta. It has been a privilege to work there, and I prize the flexibility and kindness the university has shown me. English and Comparative Literature have been good homes.

My thanks to friends and colleagues who have made such a difference to me, most particularly Daniel Aaron, Alfred and Sally Alcorn, Catherine Belsey, E. D. Blodgett, J. Edward Chamberlin, Ross Chambers, Patricia Clements, Brian Edwards, Margaret Ferguson, Stephen Ferguson, Luis Galván, Robyn Gardner, Teresa Grant, Judith Hanson, Tom Healy, Shelagh Heffernan, Dolores Herrero Granado, Roland Le Huenen, Linda Hutcheon, Olaf Kaltmeier, Timothy Kilbourn, Wladmir Krysinski, Eva Kushner, Michèle Lamont, Maria Felisa López Liquete, Juliet McMaster, Stephen Mobbs, J. Hillis Miller, Kenneth Munro, Lenore Muskett, Thomas Pavel, Michael Pretina, Ricardo Quinones, Josef Raab, Harold Shapiro, Peter Sinclair, Irene Sywenky, Pauline Thomas, Sebastian Thies, Massimo Verdicchio, and Michael Worton. My thanks also to Cindy

Chopoidalo and Jane Wong at Alberta for help with the technical matters of the manuscript.

To the librarians at Toronto Reference Library, Toronto, Harvard, Alberta, Princeton, Cambridge, Oxford, the British Library, the Bibliothèque Nationale, and elsewhere, my thanks. For my hosts and associations where I lectured or participated in seminars about Shakespeare, theory, poetics, and the Renaissance, I thank the Shakespeare Association of America, the Renaissance Society of America, the Canadian Society for Renaissance Studies, the Pacific Northwest Renaissance Society, the Marlowe Society of America, the American Historical Association, the Modern Language Association of America, the American Comparative Literature Association, the Canadian Comparative Literature Association, and the International Comparative Literature Association, and my hosts at Oxford (Terence Cave and Nigel Smith), Wales (Catherine Belsey, Terence Hawkes, and Christopher Norris), Hull (Tom McAlindon and Roland Wymer), Southampton (Ken Hirschkop), Montpellier III (Jean and Angela Maguin), Birkbeck (Tom Healy), Saarlandes (Klaus Martens), Tartu (Jüri Talvet), the Estonian Institute of Humanities (Ülar Ploom),Utrecht (Hans Bertens), Bielefeld (Barbara Job, Josef Raab, and Sebastian Thies),Navarra (Luis Galván), the University of the Basque Country (María Felisa López Liquete), Zaragosa (Dolores Herrero Granado and Susana Onega Jaén), Sorbonne Nouvelle–Paris III (Philippe Daros and Stéphane Michaud), Ljubljana and Villenica (Vanesa Matajc, Darja Pavlič, and Gašper Troha), Institute for Slovene Literature and Literary Sciences (Marko Juvan and Jola Škulj), Koper (Andrej Blatnik, Krištof Jacek Kozak, Vesna Mikolič, and Marcello Potocco), Calgary (Ron Bond, James Ellis, Pamela McCallum, and Mary Polito), and Duke University (Gilbert Merkx, Jane Moss, John Herd Thompson); Cambridge and Harvard (my many hosts in the two Cambridges). To my hosts for talks in other related fields sponsored by or at Sangmyung University in Seoul and Cheonan, Hong Kong, Nanjing Normal in Nanjing, Melbourne, Deakin, Montréal, Toronto, Princeton, Yale, Brown, and elsewhere, I thank you for your many kindnesses. My gratitude also for fellowships from the Social Science and Humanities Council of Canada, and the Fulbright and the Carmargo Foundations, as well as visiting fellowships at Toronto, Harvard, Cambridge, Princeton, and elsewhere. Thanks also to the University of Toronto for granting me the honor of being the Northrop Frye Professor. To the editors and publishers of *Canadian Review of Comparative Literature/Revue Canadienne de la Littérature Comparée, CIEFL Bulletin, English, Language and Style,* Palgrave Macmillan and Taylor Francis go my thanks for publishing my work and for the permission and the courtesy to reprint earlier versions of material in the chapters (specific debts occur in the notes). My editor at Palgrave Macmillan, most recently, and Brigitte Shull, deserve praise and thanks. I also wish to thank Colleen Cantrell at Scribe and Lee Norton, Joanna Roberts, and Ciara Vincent at Palgrave. It has been a pleasure to work with Palgrave for so many of my books.

Thanks also to members of my family for their inspiration and support. I thank my father George and remember my mother, Jean. Many thanks to my brothers, Charles and Alan, and my sisters, Gwendolyn, Deborah, and Jennifer.

A particular debt to my wife, Mary Marshall, and our twins, Julia and James. I also thank my aunt, Helen Fitzsimon, and my cousin, Betty Bednarski, herself a literary scholar and translator, and remember my aunt, Nan Herman.

As I said in the preface to *Shakespeare*, I have set out some of the benefits in being slow to put this book together, my one regret is that I did not finish it earlier for those friends and family I have lost along the way. Sometimes an author feels like Falstaff, having much to say in his own defense, or Maurice Morgann, defending the "Courage and Military Character" of the fat knight with the American War of Independence swirling about him (Morgann, *On The Essay on the Dramatic Character of Sir John Falſtaff* [London: T. Davies, 1777], 1, see A). This book has been slow and wayward, so I hope that it may have slimmed down in penitence, while keeping some of its pleasures, and that some of the wait was worth it.

Introduction

Strictly speaking, William Shakespeare and his contemporaries means those who lived from some time in April 1564 to April 1616, old calendar, and in some senses this book adheres to that interpretation, but it also is more latitudinal in interpreting the word "contemporary." It stretches Shakespeare's intellectual contemporaries out into the Renaissance, those before and after him as well as those who were affected by the concentration on reconsidering the classical past. The study also flirts with the notion of Shakespeare as our contemporary, as Jan Kott once suggested.[1] Just as Shakespeare engaged with his past, we engage with him as part of our past. This creates the classical interpretative situation of past and present. We are not in the past but we are of it. Communication is both historical and transhistorical. We were not there for the first performances of Shakespeare's plays, but we have the traces of the performance texts in print. The plays were meant to be performed, but some were printed during Shakespeare's life and were intended to be read, so they have an oral and written dimension. We lose something and gain something.

Here, I center on Shakespeare while decentering him. The book begins not with Shakespeare and his sceptered isle of England, but with the expansion of England and with Shakespeare's contemporaries, Christopher Marlowe and Robert Greene, both university wits who had attended Cambridge. Shakespeare does not seem to have been at Oxford or Cambridge, although university training does not appear to have been necessary for success as a playwright.[2] Marlowe and Greene both died relatively young while Shakespeare made it into his early fifties. And Marlowe, who was very close to Shakespeare in age, was a great talent whose presence in poetry and drama Shakespeare could not help but notice. Greene, who carped about Shakespeare in a famous passage, provided source material and shared many interests with Shakespeare, including comedy in the widest sense and romance in particular. So the book begins with the halting course of empire, with the power of Spain in the expansion of Western Europe, and the relative vulnerability of England. There was no certain course that England would become Britain and create a British Empire, larger in land mass and extent than any empire before or since. That would be a teleological view that would read ahead by reading what we know backward into the minds of Shakespeare's predecessors, contemporaries, and successors.[3] The uncertainty that I am emphasizing qualifies the once traditional view of England and the Spanish Armada and how Shakespeare and his contemporaries from 1588 blossomed in the newfound confidence of English power and counterbalance to the greatness of Spain. While there is some truth to this flowering of English literature at this time and some of it might have derived from this confidence in the defeat of Spain in this one "battle," there is much more to it. It is difficult to say why some periods produce an efflorescence of creativity in literature and the arts. This is not really the question this book tries to answer. Instead, it takes some different vantages, with England gnawing at the edges of the Spanish Empire, and Shakespeare being deferred and then placed in conversation with writers in England and on the Continent in the sixteenth and seventeenth centuries. England is unto itself and not.[4]

The central concerns of my study are language, genre, drama, and literary and historical narrative. Within language, I focus on the connection between rhetoric and poetics, between presence and absence, how words call up worlds and also efface them, how they represent matters of life and death.[5] Marlowe's language is a good place to examine these dynamics. In genre, I focus a good deal on the wider vision of comedy, including what we consider to be prose romance and dramatic romance, and in those instances I concentrate on Greene and Shakespeare. Between these romantic bookends, I also analyze the comedy of Shakespeare and Ben Jonson in the context of some important plays from Italy, Spain, and France in the sixteenth and seventeenth centuries. My discussion includes romantic and satirical comedies. Shakespeare is European as well as English. I am also interested in the ways that writers represent stories about the past, how histories past and present work in different kinds of writing. History plays and prose histories may well depend on the historical dramatist being foremost a poet while also serving the role of historian. Narrative or stories in drama, a topic that has not received the attention it deserves, is a key subject in the book. I ask how narrative functions in plays and relate theory to practice, drawing on classical, Renaissance and later theorists. Since Greek drama, plays have used showing and telling to appeal to audiences, but sometimes the telling gets less notice. Dramatic history combines literariness and the craft of the historian, and what history is or what we think it is has shifted with the sands of historiography from Herodotus onward. By necessity, compression is a key to dramatic history, because plays tend to be brief compared to some prose histories. The invention of the poet, as Aristotle noted, distinguished him from the historian, who could not invent or rearrange events but had to follow what happened.[6] Shakespeare is one of the most read historical dramatists, and if we accept this genre of history writing as one of the many historians use, then Shakespeare is one of the most read and watched historians. Rhetorical history, or history as a literary art with narrative, and history as inquiry, as an analytical discipline, especially came into collision in the twentieth century. History as narrative, as an art, never left us, but it was under some pressure before its return in the past few decades. How one sees this debate and how scientific one thinks history is will affect one's view of whether Shakespeare can be a historian.[7] I think he is a historical dramatist and so is both even if some might think that history gets in the way of some of his dramatic power in the *Henry VI* plays and others might consider his drama blocking his way to the title of historian, as when he changes the age of Hotspur in the *Henry IV* plays for greater dramatic effect because they make him the young rival of Hal. It is also important to remember that there were many other authors of chronicle and history plays besides Shakespeare. Invention and tall tales and miraculous rebirth or regeneration become the stuff of *Cymbeline* and *The Winter's Tale*.

My examination of literary or dramatic texts begins with Christopher Marlowe, whose youthful language is like a force of nature. Its high astounding terms, its rhetorical power, create a great effect. His use of rhetoric, especially of apostrophe, can tell us a great deal about questions of absence and presence, which are so key to drama. Art and life deal with what once was and what might be, as well as what is. Across the genres, Marlowe's characters use language as a seduction or a weapon, as something overreaching itself and bumping up against its limits. Tamburlaine's address to the dead Zenocrate is a case in point. What is the relation of apostrophe to direct address and, by extension, of the living to the dead is one question that Marlowe seems to be raising. Word and world appear connected and disconnected. Like Shakespeare, Marlowe explores English history, and the language of *Edward II* makes its own contribution to historical drama and to historiography. Apostrophe, for Edward, creates a different characterization from the extended metaphor in prison that Shakespeare's Richard II makes. Edward's theatricality can be apostrophic and makes for a different form of self-regard. Paradoxically, like Faustus, Edward II moves toward the general, public, and impersonal through self-dramatization. The audience is carried away in the sweep of eloquence, but that eloquence can be suspicious of itself. Marlowe's language is a little like Helen's face in his famous speech.

Robert Greene is also a writer worthy of notice, although he does not have the linguistic verve of Marlowe. Greene's *Pandosto, The Triumph of Time* (1588), although a source of Shakespeare's *The Winter's Tale*, deserves close scrutiny on its own merits. This romance involves sympathy, estrangement, and supplement, so that this genre explores in its fabulous adventures the most important questions about art and about its relation to life. Paradoxically, romance is an escape from the world in order to see the world more fully. Although romance did not have the authority of Plato or Aristotle to legitimize it in the Renaissance, writers like Tasso and Cinthio elaborate on romance and heroic poetry. The divide between poetry and prose seems sometimes to create two solitudes in the world of romance. Greene, who wrote romance within a critical and poetic context, creates an interesting text in *Pandosto* partly because it exemplifies the intricacy of the best romances in their mixed representation of sympathy, alienation, and supplement.

Romance and comedy are kindred. Shakespeare appears here in a European context. I maintain that in Italian, Spanish, English, and French comedies of the early modern period, the way the plays end involves disjunction, stress, and rupture. Thus, while they represent a return to order, it is a restoration with loose ends. In this chapter, I concentrate mostly on two kinds. First, I discuss the "romantic pastoral," exemplified by Guarini's *Il Pastor Fido* (1590), Shakespeare's *As You Like It* (1599) and *Twelfth Night* (ca. 1600–1601), and Calderón's *No hay burlas con el amor* (ca. 1634–35). This last play I discuss at some length. Second, I briefly examine "satirical comedy," represented by Jonson's *Volpone* (1607) and Molière's *Tartuffe* (1664). I argue that these comedies constitute the poles of romantic comedy and romance (tragicomedy) and that of satire. As with romance, a flight from reality can be a way of examining reality more closely. Even in the most romantic of these comedies, there is some struggle and some elements of actuality.

Narrative in the drama has important dimensions in theory and practice. I shall consider the classical, medieval, and modern contexts for the Renaissance and also suggest that narrative in the drama possesses four primary functions. Exposition, suggestion, compression, and address are keys to dramatic telling. Exposition consists of commentary and explanation. Suggestion comprises description and reports of off-stage action. Compression involves action that would be protracted if represented. Address can be the speech of a chorus addressing the audience or another character. It can also include a character telling a story to another character with that character in mind or being overheard by the audience or another character. Each category is something I discuss as a way of clarifying the larger role of narrative in plays. I also analyze literary narrative and theories of narrative that are germane to a discussion of drama. Situation, presence, form, and social acts are all part of storytelling in history, literature and drama. The nature of diegesis and mimesis, of narrative and dialogue, becomes an element of my discussion. From Plato and Aristotle to Genette and Derrida, these aspects of story are important.[8] In the 1540s and 1570s, respectively, Robertello and Castelvetro discussed the role of imitation in drama. In the sixteenth and seventeenth centuries, Spanish, Dutch, English, and French writers and theorists also weighed in on the nature of drama and how it is constructed, which often means how much can be shown or told and what is the nature of verisimilitude. Choosing examples from plays, including Shakespeare's, I discuss the elements of narrative.

The relations among story, play and history are also suggestive. The questions of narrative and language are closely related. Language constitutes structure, and structure determines the difference between the representation of events and what happened. There is often a difference between how a tale is told or a play is presented and the sequence of events. The matter of story need not be solemn. Rabelais, Cervantes and Shakespeare provide instances of a ludic attitude toward narrative. Moreover, at the end of *Hamlet*, the dying prince asks Horatio to tell his story although the audience already knows it. This incident says much about the connection between narrative to drama. Shakespeare's Second Tetralogy— *Richard II, 1* and *2 Henry IV*, and *Henry V*—makes a vital contribution to history and the history play and does so with powerful telling and showing. Irony plays a role in this success. Irony of words, structure, and theatre are ways to an intricate representation of history.[9] Philip Sidney, Walter Ralegh, William Camden, and others also weigh in on the practice and theory of history. Genre becomes a significant aspect of representing the past. To Shakespeare's representation of history, we also contend with the representation of Shakespeare in subsequent times as part of culture history in England and in English.

Dramatic history challenges fictionality and historicity. Chronicle and history plays are fictional works in the pursuit of truth. Who interprets the past and how becomes a key issue, and the multiplicity of points of view in historical drama complicates this question. However significant Shakespeare's contribution to the history play, others also contributed much to create history on the stage in Renaissance England. The morality elements of humanist drama were refracted into chronicle and history plays. Whereas in John Skelton's *Magnyficence* morality figures are allegorical abstractions, in later history plays characters become more particular and historical. *King Johan, Respublica*, and *Gorbuduc* helped to make this transition. *Cambises* and *Richardus Tertius* (1579–80) also explore kingship, a theme that Marlowe and Shakespeare represent to great effect, and Shakespeare does so explicitly on many occasions. Irony and history are important concerns in chronicle plays by Elizabethan authors and not simply in Shakespeare's histories. In plays by Shakespeare's contemporaries from *The Famous Victories of Henry the Fifth* (ca. 1586–88) to *Woodstock* (ca. 1590–94), many themes, like kingship and rebellion, occur that also figure importantly in Shakespeare's historical drama. *The Troublesome Raigne of King John* (ca. 1588) shows how influential *Tamburlaine* was on the Elizabethan stage. Shakespeare's *1 Henry VI* (ca. 1590), which has its share of irony, benefits from being examined in the context of these other plays by his contemporaries. *Woodstock* represents kingship in relation to Richard II just as Shakespeare's eponymous play does, yet its representation provides another powerful but different views. Shakespeare explores the implications of the fall of Richard in the Second Tetralogy and beforehand when he wrote the end of the story with the decline and fall of Henry VI in the First Tetralogy. Marlowe explores history in *Dido, Queen of Carthage* and *Tamburlaine*, as well as in *Edward II*, although I am concentrating on English history in this book. In the first decade of the seventeenth century, Ben Jonson wrote *Sejanus* and *Cataline*, and, at his death, he left unfinished his only English history play, *Mortimer, His Fall*. Plays about history varied from Thomas Dekker's *Shoemaker's Holiday* (ca. 1600) to John Ford's *Perkin Warbeck* (ca. 1632–34). In the interim, Elizabeth Cary's historical plays, *Mariam* (1602–4) and *The History of Edward II* (1627), are noteworthy. History on stage is both exciting and precarious.

Shakespeare's art also extends from history to comedy and romance. In the First Folio (1623), seven years after the death of Shakespeare, John Heminge and Henry Condell divided the plays into comedies, histories, and tragedies and so did not recognize the category of romances for Shakespeare's plays. They placed *The Winter's Tale* under comedies but do not include *Cymbeline* in the volume.[10] In *Cymbeline* and *The Winter's Tale*, Shakespeare's self-conscious technique underscores wonder through the interplay of miracle and theatre. Although Aristotle does include estrangement in his notion of representation, Bertolt Brecht emphasizes alienation, and that is a theme I take up, a way to use twentieth-century dramatic theory to read Shakespeare. Brecht himself would have been influenced by Shakespeare, and it is not as if Shakespeare is a stranger to self-conscious theatricality, to the breaking of the illusion of the theatre. Shakespeare also denatures the naturalization of nature, as Roland Barthes does, and the meeting of past and present should help a reader from the late twentieth or early twenty-first century see an aspect of Shakespeare's romance more clearly. The dramaturgy of *Cymbeline* and *The Winter's Tale* shares some of the characteristics of the alienation effect of Brecht and the "double" sign of Barthes but with a difference. Ideology and historical context represent part of this difference. Shakespeare's critical estrangement calls attention to illusion. Both romances use their dramaturgy to make the audience critical of the relation of art and life and of the theatre itself. Through dramatic irony, these plays alienate the audience.

This book begins with the expansion of Europe in the world and with the tentative situation of England. This strategy estranges later times when the hegemony of English language, though British and American expansion, took hold from the defeat of Napoleon in 1815. The rise of Shakespeare, England, and English was not inevitable, and to read history forward as if backward was something I wanted to try to avoid. The power of Marlowe's dramatic language is another way of remembering that Shakespeare lived among great contemporaries and that the drama of Renaissance English and English literature would be remarkable without Shakespeare. Robert Greene's *Pandosto* was a source for Shakespeare's *The Winter Tale* but can also tell us about the way romance uncovers more about actuality by seeking to escape it. The ends of Renaissance comedy put the endings or goals of Shakespeare's comedies into a western European context. Shakespeare, the European, complicates Shakespeare, the Englishman. Mimesis includes telling as well as showing, so that the relations among theory, narrative, and drama are intertwined. In exploring genres in context, I call attention to history and the history play. In Renaissance England, histories are both stories and stories about the past. Historical drama is suggestive because of the way it calls attention to its fictional nature while also claiming the truth of history. In the next chapter, I turn to apostrophe as a telling trope, as an indicative strategy in language that gestures beyond itself in the range of Christopher Marlowe's plays. Although it is not possible to catch the astonishment that many members of the Elizabethan audience most probably felt in first hearing Marlowe's mighty line on stage, the shock of discovery of this hitherto undiscovered world made of his words can be partially imagined in remembering our first encounters with the plays. If this discovery can be imagined about four hundred years later, with all the flow of English between, imagine coming into that theatre in the 1580s and early 1590s for the first time. Perhaps in the boast of language then, Marlowe would seem less daring. Perhaps all the contemporaries and the members of the audience lived in a great age of innovation in the English language and might take this brilliance for granted, but even still there is something astonishing in the overreach of Marlowe.[11] By examining Marlowe's use of a trope in detail, I hope to help us to see the world in this grain of sand.

CHAPTER 1

England and Empire

Shakespeare and empire is a tale of the representation of Greece and Rome, of how the Roman Republic became the Roman Empire, how Roman Britain made its peace with Rome, how England expanded into France and contracted through civil war and other mishaps and how a shipwreck in the Virgilian mode in the Mediterranean became, through allusion and other means, a parable of the New World and the vexed nature not just of Bermuda but of colonies and empires. England and empire is something more.[1] Although I will concentrate most on the time between Shakespeare's birth in 1564 and his death in 1616, with a little blurring into the 1550s and into the 1620s and the age of the First Folio (1623), I will focus more on his "contemporaries" and place England in a wider context. Broader backgrounds will be unavoidable, but I will try to keep them to a minimum. Portugal and Spain were the examples of states that expanded beyond Europe, and England and France often tried to play catch-up with them. In this chapter, I will explore brief themes of empire as something suggestive and not in the more expansive ways I have in my books on empire and colonies, colonization and decolonization.

One of the important aspects of this chapter is that while the frame is roughly the lifetime of Shakespeare, it examines a context in the wider world of court, university, and colonies, where, unlike literature and theatre, he did not play a leading role. Before concentrating on Shakespeare increasingly at the end of the book, I seek to decenter him. What follows also attempts to decenter England by examining it in terms of its neighbors and Spain, the great power at the time, so that Shakespeare and his English contemporaries in drama and literature seem all the more remarkable as they are not at the center of Europe or the world and even within England, they do not hold sway in the powerful institutions of the law, universities and court.[2] The context of a changing world with an expanding view, which shrinks England and Europe, while attempting to extend it linguistically, culturally, and in other ways, is an exciting milieu for the travel, literary, and other texts that lie at the heart of this study.[3] Let us start with trade with Asia.

Backgrounds

The role of Columbus and other Spaniards in the western Atlantic is sometimes better known than that of the story of the Portuguese and Dutch in the age of empire.[4] The expansion to Asia was also key in the middle years of the sixteenth century. No power could defeat Portugal in the Indian Ocean, but the Chinese could in the China Sea. Nonetheless, they found it convenient, in about 1557, to permit a controlled Portuguese settlement near Canton at Macao. China, which had prohibited contact with Japan because of its piracy, could trade silks for Japanese silver. In 1571, the Japanese allowed the Portuguese to settle at Nagasaki. The Portuguese behaved as peaceful merchants rather than those who enforced trade with military power as they did in the Indian Ocean. They brought with them the Jesuits, who were involved in the trade between Nagasaki and Macao. The Spaniards, who in the wake of Columbus had crossed the Pacific from Mexico and established Manila during the 1570s, carried Dominican and Franciscan missionaries with them. By 1600, there seem to have been hundreds of thousands of Christian converts in Japan. In reaction, Japan expelled the Portuguese in 1639. Although Lisbon was the great European center for Asian trade, the distribution of these imports lay in the hands of the Netherlands. Owing to its experience in the fisheries of the Baltic and North Sea, the Netherlands had the largest merchant fleet in Europe.[5]

This relation between the Portuguese and Dutch became a cause for friction. King Sebastian of Portugal died during his invasion of Morocco in 1578. This death led to the union of Spain and Portugal under Philip II in 1580. The Spanish Netherlands fought for its independence at this time and sought the help of Elizabeth I of England. Even if Francis Drake sailed round the world in 1580 and James Lancaster searched out Portuguese ships to plunder and reached the northern part of Sumatra in 1591, the English did not do as much as the Netherlanders to challenge Portuguese trade in Asia. The Dutch had a long association with Portugal, so that they were able to use their maps and knowledge of sailing and this Asian trade to make inroads. This group included Catholics in the Netherlands who had served with the Portuguese in Asia. In 1595 the Dutch set out to Asia. By 1602, this commerce was important enough to set up the Vereenigde Oostindische Compagnie (the United East India Company). Perhaps sensing a threat to their Levant trade from the Dutch in the 1590s, the English formed the Company of Merchants of London Trading into the East Indies. Owing to the union of the Iberian crowns and the Dutch Revolt, a rivalry among the Portuguese, Spanish, Dutch, and English had arisen from political as well as economic pressures.

The English tried to protect their interests and keep up with their rivals. On December 31, 1600, Elizabeth I issued a charter for the founding of the East India Company. It had 218 subscribers and possessed a monopoly for English trade in Asia and the Pacific. The first four company ships left Woolich on February 13, 1601. They arrived in Bantam, which is now in Indonesia, on December 16, 1602, over five years after the first Dutch ship reached there. The ships returned safely to England by September 1603. James Lancaster had raided Portuguese ships in the early 1591 as far as Sumatra and his ship, along with a Dutch ship, fought and captured a Portuguese carrack in the Straits of Sumatra on October 3–4, 1602. The Portuguese and the Chinese traded in Bantam, which pepper had helped to develop. After landing that first time, the English rented accommodation in the Chinese quarter. Although the English first used Portuguese to communicate in the area, they soon switched to Malay, which the Chinese had used as the *lingua franca* in Southeast Asia before the arrival of the Europeans. *A true and large discourse of the voyage . . . to the East Indies* (1603) and *Dialogues in the English and Malay* (1614) were the first publications from the East India Company and were manuals to learn to trade in Malay. In looking back from a time in which English is a global language, it is easy but unwise to project this situation from the past and provide a kind of teleology that did not take into account the tentative and precarious situation of England and English before greater states and languages. Thus, it is important to remember that English was not a trading language in these and perhaps in any parts beyond the British Isles.

A number of voyages were made to Bantam thereafter. The voyage of 1612 was the most profitable with a return of 220 percent. The principal products of England were woolen broadcloth and lighter cloths like serges, kerseys, and baize. The merchants soon realized this merchandise would not be in demand in extreme climates. In *Discourse on Western Planting* (1584) Richard Hakluyt hoped for sales of woolen cloth to the Natives in Canada.[6] The East India Company soon learned that bartering Asian goods, especially Indian textiles, for other Asian goods was the most profitable trade. They sailed the first English ships to India in 1608. However, the Mughal governor at Surat was anxious not to anger the Portuguese. He thus ordered the departure of an English fleet in 1610. This action caused Sir Henry Middleton to intercept the annual Haj pilgrimage ships from Surat at the entrance to the Red Sea. To avoid the name of pirate, he forced an exchange of Indian cloth for broadcloth. In 1611, other ships opened relations with the other coast of India that was outside the Mughal Empire. In 1613, the East India Company opened a factory at Hirado in Japan. An English pilot, William Adams, sailed in 1598 with a Dutch fleet en route to Indonesia via the Straits of Magellan, and his ship alone reached Japan in April 1600. Imprisonment and interviews with the Shogun Ieyasu, through a hostile interpreter, a Portuguese Jesuit, João Rodrigues, followed, but in time Adams became a retainer of Ieyasu and replaced Rodrigues as official interpreter for Europeans in that region. He thereby helped the Dutch East India Company to set up a factory at Hirado in 1609 and was friendly to the English four years later. Adams died in Japan in 1620.[7] The Dutch were stronger than the Portuguese and English. In 1601, in the Bay of Bantam, they defeated a Portuguese fleet. The English found at Bantam and elsewhere that the Dutch had more money, ships, men, and purpose.[8]

Rather suddenly in the late sixteenth and early seventeenth century, the Netherlands became a European power and empire to be reckoned with. The Dutch, to control the fine spice trade in Asia, offered, through treaties, protection in exchange for a monopoly over the spices. They imitated the Portuguese example of Goa in India by establishing Batavia (now Jakarta) as a hub or rendezvous for its trade. The Dutch and English cooperated for a few years. However, in February 1623 the Dutch governor, Herman van Speult, put to death Gabriel Towerson, the English leader on Amboina, nine other company employees, nine Japanese samurai, and a Portuguese. A propaganda battle broke out between London and Amsterdam, and in England something akin to the Black Legend of the Netherlands developed for fifty years or more. One text that reflects this conflict is *A True Relation of the Unjust, Cruell and Barbarous Proceeding against the English.*[9] A comparative context shows that England had more rivals than Spain and that its language and culture, although important, were far from being central in trade and empire. Shakespeare was not the great poet of an imperial language in a preeminent power or empire. The year of the First Folio, seven years after his death, the Dutch were not afraid to challenge the English in Asia. Jamestown and the Mayflower should also be seen in this tentative light and not simply as harbingers to a great First British Empire or of the United States. The shadow of slave labor also began in other European colonies before Shakespeare died, but only a few years after his death did it begin, however haltingly, in English colonies. This would change the English-speaking world in ways whose wounds and scars are still healing.

Slavery

The kidnapping and treating of African people as chattel or beasts for labor without regard for their very humanity drove national and imperial expansion.[10] Legal and illicit trade was interwoven in this period, and this was also the case in slavery. Piracy was an ancient practice: it was always a part of commerce on the Atlantic. Even in the fifteenth century, French pirates benefited from Portuguese shipments. Jean Ango of Dieppe built ships for his king but also plundered for him when the opportunities arose with Portuguese and Spanish ships from Africa and Asia. Even a Portuguese, João Affonso, known in France as Jean Alfonse, sailed under a French flag to take advantage of this triangular trade between Africa, America, and Europe. The English and French traded goods with Africa as the Portuguese did. John Hawkins was interested in slaving: however, Elizabeth I wanted slaves taken only of their free volition because otherwise divine vengeance would punish those who did otherwise. Even this contradiction and ambivalence, as in the case of the Dutch, did not prevent slaving from proceeding. The queen herself came to invest in Hawkins' ventures. In 1572, black African slaves were sold for almost three times what Native slaves were bought for in Brazil. By 1580, the Spanish officials in Mexico and Peru (where the vast silver mine at Potosí was located) decided to feed Spain's hunger for precious metals with a flow of black African workers. In that year, the merger of Spain and Portugal under one crown meant that the Spanish acquired the Portuguese expertise in slaving and its trading posts in Africa.

For the next sixty years, Spain tried to keep foreigners, especially the Dutch and English, from its overseas trade. The Dutch Revolt meant a challenge to

Spain not just for independence but for commerce. As Portugal was joined with Spain through the Crown, the Netherlands attacked Iberian interests in Brazil as well as elsewhere. In the 1590s, Amsterdam and Middelburg refused to allow Dutch ships to trade in slaves in their ports. By 1600, the Dutch carried about half the goods from Brazil to Europe. In time the Dutch settlements in Brazil started to import slaves. The French, too, had early scruples about trading in slaves: during the 1570s, a court in Bordeaux forbade trading slaves there. But France also gave into the temptation of slavery.

Slavery was long part of the Iberian trade that the French and English disrupted. In 1545, Pierre Crignon wrote a discourse about Jean Parmentier, a sea captain from Dieppe, and described Norumbega, which he said was discovered by Verrazzano 15 years before. In *La Cosmographie*, Jean Alfonse, Roberval's pilot, enhanced Crignon's description of Norumbega, but in his *Les voyages avantureux* (1559), a work on navigation, Alfonse thought that it was illegal to reduce the indigenes to slavery because they were delicate: "The men of this land of Peru are small, feeble and good. But the Spaniards mistreat them and make them their slaves."[11] In addition to the Spanish involvement with slavery, the Portuguese were involved in the black African slave trade in the fifteenth and sixteenth centuries and beyond. The Portuguese, according to André Thevet, altered their tactics when French corsairs and English privateers attacked a caravel, which had slaves as a crew.[12] This is the context for Nicolas Durand de Villegagnon's voyage to Brazil in 1555. Jean de Léry commented on the monopoly that Portugal and Spain held so dear, the Spanish and Portuguese claiming to be the lords of the countries whereas the French maintained and defended themselves valiantly.[13] If Portugal had rivals to its power, so too did Spain.

The Netherlands rebelled against Spain in 1568, and the rebellion occurred on and off for eighty years. In the final years of the sixteenth century the Dutch attacked Iberian colonies. When Spain and Portugal were united under Philip, the arrangement prohibited Spaniards from settling or trading in the Portuguese Empire and the Portuguese from doing the same in the Spanish Empire. This long colonial war against the Netherlands was for the sugar trade in Brazil, the slave trade in West Africa, and the spice trade in Asia. The Portuguese won the war in Brazil, drew in West Africa, and lost in Asia.[14] The Portuguese contested first with France and then with the Netherlands.

Various empires vied for the possession of key overseas territories. Each empire used various ceremonial means of possessing territories. The French and English still occupied and wanted to occupy the lands of the Natives, something that, with good reason, met with resistance, even as they differed from more horrific forms of Spanish possession. The one Las Casas focused on was the *Requerimento*, or Requirement, which traced the history of creation, gave the grounds for Spanish possession, and threatened the Natives in a language they could not understand with enslavement and loss of their lands if they resisted.[15] The Natives of the New World were attacked, displaced, and enslaved.

In the seventeenth century the slave trade in the English, Dutch, and French colonies had ambivalent beginnings, as people favored and opposed it. Early on, the Dutch had also been weary of or had opposed the slave trade with Africa. In 1596, the city fathers in Middelburg had freed a hundred slaves brought as cargo there and in 1608, Usselincx had opposed the use of black slaves in Dutch America. A Dutch ship brought twenty black slaves to Virginia in 1619, perhaps having captured them through piracy from a Portuguese slaving ship. Like sugar before it and cotton afterward, tobacco came to rely on slave labor. Conquest has many sides and representations in the public and private realms.

Images, Maps, and Sex

Conquest is an old theme of empire.[16] The conquest, portrayed in Jan Mostaert's *A West Indian Scene* or *West Indian Landscape* (ca. 1540–50), was first mentioned in *Het Schilder-boeck* (Alkmaar, 1604) by Carel van Mander, a painter and art historian. This painting, which placed the Natives in the foreground and pushed the Spanish off to one side (the right hand), invites the viewer to observe the naked Natives fighting with the armed Spanish in full armor. It is quite possible, as Hugh Honour suggests, that Mostaert is using parallels here between the Spanish advance in the New World and that in the Netherlands.[17] The painting may encourage the viewer to take sides with the Natives and with the Netherlands against Spain at the height of the Dutch Revolt, but this invasion may be an intrusion into an Ovidian golden age. Ambivalent tensions occurred between positive and negative representations of Europeans and Natives in visual images of the New World.

Maps could also show the power of Spain. There was, for instance, one apparently made for Mary Tudor in the 1550s that displayed the extent of the empire over which her husband, Philip II, reigned. This map derives from an atlas of nine maps: one of the maps represented the British Isles with a shield that bears the arms of Philip II impaling those of Mary I. Diogo Homem's map of the world, which bears the royal arms of England, divided overseas possessions between Spain and Portugal as they were determined by the Treaty of Tordesillas during the 1490s, a division that Spain insisted be respected long after.[18] A joint Spanish and English rule at home and overseas was a possibility and something that Richard Eden advocated in the 1550s. The greatness of Spain was also a matter of reach, overreach, and hubris. In Bernardo de Vargas Machuca's *Milicia y Descripcion de las Indias* (Madrid, 1599), there is an image of a conqueror who rests his left hand on his sword and his right on a compass that divides the world. At the bottom is a message: "Ala espada y el compas / Mas. y mas. y mas. Y mas" (With the sword and the compass / More. And more. And more. And more).[19] In time, England would come to this point. For a long time, the printing of travel narratives in English was not viable.[20]

Ambivalence was common in the reactions to Spanish colonization of the New World. In the middle of the sixteenth century, the English and French continued to see Columbus and Spain as a model for colonization in the Americas. In 1555, Richard Eden, who had proclaimed: "The Spanyardes haue shewed a good exemple to all Chrystian nations to folowe," justified the gold and God of empire.[21] In France, André Thevet's *Universal Cosmography* (1575) derived from his experience with Villegagnon in Brazil and represented Spain in a positive light.[22] The Spaniards were the first to discover Peru and to see "the way of life of these poor barbarians and Savages, cruel through and through, and without civility, not more than beasts."[23] The first part of Martin Fumée's French translation of Gómara's *La Historia* in 1578 described Columbus, his enterprise, and Hispaniola.[24] Urbain Chauveton was critical of Spanish abuses in the New World.[25] Chauveton's summary described Benzoni's account of the Spanish, "that is to say judgements of God on the head of those who have oppressed this poor people."[26] In 1589 Richard Hakluyt's *The Principall Navigations* included a map between the "To the Reader" and the dedicatory poems in Greek and Latin, which records that America was first detected by Columbus in 1492 in the name of the king of Castile.[27] John Smith fashioned himself on the heroic model of Cortés and commended Columbus and Queen Isabella for having the vision to back him but could proclaim, "And though I can promise no Mines of gold, yet the warlike Hollanders let vs imitate, but not hate, whose wealth and strength are good testimonies of their treasure gotten by fishing."[28] The rehashing of the origins of America and the first European contact with it occurred in French and English writing from the sixteenth century onward. The figure of Columbus, and later Las Casas, became part of the French and English archive of the Americas. Moreover, the revisiting of origins to the right to settle the New World was something that the French and English felt compelled to repeat. Certain traumatic events recurred. Columbus' discovery of the New World, the papal donation of the new lands to Spain and Portugal, the first meetings of Natives and Europeans, the death of the Huguenots in Florida, the revolt in the Netherlands, the Spanish Armada came up over and over in the French and English writings about the New World.[29]

Walter Ralegh, in his *Discoverie of Guiana* (1596), suggested that England emulate, rival, and displace Spain in parts of South America. Near the end, when Ralegh attempted to make a final rhetorical appeal to Elizabeth I to back a conquest, he brought the ancient lost opportunity that Henry VII had to employ Columbus in his enterprise: "The West Indies were first offered to her Maiesties Grandfather by Columbus."[30] Henry's lost chance to have backed the enterprise of the Indies and the "discovery" of America comes up. This regret over Henry VII not having Columbus in his service is a much-rehearsed regret in the annals of the English colonization of America.[31] Ralegh's book concentrated a good deal on the power and riches the Spaniards reaped in the New World and what that did to the balance of power in Europe. England should emulate Spain to rival it in South America. It was time for an English Columbus, for Ralegh. Although Ralegh identifies himself with Columbus, he also distinguishes himself from him when he wants to minimize the risk for Elizabeth. Whereas Columbus discovered new lands, Ralegh was in a region already discovered, so that this involved less risk and the Natives were a known quantity and could be used to subvert the seemingly invincible Spaniards. Ralegh had already presented Guiana as a virgin land that, in a twist, the Virgin Queen is to enter.

Besides the pleasures of the flesh was the disgust over the eating of flesh. Columbus comes back to cannibals over and over again in his texts. Jean de Léry set out a typological view of such flesh eating between the New World and civil war France.[32] Some texts show a fear of sodomy while a lust for and fright of women happens in a number of the works. Other works suggest an alternative or opposition to such a view. As in Shakespeare's poetry, an erotics or the rhetoric of seduction occurs, and in the process the reader then and now may well become implicated in what is put on display.[33] The act of reading or viewing may become part of seduction. There is a fine line between the exotic and the erotic, between the world and the imaginary. The fantastic calls up short the real.[34] The seduction of expansion could also include the mixing, reversal or overturning of sex roles, suggesting intricate motives. Amazons, cannibals, and sodomites were images and "asserted realities" in the dreams and texts for at least a century after Columbus and in the time of Shakespeare.

There were figures of Amazons long before the birth of Columbus or his landfall in the Caribbean. The myth of the Amazons derives from classical antiquity. In Book 6 of the *Iliad*, Hercules and Bellerophon fought against them. Herodotus discussed them in Book 4 of the *Histories* and described how the Amazon mothers burn the right breast of their daughters with a copper device, a practice that helped their archery.[35] As in many areas concerning the New World, the Portuguese and Spanish developed their textual archive before the French and English. One such important instance is Antonio de Herrera's description in his account of Francisco de Orellana's journey down the Amazon river.[36] Another account of the Amazons took place in Father Cristoval de Acuna's "A New Discovery of the Great River of the Amazons," which is quite different from Herrera's report.[37] The real villains of the piece, for Acuna, are the Portuguese men, not the Amazons. Acuna told of Portuguese abuse of the "Indians."[38] Acuna then referred to "the cruelty of the Portuguese" twice and asked the Spanish king to restore peace to the land that was so troubled by the cruelty, and tyrannical rule, of the Portuguese.[39] This is a similar argument to the one Ralegh would later use to move Elizabeth to action against the "cruel" Spaniards in Guiana.

Visual representations of America as woman also complicate the sexual representations of this New World. The title page of Abraham Ortelius' *Theatrum Orbis Terrarum* (Antwerp, 1570) is an allegorical depiction of America, who is a naked woman in the foreground. Philippe Galle, a Flemish artist, produced an American allegory from circa 1579 to 1600 that is of a naked and armed Amazon carrying the head of a man, and he engraved an image about 1580 that contains a woman with a club, who is situated at the center of a variety other creatures, human and nonhuman, in the New World.[40] The Galle engraving also includes an inscription describing America as a female glutton who devours men. There were also significant images like *Vespucci Discovering America* by Jan van der Street, called Stradamus, in pen and ink in 1589; Plaquette's *America*, produced in Germany circa 1580 to 1590 in lead with gilt; *America* by Marcus Gheerarts, an engraving about 1590 to 1600.[41] There are also many representations of America as a woman in different contexts. The first painting of America as woman occurred in 1574. It is in a fresco at the palace, built for Cardinal Alessandro Farnese, at Caprarola, near Rome. Giovanni de' Vecchi represented the Western hemisphere of a world map with allegories of the continents (1574). Jost Amman, a Swiss artist, produced four prints of the four continents as landscapes with figures (1577). Maarten de Vos' (1594) sketch was commonly copied for over a hundred years.[42] The range of sexual representations of America is wide, from the erotic and violent representations of Amazons and cannibals to images of America as a woman and to anxieties over sodomy.

Spain and the Black Legend: An Overview

Anxiety over Spain or an accommodation of it was a key to Elizabethan and Jacobean England. One aspect of that context was the "Black Legend" or "La Leyenda Negra." This legend may have developed in the reaction of Italy to Spanish hegemony or in Reformation Germany, or grown out of the encounter with the New World and the Wars of Religion in the sixteenth century, or begun with William of Orange's *Apologia* (1580) in response to Philip II's ban or proscription of the leader of the revolt in the Netherlands.[43] The charges against Philip in the Netherlands came to be applied to Spain as a nation in its policy there and also in connection with its role in the Inquisition and in the conquest of America.[44] Bartolomé de Las Casas played a central role in this legend as the French and English translated his work at times of crisis from 1579 onward. He is controversial because he is often praised for his representation, or is blamed for his misrepresentation, of Spanish colonization in the New World. Other countries translated Las Casas and used his work to build anti-Spanish propaganda. At first, the French and English sought to imitate Spain but then, along with the Dutch, they drew on writers like Las Casas to develop the Black Legend of Spain. Lewis Hanke, for instance, tried to stress this penchant of the Spanish for self-criticism.[45] French and English writers advocated attacks on Spain and its displacement, a good example of which was Philippe Du Plessis-Mornay's *Discours . . . sur les moyens de diminuer l'Espagnol* (1584).[46]

The translation of study was part of the translation of empire. In 1603, Michel de Montaigne's English translator, John Florio, asked whether he should apologize for translation, which gave birth to all science, while still upholding the name of the Greeks.[47] The translation of influence from the Spanish to the French and English can be seen in Montaigne's relation to the Spanish and in Florio's translation of Montaigne into English.[48] For Florio, translation moved knowledge from the universities into the commons, which was a good process.[49] The world of the western Atlantic was new to Europeans but not to the Natives.

The Protestants in Europe faced a strong Catholic Spain. Nicolas Le Challeux's account of the Spanish massacre in Florida was a turning point in representations of the Spanish in Europe. It analyzes the praise for Spain in England during the reign of Mary. It is the first important French description of Spanish cruelty in the New World. The anti-Spanish tracts of the 1560s and 1570s to the narratives leading up to the Armada (1567–88) were also part of the age of

Shakespeare. An intensification of rivalry with Spain when both France and England were trying to expand and establish colonies until the end of the first decade of the seventeenth century. The ascension to the throne of Henry IV in France and the appearance of Richard Hakluyt's *Principal Navigations* in England occur when Shakespeare was writing his history plays. Ambivalent and contradictory representations of Spain in the New World were not—as in Marc Lescarbot's *L'Histoire de la Nouvelle France* (1609)—simply a matter of religion. Once France and England established permanent colonies in the New World and Spain began to decline in this period (especially after the death of Shakespeare), the sustained intensity of anti-Spanish sentiment abated into periodic eruptions of the Black Legend of Spain. The years 1554 to 1608, but particularly up to 1588, the defeat of the Armada, were crucial because after the French and English established permanent colonies and Spain began to decline and collapse, the representations of Spain were not as concentrated and as extensive. The French and English texts about the New World, travel and expansion in the 1550s through to the early years of the seventeenth century were obsessed with Spain. These texts were advocating emulation of its power to create American colonies while also finding it to be a block to the ambitions expressed in English and French works. Once England and France had a foothold in North America and established spheres of influence, the problems of origins, legitimacy, and rivalry continued but were less pressing.

The 1550s and 1560s

Between the publication of Thevet's *Singularitez* (1557) and *Cosmographie* (1575), the French tried and failed to establish permanent settlements in Florida, which the Spanish claimed for their own. The first French voyage under Jean Ribault in 1562 was a failure partly because the French depended on the Natives, who came to resent them, rather than on farming. The second voyage under René Goulaine de Laudonnière in 1564 did not succeed because the settlers dreamed of riches, became involved in the wars of the Natives, traded guns to them, and practiced piracy against the Spaniards in the Caribbean. The third voyage under Ribault reinforced the settlers with laborers, artisans, and soldiers but was primarily a military venture to attack Spanish commerce in the West Indies. This voyage failed because a storm drove Ribault's fleet off course as he was attacking Pedro Menéndez de Avilés, who had been sent to battle the French. Avilés later massacred 132 French at Fort Caroline. He may have tricked Ribault into surrendering so he could kill him and his men.[50] Menéndez, who had Philip II's approval, seemed to have thought that he had saved the West Indies for the Spanish by preventing Ribault from joining forces with the Huguenot pirate, Jacques de Sores.[51] There were Huguenot pamphlets against Spain at this time. Dominique de Gourgues, a French Protestant noble, raised volunteers and in 1568 took two Spanish forts in the New World and hanged his prisoners in a similar fashion to the way Menéndez had the Huguenots.[52] The massacre of the Huguenots helped to turn English opinion against the Spanish and motivate the

English seadogs and the intervention of England in America.[53] This piracy had a long history. French privateering intensified and led to the burning of Havana in 1555. The massacres in the 1560s were a continuation of this conflict between the French and Spanish, a struggle in which the English became involved.

On the fourth voyage, led by Jean Ribault, Nicolas Le Challeux, one of the survivors of the slaughter, acted as the chronicler.[54] At the opening of *The Whole and True Discovery of Terra Florida* (1562), Ribault said that the admiral (Coligny, the Huguenot leader) had long wished for the day when France could make new discoveries and find regions full of riches and commodities. The massacre of the French in Florida in 1565 evoked a strong reaction in France. The Spanish failure to conquer Florida seems to have created a vacuum for the French. Various editions of Le Challeux's text appeared in 1566, with and without the additional request to the king for redress.[55] Le Challeux included an appeal to emotion also represented the Spanish as contravening the authority of the king of France, a loss and wrong to all the kingdom.[56] Le Challeux's book pointed a lesson: we should not be carried away by our desires for those things God forbids.[57] Not once here, where rhetoric and polemic might demand it, did Le Challeux talk about the Spanish, let alone vilify them, and his eight-line poem did not mention Spain but concentrated on the personal journey of the author.[58]

In 1566, *A true and perfect description, of the last voyage or Nauigation, attempted by Capitaine Iohn Rybaut, deputie and generall for the French men into Terra Florida, this year past. 1565. Truelly sette forth by those that returned from thence, wherein are contayned things as lamentable to heare as they haue bene cruelly executed* appeared in London. The title of Thomas Hacket's translation of Le Challeux emphasized the cruelty the French suffered without naming the Spanish perpetrators. The speed of this translation showed how much interest in these events there was in England. As Jean Ribault's account exists only in the English, which Hakluyt later published, and Laudonnière's *L'Histoire notable de La Floride . . .* was published in Paris in 1586, Le Challeux's narrative was the one that made an immediate impact in the French-speaking world.[59] Hacket's English translation added at the end of his English edition a moral about covetousness and a prayer that God keep England from "murther and bloudeshedde" that did not appear in the French original.[60] The events in Florida and the ways in which the French and English represented them were instrumental in developing a rhetoric of blame against the Spaniards, but they did reserve some doubts about their own designs on the New World. A typology between the New World and the Old began to take hold. If the Spaniards had behaved cruelly in the Americas, then they would do the same in Europe. The suffering of the French in Florida would give the English ground on which to use Las Casas' descriptions of Spanish cruelty against the Natives in the New World and to raise the alarm against Spain's actions in the Netherlands.

The events in Florida moved Protestants in France and England to protest against the Spanish.[61] France's failure in Brazil led them to seek success in Florida. In *Les Singvlaritez*, Thevet gave his account of his voyage to Brazil with Villegagnon in 1555, including his preference for the religion of the Natives, who recognized the eternal God, and the Protestants.[62] Apparently, Elizabeth I and Hawkins were playing both sides of the French and Spanish rivalry in order to give England an entry into the West Indian trade. They would learn over the next year, however, that Spain would not tolerate an English intrusion any more than a French incursion. Later, Elizabeth I's letter to Mendoza, the Spanish ambassador, would show that she was not interested in abiding strictly by the papal rules of empire.[63] The vision Richard Eden had expressed in the 1550s of Spain and England building an American empire together was something that would appear increasingly fantastic just over a decade afterward.

During much of the sixteenth century, England had sought a foreign policy that would guarantee its own independence. This policy relied on three factors. First, England developed sea power to protect its coast. Second, it sought to neutralize Scotland and Ireland. Third, it worked for a balance between France and Spain, so that the one would defend England if the other attacked it.[64] Although Spain and England were divided by religion, the Spanish often sought good relations with England. Spain sometimes wanted a balance against France. The *Empresa de Inglaterra*, or the enterprise of England, had religious as well as economic and political dimensions. This enterprise involved a Catholic power fighting with a Protestant country, but Philip II had strained relations with the papacy after the election of Sixtus V. Philip had not given unconditional support to putting Mary Stuart on the throne as he feared that the Guise and France would control her. He resisted the excommunication of Elizabeth I. Moreover, Philip refused to permit the excommunication of 1570 to be published in all his territories.[65]

Until the 1560s, France was an ally to Scotland and was the greatest threat to England. But Spain replaced France in that role. With the ascension of Elizabeth I, England made its final break with Rome. This division rendered relations with France and Spain difficult and helped create more friendly relations with Reformed Scotland. In 1567, Spain sent an army into the Netherlands to crush the rebels and Protestantism. This action also damaged England's most lucrative overseas market. When the English sought alternative markets, they came up against Spanish power. At the end of 1584, the secret Treaty of Joinville meant that the Catholic League became a dependent ally of Spain. Thus, France could not pursue her policy of balancing the power of Spain. In August 1585 by the Treaty of Nonsuch, Elizabeth I committed seven thousand troops to protect the Netherlands. A clash occurred between England and Spain in 1588.[66] The fear of Spain and the Catholic League in France had already helped to turn up the anti-Spanish and pro-Huguenot rhetoric in England. This turn can be observed from the translations of narratives concerning the Spanish massacre of the French Protestants in Florida from the 1560s to Richard Hakluyt the Younger's *Western Discourse* in 1584.

Through their written accounts, explorers and pirates like Hawkins and Gourges justified their actions, the one for breaking Spanish laws and the other for wreaking revenge on Spain. English and French narratives were instrumental. Their ends were often political and economic, even as they protested motives of religion and liberty.[67] Hawkins and Martin Frobisher were involved in the war against Spain.[68] The English thought they could balance Spain and France to gain entry into the slave trade or piracy in the West Indies. In 1567 John Hawkins made yet another slaving voyage, taking his cargo of five hundred Africans from Sierra Leone to the Spanish Main.[69] Hawkins' account in 1569 was like Le Challeux's narrative about Florida. Both were about failure and martyrdom in the face of Spanish reprisal and cruelty.[70] The English had learned a similar lesson to the French: Spain would not tolerate piracy or trade that encroached on its monopoly in the New World. That lesson was something the Huguenots would not accept, so that they concentrated on the Spanish cruelty. In 1568, the *Histoire memorable de la reprinse de L'Isle de la Floride*, by Dominique de Gourgues or one of the members of his mission in Florida that avenged the death of Ribault and his compatriots, appeared. The *Histoire memorable* began with a claim that the French had discovered Florida, sent men and women to settle it and soldiers to guard them under the charge of captains Ribault and Laudonnière. The French had built a fort and cultivated the earth, but the Spanish were jealous and murdered them.[71] This narrative alluded to Le Challeux's description of the inhuman cruelties of the Spaniards. The account told the story of Gourgues and how in April 1568 he set out to avenge this massacre. He had to convince the Natives that he was not Portuguese or Spanish, and the French sang psalms to prove it.

Discovering a sea route to Asia was one way the English thought they could challenge Spain. The dream of a northwest passage continued to motivate the English. Humphrey Gilbert took an active interest in reviving interest in discovering that route to Asia, which John Cabot had kindled. In 1566, Gilbert petitioned the queen for the right to discover it and for a monopoly in the passage.

The 1570s and 1580s

Many of those who supported such a northwest venture—Gilbert, Martin Frobisher, Henry Sidney—were in Elizabeth's service in Ireland.[72] Ireland was, for Protestants, like Florida—a place to colonize.[73] Ireland was a testing ground for expansion for England. Humphrey Gilbert was an important figure in the renewed strategy of exploring a northwest passage as a route to China in order to challenge Spain. Composed in 1566 but printed in 1576, Gilbert's *Discourse of a Discoverie for a New Passage to Cataia* was an attempt to have the queen give him permission to sail in search of this passage and for a monopoly there. However, Gilbert's efforts to that end were unsuccessful. Gilbert revised *Discourse* considerably after his return from Ireland in 1570.[74] The question of first contact and the origins of discovery arose once again. Gilbert attributed the discovery of America at least as far back as Pliny. This origin would undermine the claim of Spain to America.[75]

Before Martin Frobisher's first voyage, the state papers included a document, a brief *summa avant la lettre* of Hakluyt's *Discourse* that set out an English colonial policy that sanctioned the discovery of lands that were unoccupied, the use of the commodities found there, and the spread of the Christian faith in that territory.[76]

This document suggested that the queen take up the lands toward the South Pole, which no other countries had possessed or subdued, so that providence had given the Spanish the west, the Portuguese the east, and the English the south and would allow England to bring "in grete tresure of gold, sylver and perle."[77] During the 1560s, the French and the English almost seemed ready to join forces in Florida against Spain. In the 1570s, this anonymous advisor was trying to have Elizabeth's government use Florida and the voyage of Hawkins, which wavered between slaving for the Spanish and pirating with the French, as precedents to trading and settling in the New World.

Like Gilbert and the anonymous advisor, Frobisher represented the challenge to Spain in the New World. His first expedition departed England on May 15, 1576, part of the search for a northwest passage preoccupied the English, French, Spanish, and Portuguese after John Cabot's voyage in 1497. England was trying to reestablish itself in the northern part of America, which it had been instrumental in calling attention to the rest of Europe and whose example in this context the western European powers had followed. The English had been quite negligent in and about Newfoundland and had lost their advantage to other nations, particularly France. In October 1576, Frobisher returned to England. He seems to have thought that he had found the northwest passage, bringing with him an Inuit, and having discovered what he considered gold. The hope was not for markets for English wool and merchandise but "an arctic Peru."[78] Frobisher's second voyage, which set out on May 26, 1577, had a chronicler in one of the participants, Dionyse Settle, author of *True Reporte of the Laste Voyage into the West and Northwest Regions* (1577).[79] Settle's "Epistle to the Christian Reader" called the English to the conversion of the Natives and recommended that England look for a northwest passage.[80] In *A True Discourse* (1578), an account of the three voyages Frobisher made, George Beste addressed a dedication to Sir Christopher Hatton, a member of the Privy Council.[81] The anxiety of origination continued to afflict the English when they were under pressure to compete with the exploration and riches of Spain and Portugal. Settle was translated into French in 1578, Latin and German in 1580, and Italian in 1582. Translation went both ways between England and the Continent.

When in 1580 Francis Drake returned from his circumnavigation, his ship was full of Spanish gold. He came home to a nation with factions for and against Spain. In Thomas Nicholas' translation of Augustín de Zárate's *Discovery and Conquest of the Provinces of Peru* in 1581, there was praise for Drake. Nicholas saw Drake as an example for the English to rival Spain in the context of conquest, gold, and silver.[82] During this period, Gilbert and Hakluyt the Younger thought that North America would provide bases against Spain, a policy that Coligny had tried during the 1560s.

Translations were a primary means for the French and the English of learning from the Spanish. Although the work of Las Casas is the central example of a translated text, many translations affected England and France in their rivalry with Spain. The translation of empire and the translation of study, narrative and technology coexisted. The Revolt of the Netherlands provided a background to the typology of Spanish cruelty in the New World and in the Netherlands that is best exemplified in Cloppenburch's volume (including Miggrode's translation of Las Casas), *Le Miroir De la Tyrannie Espagnole Perpetree aux Indies Occidentales* (1620). It is quite possible that Jacques de Miggrode, the translator of Las Casas, was Flemish. These groups were using the texts of Spaniards, like Las Casas, and of others, like Benzoni, who worked in the Spanish colonies, as testimony of Spanish cruelty.

During the 1570s and 1580s, the Black Legend of Spain took off in both France and England. The growing body of translations concerning the New World that the French and English produced, which was part of their growing production of texts generally about the New World, may have arisen from a growing sense that they should challenge Spanish hegemony in the western Atlantic. Although these translations served as a means of gaining information about Spain and about the New World generally and as a weapon in a war of propaganda, they had more varied functions. The French and the English also translated each other's works, so that they were supports and rivals in their challenge to Spain. Hacket published his third translation on the New World, his English version of Thevet's *Les Singularitez de la France Antarctique*, dedicated to Henry Sidney, lord deputy of Ireland and lord president of Wales. With this book, English readers seem to have had their first comprehensive view of the New World, a claim that may well have been true for a unilingual readership. Although Richard Eden's translations had been informative, they had not covered the ground from the East Indies to Newfoundland. Martin Frobisher took Hacket's translation of Thevet with him eight years later, although he also had a recent edition of Mandeville's travels.

From the mid-1550s, French and English translations were sending out mixed messages about the Natives through Spanish eyes. Besides Hakluyt, who translated or commissioned translations from the Spanish, other principal translators were Richard Eden, John Frampton, and Thomas Nicholas. The English adapted Spanish writings that glorified the Spanish conquest for their own purposes such as providing propaganda to encourage potential investors and settlers and often adopted Spanish representations of the New World and the Native. The Spanish authors most translated into English, such as Peter Martyr, Oviedo, and López de Gómara often emphasized the glory of Spain in the face of Native American betrayal and barbarism. Sometimes they advocated conversion and condemned Spaniards for mistreating the Natives.

Even though Las Casas considered the work of his compatriots in the New World to be important, he was not one to emphasize Spain's colonization of the New World and its treatment of the Natives as full of glory. Those Spanish authors who glorified Spain were the most often translated into English. Only one edition of Las Casas' *Brevissima relación* appeared in English (*The Spanish Colonie*, 1583).[83] This translation was filtered through the French translation from which the Preface was taken. The Preface encouraged support for the Dutch revolt against Spain.[84] Much the same situation in the publication of translations of Spanish works concerning the New World occurred in France as in England. In French the translation of the anti-Indian work of Gómara, *La Historia*

(1552), went through at least six printings of Part I between 1568 and 1580, and a minimum of 6 more printings of Parts I and II in the next 26 years (1584, 1587, 1601, 1605, 1606 [twice]) and one printing of Part II (the conquest of Mexico, 1588). Las Casas' pro-Native *Brevissima relación* (1552) was translated, often the first of the nine constituent tracts or the first and some selections from the remaining tracts, into French in various guises and under different titles: *Tyrannies et cruautez des Espagnols* (Paris, 1579; Paris, 1582; Rouen, 1630), *Histoire admirable des horribles insolences* (Geneva, 1582), *Le miroir de la tyrannie espagnole* (Amsterdam, 1620), and, in the same place and time and with the same publisher, in a larger volume by Johannes Gypsius with the even more hyperbolically denunciatory title, *Le miroir de la cruelle & horrible tyrannie espagnole*.[85] Las Casas was translated into English in 1583: Léry first appeared in English in Purchas (1613–25).

The heroic example of Cortés and his conquest also became available in England, for in 1578 Nicholas translated Part II of Gómara's *Historia General* (1552). In addition to translating accounts of its glorious history, this translator had hard personal experience with Spain. The second part of this popular work, which chronicled Spanish expansion in the New World to 1551, concentrated on the conquest of Mexico. In fact, Nicholas' free translation omitted over 230 pages of the original.[86] It is important to remember the positive example that some Englishmen found in Spain's colonization of the New World. The shift or disjunction between Nicholas and Hakluyt, both addressing Walsingham and therefore the queen, in 1578 and 1584, respectively, was stark.

Patrons, like Walsingham, often reflected the complex interests of England in Ireland, the Netherlands, and the New World.[87] The context is instructive here. The year 1577 was the closest the English came to aiding the Netherlands against Spain before 1585.[88] At this time Nicholas held up Cortés and his cohorts as heroic examples of colonizers.[89] How different would be the advice that Hakluyt gave to Walsingham in 1584, when anti-Spanish sentiment percolated through "Discourse on Western Planting."

Translations could also treat of traumatic encounters with the power of Spain. One of the events that turned the rhetoric of Huguenots against Spain was the massacre of the French colonists in Florida in 1565. Las Casas was not the only source for the Black Legend. The title page of Urbain Chauveton's text of 1579, which included a translation of Benzoni, demonstrated that the Italians, as well as the Dutch, French, and English, fed this legend. Fifteen years later Theodore de Bry's illustrations in Frankfurt would indicate the participation of artists and printers in Germany in anti-Spanish tracts. Chauveton's title emphasized "the rude treatment that they [the Spanish] have shown to these peoples there [in the New World]" and that the book is "A little History of a Massacre committed by the Spaniards against the French in Florida."[90]

A key translation in the establishment of the example of Spain in France and England was that of Bartolomé de Las Casas' *A Short Account of the Destruction of the Indies* (1542, pub. 1552). Miggrode's translation of Las Casas' *Brevissima relación*, which was printed in Antwerp (1579), then in Paris (1582), and finally in Lyon (1630), emphasized the tyranny and cruelty of the Spaniards in its title.[91] The English translation of Las Casas, *The Spanish Colonie, Or Briefe Chronicle of the Acts and gestes of the Spaniards in the West Indies, called the newe World . . .* (1583), owed a debt to the French version of Miggrode. Translated by M. M. S., the English text was more than an indirect translation of Las Casas' *Brevissima relación.* The printer added a supplement of remedies that Las Casas recommended to the government of Spain and a summary of the debate between Juan Ginés de Sepúlveda and Las Casas at Vallodolid in 1550–51.[92] Whereas Sepúlveda, following Aristotle's doctrine of natural slavery, argued that the Spaniards could subjugate the Natives as slaves because they were of a lower order of nature, Las Casas opposed this view. In this opposition he related Spanish atrocities that the English and Dutch, enemies of Spain, as well as the French, seized on and used to help create the Black Legend of Spain.

The work of Huguenot histories, by Jean de Léry, Lancelot Voisin, sieur de La Popelinière, and Martin Basanier suggest that even as France was tearing itself apart over religion, authors could still attack Spain. The motives were complex and could be as much about national as religious differences. These Huguenot historians viewed Spain and Portugal as threats to the desires of some French Protestants, in the face of religious tensions at home, for refuge in the New World, and not simply to the national interests of France there. The French wrote significant examples of histories of parts of the New World whether the author had been there, like Léry, or not, like La Popelinière. Léry's account of Brazil revisited the same occurrences Thevet described there. These controversial events that the French experienced in Brazil, like those in Florida, left an impression on the English and, during the French Wars of Religion, left a vacuum for England to fill in the New World. Hakluyt the Younger came to draw on the French and to urge the English to take up their challenge in the New World.

Three histories, one by Léry that describes French colonization in Brazil during the 1550s, another by La Popelinière that is about France but that includes discussions of the New World, and still another by Basanier that brought together French writings about the events in Florida during the 1560s, provide strong examples of works that, while examining France in the New World, reveal the friction within France during its internal divisions. Léry expanded his use of Las Casas in subsequent editions of his history. Variants of a typology between New World and Old World are something we will notice in the uses to which France, England, and the Netherlands put Las Casas. Spanish cruelty to "Amerindians" meant a similar cruelty to Europeans was possible and even likely.

Jean de Léry's *Histoire d'vn voyage faict en la terre dv Bresil, avtrement dite Amerique* (1578, revised 1580) was about his voyage to Brazil in 1556.[93] Its dedication was addressed to François de Coligny, the son of Gaspar de Coligny, the admiral of France, who had obtained royal support for Villegagnon's colony in Brazil and who, as the leader of Protestants in France, was killed in the Massacre of Saint Bartholomew's Day in 1572.[94] Chauveton, De Bry, Montaigne, Purchas, Lescarbot, Claude d'Abbeville, and others made use of Léry.[95]

Jean de Léry presented views of the French in Brazil and in France. The 1580 edition of Léry's *History of a Voyage to the Land of Brazil* is more readily available in French and English than that of 1578 and did not accrue to itself the material concerning Spanish cruelty as taken from Las Casas that Léry's subsequent editions did. Like Montaigne, Léry could criticize the French above the Natives in a typological comparison of the Old World and the New. Brazil became a point of comparison for Léry during the Wars of Religion that were tearing France apart. Besides having been to Brazil in the 1550s and having nearly starved on the voyage back, Léry had witnessed the Saint Bartholomew's Massacre in La Charité sur-Loire and lived through and wrote about the siege of Sancerre from January to August of 1573 in which many had little or nothing to eat.[96] These terrible experiences made him aware of the barbarity in Europe, so that he could be more critical of his compatriots than he could of the Natives in Brazil, even if he saw their shortcomings and his own as well. In the 1580 edition, he spoke about how cruel and barbarous both the Natives of Brazil and the people of France were.[97] After cataloguing "the cruelty of the savages" in the edition of 1580, Léry reminded his readers that he wanted them to "think more carefully about the things that go on every day over here, among us."[98] In the 1585 edition, Léry added other atrocities from the Old World. In the 1611 edition, he expanded the material about Spanish cruelty in the New World taken from Las Casas, so this typology could be seen less starkly. It is for the French in the Wars of Religion (1562–98) that Léry saves his harshest words: "(I am French, and it grieves me to say it.)"[99] In 1574, Léry had published his account of the siege of Sancerre, which he had experienced firsthand. Here was an eyewitness who had lived through hardship in the Old World and New. Looking back on Brazil, where he had arrived in 1556 and where Nicolas Durand de Villegagnon had led the French expedition, through the civil strife of France only a few years after his return in 1558, Léry provided a lament for his people.

The French and English influenced each other in relation to colonization in the New World and in their representation of Spain. The Wars of Religion in France made Huguenot exploration and settlement in the New World increasingly difficult. An important writer in this regard, although less renowned than Montaigne, was Lancelot Voisin, sieur de La Popelinière. In 1581, he published anonymously *L'Histoire de France . . .,* which discussed events beginning in 1550, or, as he mentioned in the dedication "To the King," since the time of the king's father, François I, to the present. This was the author whom Hakluyt would use in his prefatory matter to *Principal Navigations* (1589) in order to goad the English into a new navigation policy because he thought French scorn for the lag in English sailing and exploration would motivate, queen, court, and country. La Popelinière's dedication also included an offer of history as an example to the king and his councilors as well as a wish and a prayer for peace, an end to the "detestable effects of the bloody French mutinies."[100]

Martin Basanier's *Histoire notable de la Floride . . .* (1586), another example of a Huguenot history of French colonization, represented this intricate triangular relation and made Walter Ralegh a focus. Martin Basanier, a gentleman and mathematician, included a dedication to Ralegh in his *Histoire . . .*, which collected three chapters on the French expeditions in Florida of 1562 and of 1564–65, the work of Captain Goulaine de Laudonnière, and another chapter concerning the revenge of Dominique de Gourges, a Gascon captain, against the Spanish in Florida, written by Gourges. For French Protestants in the middle of the Wars of Religion, the events in Florida were still a controversy to keep alive. Basanier's "Epistle" used the common trope of the mirror of history. In representing the New World of Laudonnière and Gourges to Ralegh, Basanier drew out the moral and exemplary dimension of history and thereby kept within the Ciceronian notion of historical representation.[101]

In their histories that relate to the New World, Léry, La Popelinière, and Basanier, like Montaigne in his *Essais*, all represented Spain in a complex fashion. Religious conflict is not as obvious in their work as the terrible divisions in France might lead us to expect. The Huguenots with a stake in the New World were, as we can see expressly in Basanier's address to Ralegh, closely connected to English Protestants involved in the exploration of the Americas. A good example of the debt of this group that benefited from the experience of the French Protestants in, as well as the knowledge of concerning, the New World is Hakluyt the Younger, who spent crucial time in Paris in the early 1580s and brought back the benefit of what he learned to London. It is probably not an exaggeration to say that the Huguenots are the unsung begetters of English designs, from about 1580 to 1630, to establish permanent settlements on the eastern coast of North America.

At the heart of this English colonial design was the textual enterprise, that is the collecting, scholarship, translation, and editing that Richard Hakluyt the Younger oversaw. A promoter of colonies, Hakluyt shared a number of ideas with Gilbert. His work supported and promoted Gilbert's plan for a westward voyage. Hakluyt worked in France, where he learned from many sources. In the context of our discussions, the role of the Huguenots is of central importance. The most crucial text concerning the example of Spain that Hakluyt produced was "Discourse on Western Planting" (1584), but there are a few germane aspects of *Divers Voyages* (1582) that we should first touch on.

In the "Epistle Dedicatory" to Philip Sidney in *Divers Voyages*, Hakluyt included a list of geographers and travelers and an argument for the northwest passage. Some of the themes that would appear in "Discourse on Western Planting" occurred in the dedication in a much briefer form.[102] At the opening of the address to Sidney, Hakluyt expressed the ambivalence to Spain and Portugal: They had come to possess the most temperate lands, but even though the English had missed this opportunity, the Portuguese were past their prime and "the nakednesse of the Spaniards" was apparent, so that the English could hope to share America with the Iberian powers.[103] Hakluyt's "Discourse on Western Planting" (1584) is a private document prepared for the government of England and presented to Elizabeth I in October 1584.[104] The Reverend Mr. Richard Hakluyt, chaplain and secretary to Sir Edward Stafford at the English embassy in Paris, wrote his work in this city, which was a substitute for a listening post at Madrid, where the English had no envoy.[105] Sir Francis Walsingham, secretary of state, seemed to have employed Hakluyt as a support to Ralegh. In the spring of 1584, Ralegh had sent Philip Amadas and Richard Barlowe to look for a suitable site for a colony. Hakluyt might have been used to give advice and to persuade the queen to back the venture.[106] As Walsingham was a central force in English expansion, it is not surprising that Hakluyt, like Thomas Nicholas, worked within the secretary of state's network of patronage. Hakluyt was busy gathering information on rivals in North American colonization, especially on Spain. He knew the work of Peter Martyr, Gómara, Oviedo, Benzoni and others who wrote about Spanish colonization and others, like La Popelinière (Lancelot Voisin) who wrote about French colonies. Moreover, Hakluyt seemed to have sought out pro-Dutch and anti-Spanish work.[107]

In Paris, Hakluyt may have met with Duplessis-Mornay (Philippe de Mornay, seigneur du Plessis-Marly), a Huguenot hostile to Spain, and a diplomat who, serving Henri de Navarre as his ambassador in London in 1577–78, knew Walsingham and Lady Stafford. On April 24, 1584, Mornay presented to the French king an unpublished work, "Discourse to Henri III. On the ways of diminishing the Spaniard," which was probably known to Hakluyt.[108] Duplessis-Mornay, reflecting the views of Henri de Navarre, asserted that Philip II was a tyrant who was undermining France, destroying the Netherlands and Europe; that the French should, along with England, blockade the English Channel from Spanish shipping; and that France should attack the Spanish Empire in the New World to seize it and to prevent the king of Spain from receiving the bullion that allowed him to tyrannize Europe. These anti-Spanish themes echoed similar positions in Drake and Coligny and foreshadowed those in Hakluyt. For Duplessis-Mornay, the French conquest would involve good treatment of the Natives, who should be enlisted against the Spanish conquerors who had exploited them.[109]

In the "Discourse" Hakluyt argued for the English colonization of North America. To that end he concentrated on Spanish aggression in its colonies in the New World and envisioned the English American colonies as a curb to that abusive Spanish power. The Church of England was to help evangelize the Natives, who might also prove useful in the fight against Spain, whose Jesuits had had a head start in their mission. Hakluyt then argued for colonial expansion to North America as a means of addressing problems of trade arising out of the disruption of trade with the Netherlands and Spain (particularly in the cloth trade) and the civil war in France (even with its lulls as in 1584). North America was full of abundant resources to make England rich and keep masterless men at work.[110]

Hakluyt's "Discourse on Western Planting" is a key text that helped to consolidate the work of earlier instructions as well as Gilbert's writing. It is part of an effort to advance English colonial interests in the northern parts of America. This remarkable document, meant for the private consumption of the queen and her counselors, fell between the voyages of Frobisher and Gilbert on the one hand and Ralegh's Roanoke and Chesapeake voyages on the other. The secretary of state, Sir Francis Walsingham, as mentioned earlier, appears to have employed Hakluyt as a means to support Ralegh.

Ralegh's example as a colonizer was known in France, particularly among the Huguenots, whose leader Coligny was dead and who could find few leaders interested in colonization during the French Wars of Religion. At this crucial moment, English Protestants were pursuing settlement in "Florida" now that French Protestants had abandoned the project. The similarity in the two designs was a kind of colonization that would thwart Catholic Spain and develop a Protestant colony to the north of the Spanish holdings in America.

While Hakluyt's "Discourse" may have helped to prepare the way for Ralegh's ventures in North America, it would not be a prophecy of successful and permanent English colonies because English colonization over the next two decades was still halting and erratic.[111] It was clear that Ralegh was now the leading force in England concerning the colonization of America. However, neither of his ventures of 1585 and 1587 succeeded. The Armada and the subsequent war with Spain slowed but did not stop Ralegh's push for permanent English settlements in the New World. Hakluyt would have more to say but did not live long enough to witness strong and vital permanent colonies in what would come to be known as English America.

After the Armada: 1588

The defeat of the Spanish Armada in 1588 was not the end of Spanish power. Between 1580 and 1640, the two great overseas empires of Portugal and Spain were united under the Spanish crown, so that to speak of the decline of Spain is to suggest a relative decline in a world power and not to confuse the anti-Spanish rhetoric of the rivals of Spain with its actual political and economic wealth and influence.

An instance of anti-Spanish sentiment occurred in a French text, Antoine Arnauld's *Anti-Espagnol, avtrement Les Philippiques d'vn Demostenes françois touchant les menees & rvses de Philippe roy d'Espagne* (n.p. [Paris?], 1590), which was translated into English during the same year as *The Coppie of the Anti-Spaniard, Made at Paris, by a Frenchman* (London, 1590). Arnauld attacked the designs Philip II had on the French crown and referred to the Spanish destruction of the French in Florida. During the 1590s, Arnauld's book was reprinted numerous times and was translated into several languages and published in Protestant centers like London, Leyden, The Hague, and Geneva. The French also noted the effects of Spanish wealth from the Indies on Spain's politics in Europe as in *Discovrs svr l'estat de France* (1591).[112]

Even at the height of the Armada and the subsequent war between Elizabeth and Philip, the English did not avoid the double action of imitation and displacement. The English texts wonder after Spanish riches while reviling them. The English continued to learn from the Spanish in translation such as Pedro de Medina, *The Arte of Navigation Translated out of the Spanish* . . . by John Frampton (London, 1595), a reprint of the first edition of 1581. This attention to navigation was one of the ideas that Gilbert and Hakluyt urged upon England. Hakluyt used Spanish descriptions of the land and the indigenous inhabitants to give the English information to rival the colonies of Spain in the New World. The permanent colonies the Spanish had planted would serve as exempla for those the English wished to plant.

Paradoxically, at the height of Spanish power, the English and French established their first permanent colonies, at Jamestown in 1607 and at Québec in 1608, respectively. Sixteen years after the Armada, James I signed a peace treaty with Spain, so the balance of power among Spain, France, and England shifted once more. For over three decades after the defeat of the Armada, Spain was still a great power, but it soon began to decline. How much contemporary rivals wished for this decline and how much they knew about it is hard to say. Between 1621 and 1641, the Spanish Empire in the New World began to collapse.[113] Silver remittances from the Indies declined, and Spain lost dominion over the seas. In an effort to reduce the Dutch trade in Spanish and Portuguese overseas possessions, Spain made an ill-fated decision to resume war with the United Provinces in 1621. The Dutch gained a foothold in Brazil, which divided the Portuguese and the Spanish, who were both under the Spanish monarchy. The great collapse of the power of Spain came in 1639–40.[114]

None of this decline and collapse could the French and English have known about or surmised. In this period there are important texts about exploration and the expansion of England or France by Robert Payne, Hakluyt, Ralegh, Samuel de Champlain, Lescarbot, Robert Johnson, William Strachey, Samuel Purchas and others, a mixture of collections about travel and eyewitness accounts of America.[115] In Hakluyt, Lescarbot, and Purchas particularly, whose works were wholly or in part collections (even though Lescarbot called his work a history), translation was a significant aspect of their books. Lescarbot could criticize Spain in the New World but found Spanish sources to be indispensable. During the sixteenth century, English ideas about colonization, while deriving from classical and medieval concepts and from the involvement of England in Ireland, depended most heavily on continental sources. Even in the early seventeenth century, English promotional literature about America most often involved translations of continental authors, especially from Spain.[116]

Just as the Canary Islands were the prelude and testing ground for Spanish colonization, so too was Ireland for the expansion of England to the New World. There was, for the English, a kind of typological relation between Ireland and Virginia. Spanish influence or presence in Ireland caused anxiety in England, especially in the Protestant circles at court. The Armada was still fresh in mind, so that any comments concerning the Spanish in Robert Payne's *A Briefe Description of Ireland: Made in this yeare, 1589* . . . would not have fallen on deaf ears.[117] There was, according to Payne, a double threat to England: Catholic Ireland and Catholic Spain.[118] Payne's ambivalent representation of the equivocal response of the Irish to the Spaniards was explicit about the typology between the New World and the Old. The events of the shipwrecked Spanish ships from the Armada haunted the text: "Most of t[he] better sort of t[*he*] Irish haue read of their mo[n]sterous cruelties in t[he] west Indias."[119] This "better sort" would have read about the Spanish cruelties in the West Indies and would realize that the Spaniards would be capable of like atrocities in Ireland. This was a similar strategy to the one used in the typology of the New World and the Netherlands, especially in translations of Las Casas, which warned that the Spanish would be as cruel to people of the Netherlands as they were to the American Indians. It comes as no surprise that Payne invoked Las Casas. He had already written about the Spanish having killed millions of Natives. In addressing the reader, Payne told of Las Casas: "a learned Bishop of their owne countrey" and "afterwardes translated into English & diuers other languages, to make their monsterous tyrannie knowne to the worlde."[120] Payne was cogent on the intentions Las Casas had had for his text and how England and other nations had used it to expose Spain, "to make their monsterous tyrannie knowne to the worlde." The Black Legend persisted. This expatiation on Ireland and Spain also had a direct bearing on domestic affairs in England. The aftermath of Mary Queen of Scots and the Armada focused Payne's attention on English Catholics, something that occurred in Hakluyt's "Discourse on Western Planting." The English readers were supposed to pass on Las Casas to their Catholic neighbors as a warning of Spanish cruelty not unlike, if the analogical, anagogical, typological, and allegorical urges in Payne's text are kept in mind, the one he had issued to the Irish.[121]

In *Principall Navigations* (1589) Hakluyt could not avoid the example of Spain, but his purview was larger than that. He began with a story about his own life in order to remind Walsingham of his connections to the crown and to Walsingham himself.[122] Hakluyt explained that he read about discoveries in Greek, Latin, Italian, Spanish, Portuguese, French, and English. Hakluyt used French texts to spur English interest in the New World. Hakluyt's comparison between other European nations and England was meant to show the shortcomings of his own country.[123] Hakluyt's interest in the Protestant La Popelinière had a certain strategic value: His patrons and he himself were advocates of Protestantism, and the Huguenot experience in the New World was an object lesson to those English Protestants interested in colonization in the Americas. In the dedication to a work devoted to translating accounts that were not in English and placing them beside those in English, Hakluyt chose to emphasize the foreignness of La Popelinière by quoting him in the original French. In *Principall Navigations* Hakluyt did not pay much attention to the champion of the Indians—Las Casas. Whereas the first edition contained no mention of Las Casas, the second alluded directly to him only twice. Only in a work that remained unpublished until the late nineteenth century—the "Particular Discourse" or what is also called "Discourse of Western Planting"—did Hakluyt show a clearly anti-Spanish and pro-Native stance.[124] In the Introduction to *Virginia Richly Valued* (London, 1609), Hakluyt assumed the Spanish view that the Natives were liars and dissemblers. Moreover, he suggested that if the inhabitants of America could not be converted, then English soldiers trained in the Netherlands against Spain should prepare the Natives for the hands of English preachers.[125]

In his own way Sir Walter Ralegh, like Sir Francis Walsingham, set out to affect attitudes at court toward the English prospects for colonies. Hakluyt was someone both men called on to get the message out. Ralegh himself was, among many other things, an able poet, rhetorician, and historian who could also advance his own cause.

The career of Walter Ralegh shows the two-sidedness of English attitudes toward Spain but also provides an opportunity to study someone who was a colonizer, courtier, and historian and the texts he produced on the subject over a period of more than 25 years. Although Ralegh encouraged Hakluyt's "Discourse," he also wrote to persuade queen and country into supporting the American option. Nearly four decades after Las Casas' *Short Account* but only eight years after the English translation, in the aftermath of the defeat of the Spanish Armada, Ralegh, who lived as the enemy of Spain and died in 1618 as an alleged friend of Spain, represented the dark side of the propaganda of the Spaniards.

Ralegh's *A Report of the Trvth of the fight about the Isles of Açores, this last Sommer. Betwixt The Reuenge, one of her Maiesties Shippes, And an Armada of the King of Spaine* (1591) began with a denunciation of Spanish lies in the face of the author's truth.[126] In the author's mind there was a typological connection between the Low Countries and the New World: Spain pillaged both. Ralegh told the ironic story of the burgher of Antwerp who thought that the Spanish would spare him because he was a Catholic: they did but looted his house because his goods were all heretical. With sarcasm, Ralegh called Spain "that holie and charitable nation."[127] Ralegh connected the Low Countries and the New World, where Spanish cruelty should act as a negative example even to Flemish and English Catholics: "The Storie whereof is at large written by a Bishop of their owne nation cal-[led] Bartolome de las Casas, and translated into English and manie other languages, intituled *The Spanish cruelties*."[128] His Las Casas became a witness against Spanish aggression in Europe and the New World: the Dutch and English were, by implication, innocent victims like the Indians.

Ralegh's *The Discouerie of the Large, Rich, and Bewtiful Empyre of Guiana* (1596) tended toward the anti-Spanish and pro-Native position of the literature of the Black Legend. However, it also echoed the Spanish dreams of gold, God and a land to be exploited.[129] In the "Epistle Dedicatorie," Ralegh set for his goal, 'that mighty, rich, and beawtifull Empire of Guiana, and . . . that great and Golden City, which the Spanyards call El Dorado, and the naturalls Manoa."[130] In the address "To the Reader," Ralegh connects political expansion with breaking the hymen of a virgin. Charles V "has the Maydenhead of Peru, & the aboundant treasures of Atabalipa," and his successor has consequently held power over Europe: "It is his Indian Golde that indaungereth and disturbeth all the nations of Europe, it purchaseth intelligence, creepeth into Councels, and setteth bound loyalty at libertie, in the greatest Monarchies of Europe."[131] Anyone, like Ralegh, given such a chance, "shall performe more then euer was done in Mexico by Cortez, or in Peru by Pacaro."[132] Clearly, Spanish goals and influences affected English views of the New World even if Ralegh wanted to exceed Spain in the Americas. In addition to reading the Spanish, Ralegh also made use of French texts, like the work of André Thevet: "And vpon the riuer of Amazones Theuet writeth that the people weare Croissants of gold."[133] Ralegh dedicated his work to his kinsman, Charles Howard, and to Robert Cecil, but his text, like Hakluyt's "Discourse," was ultimately meant for the notice of the queen.

The Black Legend of Spain made its appearance in Ralegh as it had in Hakluyt's "Discourse" (1584). To this liberational narrative, Ralegh added the prophecy among the Incans that the Spaniard Berreo confessed to him and others: "from Inglatierra those Ingas shoulde be againe in time to come restored, and deliuered from the seruitude of the said Conquerors."[134] In Ralegh's view, if Elizabeth were to act and take Guiana and beyond, she would gain reputation. Over a decade after the death of Elizabeth I, Ralegh found himself unpopular with James I but never gave up his dream of El Dorado and the hope for redemption with his new sovereign, who had made peace with Spain in 1604.[135] Ralegh's *History of the World . . .* (2 vols., London, 1614), like Pierre d'Avity's work, often represented a providential history but also compared the Romans negatively to the Spanish in the New World. Some of Ralegh's friends tried directly and indirectly to rehabilitate his reputation with James I.[136]

The translation of texts about far-off places from other rival states continued to be an important part of the English effort at expansion. Spain was a good source of such texts. In a translation in 1612 of Peter Martyr's *De nouo orbe*, Michael Lok (Locke) made additions to Richard Eden's translation decades before. Lok included a preface "To the Reader," in which he spoke about how Martyr's book "containeth the first discouery of the west Indies, together with the subiection, and conquest therof."[137] The address to the reader stresses what the book is supposed to accomplish: "We are chiefly to consider, the industry, and trauailes of the Spanyarde" and "All whiche, may bee exemplary vnto vs, to performe the like in our Virginea."[138] Lok called attention to the example Spain set for England.[139] The sympathy with the Natives as casualties of the Spanish conquest is something echoed in English texts during the sixteenth and seventeenth centuries. This ambivalent attitude in these works toward the Spaniards long persisted: the relation to the Natives was also equivocal.

The English and French representations of the New World, which included translation and editing, involved shifting emphases within the model of the imitation, displacement, and rejection of Spain. In 1603, Pierre du Gua, sieur de Monts, was granted a monopoly in Acadia for ten years, and his main goal was to find rich mineral deposits. In 1607, the French merchants who had opposed these monopolies in the New World, succeeded in challenging the exclusive rights of de Monts and others.[140] The Acadian settlement was abandoned the same year Jamestown was established. After the Armada, England could concentrate more on colonization. One of the key figures in the colonization of New France was Samuel de Champlain, who was an associate of de Monts before he founded Québec in 1608. Champlain's, Lescarbot's and Pierre d'Avity's work embodied contradiction and ambivalence toward the Spanish in the New World but also complicated ideas of the French representation of the example of Spain. Like the English, the French demonstrated a marked ambivalence toward the Spanish Empire. At the moment that France was on the verge of establishing permanent settlements in North America, its colonizers and writers were learning from Spain as well as posing a serious threat to it. In this period, however, the French still seemed closer to the Spanish despite James I's policy of peace with Spain.

More than Champlain, Marc Lescarbot became the chronicler of Acadia and was more apt to comment on Spain. Lescarbot lived in the Port-Royal colony from July 1606 to the next summer when the expiration of de Monts' license meant the return of the entire colony to France. He was a Catholic but maintained friendships with Protestants.[141] Although there was a strong tendency for anti-Spanish sentiment to be Protestant, there were Catholic examples of the Black Legend.[142] Lescarbot's history of New France was popular in England as well as in France. It appeared in two English translations by Pierre Erondelle in 1609 and, subsequently, by Samuel Purchas.[143] The original French versions of Lescarbot's text best illustrate the example of Spain in France. Lescarbot concentrated on French discoveries in the New World.[144] Like Hakluyt, Lescarbot envisaged discontents and unemployed tradesmen going to the colonies rather than being lost to foreign lands. However, he emphasized the arts and spoke about "men of courage" settling in the New World.[145] Lescarbot mostly borrowed from Léry (10 chapters) and defended Thevet's imaginative Brazil as a means of convincing others to support and transform the colony.[146]

Pierre d'Avity, sieur de Montmartin, like Hakluyt and Lescarbot, collected information about the New World. He was more interested than they were in Catholicism as a key factor in colonial policy and relations with Spain. The writers in France could frequently be more generous toward Spain than the English were. Often, but not always, this generosity stemmed from a shared Catholicism. While assuming an ideology of a united Catholicism, d'Avity concentrated most on geographical information and described America in his *Les Estats, empires et principavtez dv monde . . .* (1613).[147] The sheer bulk in d'Avity devoted to the description of the Spanish Empire attested to its preeminence. D'Avity also lauded them for their work of conversion, bringing the eternal word of Christ to the New World. Two years later an English edition of d'Avity appeared in London, but Edward Grimstone, its translator, sometimes made changes that indicated different and supplementary attitudes to Spain, a carrying over or "translation" that was part of the larger project of ideological editing in France and England during this period.

A little before the time that Shakespeare was born, the French Protestants were trying to establish colonies in Florida owing to the problems with the colony in Brazil in the 1550s. By this time, there was not, if there had ever been, an isolated England. It was part of a European and world context. Shakespeare and his contemporaries could not seal off the country from the outside world. Even when Shakespeare wrote about English history plays, they represent those neighboring lands. Marlowe's Tamburlaine and Greene's Pandosto are from other lands even as they speak English in their texts. England and empire is of that time but also of the past and future, of the ancients and moderns. Shakespeare and his contemporaries had a wide range, and that is one reason I chose the context of empire and especially at a time when Spain was the great European power with an imperial reach and England was often in a reactive and defensive position. The story of English then was not of an inevitable growth to a language that would be the engine of a culture, politics, and economics with a global reach. What follows is a story about language that reaches and overreaches in a tentative time made bold by poets, dramatists and prose writers. Shakespeare is a big part of this time's argument, but he is not alone. This chapter has been about many writers in England and beyond and the next two chapters will be about writers whose works Shakespeare knew, used and echoed: Christopher Marlowe and Robert Greene.

CHAPTER 2

Marlowe's Apostrophe

As England faced the power of Spain with so many strategies—accommodation, opposition, circumvention—its writers, especially from Richard Eden onward came to terms with an England that was both ambitious and defensive, culturally dependent on translation and bold in expanding the capabilities of the English language. This was an age of innovation that seemed to intensify in the 1580s for two or three decades. England, and its European neighbors, had contended with the Reformation, with England's break with Rome, with the French civil wars in which Catholics and Protestants killed each other. This was also the time after Portuguese expansion south and east and Spanish expansion west until the globe was circumvented. This was the incipient "global village," as Marshall McLuhan would call it in the 1960s. This Iberian expansion affected all the other states of Europe, from Venice to France and England and beyond. That is one reason I began the body of book with this movement out.

Christopher Marlowe had a geography in his work that spanned beyond England. He wrote about the French Wars of Religion and the expanding empire of Tamburlaine. Marlowe was a great innovator of blank verse and of drama, and it is hard to image the development of English and European drama without him. Like Keats and Shelley after him, he died young, and so he left the world just as his fire was burning brightest. An almost exact contemporary of Shakespeare, Marlowe was born about two months before Shakespeare. At the same age, Marlowe was every bit as good as Shakespeare if not more accomplished. Marlowe died just beyond his twenty-ninth birthday. Imagine if Shakespeare had not survived beyond 1593. Our knowledge of the dates of the writing of Shakespeare's plays and sonnets is inexact. For argument's sake, let us assume the accepted dates or range of dates are right. In that case, the culmination of his work might be *Richard III* and *Comedy of Errors* and his minor epic, "Venus and Adonis." It is difficult to say how Marlowe would have developed as a writer, but, like Ben Jonson, he is poet and dramatist of the greatest magnitude. Shakespeare developed into the closest thing to a nonpareil in English.[1]

The "empire" of language is a central part of my book. Marlowe, Shakespeare, and the Authorized version of 1611 helped to form English. The expansion of English political and economic power in Europe and overseas, especially after the fall of Napoleon, helped to establish English as a global language. Hollywood and the might of the United States did the rest in the period after the First and Second World Wars. But what I tried to show in the last chapter was that we would be looking back as readers and projecting ahead, using a kind of retrospective teleology, to come to some providential, or inevitable or manifest destiny view of the expansion of English language and culture. Instead, England was at sea, caught up in a struggle with Spain, watching the French Wars of Religion and the Revolt of the Netherlands carefully and with some apprehension. All the while, and for whatever reason, in this age of anxiety, especially from about the time of the Spanish Armada, English poets, dramatists and prose writers experienced a great flourish. It is to this poetic and rhetorical innovation that I would like to turn. Coming to Marlowe for the first time, I remember the energy and inexorability of his language. Here, I shall examine one current in his tidal presence, one aspect of his overreaching language, his representation of inside and outside, his use of address and apostrophe. This element suggests more than itself and gestures beyond into the world Marlowe was making beyond the bounds of the one he inherited.

Apostrophe

Whether it invokes gods, addresses the absent or dead, or personifies inanimate objects, apostrophe is more important than the notice it has received in recent times. Except for Jonathan Culler, who devotes a chapter in *The Pursuit of Signs*, theorists and critics have not adequately examined this trope, which calls attention to the problems of representation.[2] I am not suggesting that apostrophe has been completely neglected, for Aristotle, Quintilian, Renaissance rhetoricians, and standard reference works in our century discuss it. In the works of Marlowe apostrophe takes on a particular importance because it gives us a better understanding of his representation of wish and power, the gap between longing and performance.[3] The Marlovian canon explores the shifting boundaries between presence and absence, direct address and apostrophe, and these relations raise significant questions about the refractory connection between drama and life. Apostrophe in Marlowe also represents problems of self-dramatization and the sense of body or physicality. The tension between body and soul, which apostrophe evokes, is bound up with notions of the self. Apostrophe tries to make something present that is absent, although the absence does not necessarily mean nonexistence but can signify wish or the disjunction between body and soul. Marlowe often shows how closely direct address and apostrophe are related, how characters address abstractions and objects, others and themselves as if they are present and absent. To speak to something that is present and other is direct address, but to call forth something that is absent is apostrophe, which resembles personification or prosopopeia, the investment of abstractions or inanimate objects with human qualities. The problem of the relation between direct address and apostrophe arises, for instance, when Tamburlaine speaks to Zenocrate's corpse. Her body is present, but her soul is absent. Tamburlaine addresses the body directly but apostrophizes her departed soul, so that "apostrophic address" is a term that might express the close and complex relation between direct address and apostrophe. When Faustus is about to die, he addresses his body and soul and dramatizes a division within himself: he also speaks to himself as if he were a third person or character. Self-address is a direct address that substitutes the first person for the usual third person or that speaks to the first person as if it were the third person, and this displacement or fiction creates a present absence or absent presence. If apostrophe represents in part the attempt of language to control or not to control the world outside the self, it also tries to shape or stabilize the self.

Sometimes the wish for the identity or union of inside and outside finds its expression in apostrophe, which embodies perhaps a wish in language to return to, in Jacques Lacan's terms, the mirror-stage, in which the infant's imagination identifies him with the reflection in the mirror.[4] If, as Lacan says, each word represents the absence it represents, apostrophe is a trope that intensifies the wish to make the absent present, so that Marlowe's characters want the unity that narcissism seemed to bring them in infancy in the very language that disjoins the signifier and referent. The child's mirror becomes the mimetic mirror, in which language filters image and identity. Lacan points out that male language represses and chains, as well as expressing ambivalently, the desire of the mother, which we may especially observe in Tamburlaine's relation to his wife and children.[5] Male and female characters in Marlowe can wish for this unity of inside and outside even as they express themselves in repressive and displacing language, although the males tend to project and impose themselves on the females, who do not appear to practice projection and imposition on the men. Direct address interests me only as much as it relates to, and interacts with, apostrophe and thereby elaborates complex notions of the relation of the self to the world. In Marlowe this attempt to control the outside or stabilize the inside often reveals the aspiration and limitation of the character, which can create in the audience sympathy for human wishes or dramatic irony when those longings seem blind or extravagant.

Apostrophe is vocative: it calls forth something. It derives from the Greek, meaning to turn away and resembles invocation and prosopopeia. A turning away from the judge to the accused or the audience in forensic rhetoric, apostrophe is increasingly recognized as a device the poets use with great effect. Like Aristotle, Quintilian discusses it in regard to the courtroom and the Roman is more favorable to it than the Greek.[6] But Quintilian also sees the literary importance of apostrophe, praising the invocation of the Muse and, in fact, invoking his own, so that God will give him inspiration.[7] Clearly, Quintilian is not embarrassed about apostrophe as Culler is, for the great rhetorician praises Cicero's and Virgil's use of the trope.[8] Quintilian is only interested in decorum, in not using too bold or dead a metaphor in apostrophe. If a modern audience is embarrassed by apostrophe—and I prefer "discomforted"—it is because some of our beliefs and conventions do not coincide with those of earlier ages. Possibly, if we are discomforted, it is owing to our fall into language: we long for unity in a time when signifier and referent were united. The occasional discomfort may have to do with the ways in which we view mimesis or the representation of inner and outer reality. Apostrophe, which concentrates in one trope the problems of many tropes, shows the aspirations and frustrations of an enterprise that is powerfully expressive and ultimately doomed: mimesis.

In the Renaissance, poets and playwrights were fond of apostrophe. Rhetoricians also discussed it. John Hoskyns, who seems indebted to Quintilian, explains apostrophe as turning one's speech away from the judge to the people or to give life to a quality or thing.[9] George Puttenham has a vivid English term for apostrophe: "the turnaway or turnetale." He says it creates recreation in the hearers' minds and cites a number of examples from poetry. Puttenham understands that apostrophe requires cunning and great discretion in calling forth something absent as if before our eyes. Here, perhaps, wariness, akin to Culler's embarrassment, creeps into Puttenham's analysis because the more supernatural or unverifiable the apostrophe, he says, the "greater wit and sharper invention" the poet needs in using it. Already Puttenham is distinguishing truth from fiction in poetic practice, for he can praise Chaucer for both the truth of apostrophe and the fiction of prosopopeia in his translation of the *Roman de la Rose*, where he personifies moral attributes like avarice and envy.[10] In light of the renewed debate on mimesis in our time, keeping before us the reminder that the discussion of representation has been going since ancient Greece, apostrophe stresses the special difficulties in relating the inside and outside, internal and external reality. Besides Paul de Man, Jacques Derrida, and Wayne Booth demonstrate the complexity and interpenetration of this opposition.[11] Marlowe and his contemporaries understood this difficult relation. Using apostrophe and direct address, Marlowe represents the aspirations and discomfort of his heroes, their attempts to create heroic notions of their selves, their wish to reconcile word and world and their trouble doing so. This difficulty the characters experience unsettles the audience and qualifies notions of heroic aspiration.[12] In the characters and in themselves, the audience recognizes, through apostrophe, the power and beauty of the language but also the disjunction between subject and object, the failure of metaphor, of human language and action more generally. Marlowe's contemporaries also made good use of apostrophe and may have learned from him. Shakespeare was aware of the potential for puns on the all and nothing of the apostrophic "O" long before Baudelaire. The Chorus of *Henry V*, for example, plays with his wooden "O," claiming that the audience in the circular theatre is all or nothing, adds and detracts from the history play.[13] Jonson also knew the powers of apostrophe: Volpone's opening speech apostrophizes the day for half a line and his gold for 26 and a half.

Apostrophe calls in the unseen from the outside inside and tries to make it visible, so that, in one sense, it attempts to make something of nothing. Marlowe seems well aware both of the instantaneous power of dramatic language and the erasure of that language.[14] Apostrophe in drama differs from that in the lyric, for the theatre is more embodied than the poem because the actor and audience represent a varying physical medium through which language is expressed and received whereas the reader recreates the poetry that the author gives to the narrator in a less physical and more unified way. A play is both a written or dramatic text and a performance or theatrical text and is more overtly fictional than an oration.[15] The fall of language may occur between the written and performance text of a play. The "O" of apostrophe may be a visual pun that differs from the aural pun or may, as in the "O" in the chorus to *Henry V*, be a metonymic or synecdochic pun for the shape of Shakespeare's wooden "O." The paradox of absent presence or present absence, to which apostrophe calls attention, finds reinforcement in the coexistence of and disjunction between actor and character. The present actor makes the past text present in his or her very enactment or presentation of the authorial representation of the character. In one body resides the uneasy alliance of fiction and nature. In a general sense, the actor represents the unstable relation between illusion and actuality that finds a more specific location in apostrophe. In addresses to a dramatized or objectified self and in apostrophe as wished erasure of the difference between speech and nature, Marlowe smudges and erases the boundaries between direct speech and apostrophe, which, in turn, complicates the divisions between inside and outside, presence and absence. It is most fruitful to examine Marlowe's complex and interactive relation between direct address and apostrophe by moving from the general to the specific, from otherness to the self. Such an examination hinges also on the interpenetration of heaven and earth, divine and human, animate and inanimate and may be pursued under four classes: turning away, personification, and calling something forth; address to place; address to the gods or another person; and address to the self.

Turning Away, Personification, and Calling Forth Something Absent

Sometimes when a character apostrophizes something, he attempts to make his wishes identical with the world or to turn his speech away from a particular person and toward a group of characters or the audience itself. This turning away makes general claims about the relation of that character to nature and society and tries to circumvent his limits. Most often, however, apostrophe involves personification or invoking something absent into presence. If Hoskyns and Puttenham acknowledge the forensic origin of apostrophe as turning away, the former recognizes that apostrophe gives life to a quality or a thing, and the latter understands how this trope tries to make the absent present, how wishes thereby express themselves. Marlowe also seems to be aware of these uses of apostrophe and, through them, reveals his characters' struggle to define the world, others, and themselves.

Marlowe's characters sometimes turn from the characters before them to make more general pronouncements. This turning away is not usually literal but may represent a vacillation between here and there or a barrier between those present by addressing something absent or personifying an abstraction or speaking deafly to others as if one's language were all rhetorical questions, soliloquies, or interior monologues, as if the hearers were not there or there amid invisible powers. On occasion, the character will apostrophize absent gods, powers, or qualities as if they were the only others present or he or she will vacillate between the visible presence and invisible absence as if they were equally real, embodied, and active. Faustus provides an especially poignant example of this turning away when he speaks with the scholars just before the clock strikes 11.[16] He exclaims, "O would I have never seen Wittenberg, never read book" and completes his address to the two scholars with the sorrowful question, "Sweet friends, what shall become of Faustus, being in hell for ever?" (V.ii.45–51 for here and following).[17] The Third Scholar does not treat this as a rhetorical question but replies that Faustus should call on God, yet Faustus cannot turn to, address or call forth God. Instead, he explains why he cannot, that he has blasphemed and says in what is a cross between a sigh and an apostrophe: "Ah my God, I would weep, but the devil draws in my tears." Faustus personifies in the devil his resistance to God and then shows his wishes in an address to his body: "Gush forth blood, instead of tears, yea life and soul." In keeping with the invocation of the invisible into the visible world and his wish that he could transform nature and his body, Faustus turns away from the realm of the scholars. He continues to vacillate between the natural and supernatural when he exclaims, "O he stays my tongue, I would lift up my hands, but see, they hold 'em, they hold 'em" (V.ii.52–57). It is not certain whether the "he" is God or the devil, but the "they," as he explains to the inquisitive scholars, are Lucifer and Mephistophilis. Even as Faustus would and would not turn away from his immediate audience of the scholars to that of God and the devils or to a more general address to the audience in the theatre as he had done at the very beginning of the play in a soliloquy, the scholars will not let him, for they answer him and engage him in dialogue. Faustus, who has given his life to and for magic and magical oaths and spells, senses that his anthropomorphism or magical thinking is ineffective.[18] On more religious grounds, the scholars will not let Faustus turn away from them and only wish that he had told them before of his dilemma, so that divines might have prayed for him. Faustus literally cannot make his language apotropaic or turn away from evil. He is unable to create a magical identity of word and thing, signifier and referent, or, in other words, cannot live Cratylus' linguistic position.[19]

Like Faustus, Edward II attempts, consciously or not, to move toward the general, public, and impersonal, which occurs, paradoxically, through self-dramatization. This theatricality makes use of apostrophe. The interaction of these two illusions of correspondence between self, word, and world calls attention to the ironic and disjunctive breaking of magic in the theatrical and apostrophic because of the self-consciousness of Marlowe's art. His king cannot suffer, for example, the illusion of absolute power and loyalty but soon learns the gap between the name and person of king. This ironic knowledge does not come without delusion or the wish for magic or omnipotence. When Matrevis and Gurney wash Edward with puddle water and shave his beard away, he seems to protect himself with apostrophe. Just when Edward is subject to a degrading and parodic ritual, and when is body is defiled, he seeks to turn away from his situation and fashion a more supernatural and friendly world:

> Immortal powers, that knows the painful cares
> That waits upon my poor distressed soul,

> O level all your looks upon these daring men,
> That wrongs their liege and sovereign, England's king.
> O Gaveston, it is for thee that I am wronged;
> For me both thou and both the Spencers died,
> And for your sakes, a thousand wronges I'll take. (V.iii.37–43)

If Edward bears his ill fortune by turning away from earth to heaven, he also tolerates his bodily pain and danger by turning from the private to the public, from his shorn and desecrated body to his royal and divine body. He is king of England. Like Faustus, Edward cannot turn away entirely and vacillates between earth and heaven. The king will not forget his favorite and his friends and apostrophizes Gaveston after invoking the heavenly powers. This shift qualifies his apostrophe and reveals the disjunction in the king's two bodies, between heaven and earth. Rather than move from an apostrophe to the human to an invocation of the divine, Edward will die in mutual sacrifice, for his friends have, in his view, died for him. As in the case of Faustus, Edward's contradictory and frustrating situation finds expression in his apostrophe. Turning away in drama is not as easy as it appears in the courtroom, where the lawyer shifts his attention from the judge to the people. In the theatre, more than in the court, the aside or change of audience is almost always overheard and is seldom confidential.

Through an apostrophe that personifies, Marlowe's characters also reveal an attempt to control the world. This manipulation of nature and of others does not necessarily achieve its ends but involves vacillation, uncertainty, and limitation, all of which the characters can admit consciously. Marlowe complicates this wavering by moving back and forth between his text and others. This literary allusiveness or intertextuality includes the echoing or invocation of an invisible, past or dead text and gives it life and breath on the stage. The reader revives Marlowe's textual corpse from the corpus just as he did Virgil in Dido and also projects or invokes an imagined performance of the play. The reader is fallen, as the audience is, between the hermeneutics of written and performance texts. The modern director is literally and literarily haunted by the projected image of the absent but once present first performance of the play. Interpretation is, then, a kind of apostrophe, which can seem like direct address. We sometimes wish for the kind of magic in writing and reception for which Dido and Aeneas yearn. At the opening of act II, scene i, Dido echoes the helpless consternation of Achates and Aeneas confronting the stone, the death within them and the world:

> O cursed tree, had'st thou but wit or sense
> To measure how I prize Æneas' love,
> Thou wouldst have leaped from out the sailors' hands
> And told me that Æneas meant to go.
> And yet I blame thee not; thou art but wood.
> The water, which our poets term a nymph,
> Why did it suffer thee to touch her breast
> And shrunk not back, knowing my love was there?

> The water is an element, no nymph.
> Why should I blame Æneas for his flight?
> O Dido, blame not him, but break his oars. (IV.iv.139–49)

In Virgil, Dido apostrophizes the gods rather than the tree-made-ship: "'pro Iuppiter! ibit / hic!, ait, 'et nostris inluserit advena regnis?'" ("'O Jupiter, shall he go,' she says, 'and our realms shall he, a stranger, have mocked?'"). In *The Aeneid* she also apostrophizes Juno, Hecate, the Furies, and the gods of dying Elisa to bring about her revenge on the unfaithful Aeneas. In both Virgil and Marlowe, she also addresses herself ("Infelix Dido!"—"O unhappy Dido") (IV: 584–620).[20] The Marlovian Dido is less vengeful and more wistful than her Virgilian model. Through apostrophe, Marlowe's Dido personifies the tree but in half a line is denying its human qualities. She is self-consciously aware of the limits of correspondences or magical thinking in language even as she has wished for such a connective magic. If the tree had sense, then it would have told Dido of Aeneas' intention to go, but, Dido reaffirms, the tree is only wood. In personifying the water, she uses another tactic. The poets call it a nymph, and if so why did it allow the wood from the tree that made the ship to touch its breast, knowing Aeneas was there? But then she denies the personification as well as its erotic and jealous implications. The poets are wrong. Dido realizes she has been using her apostrophe to blame Aeneas, if not the world, and has been calling on an animate object that becomes lifeless (but not something human) to do what she must: act. Her language considers metaphor and personification on the one hand and action and the world on the other. The greatest complication is that even her resolution to act occurs in the very language she qualifies and rejects. If her imagination is conjunctive, her reason is disjunctive. Neither Dido nor Aeneas gives up apostrophe after this speech.[21]

As Hoskyns observed, apostrophe can also personify an abstract quality, which may represent an outside force such as fortune. This abstract absence informs a concrete presence or narrative, sometimes the story a character will tell of his or her life. The narrative already includes interpretation and cannot be taken as identical to the speaker. Other characters and the audience will measure their observations with the narrative, thereby experiencing the ironic gap between the self and the other. The self can only try to get outside itself to interpret itself. A personification of fortune can also be conventional, and convention, like rhetorical schemes and tropes, can be as much a means of communication as a device to persuade and manipulate. Marlowe gives Mortimer, when he has fallen, an address in the *de casibus* tradition that is reminiscent of *A Mirror for Magistrates*: "Base Fortune, now I see that in thy wheel/ There is a point, to which when men aspire, / They tumble headlong down" (V.vi.59–61). At this most conventional point when Mortimer uses a conventional apostrophe, Marlowe provides him with a rationalization or defiance or both. Mortimer asks himself why he should grieve when he fell because he could not mount any higher. He proceeds from an apostrophe to fortune to a question to himself to a direct address to the queen, from the general and abstract through the self to the specific and concrete, the other: "Farewell fair Queen, weep not for Mortimer, / That scorns the world, and as a traveler, / Goes to discover countries yet unknown" (V.vi.64–66). The worldly Mortimer turns away from the world to heaven, if we compare his metaphor to Hamlet's "To be or not to be" soliloquy. Mortimer uses apostrophe and language more generally to console himself about the world he has lost, his rhetoric appearing as full of Christian and *de casibus* convention as of Machiavellian defiance or overreaching. In the very tropes we can observe the locus of the contradiction and energy that has split critics between the conventional and radical Marlowe. My contention is that this conjunctive disjunction involves an irresolvable paradox that enables dramatic power.

This kind of personification relates closely to a more general use of apostrophe that calls something absent into presence. Invocation often relates to a character's wish to empower himself, to change his situation or have control over nature. He reads his wish on to the world and takes back from the natural or supernatural the power he needs to manipulate nature and reality. This magical fiction attempts to create a correspondence of word and thing, wish and actuality in something akin to apostrophic feedback. Like Pygmalion, Aeneas would make a stone into a person, in this case, Priam, and then he wishes that he could be dead so that Priam could live, that he could be absent to give Priam absence. He apostrophizes Priam: "O were I not at all, so thou mightst be!" (II.i.28). This apostrophe deludes Aeneas, for he sees Priam alive in his mind's eye, which is a conflation of symbol or signifier and thing or referent. With a disjunctive rhetoric, Achates awakens Aeneas to his delusion that the wish of his language is identical with the actuality of the world. Achates tells him that Priam is dead. A less straightforward example occurs in *The Jew of Malta* when the Governor apostrophizes the soul of his dead son and addresses the corpse. The simultaneous coexistence of apostrophe and direct address calls attention to the relation between body and soul, life and death because the soul or breath or life is absent while the corpse is present (never mind the fiction of the live actor playing the dead son). Ferneze would like to bring his son Lodovick back to life: "O, that my sighs could turn to lively breath, / And these my tears to blood, that he should live" (III.ii.5–20). This apostrophic wish cannot be fulfilled no matter how much it would transform his own body to resurrect the dead man, translate his presence to make an absence present. Ferneze expresses his wish that his son might live in the presence of Mathias' mother, whose son also died in the fight with Lodovick and whose corpse also lies before them. Both parents would kill themselves as if absenting themselves from life would bring their sons back to life, but they soon come to their senses. Neither their wishful words nor their contemplated actions can change the fact of death. Sympathetic language and actions represent a magical thinking that must be denied even as it is asserted. This situation, as we shall see, also applies to the even more telling example of Tamburlaine's apostrophic address to Zenocrate's corpse. The very physicality of the stage, as opposed to apostrophe in the lyric, brings apostrophe closer to direct address. Apostrophe on the stage is more complex than that in oratory because of the actual enactment of language through characters and the author's more self-conscious use of fictions.

Address to a Place

The address to place, nature, or the heavens relates closely to the invocation or personification of abstractions and things because both represent the humanization of objects or general qualities that are absent or outside the body.[22] Invoking the gods or another person or attempting to control or manipulate them is not as alien because one is attempting to appropriate another human or humanized self whereas the calling forth of objects or qualities involves a dereification, although arguably apostrophizing a person reifies him or her and humanizing an object is symptomatic of a personality that is projecting itself on the world or is treating all otherness, human or inhuman, as an aspect of his or her self. This interpenetration of inside and outside complicates our ideas of selfhood and otherness, as if the boundaries between the two are shifting. It may be that the more narcissistic or self-reflexive the character, the more difficult it is to differentiate between direct address and apostrophe.

A character's use of these tropes reveals apparent attitudes toward the relation between body and soul, private and social selves, absence and presence and affects our view of his or her perception of context and place. An actual place can be fictionalized, contained, or sublimated into the speaker's imagination, so that it is more than the physical setting represented on the stage. Samarcanda, for instance, is an emblem of Tamburlaine's return in power and glory to the place of his humble birth, a kind of reminder of his heroic aspiration and assent, but it is also a place in his narrative about his heroic self-fashioning. At first, Tamburlaine's famous address to the city of his birth, "O Samarcanda, . . ." appears to be a direct speech to the place represented on stage (*2Tam*, IV.ii.30f.). It is soon apparent that Tamburlaine is personifying the city as an aspect of himself, for it once helped make him enjoy "the fire of his martial flesh." But Tamburlaine tells the city to blush at its disgrace, which the river Jarartes' embracing love can never wash away "from thy distained brows!" At this place, Tamburlaine says that Jove will receive this warrior's son because Calyphas is not worthy to serve the immortal part of the mortal element of Tamburlaine.[23] This direct address becomes apostrophic through personification and then, like Othello's suicide in his last speech, makes action part of the speech act. This dramatic speech perversely includes Tamburlaine's killing of his son, whom Zenocrate had once defended. Tamburlaine blames Jove for sending Calyphas such a soul, which makes Tamburlaine a worse enemy of Jove than the Titans. The defiant and hyperbolic Tamburlaine will make Jove tremble. His speech is rebellious, and he would usurp Jove's position as the sun. Tamburlaine then turns to address directly his opponents, Orcanes and the King of Jerusalem, the "cankered curs of Asia," and asserts that they will recognize his supremacy through the difference between them and the conqueror, but they find his threats revolting. If Tamburlaine can manipulate and overcome these opponents, he cannot displace Jove and redefine nature with his personification. Beginning the speech with direct address, Tamburlaine returns to it by way of an apostrophic flight. Even Tamburlaine cannot escape the ironic qualification that nature imposes on language. His body will fail him, and even if his story endures, he cannot supplant Jove in the hierarchy of mythologies. Tamburlaine's aspiring mind is full of contradictions, for he then replies to his enemies that he is the scourge of Jove or God, whose deputy he now is (IV.ii.71f.). It is as if Calyphas could not, being an "effeminate brat," be Tamburlaine's son. Tamburlaine has trouble respecting femininity because he controls and does not listen to Zenocrate and has the harlots killed as he had the virgins (V.ii.85–92, cf. *1 Tam*, V.ii.46–57). The world Tamburlaine would wish, would project on, is masculine and warlike and makes victims of women. Along with direct address and hyperbole, apostrophe emphasizes the contradictory wishes in Tamburlaine in regard to the gods and heavens and his abuse of the feminine, no matter how much he has claimed to love Zenocrate. He is caught between place and displacement.[24]

Edward feels displaced by Rome and finds himself considering this place literally and figuratively. For Edward, Rome is present and absent and would subject it with address and apostrophe, perhaps as a way of avoiding subjugation. Perhaps Edward uses these tropes to displace the events that are displacing him. Direct address and apostrophe may create fictions with which he can turn toward the world with fury or away from its harshness with harshness. Like Calyphas, Edward is effeminate in the view of men who would control kingdoms and the world. When Edward says he will obey the Archbishop of Canterbury, the representative of the Pope, he turns and makes an aside, promising to the others titles or, if this promise does not please them, to create for them equal kingdoms of his realm, "So I may have some nook or corner left / To frolic with my dearest Gaveston" (I.iv.72–73). Instead, he is forced to sign the banishment of his favorite and, left alone, apostrophizes "Proud Rome" (I.iv.97f.). Edward personifies the city or uses prosopopeia, although, having just spoken with the Pope's representative, he may also be simultaneously reversing metonymy, synecdoche and personification by substituting the whole for the part, the place for the person, Rome for the pope. The presence of Canterbury, who has just departed, has reminded Edward of the power Rome holds in England and restrains him, despite its literal presence, though absent. Edward makes Rome into a person and, by implication, the pope into a symbolic place. Like Tamburlaine, Edward uses his apostrophic speech to express his wish for violence and power: "I'll fire thy crazed buildings and enforce / The papal towers to kiss the lowly ground" (I.iv.100–101). After describing the Tiber swelling with the corpses of priests, Edward returns from this vivid absence to present England: he will execute all the peers who back the clergy, presumably because Canterbury (and thus "Rome" has been behind the move to banish Gaveston). The absent presence of Rome impinges on the present absence of Gaveston, who is about to leave England. Marlowe emphasizes the separation of Edward and Gaveston because he has the favorite enter after the soliloquy. They exchange pictures that represent their grief, the gap between the person and the image. At this crucial moment, the signifier and the referent coexist and stress the instability of the situation and of representation. Edward's love is divided: when Isabella comes upon them, he speaks cruelly to her and leaves his wife so he can walk with Gaveston. This multiplication of images of love and the resentment and hatred in Edward's language for Rome, and Isabella leaves the audience to wonder how much of a narcissistic tyrant or a wronged man the king is. Does Edward see himself more readily in the image of another man rather than the more alien image of a woman? As is often the case in a history play, the king is divided between his private and public selves even as his language reveals a wish for unity.[25]

Apostrophic addresses to nature and the heavens, things and abstractions also reveal the wish for an interpenetration of inhuman and human. Characters supplement nature in language through a linguistic contravention of natural law. Dido provides an especially good example of the wish to make nature animate. Iarbas wants to revenge the sin of Aeneas and Dido in the cave because Jove will not, so that he addresses and portrays himself, as Tamburlaine sometimes does, as an avenger that does the works that the gods will not: "Nature, why mad'st me not some poisonous beast, / That with the sharpness of my edged sting / I might have staked them both unto the earth, / Whilst they were sporting in this darksome cave" (IV.i.21–24). Not only has Iarbas abstracted nature and personified it in order to address it, but he also blames nature for his own impotence in enacting his wish to punish the lovers. Iarbas appears to transfer his sexual wishes for Dido into Aeneas' fulfillment with her in the dark cave, so that his imagined scene goads and frustrates the jealous lover. In an attempt to keep his integrity of self, he blames nature through a fiction rather than openly admitting his limitations. If he transforms nature in his fiction, in fact he cannot shape nature or possess Dido. If in Dido characters often call attention to their inability to control their fates and to manipulate the world—as in Aeneas' exclamatory apostrophe to his distant home: "O Priamus! O Troy! O Hecuba!" (II.i.105)—they sometimes delude themselves with hyperbolic apostrophe to their own power. Dido, almost prefiguring the apostrophe and hyperbole of Shakespeare's Antony and Cleopatra, says to Aeneas:

> O that the clouds were here, wherein thou fled'st,
> That thou and I unseen might sport our selves.
> Heavens, envious of our joys, is waxen pale,
> And when we whisper, then the stars fall down
> To be partakers of our honey talk. (IV.iv.50–54)

Here, Dido's magical thinking implies a correspondence or sympathy, if not a causal relation or imitation, in which nature and the heavens respond to the lovers. There is a strong sense of the pleasure of self-dramatization and language in this epic reach and tragic hubris. The apostrophe of the clouds as the means to transport the exalted lovers and the personification of the heavens as jealous of their joy looks forward to Glendower's magical account of the reaction of the heavens to his birth in Shakespeare's *I Henry IV*. Dido echoes the helpless consternation of Achates and Aeneas confronting the stone and anticipates her own apostrophe to the tree (IV.iv.139–49). Aeneas had wanted to see Priam in a stone. Apostrophizing his father, Aeneas exclaimed, "O, were I not at all, so thou mightst be!" (II.i.28). Marlowe may be punning on "not" as "nought" or the "O" of apostrophe, but whether he is or not, he represents a character using apostrophe to express longings for the divine power of bringing back the dead and his father alive. With apostrophe, Aeneas would reverse the laws of human nature, making something of nothing, reversing absence and presence, inside and outside and the movement of the generations. Language, and in this case apostrophe, can only represent the hope of achieving this new order, this redefinition of identity, this supplement to nature. Through interruption and dramatic irony, Marlowe has hinted at the frustration of apostrophe. Except through exaggeration and apostrophe—through language—humans cannot call back yesterday or attain the control of divinity. As Achates says to Aeneas, "O, where is Hecuba?/ Here she was wont to sit, but saving air, / Is nothing here. And what is this but stone?" (II.i.12–14). As hard as people may try, they cannot ultimately manipulate truth, history, and nature. As Achates has said, in the world a stone is a stone and Troy is in ruins and Hecuba is not with them.[26] Iarbas, Dido, and Aeneas all run up against the same limitations and do so, paradoxically, with words that reach beyond human power in nature. The heavens are a place that humans cannot displace, an absent presence that resists the human wish to manipulate it through invocation or the most exaggerated claims to the contrary.

Address to the Gods or Another Person

Through apostrophe, the characters attempt to break down the distinctions between earth and heaven, humans and the gods, self and other. The nature of the theatre encourages this conflation through representation. It mimics the gods with human actors. The opening scene of Dido, for instance, represents gods and humans together, Jupiter and Ganymede as well as Venus, Aeneas, and Achates. Marlowe humanizes the gods and gives humans hints of divine power. Like Edward, Jupiter is effeminate or homoerotic: his Gaveston is Ganymede. Through this "induction," which shows a homosexual love of the chief among the gods with a young Trojan prince whom Jupiter's eagle had carried to Olympus, the audience later comes to the love between Dido and Aeneas. The stage represents both Olympus and Carthage in the first scene and thereby makes the absent heavens more present and so tries to erase the division between direct address and apostrophe.

In *The Massacre at Paris* apostrophe is sometimes allied to exclamation and prayer, to surprise and an appeal to heaven to grant wishes on earth.[27] Exclamation is a calling out of a wish, a projection of the inside on the world, and so is closely related to apostrophe, which often involves a projection of a wish or human quality on to nature or the gods and then a calling in or invocation of that projection to empower or delude the speaker. A prayer is an entreaty, a wish that one projects to God or the gods and then draws back in with hope of fulfillment, so that one might say that it is apostrophic. Through apostrophe, *Massacre* frequently represents a wish for power over nature and other humans and conflates religion and politics. Navarre witnesses the poisoning of his mother: "O gracious God, what times are these! / O grant, sweet God, my days may end with hers, / That I with her may die and live again" (iii.22–24). Once again, the audience observes a character's wish to reverse the laws of nature, to resurrect the dead. This time Navarre wishes to join his mother in death and resurrection, so that his religious beliefs counter the treacherous political situation in which he finds himself. Like Navarre, the Admiral is a Protestant: he faces his death with courage as he is murdered in his bed—"O God, forgive my sins" (v.30). In this Protestant polemic, Marlowe also gives to another Protestant, Seroune, three religious apostrophes: "O, let me pray before I take my death," "O Christ, my Savior!" and "O, let me pray unto my God" (vii.6, 9, 14). This aspect of apostrophe is political and religious. The Catholics do not die with apostrophes to God. Guise dies with a recognition of the limits of his power and the wish to be revenged—"O, that I have not power to stay my life, / Nor immortality to be revenged!" (xx.79–80)—as well as with thoughts of his likeness to Caesar. When the audience first observed Guise, it witnessed an apostrophe that conflates policy, religion and the devil. He says: "My policy hath framed religion./ Religion. O Diabole!" (ii.65–66). When the friar stabs King Henry fatally, who stabs him fatally, he, as a true Jacobin, declares, "Sancte Jacobe, now have mercy on me!" (xxiii.33). King Henry, Navarre, and others qualify this apostrophe with last words that condemn the Catholic Church. The dying king hopes to live to ruin the pope and his antichristian kingdom and shares lines with Edward II: "I'll fire his crazed buildings and enforce / The papal towers to kiss the lowly earth" (xxiii. 61–62). Whether this is a textual corruption, the surrounding lines provide a context for the dead friar that denies him the same kind of apostrophe at his death. Here, apostrophe is divided along religious lines: the rhetoric of God has grown political.

Apostrophe to the gods or God is also crucial to the sense of identity of characters like Tamburlaine and Faustus that it is better to examine their ambivalent addresses to divinity in conjunction with their addresses to themselves. This close relation of all the facets of apostrophe complicates any analysis of each part, so that in the examination of the self, we shall observe this interpenetration. Before such an analysis—keeping in mind the affinity of address to place and person, heaven and gods—it is necessary to discuss the address to the person. The most interesting example of the conflation of a direct address and apostrophe is Tamburlaine's to Zenocrate when she is alive and after she is dead.

For Tamburlaine, it appears that his love or lust wants otherness in the conflation of the very wish and lack. He extends his imperial narcissism to her, capturing her in his own narrative, making himself her only referent in his mind. The magical thinking of apostrophe is like the wish for atonement with God: both want unity. Fallen, we are fallen into language. The boundary blurs between love and hope for unity with the divine and lust and yearning for power over another's body and nature. "Divine Zenocrate" depends as much on the interpretation of the audience as on Tamburlaine's speeches to and characterization of her. From one point of view, the love of the "scourge of God" can appear godlike: from another vantage, it seems blasphemous and parodic. Both views assume the gap between the divine and the human, miracle and limited power. What we do not hear enough about is Zenocrate's view of herself, especially not in relation to Tamburlaine. He bullies Zenocrate when he first meets her. He addresses her in the third person as if he were making a character of her, apostrophizing her, as if she were absent or an object (I.ii.87–105). After "Zenocrate, lovelier than the love of Jove," he alternates uses of "thy" and "thou" with the third person, "Zenocrate," so that he badgers her with a mixture of objective dramatization and subjective direct address. Tamburlaine attempts to overwhelm her with hyperbole, making her beauty greater than nature's, making his wealth greater than Zenocrate's, making his power greater than his wealth and greater than the beauty of Zenocrate. She may mean more to him than the crown of Persia, as he says, but not as much as all his earthly power. From the line, "Disdains Zenocrate to live with me?" to "And then myself to fair Zenocrate" (85, 105), Tamburlaine attempts to capture her, to enclose her with language. He is the greatest prize. It is as if Zenocrate were really a reflection of his own power and wealth. And Zenocrate is reduced to silence. Tamburlaine's follower, Techelles, speaks for her, and a soldier, who brings an urgent message of war, ensures the silence. Tamburlaine is aware that he plays the orator as well as the soldier. He soon replies to the Soldier, "Then we shall we fight courageously with them, / Or look you I should play the orator?" (I.ii.128–29).

In many ways, for Tamburlaine, Zenocrate is an absent other or a receptacle for his longing. He cannot accept her difference in life or her separation from him in death. Long after the verbal rape, Tamburlaine apostrophizes the absent Zenocrate and equates her to the stereotypical quality that men have so often wanted in women: beauty.[28] Like Dido at her death, Tamburlaine invokes the poets, this time to contend with them, to show that Zenocrate is more beautiful than all their creations and she is his. By being so, she glorifies him (V.ii.81–128). In the soliloquy he exalts his fair and divine Zenocrate and sets conditions for the poets and "their immortal flowers of poesy, / Wherein, as in a mirror, we perceive / The highest reaches of a human wit," so that they cannot compare with his representation of beauty (V.ii.103–5). The mimetic mirror is also the narcissistic mirror. The wit or image becomes more important as the person or thing represented: reflection is always a contest. Tamburlaine uses his apostrophe to conquer the poet as much as lover and soldier. He is aware of the complexity of his task. Using three conditionals, hyperbole, and the simile of the mimetic mirror to show how inexpressible language is when describing beauty (but describing it just the same), Tamburlaine wrestles with the relation between language and action, with the problem that writing or representation or speech is governed by metaphor itself. The topos of inexpressibility does not prevent him from shifting his emphasis from Zenocrate to himself, to how "effeminate" beauty is beside power. But Tamburlaine does vacillate. He sees the necessity of beauty. In a passage full of textual and editorial problems, Tamburlaine appears to admit that beauty helps shape virtue by qualifying the conceits and fashioning men with true nobility.[29] Nonetheless, Tamburlaine is interrupted and wants to know whether the caged Turkish emperor has been fed and whether the town is ransacked (V.ii.129–31). How noble beauty has made Tamburlaine. On Theridamas' suggestion, he does accept part of Zenocrate's wish—that her father be spared—but then reverts to addressing Bajazeth as "my footstool" (V.ii.133–49).

After stifling Zenocrate's expression or shaping of her own narrative of death, the rhetorical warrior nearly falls into a figurative necrophilia. The life and death struggle in the play is as much about narrative, performance and writing as it is about battle, about conquering in sex as in war. Tamburlaine smothers Zenocrate's identity. In Part Two, as Zenocrate lies dying, Tamburlaine tries to manipulate the heavens "To entertain divine Zenocrate," as he says repeatedly (II.iv.1–38). Zenocrate wants to die in peace, but Tamburlaine denies her this wish, for he blasphemes (II.iv.57–80). In this critical time Tamburlaine grows as literary as Dido, saying that Zenocrate is more beautiful than Homer's Helen and the loves of Ovid, Horace and Catullus and that she should have been "the argument/ Of every epigram or elegy"(II.iv.94–95). But at this high point in Tamburlaine's hyperbole, Zenocrate dies.[30] He resolves on war to revenge her death to "break the frame of heaven" (II.iv.104). It is not surprising that Tamburlaine takes her death personally and with jealousy, for he conjures an image of "amorous Jove" snatching his love and the gods treating her as a sexual toy (II.iv.105–18). Tamburlaine stands before her body and cries out to her soul, trying to unify life and death, earth and heaven, Zenocrate herself, Zenocrate and Tamburlaine. Zenocrate's body is present, but her soul is not, so that the cry to the soul is an apostrophe but her body makes it seem like direct address. In this highly wrought scene, he dramatizes himself, adding "the Great" to his title as death defeats him for the first time. With his mythic metaphors and apostrophes, the great warrior and rhetorician tries to unify inside and outside, but Theridamas reminds Tamburlaine that "She is dead" and that words will not bring her back (II.iv.119–24). This disjunctive reminder against magical thinking also alerts the audience to the gap between Tamburlaine's wishes, as expressed in language and, more particularly, in apostrophe. Tamburlaine twice echoes "she is dead" but addresses Zenocrate's corpse: "thou shalt stay with me" (II.iv.125–29). His reaction becomes parodic. He will pretend that Zenocrate is alive, that he has unified inside and outside, and that words and art can enliven where they only embalm. For the first time, he talks about his own death. Rather than the live tableau of mother and children he describes earlier, he envisions a burning town mourning her death and her statue rising from its ruins. She will remain his possession and, embalmed, will follow him in his wars until they are buried together When Zenocrate is alive, Tamburlaine deadens her voice, and when she is dead, he tries to revive her body but not her voice. She is a silent object on which he can project without her objection or interruption (II.iv.125–42, cf. I.iv.1–34).

The addresses to the gods and to another person relate to the projection and constitution of the self in more cases than Tamburlaine's. Addressing one's body and other self-reflexive references become especially important on the verge of a character's death. At the point of death or the abyss of absence, for the character, the soul, which is invisible, seems to take on a substance in contrast to the mortal but visible body. Absence and presence seem to be reversed. When identity appears most unstable and in crisis, the characters try to shape their identities amid the confusion of want.

Address to the Self

Marlowe's characters address themselves in the third person and thereby dramatize themselves. They also distinguish between their bodies and souls and so destabilize their identities. The characters address their souls as if apostrophizing them whereas their address to their bodies resembles direct address more. The division of the self and the anxiety over that split finds expression in the language. Perhaps the relation of address, apostrophe, and identity is the most telling. Although "identity" derives from the Latin *idem* or same and may imply a wish that one is like others or unified with the outside world, what makes a character distinct is his or her difference from others and external nature. Addresses to the self rely on difference as much as similarity, for the character dramatizes himself or herself as if speaking to a third person while also identifying the soul with his or her body.

The nature of the self lies at the heart of Marlowe's aspiring characters, so that a brief examination of several examples is desirable.[31] In his plays men and women want to control the world and to shape their identities. Apostrophe can also represent the dissolution of character. Sometimes, paradoxically, the character uses that dissolution as a means to define himself or herself. Dido is particularly apostrophic in the last scene of the eponymous play. She is distraught and curses and tries to manipulate the gods (see V.i.165–68, 216–21, 241, 248–57). When Anna, Dido's sister, provides the disjunctive objection by telling her to "leave these idle fantasies" and to remember who she is, Dido answers, "Dido I am, unless I be deceived" (V.i.264). Here Dido is being Senecan: she is being conventional while expressing the uncertainty of her identity. She resolves to erase herself: "'Ay, I must be the murderer of myself. / No, but I am not; yet I will be straight' [Aside]" (V.i.270–71). She addresses herself in the third person, "Now, Dido, with these relics burn thyself," and says that this action will make Aeneas famous for perjuring and slaughtering her, so that she implies through transference that her lover is responsible. Aeneas seems to define her language and actions (V.i.292f.). Remembering Aeneas through objects—sword, garment, words—Dido declares, "These letters, lines, and perjured papers all, / Shall burn to cinders in this precious flame" (V.i.300–301). She will burn Aeneas' representations of love and herself, as if his words will balance or substitute for her world. Marlowe has her curse Aeneas in partial translation and then gives her the original from Virgil. Dido's death is metafictional and intertextual. Marlowe uses shorthand by conflating three of Virgil's lines in Latin about thirty lines apart and by interspersing them with an English line (V: 629–30, 660). Dido's death is literary as she cries, "Live, false Æneas! Truest Dido dies! / Sic, sic juvat ire sub umbras," and throws herself into the flames. Her vengeful words are briefer in Marlowe than in Virgil and the playwright does not think it necessary to translate the Latin, leaving out the oppositions of coast against coast, waves against waves, arms against arms, the curse against the descendants of Aeneas and his men, the proclamation of delight at dying. But Dido's burning body is not from poetry, although it is staged in a play and is only a representation of the outside world. In a line she juxtaposes Aeneas' falsity and her own trueness. She still defines herself by him until she switches to Virgil and rejoices in going beneath the shades to death and so dies quoting the epic poet. The context of her death is even more complicated, for Iarbas addresses himself and then apostrophizes Dido and then kills himself, defining himself by Dido and obliterating himself when she is gone. Anna apostrophizes Iarbas, speaks about herself in the third person and so dramatizes herself, and, apostrophizing Iarbas, utters, "I come to thee!" and kills herself. She, too, defines herself by another and destroys her own identity. This wish for unity between the person and the other, of life and death, translates from language into action. When Dido ends, the oppositions between inside and outside, word and world, are seemingly obliterated in sacrifice.

In Dido the apostrophic self-immolations occur because of a failure to achieve an integrated identity or to ratify previous roles of love, power and nobility, but, in Tamburlaine, they are placed in a different context. Marlowe represents a gap between Zenocrate's view of herself and Tamburlaine's vision of her. The discrepancy in the points of view destabilizes a coherent view of Zenocrate's self or character. The audience witnesses a similar dramatic irony in the discrepancies in Tamburlaine's self-address. Zenocrate addresses herself as if to objectify and exonerate herself from Tamburlaine's pillage of Damascus and her countrymen (*1 Tam*, V.ii.256f.). Her words echo the earlier execution of the virgins (260–75, cf. V.i, ii.1–71), which immediately preceded Tamburlaine's apostrophe: "Ah, fair Zenocrate! Divine Zenocrate!" Now Zenocrate addresses herself, and her image of the deaths of the virgins is sexual and violent. In Zenocrate's speech, even the horses behave better than Tamburlaine and the horsemen with "quivering spears," because they look on the beauty of the virgins and try to restrain themselves. Enclosing the scene of rape is Zenocrate's utterance of her own name, as if the rape of the virgins were her own rape. She makes the analogy explicit when she questions Tamburlaine's "love," a word Marlowe emphasizes with epistrophe. Zenocrate observes "more tales of bleeding ruth" when she looks on the bodies of Bajazeth and Zabina. Now Zenocrate apostrophizes Earth, Jove and Mahomet, asking pardon for the cruelty and contempt that Tamburlaine and she have shown these two victims but, in the middle of this appeal, also apostrophizes her lover to behold the corpses (V.ii.284–308). Powerless to affect events directly, Zenocrate hopes that Tamburlaine will pardon her father and fiance, but Arabia is killed (V.ii.320f.). Tamburlaine forgets how beauty curbs conceits, as he had said in his apostrophe to Beauty, proclaims that Mars, Jove and Death fear him, and sees his power, "as in a mirror," in the deaths of Bajazeth, Zabina, and Arabia (412–15). He echoes the mirror imagery of the apostrophe to Beauty. It is as if the mirror is self-reflexive, is as much an image of narcissism as a reflection for magistrates. When Tamburlaine speaks about, or looks into, the mirror, he sees himself or what he calls his honor. He really does not heed Zenocrate, except to save her father. Curiously, after all this wreckage, the Soldan and Tamburlaine dwell on

Zenocrate's chastity, how pure she is. This purity did not help the imprecating virgins in Damascus. Arabia is forgotten. Both Zenocrate and her father yield to Tamburlaine's will. Zenocrate will marry Tamburlaine, "Else should I much forget myself, my lord" (416–37). She does forget her former self and suppresses or is oblivious to her doubts about Tamburlaine and herself fewer than two hundred lines ago. Tamburlaine has it all his way. He shapes the world, seems to make the outside and inside correspond with a Machiavellian or proto-Nietzschean will to power. Paradoxically, his beautiful words represent an ugly and violent world.

Tamburlaine is defiant but cannot, as hard as he tries, defy nature with a heroic rhetoric. The harnessed defeated monarchs are stage symbols of Tamburlaine's power, but his power cannot transcend human limits. Tamburlaine's language uncovers his wish to overcome nature as magical and antimagical. His words are incantatory and disjunctive at once because they lead to an expectation of the unity of inside and outside, which may be a temporary possibility in art but not in nature. In the second address to his "jades," he continues to envision himself as Jove drawn in a chariot but, as his speech proceeds, seems to forget his parody and gets carried away with his metaphors (*2Tam*, IV.iv.97–133). Later, he burns the Koran and defies Mohammed with a blasphemous apostrophe (V.i.184–85). He boasts that sickness and death will never conquer him but of course they will (187–220). His words cannot control the world. But he will try, as he threatens the heavens, personifies death and defies it (V.iii.42–115). Tamburlaine creates a new narrative: he struggles in vain but the gods will create a higher throne for him (120–22, 199–204). Like Zenocrate, Tamburlaine sees himself in heaven. He orders that Zenocrate's hearse be brought to him. He will stage his own death and thereby contain it. Tamburlaine addresses his own eyes, so that they can help his soul pierce through the coffin and gold "And glut your longings with a heaven of joy" (227). He gives advice to his son and is unrepentant. He uses Phaeton and Hippolytus as object lessons. The choice of Hippolytus is complicated, for when Phaedra married Theseus, she fell in love with her stepson and, rebuffed, accused him of dishonoring her. Theseus had his son hacked and mutilated to death as horses dragged the boy's body. The image of controlling the pampered jades of Asia is there but so is sexual jealousy and incest to the last. Calyphas, whom Tamburlaine killed, had wanted to "accompany my gracious mother" instead of conquering the world (I.iv.65–70).

As Tamburlaine dies, he sees the world in terms of himself. This sense of self Marlowe may have founded on the Homeric man, who has "no unified concept of 'soul' or 'personality,'" but, as E. R. Dodds explains, the soul in Homer is important when it departs the body. Dodds reminds us that Homer does not credit humans with a psyche, except when they are threatened by death, are at the point of fainting or death, or after they die. The Homeric sense of character hinges on reason and knowing and whatever is not rational or concerning knowledge is excluded from the self and is considered outside and alien.[32] Marlowe's view of self owes much to Homer's, but he moves beyond the thumos or breath-soul and the psyche, although he includes them, to something more contradictory and complex. Throughout both parts, the playwright does not ignore Mohammed or the Christian God in defining his protagonist's defiance and self-fashioning (others and he refer to the former 36 times and the later over 40 times). Tamburlaine divides himself into body and soul to praise himself doubly in contemplating how those present will take his death: "My body feels, my soul doth weep to see/ Your sweet desires deprived my company, / For Tamburlaine, the scourge of God, must die." (V.iii.246–48). He speaks of himself in the third person and defines his role. He dies with the word "die," somewhat of a convention in Marlowe, and one appropriate to Tamburlaine, for his last rhetorical move is to try to harmonize, or rather bend to his will, word and world, inside and outside. Beginning with an address to his eyes, his last speech ends his life with a tale, which represents either great blasphemy or the words of Jove's messenger. Tamburlaine's death becomes part of his narrative in which he addresses his lack in his audience, those who watch him die. Amyras, heir to Tamburlaine, asks heaven and earth to meet and end all things, but his apostrophic imperative cannot mend the breach. If the sheer rhetoric of Tamburlaine makes us feel his loss, it cannot fill the gap.

In *The Jew of Malta*, apostrophe and self-address show Barabas' tricks, limits and defiance as well as the gap between word and world. Dramatic irony arises from the contexts of these addresses. This irony represents the difference between the vantages of the characters and audience, so that we have a divergence of selves, although distinction depends on comparison, which is a form of similarity. If the addresses are ironic, they represent stability and instability in the relation within and between selves because an address, like irony itself, depends on a comparison of two apparently stable positions between which there is a gap or difference. The relation between similarity and difference creates tension and instability. The interpenetration of blindness and knowledge in the characters complicates their views, as well as ours, of themselves, and dramatic irony is not always a guarantee that the members of the audience have immutable selves and unassailable knowledge. The friars address Barabas with greedy joy when he promises them his wealth (IV.i.79–88). Friar Jacomo's "O happy hour—wherein I shall convert / An infidel and bring his gold into our treasury" is ironic as Barabas frames him for murder, instead (IV.iii.2f.). Barabas actually laments Ithamore's absence even as his servant is blackmailing him: "O, that he were here!" (IV.v.17). Marlowe juxtaposes Barabas' apostrophic aside—"O, that I should part with so much gold!"—with an overt apostrophe, "O, love stops my breath, / Never loved man servant as I do Ithamore," and so reveals the subtle roles that Barabas plays as he dupes others but is himself duped. He will disguise himself and observe Ithamore enjoying his wealth (IV.v.50–53). After Barabas has killed the three blackmailers, escapes in dramatic fashion, gives Malta to the Turks and is made governor, he addresses himself and considers policy, like a disciple of Machiavel who introduces himself at the beginning of the play (V.ii.26–47, cf. Prol.1f.). Like a Marlovian hero (including Guise, to whom Machiavel refers in the Prologue), Barabas does not repent, addresses himself as he is about to die (V.v.77f.). He confesses with defiance but in the torments of approaching hell cannot bring confusion on "Damned Christians, dogs, and Turkish infidels!" Although, like Tamburlaine, Barabas is unrepentant and tries to make the facts of the world comply with his word by dying with the word "die," he is more frantic and tormented as Faustus is: "Die, life! Fly, soul! Tongue, curse thy fill, and die!" (89). While his body feels "intolerable pangs," he gives his soul the apostrophic order to fly: he would do the paradoxical and the impossible, such as kill life while his cursing tongue dies. This self-conscious awareness expresses Barabas' predicament in language and the power as well as the vulnerability of his limitation. Like Faustus, he is damned but, no matter how apparently deserved his punishment, his damnation evokes some sympathy. It is not as if he were the only schemer in the play or that he did not suffer the plots of others even as those who survive him condemn him. Marlowe uses self-address and apostrophe to represent the attractions and repulsions of aspiration and the heroic shaping and assertion of the self. Even as the language of characters like Barabas falls short, its very attempt to make its wishes identical with nature appears heroic. The very failure of address and apostrophe may be their success whether the character seems admirable or not.[33]

The use of apostrophe just before death can also show the dissolution as well as the dramatization of the self. At death, teleology and ontology interact, and, in Marlowe, the characters often define their purpose and sense of self through apostrophe. Such examples occur in *The Massacre at Paris* and *Edward II*. King Charles expresses his loss of control through images of physical failure: "O, hold me up! My sight begins to fail! / My sinews shrink; my brains turn upside; / My heart doth break. I faint and die" (xii.13–15). This death is somewhat Homeric, although the dissolution of the fainting body is contained in a narrative that attempts to enclose itself by facing death with a mimetic verb "die," which represents identity, but is not nature by virtue of being language, and stasis, but with the finite movement of a verb. After his apostrophe, Guise, on the other hand, is defiant and stoic as he characterizes himself as Caesar: "Thus Caesar did go forth, and thus he died" (xx.87). Guise makes his death part of his narrative just as Othello will later do. The former plays Brutus and Caesar, killer and killed, thereby dignifying his death with Rome as well as creating a self-reflexive and conflated view of his life just as Othello is the executioner of the Turk and the Turk himself as he kills himself. Although Guise cannot prevent his death and reverse the laws of nature, he can make a heroic effort to defy death and nature through narrative control. Edward II cannot control his fate and addresses Lightborn, who does: "O spare me, or dispatch me in a trice" (V.vi.110). But Lightborn does neither, for, rather than murder Edward instantly, he has Matrevis and Gurney to stamp gently on the table so as not to bruise Edward's body. The king cannot even shape a fiction that incorporates the wish for control over his death. For his own trouble, Lightborn is stabbed by Gurney.

Ambivalence also surrounds Faustus' last uses of self-address and apostrophe. His shifting sense of self relates closely to the various ways he uses address. Faustus is caught in his eschatological rhetoric. He is literally pulled apart like Orpheus and Osiris: his words fly in many directions, and he is disembodied. Both Orpheus and Faustus attempt to harmonize animate and inanimate nature but defy the divine and suffer accordingly. Whether they are tragic figures depends, in part, on the interpreter, and Marlowe's apostrophe contributes to the contradictions in Faustus, which have divided the critics. As the clock strikes 11 and Faustus only has an hour to live, he addresses himself (V.ii.13–87). He hopes that time will stop and that he will repent but realizes he is damned and cannot control the heavens, time and the fate of his soul. This oscillation occurs repeatedly in this soliloquy. Faustus reveals this contradiction in one line: "O, I'll leap up to my God! Who pulls me down?" (142). He is caught between the hope for heaven and the despair of hell. Faustus sees Christ's blood in the firmament and will not call on him. After apostrophizing Christ then Lucifer, he sees an angry God and asks mountains and hills to fall on him in an act of self-immolation. Faustus apostrophizes the earth to hide him from divine wrath, but, fearing that this protection will not work, calls on the stars to help him to ascend into heaven. After apostrophizing God, he addresses himself and invokes Pythagoras, whose idea of metempsychosis or the transmigration of souls helps Faustus consider a transformative fiction in which he is changed into a beast until he comes back to the subject of his own damnation. He blames his parents for his damnation, then, dramatizing himself by addressing himself in the third person, he blames himself. He vacillates between blaming himself and castigating others, like Lucifer. Faustus apostrophizes his body, wishes it would turn to air, and his soul to water, so Lucifer cannot find him.[34] His psychomachia is to no avail. In his final four lines, Faustus moves from an apostrophe to God, to one of hell, Lucifer and, finally, Mephistophilis (V.ii.184–87). After echoing "My God, my God, why hast thou forsaken me?" (only more fearing than blaming God), Faustus apostrophizes adders, serpents, Lucifer and, with his last word, "Mephistophilis," in a downward spiral to hell. His language appears to reflect a division between body and soul, and mixed wishes for heaven and hell. The end of the play calls into question how much Faustus or any character governs his words and actions and how much is determined. By invoking Christ and Lucifer and so many others, Faustus attempts to define himself in a great religious struggle. The more he struggles to distinguish himself, the more he becomes Everyman, the Christian caught in an ancient and eternal struggle between good and evil. As the audience listens to Faustus' language, his apostrophes and self-addresses, it examines, among other things, its own wishes, fears, aspirations, its tendencies toward authority and rebellion.

Concluding Remarks and Transitions

Marlowe's use of apostrophe reveals a great deal about the relation between word and world: it qualifies the invocation of outside and the exvocation of inside as well as expressing the wished interpenetration of presence and absence. Apostrophe tries to make the world and self identical through the dream or wish of language. In apostrophe we observe the attempt of language to bring something into being: through the power of language, a character tries to control the world outside the self, and while this attempt can be exhilarating, as it is in Marlowe, it is inevitably limited. In some ways, the implied author and the character outlast the author, actor, and audience if the work endures, but the permanence of language questions itself and cannot transform nature to make it identical to a wished-for human nature.

Through apostrophe, characters like Faustus and Edward II personify the gods or immortal powers in order to attempt some control over the world, to make their dream of heaven identical to the way of the world. Their apostrophes humanize the heavens, but the damnation of Faustus and the murder of Edward reveal an actuality that has fallen well below their ideals. In their wish for presence, both characters call forth the lack in themselves, but they both experience death or the absence of life that they sought. The characters are often aware of the disjunctive nature of their apostrophes specifically and their language more generally. As Dido says, "The water is an element, no nymph." The contradictions and ironic qualifications create a dramatic tension with the magical thinking of apostrophe.

If the characters in Marlowe attempt to personify nature and humanize the gods, they also address a place more specifically in a rhetorical strategy that is closer to direct address, although Tamburlaine's address to Samarcanda also seems to imply a personification of his place of birth and his mythologizing of it almost as a character as part of his heroic autobiography. An interpenetration and interaction of the classes of apostrophe appears to be unavoidable. Heaven, for instance, is absent by virtue of its invisibility whereas Samarcanda is present on the stage: the personification in both cases blurs the distinction between apostrophe and direct address. Rome is absent and present in *Edward II*. Canterbury represents it, is a metonymy for it, but the city, the Vatican, and the pope are absent. When in a soliloquy Edward addresses and personifies the city, he is being apostrophic, but Canterbury has just left, so the apostrophe is not so absolute. The opening scene of Dido complicates the notion of apostrophizing the gods and other persons in this scene, and to a lesser extent in the rest of the play, because the setting is Olympus and Carthage. The play makes the heavens as physical as earth even if it represents an embodiment of personification. In *The Massacre at Paris* the characters appeal to heaven but cannot reverse the laws of nature. Apostrophe appears to be political in this play: at death, the Protestants die with apostrophes to God; the Catholics do not.

Apostrophes and addresses at death show a character attempting to come to terms with the relation of self to world. Theridamas reminds Tamburlaine that he cannot bring Zenocrate back to life, but the grieving husband parodies divine powers by embalming her and addressing her as if she were alive. This address is an apostrophe that tries to elide the difference between direct address to a living person and an address to the corpse, which is the absence of the soul and the shell of a vital body. A corpse is a signifier that has emptied itself out. When Dido addresses herself before her death, she grows literary and represents a difference from her model in Virgil, so that two addresses and deaths are occurring. Already a gap occurs in Dido's wish for unity between word and world. Her death also occurs between the literal and figurative burning of letters and the repeated falls from apostrophic address into death that Iarbas and Anna suffer. This context destabilizes notions of Dido's identity for the audience. Like Tamburlaine,

Barabas attempts to unify word and world by dying with the word "die" or one of its cognates as King Charles and Guise do. The apostrophe to death may represent an effort, as in the cases of Tamburlaine, Barabas and Guise, to control one's end with a kind of narrative closure, but the play and life go on, and any such attempt, no matter how arresting, appears ironic and disjunctive. Edward's direct address to Lightborn just before his death shows a king that might as well be apostrophizing someone absent: it cannot even pretend to control. Through sympathy or dramatic irony, or perhaps caught between both, the audience considers these apostrophes and addresses and with them questions inside and outside, notions of the world and the self.

Marlowe's plays are full of dynamic examples of direct address and apostrophe and reveal the shifting boundaries between them. Direct address is not as direct as it seems, especially in self-address, which introduces problems of self-dramatization and the multiplication of identities. Paradoxically, the mirror up to human nature, the fascination with making the self and the world one, may be the same impulse that drives a character to atonement with God. We have seen that many of Marlowe's characters are ambivalent in their apostrophic search for unity. Some tend toward the self, others toward God, although they may sometimes confuse the two. Apostrophe may represent a basic and early narcissistic wish that is at the root of emotion, poetry, and religion. It is one of the blind hopes and prayers of language. This trope, as well as others, also opposes itself by discovering breaks in the circle of magical thinking.

Marlowe provides a geography of the imagination that reaches beyond the shores of his England. His invocation and vocative reach have some parallels in romance and tragicomedy. The nature of wonder and magic and transformation through disguise and travel are also themes of romance. The romantic vision mends nature or makes it strange and can explore the forbidden, the wishes or desires that the world tolerates in fiction alone. Although Plato might denounce the poets for beautiful liars who endanger the truth and although the antitheatrical camp in Elizabethan England would attack or ban plays or at least close down the theatres or place them beyond the bounds of the city walls, these plays, as well as poems and prose works, could try to explore in the "as if" or putative space of fiction and try to circumvent the present censorship by seeking the fantastic and the exotic. This is a social and psychological role as well as a cultural and poetic mode. The power of language and imagination, as dangerous as it might be, as threatening as philosophers and councilors might find it, could express the dreams, nightmares, aspirations, and critiques of authors and audiences. Like Marlowe, Robert Greene, who himself seems to have criticized Shakespeare's overreaching, was one of the university men who set out to transform the English stage and literature. It is to his prose romance, *Pandosto*, a source for Shakespeare's *A Winter's Tale*, that we now turn. Shakespeare, a much forgiving figure, could not, it seems, pass up a good source, even if its author had attacked him with a brief parody in an allusion to one of his *Henry VI* plays.

CHAPTER 3

Greene's Romance

Robert Greene was born in the year Elizabeth I became queen and died a little while after his thirty-fifth birthday in 1592, just under six months before Christopher Marlowe was murdered. He was born in Norwich, studied in Cambridge (BA, 1580; MA, 1583), and became one of the first professional authors in England after he moved to London. Greene is connected with Shakespeare because *Greenes Groatsworth of Wit*, a posthumous pamphlet, was attributed to him and seems to allude to Shakespeare negatively, and because, despite this attack, Shakespeare used *Pandosto* (1588) as a source for *The Winter's Tale* (1610), a comedy in the First Folio (1623) and called a romance or tragicomedy by later critics. Here is Greene's advice, which contains the apparent attack on Shakespeare and like imitators of university wits or writers:

> Yes truſt them not: for there is an vpſtart Crow, beautified with our feathers, that with his *Tygers hart wrapt in a Players hyde*, ſuppoſes he is as well able to bombaſt out a blanke verſe as the beſt of you: and beeing an abſolute *Iohannes fac totum*, is in his owne conceit the onely Shake-ſcene in a countrey. O that I might intreat your rare wits to be imploied in more profitable courses: & let those Apes imitate your paſt excellence, and neuer more acquaint them with your admired inuentions.[1]

One of the obsessions with authorship in Shakespeare has been a matter of class. Could not a glover's son write so well, especially without the benefit of Cambridge that Greene and Marlowe had? It is always difficult to retrieve the author at any time, and this is especially true before copyright, and in the cooperative milieu of the London playhouses. All we seem to have close to what Shakespeare might have written is the epyllia, *Venus and Adonis* (1593) and *Rape of Lucrece* (1594). There may well have been jealousies about Shakespeare's abilities, and it seems from Greene's work that Shakespeare was imitating the university wits but was not among them. There is no mention of his university training or aristocratic lineage—so at least this allusion does not do well for Francis Bacon or the Earl of Oxford, as Shakespeare the writer.[2]

Both Greene and Shakespeare wrote in what we would now call the genre of romance. This chapter relates to the last chapter of my book on *The Winter's Tale*. The two are connected structurally and are part of the theme of imagination and regeneration that writing provides. England was expanding its literary reach as well as its political and economic extent, and I would argue that the cultural and literary contributions from about 1588 to 1616 preceded the establishment of political and economic power. Although England had defeated the Spanish Armada, Spain was still the principal power and the Netherlands were growing daily in strength while France was always a force to be reckoned with. The literary and dramatic power of the English was something that we can see was more certain, although perhaps in retrospect. Even the students at Cambridge, as we shall see in a later chapter, sensed that they had a great writer in Shakespeare.

But recognition for writers at the time was tentative, and if Greene felt he got no respect from other writers and perhaps others, Jonson may himself have called Shakespeare's comedy what we now usually call a romance, *Pericles*, a "mouldy tale." At the end of *The Newe Inn*, in "The iuſt indignation the *Author* tooke at the vulgar cenſure of his *Play,* by ſome malicious ſpectators, begat this following *Ode* to himſelfe," Jonson wrote,

> No doubt some mouldy tale,
> Like *Pericles;* and stale
> As the Shrieues custs, and nasty as his fish-
> scraps, out euery dish,
> Throwne forth, and rak'tinto the common tub,
> May keepe vp the *Play-club*[3]

In censuring the audience for its lack of appreciation, Jonson talks about *Pericles* as a "mouldy tale," and this could have referred to a play that the quarto of 1609 attributed to Shakespeare on its title page but that did not appear in the First Folio 13 years later. In *Bartholomew's Fair*, which was first staged in 1614 and first printed in 1631, the Scrivener, as part of the Induction, says,

> Hee that will ſweare, *Ieronimo,* or *Andronicus* are the beſt playes, yet, ſhall paſſe vnexcepted at, heere, as a man whoſe Iudgement ſhewes it is conſtant, and hath ſtood ſtill, theſe fiue and twentie, or thirtie yeeres. Though it be an *Ignorance,* it is a vertuous and ſtay'd ignorance; and next to *truth,* a confirm'd errour does well; ſuch a one the *Author* knowes where to finde him.[4]

Constancy, truth, ignorance, and error become themes here in the differences in taste between author and audience. Kyd's and Shakespeare's revenge plays, *The Spanish Tragedy* (probably from the 1580s) and *Titus Andronicus* (about 1594), respectively, become touchstones for old tastes. The implication is that to stick to these old Senecan tragedies of bloody revenge is ignorance with staying power and a confirmed error.

Thus, tastes change in all the genres and can do so quickly. Even years or centuries after, romance continues to fight for respectability or, more important, understanding. Prose romance is an ancient genre, but at certain times romance was so associated in poetry that the two were conflated. Sending a letter from Bolton to Cambridge, Massachusetts, on February 7, 1812, Jared Sparks wrote to John G. Palfrey about the question of what is poetry, which their old and mutual friend, Mr. Jones, "long ago believed to be unanswerable."[5] Sparks thought that this question did have an answer: "So great a resemblance exists between poetry & romance, that while we are drawing the outlines of the one, we are sketching the design of the other." He reinforced this view by asserting that "Poetry is nothing but romance beautified by the skilful hand of the artist, and decorated with tropes, figures, and metrical numbers; or rather romance is poetry divested of its gaudy decorations and artificial blandishments."[6] Sparks, who later became the editor of *The North American Review* and president of Harvard and the first Harvard professor to teach a course in American history, was a literary figure as well as an historian. Writing in the same letter about Walter Scott's *Marmion*, he said, "Believe me, when Milton, Pope, Dryden, Young, and Thompson, and many others, shall be read with admiration and renewed delight, by our philosophers, divines, poets, and all men of taste and education, and shall occupy a distinguished station in their libraries; the works of Walter Scott will only be found huddled together with a promiscuous collection of romances and trivial plays, in the libraries of a few puny poetasters and crazy novel readers."[7]

Romances, plays, and novels do not have the high seriousness of poetry or poetic romance for this American Romantic. For Sparks, it is unclear whether romances of inferior poetry are as bad as prose romance and novels. In the Renaissance, there were different kinds of romance, and it is possible that some prose romances were more read than appreciated. There was less critical discourse printed then, so that is hard to know. In any case, the poetic romances of Spenser and Shakespeare were not the only kind of romance available in England at the time. Here I would like to concentrate on a prose romance by Greene, which is often taken up because it appears to be a source for Shakespeare's *The Winter's Tale*. It is a work that stands well on its own and deserves more attention, so that while I relate it to Shakespeare's play, I shall also consider it on its own terms and in the context of romance. The theme of this chapter is the end of time, and it discusses Greene's *Pandosto* as a Renaissance romance and assumes that this genre yields something important, whether in poetry or prose.

Arcadia Once More and Theoretical Background

The woods of Arcady are not dead. The best of Renaissance romance, as with the best of any genre, is worth discussing.[8] After looking briefly at the critical background of Renaissance romance, I shall argue that Greene's romance, *Pandosto, The Triumph of Time* (1588), involves sympathy or identification, estrangement or alienation, and supplement, so that romance explores in its fabulous adventures the most important questions about art and, more specifically, about its relation to life. This paradox, that romance is an escape from the world only to investigate the world more fully, has been increasingly recognized.[9] Rather than thinking that we have lost "a world of fine fabling," I shall argue that the vitality of Greene's romances derives in part from the tensions among sympathy, alienation, and supplement.[10] *Pandosto*, which is too often considered only as the main source for Shakespeare's *The Winter's Tale*, deserves close attention in its own right. It is not wise to underestimate Greene's work and censure him for not writing Shakespeare's play years after his premature death. Greene achieves some intriguing effects of his own.

Romance did not have the authority of Plato or Aristotle to legitimize it in the Renaissance. That did not keep Renaissance poets from trying to justify their practices by appealing to Aristotle or by denying his authority. Although Aristotle's view of representation is various and recognizes mimetic differences among the genres, saying, for instance, that "tragedy attempts to imitate men who are better and comedy men who are worse than those about us," he also takes into account the differences in narrative technique or point of view in representation, and because he defines poetry as involving fictitious characters and invention whereas history does not, Aristotle's insistence on the possible and his ignoring of romance seems to have caused anxiety among Renaissance poets.[11] Philip Sidney was not alone in defending poetry, in asserting imaginative freedom for the poet and in trying to limit the influence of Aristotle and philosophers where it did not serve poetry. Before examining sympathy, alienation, and supplement in *Pandosto*, it is necessary to establish the background in the Renaissance for each of these attributes of romance.

Sympathy or identification is part of the response of the reader and audience to romance.[12] The suspicions of the ill effects of mimesis on the audience that the Platonic Socrates experiences admits a sympathetic response to those who come under the influence of poetry. In *Poetics* Aristotle discusses the effects on the audience of the laughable in comedy and of catharsis in tragedy. Sidney defines poetry in Aristotelian and Horatian terms, saying it is "an art of imitation, . . . a representing, counterfeiting, or figuring forth—to speak metaphorically, a speaking picture." In *Discourses on the Heroic Poem* (1594), Tasso argues that truth and verisimilitude are intrinsic to poetry and that reality and truth may have broader Christian definitions, ones that include earth and heaven, the natural and the marvelous.[13] Mimesis becomes a more encompassing idea in the Renaissance, attempting to enclose the classical and the Christian views of reality. Sympathy, alienation, and supplement become part of this Christianized mimesis. When Sidney, Tasso, and others seek to broaden the bounds of poetry, they do not generally reject its mimetic basis or that poems represent reality. They try to extend the terms "mimesis" and "reality" and in doing so argue for a more far-reaching art.

Alienation or estrangement, closely allied to sympathy or identification, also relates to supplement. Inasmuch as someone can identify with nature, that person displays sympathy, but to the extent that he experiences a distance from nature, he shows alienation. That is also true of the relation between reader and work, audience and play. Alienation is, for many Renaissance theologians and poets, a consequence of the Fall, the demise of humankind from primary to secondary nature, from the prelapsarian to the postlapsarian. Boccaccio, Sidney, and Tasso, for example, all understand that poetry should fill the gap in fallen nature, an idea Milton later develops with such power. In *The Life of Dante* (1363–64) Boccaccio makes the poetic making of beauty a moral act, an atonement for original sin, for human alienation in nature.[14] This biblical translation of the classics is one form of secular scripture. Second nature, the fall of Adam, and how humankind's most divine means of learning about the perfection it lost and hopes to regain become more explicit in Sidney's *Defence*. For Sidney, the purifying of wit, which poetry achieves most, moves, leads, draws men to the final end of learning, "to as high a perfection as our degenerate souls, made worse by their clay lodgings, can be capable of." Tasso also observes a close relation between poetry and theology, comparing poetic images of virtue and vice that teach people in an imperfect world to seek paradise and shun hell, also implying that classical views of experience are too circumscribed.[15]

That romance is a supplement does not contradict views in the Renaissance of poetry more generally and of romance or tragicomedy more specifically. The existence of alienation or the Fall as well as identification with the fallen and the wish to be atoned, united or in a state of grace bring many poets of the Renaissance to a moral view of art. Repairing the ruins becomes a professed objective of the writers of romance, even if they sometimes do so in secular ways. Ostensibly, romance consists of poetic justice and representing what should be rather that what is in second nature. The moral becomes the aesthetic. Strange events, strong passions, great wonder, and poetic justice help compose the moral universe of Renaissance romance. There is no dearth of poets who emphasize the moral nature of poetry or who defend romance as a genre. Like the theology of the scriptures, Boccaccio says that "poetry, with fictions about various gods, with transmutations of men in varied forms, and with pleasant persuasions show us the causes of things, the effects of virtues and vices, and what we should follow, in order that by working righteousness we may attain that end which they who did not fully know the true God thought was complete blessedness."[16]

Like scriptural teaching, the nature of the divine Word and the miracles of the life of Christ, poetry can, according to Boccaccio, instruct moral lessons even if it is classical and pagan. Paradoxically, in Christian terms, the breaking of the laws of nature or the supplement to the natural order is the most real act in nature, so that, like the incarnation, allegorical narrative does not represent simply the fallen world but elaborates its relation to heaven, in short, its essence. Over two centuries later, Sidney makes a similar point in *The Defense*. Renaissance romances, like *Arcadia*, *The Faerie Queene*, and *The Winter's Tale*, contain miraculous transformation.

Boccaccio, Elyot, Cinthio, Mazzoni, Sidney, and Tasso all argue that poetry is moral, although each writer varies slightly on his view of how poetry attains morality.[17] Renaissance writers appeal to Aristotle but also modify and argue against his tenets on poetry. In *Poetics they* find wanting a full treatment of the marvelous and any treatment of literary freedom and romance. For instance, Cinthio argues that classical principles do not apply to Renaissance romance and that the nature of the poet is to feign and make marvelous things—such as transformations of the animate into the inanimate and the converse—that extend beyond those that exist in nature.[18] Sidney shares the moral vision of the Italian critics. In a well-known passage in *The Defence*, Sidney argues for poetic freedom, exalting the poet's invention and lack of subjection; giving examples of this creative liberty such as heroes, cyclops, and furies; and concluding that nature's "world is brazen, the poets only deliver a golden." Sidney also praises poetic justice and says that in poetry, and not in history, "a man should see virtue exalted and vice punished."[19] In his letter to Ralegh, Spenser states the moral aim of *The Faerie Queene*: "The generall end therefore of all the booke is to fashion a gentleman or noble person in vertuous and gentle discipline."[20] Greene wrote romance in a well-established critical and poetic context that justified the ways of romance to those who admired Aristotle and the ancient views of literature. The Renaissance took romance seriously, and it became a sign of poetic liberty and exploration for modern Europe. *Pandosto* exemplifies the complexity of the best romances, and it is their mixture of sympathy, alienation, and supplement in a moral aesthetic or aesthetic moral that most distinguishes them.

Sympathy and Alienation

Sympathy or identification is the first apparent effect of romance. As it is the most ostensible effect, we shall consider it more in conjunction with alienation and supplement than by itself. The identification of reader or audience with characters is a consequence of mimesis, for in this state the response to the characters supposes that they are people or, at least, much like them. In *Pandosto* Greene creates sympathy for Bellaria and Fawnia as Shakespeare later does for Hermione and Perdita but with different ends. Although Bellaria suffers as Hermione will, Greene chooses a different fate for her as she dies whereas Hermione experiences a sort of resurrection that Paulina arranges for her. Even though Bellaria and Hermione both face obstacles, Bellaria's prove to be tragic for her, although her death is part of a larger comic scheme, that is, of poetic justice, the punishment of vice, and the reward of virtue. In one sense Greene complicates the notion of poetic justice because he punishes Pandosto, who in despair over his past injustice commits suicide, but also the virtuous Bellaria, the victim of his sudden jealousy. The audience sympathizes with Bellaria, whose death, as James Joyce might say, lacks poetry and justice. To qualify the ending further, it is not certain whether Fawnia dies, an issue we shall leave for the moment but one that will differentiate Greene's triumph of time even more from Shakespeare's. In its own way the conclusion of *Pandosto* is as provocative as that of *The Winter's Tale*.[21] Greene concentrates more than Shakespeare on tragic identification, on loss and death, on pity and fear, shows the mortal danger of vice to virtue and dwells on alienation. Whether or not Greene's work purges pity and fear is less certain than the interest that the deaths of Bellaria, Pandosto, and perhaps Fawnia create, for his view of time and morality is not conventional. Romances usually have happy endings.

Pandosto represents a distinct alienation. Addressing the reader, Greene speaks of the triumph of time, but his time is harsh and retributive. Pandosto's jealousy is less sudden and perhaps less alienating than Leontes', for the narrator provides motives whereas Shakespeare's play lacks such preparatory and explanatory narration. Pandosto sees Bellaria and Egistus as lovers, "thinking that love was above all laws and, therefore, to be stayed with no law" (186). Strangely, in the opening paragraph the narrator called the jealousy "causeless" (184). His ambiguous explanation potentially implies a cause for the jealousy as he speaks about the so-called lovers, about "a secret uniting of their affections" (186). Although Greene represents motive more than Shakespeare—as in Franion's statement of his dilemma, whether to obey Pandosto and murder the innocent Egistus or warn Egistus—he complicates motive, also supplementing narrative explanation with the device of Fortune as Machiavelli does in *The Prince* (e.g., 188–90, 192–94, 200–204). If Fortune is blind, so too is Pandosto, a fallen man who, for a crucial time, doubts other people and forgets the gods. Bellaria apostrophizes herself as if she were a character in a moral, subject to fortune in plenty (191–92). She is alienated from herself, weighing the woes of the great as opposed to the humble, as Richard II, Henry IV, and Henry V bewail the king's two bodies in the Second Tetralogy. Divine retribution, Greene implies through his narrator, punishes Pandosto's sin: his son, Garinter, dies suddenly, and Bellaria dies as a result of this news. Pandosto has been alienated from himself through jealousy, and now he reproaches himself and rails against his jealousy. Like Bellaria, Pandosto apostrophizes himself as if he is alienated from his former self, and self-recognition disgusts him and shames him. He cannot make sense of why the gods would punish his innocent son and not him. Their imperfect justice baffles Pandosto, so much so that the alienation of death and sin makes him want to kill himself, but his peers prevent that action (198). Paradoxically, the more Pandosto realizes his wrong and his alienation, the more sympathy the audience is likely to have for him. (Later, the author will ensure the distance, if not repugnance, of the audience.)

Greene shifts the perspective from the repentant Pandosto to the daughter he cast away. Fawnia is beautiful, her virtue contrasting to her father's vice, so that she gains the audience's sympathy (199f.). Egistus' advice to his son, Dorastus, applies to all the characters but perhaps most to Pandosto: "Time passed with folly may be repented, but not recalled" (203). But even repentance does not seem enough in this romance. Nor does the love between Dorastus and Fawnia ultimately repair the ruins. Greene frames Dorastus' love at first sight for Fawnia in ambivalent terms: "casting his eye suddenly on Fawnia, he was half afraid, fearing that with Actaeon he had seen Diana; for he thought such exquisite perfection could not be found in any mortal creature" (204). He fawns on Fawnia, but, as *The Metamorphoses* relates, Actaeon, a hunter, coming across a naked Diana, becomes hunted as she turns him into a stag and has him torn by his own hounds.[22] In *Pandosto* Dorastus' use of this transformation is obviously hyperbolic, but the hunt turns on itself: male anxiety over female power and revenge, the change of man into beast, and violence all modify the innocence of love at first sight. This ambivalence may be in keeping with the idealization of women in conjunction with misogynist remarks and class bias that occur especially in the second half of the story (e.g., 200–206). In his love for Fawnia, Dorastus experiences attraction and sympathy on the one hand and estrangement or alienation on the other. Fawnia's first sight of Dorastus also brings the attractive alienation of love, for she, as the narrator reports, "seeing his face so well featured, and each limb so perfectly framed, began greatly to praise his perfection, commending him so long till she found herself faulty" (204–5). Both cannot rest and feel ill at ease in their love. Dorastus is practical enough, however, to consider the social disadvantages that Fawnia would bring him until Love wounds him again and quenches the rage he had against himself (205).

This alienation in love persists in a sequence of the lovers' self-reflexive and self-apostrophizing soliloquies. Dorastus asks himself as if he were someone else whether he is himself. He also addresses love and explores its paradoxes, considering his dilemma serious enough—after all, an heir to the throne should not marry a shepherdess—to contemplate suicide, if only for a moment (205). In obedience to the gods' love of beauty and to the unbending laws of love, Dorastus says, "Fawnia, yea Fawnia shall be my fortune in spite of fortune" (205). But Dorastus vacillates again and apostrophizes himself for forgetting himself, allowing love to "violate" his honor, for loving Fawnia and dishonoring his father. The paradoxes nearly overwhelm Dorastus: he resolves, "cease to love her whom thou couldst not love, unless blinded with too much love," and he adds, "Tush, I talk to the wind, and in seeking to prevent the causes I further the effects" (205). In another shift, Dorastus, who speaks to the wind and himself at the same time (as apostrophe does precisely that), decides to love and honor Fawnia (206). Nor in an adjacent soliloquy is Fawnia spared further alienation. She depicts herself in this apostrophe as a female Tamburlaine, an ambitious shepherd, though she does not know (as the audience does) that she is a princess by birth: "Unfortunate Fawnia, and therefore unfortunate because Fawnia! Thy shepherd's hook sheweth thy poor state, thy proud desires an aspiring mind: the one declareth thy want, the other thy pride" (206). In 1588 Greene had *Tamburlaine* very much in mind as he probably also produced in that year, *Alphonsus, King of Aragon*, a dramatic imitation of Marlowe's play. The self-reflexive paradoxes continue. She also thinks it against "nature" to love a prince and, in accordance with the wheel of fortune and the *de casibus* tradition, she warns herself as if she were a parent giving advice to a child (as Egistus had Dorastus): "if thou climb thou art sure to fall." In Fawnia's speech Greene amplifies his moral—that time, fortune, and the gods will punish those who defy the order of the world: "Daring affections that pass measure are cut short by time or fortune: suppress, then, Fawnia, those thoughts which thou mayest shame to express" (206). She is all too aware of the drawbacks of her class, concludes, much as Dorastus had, "better were it to die with grief, than to live with shame," though she will try to "sigh out" love and be more patient than Dorastus. The prince becomes increasingly disquieted and estranged from himself. Greene uses a hunting image when his narrator describes Dorastus' decision to pursue Fawnia, though he qualifies this disturbing but common image with the prince's bungling this new kind of chase, finding Fawnia (her name suggests that she is a deer) harder to quarry than a partridge.

If Greene alienates the two lovers from themselves, he uses dramatic irony to show Fawnia's estrangement through circumstance and ignorance from Dorastus as well as from a part of herself. She salutes "the prince with such modest *curtesies* as he wondered how a country maid could afford such courtly behaviour" (207). Fawnia differentiates shepherds from courtiers by various means, one of which is identifying the pastoral with Pan and the courtly with Venus. As if Fawnia did not know herself or was subject to the division between public and private, she denies and objectifies ambition whereas before she admitted it as part of her identity: "Envy looketh not so low as shepherds: shepherds gaze not so high as ambition" (207). She also generalizes her desire for fortune and honor, saying that beggars should not strive against fortune or gaze after honor, protesting perhaps too much that her "nature" is unfit for the "nurture" of courtiers. Custom supplements and transforms nature. If Fawnia speaks to Dorastus about the simple pleasures of shepherds such as "oft singing and telling tales," their discussions about the art of love reveal a love of art (208).

An innocent art or artful innocence occurs in the relation between the two lovers. This oxymoron and antimetabole shows the identification and estrangement, the similarity and difference between Fawnia and Dorastus. When Dorastus says that Cupid is a child and Venus is freshly painted though old, Fawnia replies that "age may be painted with new shadows, and youth may have imperfect affections; but what art concealeth in one ignorance revealeth in the other" (208–9). Her observation emphasizes the dramatic irony that she is ignorant of her origins while the reader is not and that both the lovers conceal with art their intentions. Pandosto concealed while Bellaria suffered in ignorance. Fawnia's wit about art and love make her even more attractive to Dorastus, and her virtue will lead the prince to descend the social scale and become a shepherd. The arrival of Dorastus' companions separates them, which sets up another series of self-apostrophizing soliloquies. Rather than repeat observations on Greene's repetition, I shall only note Fawnia's repetition of aspiration and its fall, her division within—"thou hast denial at thy tongue's end, and desire at thy heart's bottom" (including this woman's blame of herself as a woman, presumably through a male narrator), and her suggestion that she should die because the prince jests in his love (209).

Dorastus is also suddenly changed, his identity altered as Fawnia's has been and will be even more so. He will let love conquer honor, though the narrator attributes "hot desires" to the prince. Disguised as a shepherd, Dorastus addresses himself, concentrating on his base transformation and still worried about Fawnia's social rank. He admits his "base desires" or "crooked desires" and justifies his transformation by comparing it with Neptune's change into a ram, Jupiter's into a bull, and Apollo's into a shepherd. Greene has a particular passage from *The Metamorphoses* in mind when he gives this language to Dorastus (210). In Book Six, Ovid represents Minerva, Jupiter's favorite daughter, being pleased with the muses' songs of stories of rape or attempted rape. All these involve transformation, such as the rape of Proserpine and Arethusa's flight, as well as the boy Triptol-emus' escape and the transformation of the Macedonian women into magpies (see Book V). These songs make Minerva think about Arachne, a mortal who had thought that her tapestries were better than Minerva's. Pallas Athena, or Minerva, had disguised herself as an old woman and had warned Arachne against defying a goddess, but even after she revealed herself to the mortal, Arachne remained proud and defiant, so that the contest continued. Pallas' tapestry showed the rock of Mars, the 12 gods, Pallas among them, surrounding Jupiter, all them "gazing in awe at this miracle," that is at the place where Pallas' spear had struck the earth and an olive tree had sprung. To this image, Pallas added the figure of Victory, and "to give her rival illustrations of the reward she might expect for her insane audacity," placed in the corners four scenes of mortals—Haemon and Rhodope, the queen of the pygmies, Antigone, the daughter of Cinyras—the first two transformed into mountains, the queen into a crane, Antigone into a bird, the limbs of the last into temple steps. Paradoxically, Pallas makes these corners enclose Pallas' triumph, the aspiring, powerless, and defeated mortals being mar-ginal rather than containing the gods.

Greene's allusiveness is more complex still. Dorastus refers to a context in Ovid in which Minerva, hearing the muses' tales in songs, remembers her tapestry that contains moral images within moral images, self-reflexive triumphs within reflec-tion. The transformations on the tapestry warn of human overreaching and the consequence of human retribution, a central concern of *Pandosto*. Transformed in love and lust, caught between sympathy and alienation, Dorastus apostro-phizes himself and alludes to a goddess whose self-reflexive remembrances con-tain his allusion to the transformations of Neptune, Jupiter, and Apollo. These transformations are even more complex, for they occur as part of Arachne's tap-estry. If Minerva's tapestry depicts the gods' victory over proud mortals, Arachne shows the disguises that the gods take on to rape mortal women, including, in the shape of a bull, Jupiter's rape of Europa; as a ram, Neptune's "deceiving" of Bisaltis; in shepherd's clothes, Phoebus' or Apollo's "deceit" of Isse. There are rapes in Arcadia, as Diana learned when Jupiter raped one of her nymphs. Nei-ther Jealousy nor Minerva can find any fault with Arachne's tapestry, so that in rage the goddess beats her rival, then transforms Arachne, who wants to hang herself, into a spider who hangs and weaves and is an artist. Ovid then tells the story of Arachne's friend, another mortal punished for her aspiration, Niobe, so that the context makes the moral clear and aesthetic (Book VI, pp. 136–38, see 62, 72–73). It appears to be no accident that Greene uses this allusion as an inset for a story about jealousy, aspiration, lust, despair, and divine retribution. Dorastus sees "love" or lust in himself, a prince who likens himself to a god who would seduce a mortal. By analogy, he makes Fawnia into a victim, qualifies the courtship with rape, his innocence with baser thoughts. Greene's exploration of art of love and of romantic transformation echoes Ovid's.

The love is strange in other ways. Fawnia would love the shepherd and then sees that he is Dorastus, who with a kiss begins "to lay the battery." Dorastus calls attention to the estrangement: "If thou marvel, Fawnia, at my strange attire, thou wouldest more muse at my unaccustomed thoughts: the one disgraceth but my outward shape, the other disturbeth my inward senses." Greene represents the tension between inward and outward; disguise and appearances destabilize identity for both Fawnia and Dorastus. As usual, Fawnia relates this problem of alienation to the relation between art and life: "Zeuxis' grapes were like grapes, yet shadows" (211). This image, which is one among many that she uses, relates to the contest between Minerva and Arachne, for all these images are examples of art being lifelike, but Fawnia is also saying that appearance is not actuality. Transformations, she implies, can be fictions, and although they represent nature they are not natural. Dorastus warns that time withers beauty and, setting aside his language of lust, he proposes to Fawnia. The narrator's description reveals the sympathy and alienation, the oxymoron: Fawnia "yielded up the fort in these friendly terms." Her profession of love is conditional, for she says, "I yield, . . . ready to obey his will, if no prejudice at all to his honour, nor to my credit" (211–12). The difference in class creates a parental obstacle to their marriage, namely Egistus, so that Dorastus decided that they should leave Sicilia, "as soon as time and opportunity would give them leave." Haste and danger surround their love. Dorastus rejoices in their love but must pretend to the court to have recovered his health. Whereas Dorastus cannot decide whether he is spiting the destinies, she, though fearful, thought that fortune was rewarding her (212).

Greene has his characters dwell on the class differences—Porrus is worried that a prince can get away with his dalliance because "it is a hard case where kings' lusts are laws, and that they should blind poor men to that which they themselves wilfully break" (212). Mopsa is as practical as many wives in folk tales, for she admonishes her husband, "Do what you can, but no more than you may, lest in saving Fawnia's maidenhead you lose your own head" (213). So Fawnia's adoptive father resolves to take the chain and the jewels to the king to please both Egistus and Dorastus with Fawnia's high birth. He is worried that the prince will make Fawnia pregnant, so that the shepherd and his wife equate the love with sex and power and not with chastity and idealism (213). The lovers plan to go to a strange country, so that they can be as they wish. Capnio, an old servant of Dorastus', agrees to help, and Fortune, who does not always seem predictable, shows Porrus "a little false play" and prevents him from showing the jewels to the king as evidence of his adopted daughter's noble birth. The old servant, a coffer under his arm, tricks the old shepherd, having him put forcibly on the ship, where he sees Dorastus and Fawnia, who was dressed in rich attire that "so increased her beauty that she resembled rather an angel than a mortal creature" (213). There is art and appearance in this love. Seeing Porras, the two lovers, the narrator says, are "half astonished" but also "marvelling greatly," although he notes that Dorastus "praised greatly his man's device" while Fawnia was ashamed for having put Porras in such a predicament. The old shepherd's grief and Dorastus' denial of Fawnia's plea to listen to her "father's" request to go home also qualify the celebration of love and increase alienation (216).

The End and Ends of Time

The ending of Pandosto creates a complex poetic justice. Greene's supplement is ambiguous because the pattern involves a mixture of sympathy and alienation. The king fears that Dorastus has been devoured by wild beasts, but when he finds out what has happened, he is "half dead for sorrow," and, thinking about the base birth of Fawnia, Egistus falls into a quartan fever, a severe illness with paroxysms. This is another example of the parental obstacles to marriage that occur often in comedies but also in tragedies like *Romeo and Juliet* and *Hamlet*. Dorastus, the narrator reports, thought little of father or country and, until a tempest rises, receives from Fortune good winds for his escape. Fortune is capricious as everyone now seems sick, uncomfortable or in danger. The threat of death subsides and the lovers are joyful until Dorastus hears that they have landed in Bohemia, the kingdom of Pandosto, the man his father hates most. The ambivalence persists (216–17). Capnio counsels Dorastus to disguise himself, and the prince will lie to Pandosto about his identity. The king of Bohemia, with "young and fresh affections," wants to see the beauty of Fawnia. The audience knows that Pandosto is Fawnia's father, so that the estrangement of dramatic irony builds as Pandosto's incestuous infatuation grows and he attempts to act on his desire. The figure of Pandosto is problematic, for he sends guards to apprehend the lovers and their party as spies only after he hears that they are no threat. Neither is his wonder complete, being by halves and almosts: "Pandosto, amazed at the singular perfection of Fawnia, stood half astonished, viewing her beauty, so that he had almost forgot himself what he had to do" (217). He also doubts the truth of Dorastus' tale, and the two quarrel until Pandosto throws the prince and the shipmen into prison while beginning to woo Fawnia with his "courtesy" (218–19).

Pandosto is a story of devices, both Greene's and the characters'. One of Greene's favorite techniques is the soliloquy: in Pandosto's we witness, as the narrator notes, "a thousand new devices" (219). As Dorastus and Fawnia do, Pandosto apostrophizes himself but is alienated from himself. In the imagery Greene plays on a conflict beyond the one Pandosto is experiencing, that of incest, of feeding on one's young. Of his desire for Fawnia, the king says, "I reach at that with my hand which my heart would fain refuse; playing like the bird Ibis in Egypt, which hateth serpents, yet feedeth on her [their] eggs" (219). Greene also has Pandosto consider aspiration—"king's thoughts ought not to climb so high as the heavens, but to look no lower than honour"—as he had Fawnia do. Like Dorastus and Fawnia, Pandosto says that he would rather die with honor than to live in "unfit love." Pandosto equates a woman's beauty with unchastity, blaming his victim. For him, the lure is Fawnia, "whose eyes are framed by art to enamour, whose heart is framed by nature to enchant," so that she is armed with both art and nature, which are complementary and not opposed (219). Just when Pandosto looks like he will obey reason and control his passion, he sends for Fawnia and asks her to forsake Dorastus, who called himself Sir Meleagrus for the power, prestige, and wealth of the king of Bohemia. Fawnia denies the advance of the man who has imprisoned her love "without cause," and Pandosto leaves her, hoping that time will make her reconsider, which leaves her one of the central devices of the story—the self-apostrophic soliloquy: "Ah, unfortunate Fawnia! thou seest to desire above fortune is to strive against the gods and fortune" (220). An important moral in this romance is to avoid affronting the gods with aspiration. To gaze at the sun, Fawnia says, leads to a fall, and she wishes that she had remained a shepherd, a remark that wrings with dramatic irony. The readers do not share her point of view as they know that she does and does not aspire, for she is not entirely what she seems to herself. She blames herself for the imprisonment of Dorastus, who pretends to be someone he is not. The narrator reports that Dorastus sometimes blames himself for his predicament because of his folly or his disobedience to his parents and at other times censures the gods and fortune.

Greene continues to use the structural technique of juxtaposing the lovers' self-reflexive apostrophizing soliloquies. In a soliloquy the prince upbraids himself like a dishonorable character that has not honored and obeyed his father, and, like Fawnia, he thinks of the suffering of his lover and welcomes his own death as a solution (220–21). Pandosto, as Egistus had before, threatens the identity and happiness of the couple. The narrator tells about the conflict in Pandosto, about his "broiling at the heat of unlawful lust" and his disquieted mind that make his subjects marvel greatly but also about his courteous entertainment of Fawnia. Pandosto does not know how unlawful his lust really is. Rape and seduction surface once more. Fawnia asserts that if the body yields, the mind will not. She also prefers honesty to honor and gold, but Pandosto depicts his behavior before her differently than he does in private, for he says he is doing her a good turn. When Fawnia still denies him, saying, as characters do repeatedly in this romance, that she would rather die with her reputation than live in dishonor, Pandosto threatens her with force as he thinks that "reason" has failed him. She despises the man who is actually her father.

This is a hard tale. Egistus hears about his son's imprisonment and would try to save him but would seek the death of Fawnia and her father. Sorry for his previous wrong against Egistus, Pandosto shows the King of Sicilia courtesy when his ambassadors arrive in Bohemia. The ambassadors interpret Pandosto's recounting of Dorastus' tale, guess the prince's identity, and, confirming it, convey Egistus' wish for retribution, adding Capnio to the death list. Despite his lust for Fawnia, in light of his former wrongs, Pandosto will comply with Egistus' request. If Pandosto marvels, so does Dorastus when he is released from prison (222–23). Both Pandosto and Dorastus experience ambivalence, Pandosto caught between lust and penitence, Dorastus between freedom and sorrow. The prince laments the death sentence for Fawnia, against whom Pandosto vents his hate, now transformed from "love." The enraged king rails against Fawnia, chastising her for, among other things, having "an aspiring mind." His apostrophic sermon to Fawnia and Porrus, which dwells on their abuse of honor, social position, and wisdom, is ironic as she is his daughter and is not an aspirant while his sin is more damning than the ones of which he accuses them. An example of the irony arising from Pandosto's brazen hypocrisy occurs in his speech to Capnio: "thou which hast betrayed the king, and hast consented to the unlawful lust of thy lord and master, I know not how justly I may plague thee: death is too easy a punishment for thy falsehood, and to live (if not in extreme misery) were not to shew thee equity" (223). The lustful and unjust Pandosto, under the guise of justice, judges Capnio for abetting lust. The suggested punishment is sadistic and tyrannical: he proposes to have Capnio's eyes put out and to have him ground in a mill "like a brute beast."

At the climactic moment of Pandosto's tyranny, Porrus reveals his story (223–24). Greene maximizes the dramatic effect. The old shepherd's tale is of the shipwreck of a foundling and of the identifying chain and jewels, a narrative the reader has already read but one that transforms the characters. So animated is Pandosto that he can hardly let the old shepherd tell out his tale. After questioning Porrus, Pandosto leaps up and, amid tears, kisses Fawnia, calling her his daughter, which drives the other characters "into a maze," but the reader is only amazed insofar as their amazement is contagious and not as a result of surprise or new revelations. Pandosto now tells the other half of Porrus' story, relates his own mistreatment of Bellaria and the abandoning of the child to the seas. It is as if Pandosto and Fawnia have forgotten the earlier sexual tension between them and as if the question of her high birth and the possibility of reuniting the friendship of Sicilia and Bohemia become, for them, most important.

The narrator prepares us for a comic ending, the obstacles overcome and the long enmity between the kingdoms over. He reports that the Sicilian ambassadors, admittedly from a limited point of view, rejoice at the prince's choice, that the kingdoms "should now through perpetual amity be united and reconciled" (224). The people, the narrator adds, celebrate the reunion and discovery of an heir with a bonfire while the courtiers appointed jousts and tourneys. The wish fulfillment and communal celebration continue for 18 days: Pandosto makes Porrus a knight, and the party moves to Sicily, where Egistus provides princely entertainment. Another preparation for a comic ending occurs when the narrator describes Egistus' view of the outcome as a "comical event," his rejoicing, and his desire that the couple experience "perpetual joy" through marriage. The ending becomes more complex as Greene complicates his representation of poetic justice and the self-conscious mixing of tragedy and comedy. Pandosto, the key to this ending, "calling to mind how first he betrayed his friend Egistus, how his jealousy was the cause of Bellaria's death," recalls "that contrary to the law of nature, he had lusted after his own daughter. Moved with these desperate thoughts," the narrator notes, Pandosto falls "into a melancholy fit, and, to close up the comedy with a tragical strategem, he slew himself" (225). Another tragic qualification does not allow a full comic celebration in which the reader can identify with the characters. There is a tension in poetic justice, which by necessity involves the "tragedy" of punishment and the "comedy" of reward. The tragedy may surprise the reader who expects the usual happy ending of romance rather than the poetic justice that Greene prepares him for since the beginning of *Pandosto*. In the last few paragraphs of the romance, Greene lulls the reader into the expectation of comedy but then, at least in part, surprises him. The last disjunction lies in the ambiguity of the end of the long last sentence. After the mourning for Pandosto, Dorastus left his father and "went with his wife and the dead corpse into Bohemia, where, after they were sumptuously entombed, Dorastus ended his days in contented quiet" (225). The "they" is ambiguous and seems to refer to the death of Fawnia and Pandosto, but if this reading is right, it makes us wonder why Dorastus later died in "contented quiet" and why the narrator does not mention how Fawnia lived out her days. This problem may be textual, but if we assume that Fawnia is dead and Dorastus lives, we might question the basis for the poetic justice because how did she defy the gods any more than Dorastus. Even if we try to ignore the terse and unmoralized "they," after the motives for Pandosto's death have been set out, we can still question the poetic justice in his suicide, for he did not know that he was seducing his daughter, although he was engaged in seduction, and seems to be reconciled to Fawnia. On the other hand, Greene emphasizes the celebration of the marriage and not Pandosto's guilt, apology, and penitence, except as an explanation for the suicide. Greene creates an end that is distinct from that of *The Winter's Tale* (which tends more toward penitence, reconciliation, regeneration, wonder, and a lasting happy ending and which gains some of its effect from a tension between the dramatic representation of Act V, Scenes i and iii and the narrative representation of Act V, Scene iii). After representing the marvelous and supplemental conventions of romance—the foundling, the disguise, the shipwreck, the discovery and identification of the foundling as being someone of high birth—Greene gives the ending the alienation of tragedy and the identification of comedy, and, for the breaking of the laws of nature, he attempts to punish and reward like God on high, repairing a fallen world with this moral overview.

Romance and comedy are closely connected, so much so that Heminge and Condell divided Shakespeare's First Folio into tragedies, comedies, and histories, and they placed plays we might now consider romances or tragicomedies into the section under comedy. In this chapter I sought to show the fragility and lack of respect that romance could have from Ben Jonson's allusion to *Pericles* and to Jared Sparks placing romance in a list of lighter and lesser kinds. I also placed romance in the context of Renaissance theories of poetry, comedy, tragicomedy, and romance before examining sympathy, alienation, and supplement in Greene's *Pandosto*, with some reference to Shakespeare's *The Winter's Tale*. In the next chapter, I would like to turn to the ends of comedy on the Renaissance stage, that is, the motives and goals and the loose ends when all is said and done. In a sense, this will be an analysis of the practice of comedy in plays in Italy, England, Spain, and France. More specially, I shall find examples in Guarini, Shakespeare, Jonson, Calderón, and Molière's from about 1590 to 1664 and stretch Shakespeare's contemporaries to roughly when his granddaughter, Elizabeth Hall, the last of his direct line, died childless in 1670.

CHAPTER 4

Renaissance Comedy

There is no denying the order brought to bear at the end of most Renaissance comedies. Criticism has often emphasized the happy ending of comedy and the movement from order through disorder to order.[1] This assumption is sound, but it needs modification. One of the recent qualifications has been, in the English-speaking world at least, to see the ends of comedy, both the endings and the purpose of the plays, as a kind of ideological containment. While these arguments, which find their inspiration in Derrida's breaking down of binary opposites and in Foucault's analysis of power, are suggestive and have provided new perspectives with which to view literary texts in general, and Renaissance comedy in particular, the interests of this chapter lie elsewhere.[2] I would like to argue that in Italian, Spanish, English, and French comedies of the early modern period, the very structure of the plays, the way they end, involves disjunction, stress, and rupture. The ends of comedy represent a return to order, but a restoration with loose ends. They are often asymmetrical and leave doubt in and with the audience. Here the exception, while not proving the rule, complicates it, and the comedies are not simply apologies for utopian hope or the existing social and political order. What I am proposing—to see the tragic in the comic, disorder in order, as an unsettling of the end of comedy—is not novel. The difference is one of emphasis, serving as a reminder that the complex ways of representing and seeing the endings of comedy from sixteenth-century Italy to seventeenth-century France can be forgotten in a fascination with order and pattern.[3]

The pleasure principle of comedy may predominate in the happy marriage that ends New Comedy and becomes popular in the romantic comedy of Shakespeare and his contemporaries, but, the "agonistic principle," to use Harry Levin's phrase, pushes the ends of comedy toward Freud's reality principle.[4] The stresses, ruptures, and the mixing of generic imperatives occur in many Renaissance comedies, including the ones most discussed here. Rather than examine the whole range of comedy, I shall concentrate primarily on two kinds or aspects, first the "romantic pastoral" Guarini's *Il Pastor Fido* (1590), Shakespeare's *As You Like*

It (1599), and *Twelfth Night* (ca. 1600–1601), particularly Calderón' s *No hay burlas con el amor* (ca. 1634–35)—second, and more briefly, "satirical comedy"—Ben Jonson's *Volpone* (1607) and Molière's *Tartuffe* (1664).[5] These comedies represent the poles of romantic comedy and romance (tragicomedy) and that of satire. Even in the most romantic of these comedies there is an admission of agon and reality.

Pastoral and Romantic Comedy

Pastoral and romantic comedy involve compensation and escape from the tensions of the world. The idyll of the pastoral contains implicit and explicit reference to its opposite. This absent other might be a social order that needs renewal, a household in which the *senex,* or old man, blocks the romantic yearnings of the young, or a world that has fallen from some kind of golden age or Eden. The tragic stress or potential chaos often occurs when the city or court threatens to impinge on the pasture or forest, what Northrop Frye has called the "green world."[6] Sheer confusion can seem, to the characters at least, a threat to their happiness. But even at the end, after the comic recognition has resolved the near catastrophe, there are loose ends and suggestions that the dark and tragic side of life is still there and can reassert itself at any time. This tragic potential is only suggested and in varying degrees, sometimes to the point of being in a very minor key.

Romantic comedy or what I have also called "romantic pastoral" represents the tragic or disorder on a sliding scale. These darker elements coexist with the more dominant celebratory aspects. If one accepts the origins of Greek comedy that critics like Francis Cornford set out, then the romantic element of comedy can be related to the Greek religious rites that probably involved ceremonies of sexual initiation for the young, whose *komoidia* or revel songs developed into Greek comedy.[7] Although I am concentrating on the period of romantic comedy from about 1590 to 1635, *Gl'Ingannati* (1537) contains many of the elements of plot that Shakespeare later uses in *Twelfth Night,* a comedy from the turn of the seventeenth century. Before Shakespeare's play, *Gl'Ingannati* represents a brother and sister parted by accident and ultimately reunited, a heroine who disguises herself as a boy and has to court a woman for the master she herself loves. The ending, however, lacks a comic scapegoat, like Malvolio, swearing revenge. Comedies share conventions but also distinguish themselves.

In *Il Pastor Fido,* Baptista Guarini represents characters who are blind and chase illusions in their pastoral Arcadia and whose recognition brings about a peripeteia. Guarini doubles the action.[8] At first, Silvio alone seeks Amarillo's love, but then Mirtillo is also in love with her. By a peripeteia, Mirtillo's fortunes are reversed and, through faithfulness, he wins Amarillo's hand. Dorinda loves Silvio without much hope, but through a peripeteia, she finds that he loves her. Silvio, blind in love and in the hunt, has wounded the disguised Dorinda with his arrow and wounds himself when he sees what he has done, a more concrete version of Romeo's poisoning of himself after he sees the sleeping Juliet and thinks her dead. When Dorinda asks Linco, an old servant of Montano, Silvio's father, not to carry her home disguised in the clothes she is wearing, Silvio says,

> Why should Dorinda go to any house
> But Silvio's? surely she shall be my Spouse
> 'Ere it be night, either alive, or dead.
> And Silvio in life or death will wed
> Dorinda. (IV.ix; 319)[9]

Here is a moment of love in life or death, tragedy in comedy and comedy in tragedy, a kind of transcendence of love that Shakespeare's Romeo and Cleopatra espouse in their respective plays. The marriage of spirits is part of Guarini's tragicomedy. Linco reinforces this Neo-Platonic element and also emphasizes the reversal and the doubling of the plot ("Now she may become thy Wife . . .," IV.ix.319f).[10] As Amarilli is lost to marriage, life, and virtue, Dorinda can become Silvio's wife. Linco prays to the gods for a cure for them both. They are wounded in a pastoral paradise in a kind of oxymoronic love where pain and pleasure, life and death are joined.

Corisca, a nymph who is in love with Mirtillo, is willing to sacrifice Amarilli. Guarini has her repent, and she is left by herself, so that there are not three couples paired, leading to a culmination at the end with the pairing of Mirtillo and Amarilli. To Mirtillo, Corisca says, "Thy pardon is to me a better feast: /A greater joy, my conscience now at rest."[11] Despite the asymmetrical ending, which J. H. Whitfield has observed, love triumphs.[12] Guarini separates the pairing of Silvio and Dorinda from that of Mirtillo and Amarilli by an act. Despite this double climax, which is reflective and splintering, the playwright is still proud of what he conceives to be an observance of Aristotle's unities in the play. In *Compendio della poesia tragicomica* (1601), Guarini asserts, "it seems to me that the *Pastor fido* has a great deal of this, since in it the precept of unity, taught to use by the great Aristotle, is exquisitely observed."[13]

The end of *Il Pastor Fido* represents the shepherds twice calling on Hymen to bless the marriage before and after Mirtillo's speaking of the joy and anguish he has experienced at once and his wondering, before Amarilli, whether he is in a state of sweet wakefulness rather than in a dream of bliss. At the very end, the Chorus also emphasizes the pairing of pain and pleasure in Guarini's tragicomedy ("O Happy couple!" [V.x.411]).[14] Here the Chorus moralizes about what a foil the couple's fears play to their joys, the blindness of mortals in love and life, true joy born from virtue after suffering. In this pastoral romantic comedy, which Guarini calls a tragicomedy, the tragic elements express themselves thematically and structurally, for instance, in the words of the Chorus and in the double mirror of the two couples, where likeness and difference appear.

Shakespeare also writes a romantic and pastoral comedy about faith in love: *As You Like It* (1599). Here disguise involves less talk of pain than in *Il Pastor Fido*, but both plays rely on Hymen's blessing, in the shepherd's choric prayer in Guarini's play and in person in a masque in Shakespeare's. The recognition scene in *As You Like It* involves Rosalind's disguise as Ganymede in which she promises to bring Rosalind forth and then appears, with Hymen and Celia, as "herself" (V.iv). The dramatic irony underscores the audience's knowledge and the exploration of identity in this comedy:

> *Duke Senior.* I do remember in this shepherd boy
> Some lively touches of my daughter's favor.
> *Orlando.* My lord, the first time that I ever saw him
> Methought he was a brother to your daughter. (V.iv.26–29)

Jaques' satirical presence and humor qualify the romance and give the comedy another dimension. He is wry about the movement toward the multiple pairings of lovers: "There is sure another flood toward, and these couples are coming to the ark" (V.iv.35–36). He calls Touchstone and Audrey "very strange beasts," that is, fools. Touchstone displays the wit of a fool on the topics of women, marriage, and the court before Jaques and Duke Senior but must leave off when the god of marriage, Hymen, enters. Touchstone has used "if" thematically and rhetorically to hold together his tale of the courtier and has spoken about "if" as a peacemaker full of virtue, and now Shakespeare pins his recognition scene on the anaphoric "ifs" of Duke Senior, Orlando, and Phebe as they discover Rosalind's identity. The playwright uses these serial "ifs" to lead from the climax of the Duke's recognition of his daughter and Orlando's of his love to the anticlimax of Phebe's *cognitio* that Rosalind cannot be hers because Ganymede is a woman: "If sight and shape be true, / Why then my love adieu!" (V.iv.120–21). As Ganymede, Rosalind exacted a "compact" from everyone before she left to change her costume, so that on refusal of Ganymede/Rosalind, she must marry the shepherd Silvius (V.iv.5–34). Hymen bars the confusion of identity that Rosalind's triple "if . . . not," in regard to father, husband, and woman, questions. Even Hymen, as he blesses the four couples with marriage and fertility, cannot resist a joke about the match between Audrey and Touchstone: do we know which is winter and which is foul weather (V.iv.135–36)? Duke Senior welcomes Celia and Rosalind while Phebe greets Silvius.

The next movement in the ending occurs with the entrance of Orlando's brother Jaques de Boys. He announces that Duke Frederick marshaled a great power to take the forest and to put his brother, Duke Senior, to the sword, but, after meeting a religious man, the Duke "was converted / Both from his enterprise and from the world" (V.iv.161–62). This report—which allows narrative to soften the romance nature of the conversion, the ultimate in reversals—includes the information that Duke Frederick has given back the crown and lands to his banished brother. This is a sequel to Oliver's conversion, so that this Jaques, and not the satirical one, is just in time, as Duke Senior tells him, for his two brothers' weddings. Duke Senior's proclamation applies as much to romantic comedy in general as to *As You Like It* in particular: "First, in this forest let us do those ends / That here were well begun and well begot" (V.iv.170–71). They return to order, love, and good fortune. After Duke Senior asks the couples to dance, melancholy

Jaques says he wants to join Duke Frederick in his religious life away from court for the sake of what is "to be heard and learn'd" (V.iv.185). In a role that would usually fall to Duke Senior, Jaques gives his blessing to the restored Duke and to the other males in the pairs of lovers. He cannot resist a parting shot in his interrupted badinage with Touchstone:

> And you to wrangling, for thy loving voyage
> Is but for two months victuall'd. So to your pleasures,
> I am for other than for dancing measures. (V.iv. 193)

But the Duke's response, "Stay, Jaques, stay" (V.iv.194), meets with Jaques' ambivalent response and not outright rejection. Jaques will not stay to see this dancing pastime, but he will stay to hear out the Duke at his cave: "What you would have I'll stay to know at your abandon'd cave" (V.iv.195–96). By pronouncing the shortness of Touchstone's proposed marriage and by not remaining for the marriage dance, Jaques does provide a satirical qualification to the comic order. The comic dance, as Anne Barton reminds us and as this chapter argues, cannot contain all elements of human experience, but whether Jaques goes off to search with Duke Frederick (368) is much more ambiguous than most critics, like Barton, assume.[15] In his discussion with the other Jaques, Jaques has stated his intention of joining Duke Frederick, but his reply to Duke Senior shows that he respects this brother's authority. Jaques will attend to him in the Duke's cave to know his wishes, which may be for Jaques to stay. If Jaques may be moving beyond the world of comedy, he is still perched on its outskirts. He may go and he may leave, but that, like the marriage itself, is left for the future in allusion: "Proceed, proceed. We'll begin these rites, / As we do trust they'll end, in true delights" (V.iv.197–98).

Like other begging choruses in Shakespeare's oeuvre, the Epilogue to *As You Like It* plays games with the audience. Just as Jaques qualified but respected the authority of Duke Senior at the end of the play, here Rosalind says that "It is not the fashion to see the lady as the epilogue" (1–2), but in challenging the convention, she softens the challenge through normative analogies, the lord as prologue, and the bush as the vintner's sign. Although a good play does not need an epilogue, Rosalind says, it can benefit from its supplement. Rosalind's wit shows that she begs as she denies it and implies that the audience knows what she is doing and enjoys it. She asks the men and women to let the play please as they love each other. But then the boy actor playing Rosalind is given the opportunity to make part of the delight of the play a playing with the gender boundaries of the comedy, which has relied on the dance of heterosexual marriage at the end to achieve order: "If I were a woman I would kiss as many of you as had beards that pleas'd me, complexions that lik'd me, and breaths that I defied not; and I am sure, as many as have good beards, or good faces, or sweet breaths, will for my kind offer, when I make curtsy, bid me farewell." (18–23) Here is the "If" that ends as conditionally as the "If" that begins Shakespeare's *Twelfth Night*. The boy actor is dressed as a woman and is thus in Shakespeare's fiction (when not dressed as the boy Ganymede), but in the after-shadows of the Epilogue, the character must also give way to the boy actor who lives in the world. The boy actor is, nevertheless, still in role because he will curtsy if they applaud Rosalind for her offer. The offer is fictional, an appeal to the desire of the men in the audience. They do not expect an actual parade of kisses. The last ambiguity is that this offer to the men (though women also have good faces and sweet breaths) ends the play, as if the applause is for the offer of kissing and not the pleasure of the play. But it also has to be an appeal to the women in the audience, as the appeal for applause and approval is also to them. It is hardly likely that Shakespeare expects only the men in the audience to applaud. In this play with gender boundaries, the playwright elides the difference between the offer of kissing and the play itself as well as the differences between men and women on stage and in the audience. The end of the body of this comedy and the Epilogue allow for wit and satire, the dance and the critic, conventional marriage and other desires.

The fifth and final act of *Twelfth Night* has more tragic force than the end of *As You Like It* and pushes harder toward catastrophe before the comic anagnorisis resolves the confusion over identity through the double image of Sebastian and Viola, which leads to the pairings of Sebastian and Olivia, Viola and Orsino. Feste clowns with the Duke just as Touchstone has with Jaques, playing on grammar and logic, in this case for gold, as Orsino waits for Olivia. After Feste and Fabian exit, Cesario/Viola recognizes Antonio as the man who rescued him (her, though she is still in disguise as Cesario, Orsino's servant). Unfortunately, for Antonio, the first officer identifies him as Orsino's enemy who, among other things, "did the Tiger board, / When your young nephew Titus lost his leg" (V.i.62–63). When Viola says that he did her kindness but then "put strange speech upon me" (67), the audience knows that Antonio mistook her for her brother Sebastian. Orsino calls Antonio "Notable pirate, thou salt-water thief!" (69), an appellation Antonio denies. His tale begins to reverse the catastrophe in which he finds himself, by the very information Antonio provides, rescuing "That most ingrateful boy there by your side" and about giving him his purse and later being refused it back (77). The audience knows what has happened, but this begins Viola's amazement. Olivia and her attendants interrupt Orsino's declaration of the impossibility that Viola (Cesario) had spent three months at Antonio's side, when the youth had tended the Duke for that same period. Olivia is still spurning Orsino and eyeing Cesario (Viola). Orsino would make a sacrifice of Cesario because Olivia loves him and not the Duke. There is, of course, another comic misunderstanding because Olivia has already mistaken Sebastian for Cesario and the brother has not spurned her as his disguised sister has. When Cesario rebuffs Olivia here and wants to follow his true love, Orsino, Olivia heightens the drama when she calls him, reminds him with "husband." This name stuns Orsino and puts the ever-denying Cesario on the defensive. To heighten the dramatic irony even more, Shakespeare has the Priest enter. He responds to Olivia's appeal by declaring that she was betrothed to Cesario less than two hours ago.

Shakespeare extends the dramatic irony as far as he can take it in order to get the most play from this comic stress. Orsino tells Cesario to go with Olivia but not to cross his path. Cesario protests because he is Viola, who is in love with the Duke. Olivia still thinks that Cesario protests out of fear of his master because of his social superiority. But Shakespeare interrupts this strand to bring in Sir Andrew Aguecheek with another story. Narrative plays a key role in this ending. Andrew accuses Cesario of hurting Sir Toby and him. Cesario also denies this accusation but has to face Toby and Feste. Toby's accusations—"H'as hurt me, and there's th'end on't" (V.i.196–97)—are loud, and he is led, on Olivia's order, to be tended for his injury. Just when Shakespeare could play on the dramatic irony even more by stringing out the accusations of Andrew and Toby, he has them leave the stage with Feste and Fabian and brings about the moment of ultimate confusion that leads to recognition: Sebastian comes on stage. Here is the central moment in the comedy:

> *Sebastian.* I am sorry, madam, I have hurt your kinsman,
> But had it been the brother of my blood,
> I must have done no less with wit and safety.
> You throw a strange regard upon me, and by that
> I do perceive it hath offended you.
> Pardon me, sweet one, even for the vows
> We made each other but so late ago.
>
> *Duke.* One face, one voice, one habit, and two persons,
> A natural perspective, that is and is not! (V.i.209–17)

Sebastian gives the answer that Cesario is expected to give. With his words Sebastian satisfies Olivia but baffles Orsino. There are two such men in the Duke's view, as nature has produced an optical doubling that is and is not an illusion. Sebastian's warmth toward Antonio also corroborates Antonio's earlier self-defense before Orsino. Antonio pursues Orsino's puzzlement: "How have you made division of yourself? / An apple, cleft in two, is not more twin / Than these two creatures. Which is Sebastian?" (V.i.222–24). In love with one Sebastian, Olivia finds the existence of two "Most wonderful!" (225). Sebastian himself is baffled—"Do I stand there?" (226)—and it is now for Sebastian and Cesario to give the last clues to the characters and end the dramatic irony. They match backgrounds and lament the loss of each other without knowing it.

Shakespeare does string out this recognition to give the audience pleasure over the characters' discovery, especially that of brother and sister. In typical fashion, Shakespeare contrasts the joy the audience experiences in dramatic irony with the sadness the characters feel at a sense of loss. They have lost each other and remember the loss of their father without embracing each other as who they are. The audience already feels the recognition while "Cesario" and Sebastian are still in the tale of catastrophe. Sebastian's lines illustrate this contrast: "Were you a woman, as the rest goes even, / I should my tears let fall upon your cheek, / And say, 'Thrice welcome, drowned Viola!'" (239–41). Cesario/Viola recognizes her brother and eight lines later begins to reveal her feminine identity as Viola. She has an "If" of her own as she replies to Sebastian:

> If nothing lets to make us happy both
> But this my masculine usurp'd attire,
> Do not embrace me till each circumstance
> Of place, time, fortune, do cohere and jump
> That I am Viola. (V.i. 249–53)

She continues that she will confirm this claim with the evidence of the captain who saved her and who has her "maiden's weeds" (255).

Sebastian seeks to interpret this moment of recognition for Olivia as this revelation of identity affects her even more than Orsino since she has married Sebastian thinking him Cesario. So Sebastian reminds Olivia that she has been mistaken but that Nature allowed her to fall in love with someone with the likeness of Sebastian. In fact, she has married Sebastian because he looks like Cesario. But Sebastian will not be deterred in his mediation: "You would have been contracted to a maid, / Nor are you therein, by life, deceiv'd, / You are both betroth'd both to a maid and a man" (261–63). The sexual ambiguity that *As You Like It* flirts with in the body of the play and the Epilogue becomes explicit in the climax of *Twelfth Night*. But before Olivia can reply, Orsino responds as, in his interpretation, Olivia stands amazed. The Duke calls upon another romance element, "this most happy wrack" (266), which will benefit him. The ambiguity is like that in Rosalind's Epilogue: "Boy, thou hast said to me a thousand times / Thou never shouldst love woman like to me" (267–68). Orsino cannot help but yoke boy and woman in the same sentence. Still Olivia does not speak. Instead, Viola swears once more her love for the Duke, who wants to see her woman's clothes—just in case. Viola says that the Captain who has them in prison is under the order of Malvolio, a member of Olivia's household.

And so the theme of Malvolio, who had suffered a plot against him as he dreamed of Olivia's love, reemerges. Rather than respond to Sebastian and the revelation of Viola's identity, Olivia remembers Malvolio and asks that he be brought to her so that he can release the Captain, who has Viola's feminine clothes. Olivia admits that in her frenzy she forgot Malvolio. Feste discusses Malvolio's "madness" and would read Malvolio's mad letter as if he were mad. Fabian, another of Olivia's servants, reads the missive, which begins—"By the Lord, madam, you wrong me, and the world shall know it"—and which is signed—"The madly-used Malvolio" (V.i.301–2, 311). Olivia does not see much madness in Malvolio's reply, and when she finally replies to the revelations that Sebastian and Viola have uncovered, she asks the Duke "To think me as well a sister as a wife" (317), and offers to pay for both weddings at her house. The Duke offers Viola his hand, so she can now be "Your master's mistress" and, to Viola, "A sister! you are she" (326).

But here tension arises in the celebration that grows out of the characters' perception of the identities of Sebastian and Viola. Malvolio enters with Fabian and makes his famous accusation against Olivia, which echoes his letter, that she has done him "wrong, / Notorious wrong" (328–29). He wants to know why she has abused him by encouraging him with a letter and then imprisoning him "in a dark house" (342). Olivia, who says it is Maria's hand and judges evenhandedly, tells Malvolio,

> Prithee be content.
> This practice hath most shrewdly pass'd upon thee,
> But when we know the grounds and authors of it,
> Thou shalt be both the plaintiff and the judge
> Of thy own cause. (V.i.351–55)

Fabian confesses that Toby and he devised the plot against Malvolio, with Maria's aid, but did it for laughter rather than revenge, thereby letting the other characters know what the audience already knows. Fabian asks that the injuries on both sides be weighed. After Olivia says to Malvolio, "Alas, poor fool, how have they battled thee!" (361), Feste quotes some of the foolish lines that Malvolio has spoken in the play, and now the other characters recognize them for what they are because they understand the context of the trick or plot. The Fool, who says he played Sir Topas, finishes his satire on revenge, by turning Malvolio's accusations against him: "And thus the whirligig of time brings in his revenges" (376–77). To which Malvolio answers, "I'll be reveng'd on the whole pack of you" (378), and exits.

Whether that whole pack includes Olivia herself, or only the tricksters, is not entirely clear. Olivia still takes Malvolio's side, echoing Malvolio's own words to Feste—"Fool, there was never man so notoriously abus'd" (IV.ii.87–88)—when she says, "He hath been most notoriously abus'd" (379). This echo juxtaposes the plot with the exposure of the abuse. But it is not Olivia who decides what must be done, although it seems that Fabian's and Feste's pleadings have not had any demonstrable effect on her. Instead, it is Orsino who is more concerned with the evidence of the Captain, whom Malvolio imprisoned (something too often forgotten in the commentary), the evidence of the forged letter, and the wrong done against Malvolio. He does not seem concerned about the Captain, except that he can present the evidence of Viola's clothes. The Duke is speaking with the major voice of comedy when he asks (it is not clear whom) to pursue Malvolio "and entreat him to a peace" (380), so that the wronged steward's acrimony and pledge of retaliation will not usurp the music and marriage that define the order at the ends of comedy but will be played in a minor key. Knowledge of the Captain will, the Duke says, allow a marriage at a suitable time, which, he assures Olivia, they will attend.

Thus the marriage is delayed as the comic scapegoat has escaped with the last clue. Malvolio's angry flight also suspends the question of gender. The *cognitio* or comic recognition of Cesario's female identity is deferred, so that, cross-dressed, the woman under the man's clothes must wait to become Viola and Orsino's wife.[16] He addresses her as a man impatient for his return to womanhood:

> Cesario, come—
> For so you shall be while you are a man;
> But when in other habits you are seen,
> Orsino's mistress, and his fancy's queen. (V.i.385–88)

The boy actor remains in the role, so there is another layer in the garment of desire.

After these lines, the characters leave the stage, except for Feste, who sings a song. This song follows Malvolio's swearing of revenge and the damage control Olivia and the Duke may perform as members of the ruling class. As critics have long noted, this is a political scene as well because Malvolio dresses like a Puritan and may be said to represent those who dissented within and without Elizabeth's Church of England. This is another irruption, a political rebellion (although Malvolio would have been very happy to marry Olivia) that has resonances for later audiences that Shakespeare did not live to see. But this darkness is combined with foolishness. The Clown ends the play. Shakespeare used a similar refrain in the song that ends this comedy to one in the very middle of *King Lear*, where Kent and the Fool take the king into a cave out of the storm. In that play the Fool calls the king "grace" and himself a "codpiece" and "a wise man and a fool" (III.ii.40–41). The wind and rain in the tragedy are the chaos at the center of the play. Unlike Feste, Lear's fool also alludes to sexual transgression and disorder.

Why Shakespeare chooses to end *Twelfth Night* with Feste, the Clown who brought back revenge and threw it in Malvolio's face until he fled, is not clear. Shakespeare's clowns are prone to satire, and their wit can unmask and can show a wistful bent whether the context they find themselves in is happy or terrible. Feste sings a song about rain. His representation of the changes in life is a different version in the genre of Jaques' speech on the seven ages of man.[17] Feste's rendition follows the progress of the song's protagonist from when he was a tiny boy and his foolishness was taken as a toy, to "man's estate" when men shut their gate against knives and thieves (perhaps even fools), to marriage where he learned that he could never thrive by bullying, to old age when drunkards were still drunk (perhaps like Toby and Aguecheek). But no specific allegory is attached to the song, and it is built on tautology: rain usually rains and drunkards are usually drunk. This is one kind of wit Shakespearean fools use. It is a kind of beautiful nonsense, apparently pregnant with meaning and rich in its simplicity. The song ends with a stanza that moves from the beginning of the world to pleasing the theatre audience:

> A great while ago the world begun,
> [With] hey ho, etc. [the wind and the rain,]
> But that's all one, our play is done,
> And we'll strive to please you every day. (V.i.405–8)

Like Rosalind's epilogue, Feste's song asks for applause, but *Twelfth Night* ends with Malvolio's sworn revenge, attempts to contain it and to bring about order in gender roles and with marriage, and a sweet and sad song about rain, spoken by the actor who is and is not in character as the Clown who tricked Malvolio and mocked him into his exit. Shakespeare thereby balances Feste's claims and Malvolio's, although Feste gets the last word. The celebratory nature of the comedy cannot escape the accusations and the shadow of the comic scapegoat even in his very absence. The mixed nature of this comedy is a productive problem, like the problematic at the end of *Henry V*, so that to use the term "problem comedy" or "problem play" to describe it, would be positive and not some deficiency that hangs on a theatrically achieved ending by a baffled playwright.[18]

The cross-dressing and sexual ambiguity in *As You Like It* and *Twelfth Night* is part of a representation of these elements on the Renaissance stage throughout Europe.[19] Calderón's *La vida es sueño* (ca. 1635) deserves more attention in this regard. It is reminiscent of *As You Like It*, perhaps by coincidence. As in the relation between Rosalind and Orlando, that between Segismundo and Rosaura involves a mixing of gender boundaries through disguise, and the recognition of the heroine's identity, now as a woman and without boyish disguise, brings about the harmonious marriage that graces so many comic endings. But the breaking down of gender boundaries qualifies the rules of that conventional marriage. Even though it seems that order and convention have triumphed, can the audience forget the world of cross-dressing and the joy and laughter it produced?[20] The representation of a return to the "normal" cannot entirely suppress female transgression. The rupture of carnival leaves an opening for the forbidden and the celebration of inversion. When in *A Midsummer Night's Dream* (1595) Theseus proclaims, "The lunatic, the lover, and the poet / Are of imagination all compact" (V.i.7–8) before the play of the rude mechanicals, he is calling attention to whether the dream in and of the *Dream* is a fiction. The audience considers whether the comic dance of premarriage is a dream both while it is going on and as they make their way out of the theatre. Puck's epilogue completes the stylized and literal comedy of Pyramus and Thisbe at Theseus' bidding. Puck speaks of actors as shadows and asks for applause from the audience, which he hopes will be less critical than the young lovers are of the production by the rude mechanicals. The very coexistence of criticism with prenuptial celebration of the marriage dance after the events of the midsummer dream produces an order of a different kind from a straight marriage dance. Shakespeare has Prospero observe at the end of the wedding mask: "We are such stuff / As dreams are made on; and our little life / Is rounded with a sleep" (*Tempest*, IV.i.156–57). Even in romance, the characters call attention to the globe dissolving and not leaving "a rack" behind. Calderón also observes the metaphysics of dream: the moment of recognition is that life is a dream.[21] This metaphor hardly possesses the solidity of comic order. But can the dream of the class and gender inversion of pastoral comedy, the land of desire, be so easily forgotten even if a rack of it, and anything else, will not be left behind? How much does the Lord of Misrule and gender transgression represent catharsis for a day or a kind of shadow structure that is often there at the end of comedy? To see the unseen is the paradox of recognition.

Comedy of Laughter and Manners

Before looking at satirical comedy, this chapter will examine a comedy devoted to laughter and manners and with only hints of darkness and tragedy, although it has its fair share of satire and parody—Calderón's *No hay burlas con el amor*, or *Love is a Laughing Matter* (1635). This comedy of intrigue and situation culminates with an ending that borders on farce. It represents themes of treachery and deceit with a lightness that Malvolio's presence does not allow in *Twelfth Night*. *No hay burlas con el amor* is a comedy that almost overthrows the argument of this chapter as it tries to evoke laughter in the representation of all things, from Leonor's tricking of her older sister, Beatriz, to Don Alonso's wound from a street fight arising from jealousy growing out of a misunderstanding of a love situation. By laughing at events that would be serious in life, even though their exaggeration heightens the dramatic irony, farce edges toward absurdity. The farce and the debate over the role of women in love and society in *No hay burlas con el amor* belong to a kind similar to Shakespeare's *The Taming of the Shrew* (1590–94), which itself draws on George Gasgoigne's *Supposes* (1566), an adaptation of Ariosto's comedy, *I Suppositi* (1509). Calderón, however, does not make much of the battles of the wills between Don Alonso and Beatriz and emphasizes their love at first sight, and he does not develop the same motifs from Roman New Comedy that Ariosto, Gasgoigne, and Shakespeare do. Nonetheless, these Renaissance comedies rely on false suppositions about characters and the situations in which they find themselves. There is, however light and pleasant we find farce, something disturbing, at least to modern audiences and perhaps to those during the Renaissance, between the machinery of laughter, slapstick jokes, and situations, and the less comic content, such as cruelty and deceit. Even if the transformations of the characters—in *No hay burlas con el amor* of Beatriz from a beautiful woman conceited with her command of language and knowledge to a woman in love, and of Don Alonso from a womanizing noble cynical about women and love to a man in love—are not explored in depth, their presence in the comedies implies that they could be and that they help constitute a shadow structure. Some of the laughter, as in the more farcical examples of English Restoration comedy, is uneasy. For the most part, the audience laughs and makes taboo topics less threatening and apparently more controllable by subjecting them to ridicule.

Comedy can also laugh at its own conventions, which is what Cruickshank and Page suggest occurs in *No hay burlas con el amor*, whose title proclaims that love is no laughing matter.[22] Comedies of the *siglo d'oro*, or the Spanish Golden Age, often share some conventions with Greek comedy. Both involve love among the young that culminates in marriage, a love that is unknown to the older generation or is actively blocked by it. The end includes a marriage that represents the triumph of youth and fertility over the winter of age (xv). Don Cruickshank and Sean Page point out that at the end of such Spanish comedies, the younger generation overcomes the older generation by joining it, so that the desire to be free finds the need to conform. While these critics think that this paradoxical tension is resolved through laughter, it may be that comic marriages, even in farces and comedies of manners, are an uneasy truce (xiv–xv). In lighter comedy it is probably too solemn to speak about the tragic dimensions of their endings, but it is still possible to see unresolved stresses or potential problems with the new society that the marriage is ushering in.

No hay burlas con el amor inverts class boundaries more than those of gender, but Beatriz has intellectual aspirations that go against conventions for women in the seventeenth century. The inversions of class occur, for instance, when Don Alonso is as cynical about women as a servant usually is (1059–88, 1515–34), while Moscatel, his servant, is in love like a noble and describes his beloved, the servant, Inés, in terms usually reserved for the nobility (697–704, 1094–96). Inés, too, sometimes uses diction more suited to a noblewoman (1251–66). The role reversals, as Cruickshank and Page note, do not turn the classes upside down: having accepted Moscatel's proposal, Inés joins him in conventional stage-servant cynicism when she refers to marriage as one of the worst things (3105–12); moreover, Don Alonzo and Beatriz defy the conventions of their class and gender but seem to end up reconciled to them.[23] Typical of the pattern of comedy, the old order moves through disorder to a new order. Sometimes, of course, the new order, except for being one generation later, is not that different from the old order.

As in *Twelfth Night*, in *No hay burlas con el amor* a trick or joke causes suffering for one of the characters, Beatriz. In this instance one woman, Leonor, thinks of a way of tricking another, Beatriz. She has the idea of introducing Don Alonso as the pretended lover of Beatriz. With Moscatel, Inés later agrees that this joke was a bad one (1925–26). Afterward, in an aside, Eleanor recognizes that the joke was a bad idea: "Oh, how I wish I'd never dreamed up that idea of getting revenge. What began as a joke is turning out to be deadly serious!" (1957–60).[24] But Leonor's first instinct, when Beatriz would not allow her to dissuade her older sister from telling their father, Don Pedro, about Leonor's love for Don Juan, was to defend herself and attribute Don Juan's letter, which the sisters tear in half as the father discovers them, to a fictional lover of Beatriz (907–61). The trick is even more necessary for the plot than the one practiced on Malvolio in *Twelfth Night*, as the steward plays the third man—or odd man out—role that Don Luis does in *No hay burlas con el amor*, rather than one of the lovers who participates in marriage at the end. As Leonor's trick unfolds, with Don Juan's help, Don Alonso becomes the invented lover whose feigned love turns to true love when he looks into Beatriz's eyes. The trickster is tricked, and the reversal soon brings in the *cognitio* or comic recognition. The situation comedy cannot do without the trick as Beatriz needs to be married, so that Don Juan can marry the younger daughter, Leonor.

In romantic comedy a sliding scale exists between disguise and deceit. Rosalind's disguise in *As You Like It* is fairly harmless; the false "disguise" of Don Alonso as Beatriz's admirer (as devised by Leonor and Don Juan) is a less harmless deceit; the disguise and trick that imprison Malvolio as a cross-gartered and not a star-crossed lover are probably more harmful than they are harmless. With each step, from simple disguise to intrigue, the role of satire, revenge, and cruelty increases. As Beatriz and Malvolio begin as self-righteous prudes, they are ready to be comic gulls, but the more cruel the revenge, the more questionable the comic movement becomes. It is as if the structure of comedy overcomes its comic content. Satire pushes comedy in the direction of tragedy, although in *No hay burlas con el amor* this movement is so incipient that it is only there potentially.

Formally, *No hay burlas con el amor* is effective, as Calderón pushes the comic catastrophe as far as possible before the comic ending. Even though the tone is so light that the audience does not fear a tragic ending, confusion reigns until the last few lines. The technique of this comic structure centers on Leonor's trick in which she reverses Beatriz's accusations against her, thereby impugning the reputation of her elder sister so that their father, Don Pedro, makes a false discovery, beginning with his discovering his daughters tearing a letter and listening to Leonor's lies about Beatriz (897–1022) and ending with him believing Leonor's second denunciation of Beatriz (1419–78, esp. 1413). The final *cognitio* begins when Don Pedro complains about his honor and speaks ambiguous lines that make Beatriz and Leonor fear that he has discovered their loves: "What's wrong is that I have met insults, though it might be truer to say insults have come calling on me in my house" (2992–95).[25] Moscatel and Inés also contribute to the dramatic irony because in hearing Don Pedro they, too, think that the daughters have been discovered. It turns out that Don Pedro is angry with Don Luis, who has told him that he must go to the wars rather than marry Beatriz (see 2638–2741). To Beatriz, he says, "Because of you Don Luis insults both my house and me" (3006–7).[26] Just when the sisters discover that their father does not know who their lovers are, Don Juan arrives and complicates the situation by appealing to Don Pedro's honor by asking him to assist him in pursuing three men from his door. Don Juan does so to spare Don Alonso the danger of dropping from the balcony again, but this backfires as Don Alonso fears that these are the men who tried to kill him.

In short, the complication moves toward catastrophe because Don Pedro then discovers Don Alonso and Moscatel. Now Don Pedro says that Don Juan must assist him in a graver matter than the one for which Don Juan had asked his assistance. This is where the danger mixes with slapstick: Don Pedro and Don Alonso fight with Don Juan, not being able to choose between them. This fighting precipitates the arrival of Don Luis and Don Diego. This arrival reminds Don Pedro that he would like to avenge himself on Don Luis, who says that such a situation was the reason he withdrew his offer of marriage to Beatriz. Don Alonso wants revenge because he now discovers that Don Luis is the man who wounded him. Don Juan then recognizes that Leonor was honorable and his jealousy unfounded. He joins Don Alonso in defending the daughters against their father, who might kill them for his honor. This situation brings about the comic resolution or climax with the recognition of the four lovers ("Don Juan," 3093–3102). Don Pedro refuses to say anything because the two men have promised marriage, something that cannot, in his view, be undone. For Don Luis, it is. The rival says nothing. The daughters have been silent since they each expressed, in a line, their sorrow over the fighting, and they remain speechless. Their father, who does not bless the marriage but is happy for what it does to his honor, does not say any more. The farce ends with the promise of marriage and with brief commentary.

The comments belong first to the two servants, Moscatel and Inés, whose master and mistress are going to be married, and to Alonso himself. The emphasis is on the reversals "de las burlas del amor" ("from the game of love") as Calderón has the two servants talk about what amounts to the laughing matter, joke, trick, game, or deception of love. Inés and Moscatel return to the role of the wry or cynical stage-servants commenting on the folly of aristocratic love. The playwright crafts their lines in a similar fashion, so that Inés' observation of the reversal that brings about the unlikely event of Beatriz's marriage supplements and echoes Moscatel's about Don Alonso's wedding:

> *Moscatel.* And so we see that the freest of men emerges from
> the game of
> love maimed and lamed and (worst of all disasters!) wed.
>
> *Inés.* And the silliest, vainest, haughtiest woman emerges from
> the game of love enamoured in spite of herself and
> (what's even worse!) wed. (3103–12)[27]

The speeches begin the same way, with "En fin," an "Anyway" that also announces the end of the comedy ("fin"). Moscatel's speech about Don Alonso uses the approximate rhyme of "sale" and "males" as Don Alonso is the most free man who "emerges" from the joke of love injured, lame, and married, the last of which is the greatest of all "wrongs" or "evils." Inés also builds her speech around a similar phrase, echoing the title, and rhymes "del amor" with "lo peor." Her use of "sale" chimes with Moscatel's rhyme. She says of Beatriz that the most mad, vain, and arrogant of women has, from the game or deception of love, emerged in love and married, which is the "worst" thing. The servants represent two reluctant lovers. Although not as witty as Millamant and Mirabel in Congreve's *The Way of the World* (1700), Beatriz and Don Alonso share their initial resistance to marriage, only to find themselves married, even if Beatriz does not have a name that alludes to a thousand lovers and does not insist on a contract that protects her rights as a woman. Despite the cynicism, Moscatel asks for Inés' hand and adds, if that is the way it has to be, they should not think about it and that the tricks and games of love, which are serious (true), are at an end. Taking Inés' hand may or may not be in marriage, but it is not a repudiation of the attraction that underlies love. Don Alonso addresses the audience directly, asking it not to laugh but to learn a lesson from him: "let everyone beware of love!" (3118).[28] These lines supplement and echo Don Alonso's direct address at the end of Act II to the men in the audience who are in love (2033–38). The last two lines of the play are a condensed version of the poet asking pardon and asking humbly, with some flattery, for the audience's approval. The audience joins the celebration of love after having been warned through satire and ironic comment on love.

Besides the wry satire, especially for modern audiences, the status of women has its stresses in Calderón's comedy. Beatriz is pompous, but she does not deserve to be duped simply because she is a woman who is a prude with intellectual pretensions. The trick against her is a plot device and serves well the symmetrical nature of comic structure. The accuser, Beatriz, becomes the accused. The reversal that the trick ushers in can be traced in the language: Beatriz says to Leonor: "Eso no, / que tener no puedo yo / hermana libidinosa" ("I am no such thing! I cannot have a libidinous sister!") (619–20), lines that Leonor later throws back in her face, except Calderón changes "Eso" to "Aqueso" (1414–16).[29] Don Alonso begins by laughing at love and ends by warning against such a course; Moscatel starts by scorning Don Alonso for mocking him for being in love and for deceiving women and finishes by wondering how such a man could wed. But the attitude toward women generally, and Beatriz particularly, in the play is traditional. Don Juan criticizes her for being conceited about her appearance and her cleverness, especially in Latin and the composition of Castilian verse, with an implicit glance at a convoluted style, perhaps worthy of Góngora: "she never utters a word except in long and convoluted sentences that nobody could possibly understand without the aid of footnotes" (305–8).[30] Moreover, Don Juan's satirical portrait of Beatriz, which follows in contrast a set-piece description of Leonora, lasts about 53 lines and precedes another description of the conflict between the sisters (see 194–392). This three-part description is more than a device to set up the situation or intrigue of the comedy: it is also a means of representing Don Juan's ideal love in contrast with the unfortunate Beatriz, who has the traditional vanity of woman and combines it with that of man. The trouble is that Beatriz and Don Alonso, who hears this long piece, usurp the role of the central lovers, and Don Alonso, himself no champion of new ways for women, does come to love Beatriz. She modifies her speech under the orders of her father and with the help of Inés, her compliant maid, but whether she leaves the old Beatriz behind entirely is debatable.

Just what else is said about women and about Beatriz? It is Don Luis who accepts Beatriz for what she is, yet he loses her, as if the structure of the comedy reinforces the approval of the changes that are imposed on her, first by Leonor's trick and second by her father's orders that arise from believing that ruse's false representation of Beatriz. The reversal in the comedy is problematic from this point of view, even if we admit that Beatriz's vanity about her appearance and her style of speech is excessive. Don Luis asks Don Diego why he should not make arrangements to marry Beatriz, which is, contrary to Don Diego's view, the right thing to do "if she is virtuous, rich, noble, beautiful and clever" (462–64).[31] But Don Diego thinks that Beatriz is too clever, and he would not like a wife who knew more than he did. This position does not impress Don Luis, who asks when can knowledge be bad? In this debate on the role of women, Don Diego answers that knowledge is bad when it is out of step and explains that women belong to the domestic sphere: "A woman should know how to spin and sew and put on patches. There's no need for her to study ancient authors and be able to write verse" (471–74).[32] Still, Don Luis will not budge. He thinks that no one should fault an excess in the harmless virtue of knowledge. Don Diego has to shift his ground as he is not winning this debate, so he concentrates on the way Beatriz scorns him, but Don Luis, the thinking man's Romeo, loves her disdain in some kind of unstated convention that she is the unobtainable beloved, perhaps from a sonnet sequence as much as from romance. In defeat, Don Diego utters the plaintive "Vamos, pues" ("Very well") (486).[33] Don Luis then delivers, in the excessive and idealistic language of lovers (not too different from Orlando's love poetry in *As You Like It*), an ode to the center of his life ("centro" 486), that is, Beatriz and her house. The style of this brief apostrophe (487–500) is elaborate. Along with Calderón's representation of Beatriz's style, it resembles Shakespeare's use of Lyly's euphuistic and pedantic style in *Love's Labour's Lost*. Don Luis' speech especially plays on the initial and medial repetition of "fuera," or "out of," to stress Don Luis' point that as a lover, being out of Beatriz's center or house, he is out of his element like the fish, bird, beast, flame, blossom, voice, life, and soul he represents in his extended metaphor. Don Luis uses *isocolon* and *conduplicatio*, that is, a kind of parallelism of clauses of about the same length and the repetition of words in adjacent clauses or phrases, respectively. His highly metaphorical use of language (often through simile and other comparison) and initial repetition (anaphora) is elaborate. Thus Don Luis builds up to the climax: his lover is translated to heaven. He is the lover and Beatriz is his heaven. With that ecstasy, he leaves with Don Diego.

Calderón represents Beatriz in all her circumlocutory and periphrastic splendor. There is no denying the satire on such language, even if the playwright did admire an ornate poet like Góngora. Beatriz refuses Leonor's request in outlandish language, but without malapropisms, and Leonor retaliates with her trick. Even Beatriz can accept the conventional view of woman while all but Don Luis (and presumably Don Pedro, until he thinks his daughter's language is connected to her supposed moral turpitude) say that she flouts the natural role of women. She condemns Leonor in unyielding terms in the speech beginning with "Desist! Seek not such propinquity with me, for you will sully the purity of my most chaste bosom and desecrate the altar of my honour" (603–16).[34] Calderón uses the rhyme and rhythm of verse to help Beatriz make her point and for the audience to get a sense of her (something that the English prose translation can only glimpse at). She speaks of honor as Don Pedro does. Beatriz will tell him of Leonor's breach of honor. Leonor says she has kept her honor.

Even if Calderón is satirizing romantic and courtly love, by allowing Don Luis to lose and Don Alonso to win Beatriz, he keeps Moscatel and Inés in love and the manservant waxing about love throughout, except at the end when he joins his own beloved in commenting wryly on the odd couple of Don Alonso and Beatriz. Besides, Don Juan is an idealistic lover of Leonor—his speech is much longer than Don Luis' and as extravagant—and he wins his love (see 192–269). Don Alonso is the playboy of comedy and gives a view of women in keeping with his role: "In my opinion, there are grounds for loving every woman and for leaving every woman."[35] Moscatel rightly fears that Don Alonso will pursue Inés, which he does, but she refuses him and teaches her lover a lesson for his false jealousy.

Both Beatriz and Inés resist stereotypes, the lady waiting for marriage and the servant available for sexual dalliance with her superiors. Inés shows herself to be an independent woman ("Tell your master, wretch" [1257–66]).[36] But Beatriz's independence is under siege when Leonor tricks Don Pedro into believing that her elder sister has soiled his honor with a tryst. The father turns on Beatriz: "It's all too plain that, if you can bring yourself to talk like that, instead of talking like everybody else, you will also behave differently from everybody else" (1440–42).[37] Don Pedro will not just judge her by connecting her bad behavior with her unusual speech, but he forbids study, poetry, and Latin books (1452–55). Calderón creates a comic situation because after all these years, Don Pedro has changed his mind and has decided that to control Beatriz morally, he must do so intellectually. He joins Don Diego's school of thought—women are for the domestic sphere, men for study: "A Book of Hours in the vernacular is quite sufficient for a woman. Let her stitch and sew and embroider, and leave studying to men" (1456–60).[38] The tone modulates with the sudden reversal. Don Pedro tells Beatriz not to look surprised at his new view and then threatens to kill her if she uses periphrasis, which he must consider to be the heart of her *bomphiologia* (*verborum bombus* or excessive bragging). But Beatriz cannot help herself, despite the patriarchal death sentence, and this drives her father into an exasperated exclamation, interrupted by *cacozelia* (affectation of diction and metaphor, awkward imitation), then followed by another such outcry:

> *Don Pedro.* So much for mending your ways, Beatriz!
> *Beatriz.* In the name of your ancestrix . . .
> *Don Pedro.* I do believe you'll drive me mad! (1474–77)[39]

Beatriz will not obey her father even as she tries to, and Don Pedro is shown to be impotent as his threat is revealed to be a figure of speech, and not an effective one. His authority does not win out. In this passage, Beatriz's Latinate response interrupts her father and then he breaks off her line by rhyming with his previous line. Despite this attempt at order in an ordered poetry—the outer lines include the rhyme of "vicio" and "juicio" (lines 1474, 1477), her vice will drive him mad because she will not banish it. Calderón gives the father, who is blind to what is going on with his daughters in his house but believes he is right, the rhyme "veo" and "Creo" (lines 1475–76; see the original Spanish in note 39).

Just as Beatriz frustrates her father's authority, so too does Inés rebuff Don Alonso's advances. Being in love with Inés, Moscatel embellishes the words she actually speaks to him, saying that she is too good to be his mistress and not good enough to be his wife, which, as we have seen, is not what she said. Don Alonso's response is both metadramatic and metonymic. He displaces his own sexual desire on to Inés, partly because she is not playing the role of available servant that plays usually represent, but, in Moscatel's report especially, she speaks like a defiant countess: "That's the kind of answer that kings in plays are forever receiving from Countesses of Amalfi or Mantua or Milan, but never from a Countess of Roguesborough! . . . *Eso a reyes de comedia / no hay condesa que no diga / de Malfi,*

Mantua o Milán, / mas no las de Picardía" (1486–89).[40] The pun on "Picardía," which this English translation turns to Roguesborough and in doing so knowingly loses the pun, plays on "pícaro, pícara" or rogue, which can also include sexual "mischief."[41] He becomes crude when he says of her, "The devil take the little slut!" (1496).[42] Moscatel, who has listened to such insults, says that like unto like, but Don Alonso can only think of Celia, the last woman he abandoned. Calderón gives the situation a little irony because Don Alonso declares, "My constancy is my undoing," which, retrospectively, will be true of his falling for Beatriz (at least from the point of view of a playboy) but in this context he rather roguishly and heartlessly says that he treats women too well when he leaves them (1510).[43] When Don Alonso tells his story about Doña Clara, Moscatel is not above trading jibes about bartering for women (1536). Don Alonso thinks he will still pursue Inés, even if only to trick or have a joke on her ("burla" is as key to the play and its ending as to its title). But then before he can tell Moscatel what to tell her, Don Juan comes in and speaks of Love—"who, after all, is but a child"—smiles today when yesterday he cried (1559).[44] He then tells of Leonor's trick and deception of Don Pedro and announces that Don Alonso must pretend to love Beatriz as part of the ruse. Don Alonso does not want to play that role and he proceeds to satirize lovers: "By God, I'd die before I'd chase a woman" (1627–28, see 1595–1642).[45] Don Alonso deprecates Beatriz in ways we have already discussed and takes up the position that Don Diego and Don Pedro have adopted: "I swear to God I'd rather fight ten illiterate men than one educated woman" (1651–53).[46] An educated woman is not, at least for now, part of Don Alonso's world, but Calderón is setting up the conversion (reversal) of a great sinner against women to the altar of Love. Don Alonso's use of the word "chistosa" (funny) to refer to Beatriz can mean that he thinks that she is pretentiously clever, but it can also mean, as it turns out, that she is witty and fond of joking. Although Beatriz is serious, she does have the last joke on Don Alonso and conceals herself to confront Leonor and him, just as her father had done to Leonor and her.

It is not surprising that in a comedy with a title, *No hay burlas con el amor*, Calderón places a joke at its center, which has reverberations at the end of the play. The joker is caught in his joke; the trickster is caught in his trick:

> *Don Juan.* I'm not asking you to be in love with her.
> only to pretend you are. The whole thing
> is just a joke.

> *Don Alonso.* I like the idea of pretending, and also of
> playing a joke on such a conceited and
> pretentious woman.

> *Moscatel [aside].*
> How quickly he rises to the bait! Let's hope
> it's not us that get caught.

> *Don Alonso.* Deceit and lies are fine by me, but wooing
> her in earnest and putting up with her
> nonsense is quite out of the question.
>
> *Don Juan.* But nobody is asking you to do that! (1665–78)[47]

In an aside, Moscatel hopes that they are not the ones to suffer from this scheme. Just before the love scene, Calderón makes Don Alonso cruel and self-satisfied in his role as trickster and bearer of false love. With alacrity, he suggests that they go at once so he can die laughing at his trick or joke in which her true love responds to his false love. When Moscatel is not sure that this joke will work out happily, Don Alonso berates him for not understanding the joke as revenge for Leonor against Beatriz before he romps with Inés, a statement that keeps up the dramatic tension between Moscatel and Don Alonso in their debate on love with which the comedy begins (1685–96). The playwright plays some more with the different forms of "burla" and "burlar," that is trick and to trick (deception and to deceive).

Of course, the trick does trap Don Alonso. Whether he is worth trapping or not may be another qualification to the happy ending of the play. How effective his conversion is, seems much more pertinent than Beatriz's change, even though the playwright has both servants comment wryly on the two lovers. Ultimately, even though, as the evidence has been showing, the text sends out intricate signals on the question of love and women, some cultural factors will affect the audience in its view of the ending.

Beatriz's style remains ornate, and she continues to use the extended metaphor of the sun, but she thinks she has reformed her speech according to her father's command. Inés, however, finds no improvement (1699–1752). Don Alonso's role as her "galán fingido" begins badly as he says in an aside that he is at a loss to speak his love even if it is false. Nonetheless, he soon regains his composure and speaks to her in a florid style not unlike hers. She calls upon her sun imagery to illustrate the transgression he has committed by being in her boudoir and echoes Góngora in the bargain. Even in his flattery of Beatriz, whom he calls "Most learned Beatriz" ("Peritísima Beatriz") and "sweet enigma" ("dulce enigma"), Don Alonso does not think that beauty and knowledge need to dwell in one woman: beauty is enough (1809–15). But in his flattering deception, Don Alonso paraphrases the next two lines of Góngora's ballad, "Cuatro o seis desnudos hombros," to which Beatriz alludes.[48] He is then a sunflower to her sun, bending to bask in her light. Meanwhile, in asides, Inés intersperses satirical remarks between his speeches, implying that Don Alonso shows the same excesses of style that Beatriz does and addressing the women in the audience about his deception: "Observe, ladies. If this is make-believe, how can we tell lying from loving?" (1833–36).[49] Is his love real or false? Who can tell? The irony soon becomes apparent because Don Alonso soon cannot tell himself and is on the verge of falling in love.

Inés and Moscatel play the same role here that they do at the end of the play—they comment on Beatriz and Don Alonso with some skepticism, but here it is in an aside for the benefit of the audience only. Both think Beatriz gullible, but, unlike Inés, Moscatel moves beyond the specific case and generalizes unfavorably about women: "In short, there's nothing as easy as fooling a woman" (1873–74).[50] It is possible, although not sure, that this last phrase echoes the familiar expression "engaña a su mujer" or "he's unfaithful to his wife," so that the verb "engañar" carries both the meaning to deceive or trick and to be unfaithful to, an ambiguity that would suggest Don Alonso's lack of faith, for which Moscatel has derided him, and his present deceit. Beatriz will not listen to her maid on her high diction, but in the midst of Don Alonso's reference to the planets, the farcical situation complicates itself as Don Juan and Leonor are talking with Don Pedro outside. This news sends Beatriz back into her planetary images and leads Don Alonso to comment wryly that this must be a play by Calderón where a hidden lover or veiled woman must appear. The shock seems to provide an immediate stylistic remedy to Beatriz, who switches, as the situation demands, to brief imperatives, statements, and questions. Don Alonso and Moscatel must hide. Don Alonso locks Don Juan out; Don Alonso takes a moment to kiss Inés; along with Moscatel, he must jump from the balcony to avoid detection. Just before Don Alonso must comply, he warns men about love.

But Beatriz cannot give up her ornate style that easily. At the beginning of Act Three, she catches herself, but then proceeds, and, in an aside, explains her awakening love for Don Alonso (2055–2118). Inés tries to console her with aureate diction: Beatriz wants to tell her of her secret love for Don Alonso, which leads the servant to tell Leonor, "Love has conquered!" ("¡Victoria por el amor!") (2165). Even Inés, who plays the independent woman, associates womanhood with love for a man: "In short, every woman is a woman in the end" (2184–85).[51] But the play is not at an end, so that this reversal from no love to love needs complication; Don Juan has heard all and now accuses Leonor of loving someone else (2190–2263, esp. 2226–29). Not to disappoint the audience with asymmetry, Don Alonso explores with his servant his awakening feelings of love and thus provides a narrative envelope for Don Juan's jealous accusations (2276–2367). Some of the most central lines in the comedy, which point to the reversal, are Don Alonso's "It would be a sad little tale if the joke turned out to be on me" (2322–24).[52] The joke is on the joker.

Through the story of the bull, Moscatel points out that Don Juan may have wanted to help Beatriz marry Don Alonso so Leonor was free to marry, rather than enlist Don Alonso's help in avenging Leonor and keeping Don Pedro off the scent of the love between Don Juan and Leonor (2352–57). Inés decides to make Moscatel jealous and teach him a lesson, so she pretends to be receiving Don Alonso's advances (2368f). The game of love is not ready to be resolved yet. But Inés has really come in Beatriz's name, saying so only after Moscatel is gone (2427). Another indication of this reluctant reversal—the false trails are still there, like Inés' flirtation with Don Alonso—is his response to Beatriz's ribbon: "What a novel turn of events" (2449).[53]

The theme of women being deficient keeps recurring. What may propel the comedy for an early seventeenth-century audience may qualify it for a late twentieth- or early twenty-first-century audience. Inés does not find Beatriz's love as novel as Don Alonso does: "I don't find it the least bit novel. I knew your love was only faked, so I realised it would succeed. Since we women never get anything right, false lovers fare better with us than true ones" (2450–55).[54] Here is a woman speaking against women, although the irony may be that Don Alonso is falling for Beatriz and so Inés' observation, even in this specific case, is not entirely accurate. Moscatel returns and misinterprets the exchange between Don Alonso and Inés, so love still remains blind (2455). Inés explains her joke or trick to Moscatel (2475–2513).

Calderón does not want to give up his complications of the movement to a comic ending, which is achieved within a few lines of the very end. Moscatel says he will leave off service in Don Alonso's house because a master in love will neglect his servant, which is a reversal of Don Alonso's threat at the beginning of the comedy to put Moscatel out because a servant in love is not much use to his master (2528–35, see 51–103). The reversal of conventional roles between master and servant is reversed. By his own admission, Don Juan's love for Leonor is finished (2548–50). The reversal is that Don Alonso is now leading Don Juan to Don Pedro's house and not the other way around. Don Alonso even admits that he wants to see Beatriz (2602). The new unexpected matchmaker is Don Alonso. The recognition of his love comes to light. Moscatel is satirical about the obliquity of expression the two nobles use to camouflage their desire to see their beloveds (2616–27). The scene is set for the comic ending, which both the views of women and the use of satire complicate. It is at this point that this chapter began its analysis of the end of this comedy. Later, with *Les précieuses ridicules* (1659), Molière would write a satire on the pretensions in speech and style of women, which helped precipitate a controversy over the education of women and their role in the education of a culture.[55] The satirical representation of women in Molière's comedy might, in a minor key, find parallels in *No hay burlas con el amor*.

Satirical Comedy

The tricksters of satirical comedy, like *Volpone* and *Tartuffe*, practice even greater enormities than Don Alonso does. Satire carries with it a tragic undertow. The Horatian satire of romantic comedy often yields to Juvenalian satire in satiric comedy. The magnitude of sin or treachery or deceit is so great in Volpone, Mosca, and Tartuffe that they almost become larger than the play. To call a comedy satiric is a matter of emphasis, as we have observed the satiric attributes of comedies that concentrated on pastoral and romantic aspects, the wry observations of Jaques, the trick on Malvolio and his isolation, and Don Alonso's cynical comments on women and the deceit of Beatriz.[56] The satire can contribute to a generic chafing between content and form, reception in the Renaissance and now. The invention of the term "problem play" or "problem comedy" in the last years of the nineteenth century and its currency in the twentieth century show how a change in audience can demand that Shaw be used to interpret Shakespeare.

The satirical aspects of Shakespeare's problem comedies help make their happy endings more problematic.

This problematic would not have surprised Ben Jonson. In *Timber, or Discoveries* he says, "The parts of comedy are the same with a tragedy, and the end is partly the same. For they both delight and teach . . . Nor is the moving of laughter always the end of comedy."[57] The end of Jonson's satirical comedy, *Volpone*, is as much about teaching as delight, a movement that involves thought and dramatic irony rather than laughter as a reflex. It is a comedy that spares no targets, male or female, in an attempt to see how blind and greedy human beings can become. *Volpone* is based on variations on a trick that extend throughout the comedy with great intricacy, providing the audience with an ironic view of the dupes, even though, ultimately and beyond the intentions of the playwright, the end of the play might dupe the audience.

The representation of women may also be a problem for a modern audience. Lady Would-be has intellectual pretensions, and she is satirized. Celia is a virtuous and obedient wife. For some, she is satirized; for others she is not (III.vii.30–31, V.xii.142–44). At one point, Lady Would-be, a voluble dupe, says to the great eponymous trickster himself: "Here's *Pastor Fido*—" (III.iv.86), and, in aside, Volpone says he will profess silence.[58] She continues to epitomize the world of the court and of romance that the fashion of Guarini's comedy represents:

> All our English writers,
> I mean such as are happy in the Italian,
> Will deign to steal out of this author mainly;
> Almost as much as from Montaignié;
> He has so modern and facile a vein,
> Fitting the time, and catching the court-ear. (III.iv.87–92)

She chatters in a satire with little sympathy for pastoral and romantic notions. Lust, greed, and competition mark Jonson's comedy, so that Lady Would-be's speech highlights the contrast between the opposite poles of comedy—pastoral/romantic and satiric. This passage follows a debate between Lady Would-be and Volpone on the nature of learning and the greatest thing for a woman. For her, the "chiefest ornament" for a woman is music, but for him, the "highest female grace" is silence, as Sophocles writes in *Ajax* (67–81). The satire here, as in *No hay burlas con el amor*, is on a woman who talks a good deal about learning, only to be opposed by men who want them silent or submissive.

Learning is not for women in these plays. Volpone would rather sing a beautifully seductive song to the young and beautiful Celia to catch her in his trick—he plays at being impotent but is not—in order to satisfy his lust than to hear Lady Would-be prattle on, even with her occasional malapropism *avant la lettre,* such as confusing the golden mean with "the golden mediocrity" (47). Women are not supposed to have any intellectual pretensions in these two comedies, although Beatriz's youth and beauty may allow her to get away with some of her cultural interests.

Volpone is a great trickster who has met his match in his parasite, Mosca. Their extended jokes and traps are of the most intricate nature, something that Jonson seemed to enjoy as he created another virtuoso performance of that kind in *The Alchemist* (1610). Their plots intertwine and are, near the end of the comedy, at cross-purposes. Mosca has taken over control of the tricks and speaks of his "Fox-trap" (V.v.18). Volpone's death is faked in order to fool the others but he, too, even in his disguises, is being fooled. The servant, Mosca, is becoming the master, while Volpone is becoming his servant. Duped by Mosca, Voltore says to him, "Well, flesh-fly, it is summer with you now; / Your winter will come on" (V.ix.1–2). There will be a reversal—a chill on the parasite's comic dance. During the trial, in an aside, Volpone begins to feel that his traps have trapped him: "I'm caught / In mine own noose" (V.x.13–14). The plot of this comedy is, as the second Avocatore observes of the situation, "a labyrinth" (V.x.42). In the street, Volpone admits that he has caught himself: "To make a snare for mine own neck! and run / My head into it, wilfully! with laughter!" (V.xi.1–2). For Voltore, Volpone comes back from the dead and begins his counterplot against Mosca.

When Mosca enters as a Clarissimo, the fourth Avocatore, clearly hoping for another kind of happy ending, says in an aside: "A proper man! and were Volpone dead, / A fit match for my daughter" (V.xii.50–51). Mosca then "buries" Volpone, who is disguised and trying to bargain with him in the courtroom, which revives the fourth Avocatore's hopes for a match for his daughter (63). Mosca will not take the half that Volpone offers him in an aside. The fourth Avocatore begins his bargaining with Mosca as "Volpone" is to be led off and whipped (84–85). This negotiation is a satire on love matches. The recognition is literal as Volpone puts off his disguise (86). He has his own sense of honor, even if it is among thieves, and he uncovers all in order to block Mosca and expose those who would feed on their own to have Volpone's fortune. The fourth Avocatore remains silent as the first three bring justice to the situation, the first Avocatore claiming this revelation a miracle and the second saying that "Nothing can be more clear" (96). Bonario agrees on the divine nature of this anagnorisis (97).

The punishments begin, which makes sense in satirical comedy but not in romantic or pastoral comedy. The second Avocatore asks that Mosca be disrobed; Celia pleads for mercy for her husband, Corvino. Celia and Bonario are vindicated. Mosca, whom the first Avocatore calls "the chiefest minister, if not plotter, / In all these lewd impostures" (108–9), is to be whipped and given life in a galley, partly because he has had the nerve to impersonate a Venetian noble. Volpone thanks the court for Mosca, who says to his master, "Bane to thy wolfish nature" (115), and is led out. The ultimate joke is the like unto like, eye for an eye, sentence the court hands to Volpone, who is a noble and cannot be given the severe sentence that Mosca received. As Volpone feigned sickness to receive wealth from those who hoped to be his heir, his fortune will be given "To the hospital of the Incurabili" (120), and he will be imprisoned in irons until he is lame and sick. Volpone's response reinforces the moral: "This is called the mortifying of a Fox" (126). Voltore is banished to a monastery to die well as he has not lived well, and all his property passes to his son. Corvino will be led through the canals with asses ears and in a pillory, "And to expiate / Thy wrongs done to thy wife, thou art to send her / Home to her father with her dowry trebled" (142–44). The first Avocatore caps the ending with a moral, so that the audience can learn from the end of *Volpone*: "Let all that see these vices thus rewarded / Take heart, and love to study 'em. Mischiefs feed / Like beasts, till they be fat, and then they bleed" (149–51). The only happy ending in this comedy is for Bonario and Celia, but with their families riven, despite the poetic justice that rights the wrongs done to them. The great characters of Mosca and Volpone, even if they are vices and must have a fall, make the end potentially tragic, as if the ghost of the rejection of Falstaff has endured.

The epilogic six lines play on this stress, between the morality of poetic justice and the great representations of vice in satire. Volpone is alone on stage and, like Rosalind, is in and out of character. Jonson plays on the convent the character asking for applause, but he does not send out Bonario. Instead, he sends the actor who played the role Volpone. The protagonist/antagonist for whom the comedy is named has suffered an unhappy ending, but he asks that the audience applaud if they are happy with the play. The first and sixth lines request applause. Volpone says that although the law has punished the Fox, he hopes that he has not done anything to make the audience suffer, that is, tricked them or let them down in the entertainment. If he has, censure him; if not, applaud. Thus, Volpone is resurrected by the audience who has to wonder whether it is not simply applauding a good representation of vice but the Vice character himself. Is this a trick, where the frame qualifies the punishment of Volpone and the words that would make him an example, which the first Avocatore pointed out in the previous lines? Volpone is not in leg irons, and although the epilogue serves to break the illusion and usher the audience back into the world, it also reaffirms that the trickster is free. Perhaps, after all, there is a happy ending to *Volpone* for the eponymous character as much as for Bonario. Whatever the audience decides, there is a fascinating stress between the judgment of Volpone at the end of the comedy and his resurrection in this epilogue.

Molière's *Le Tartuffe ou L'Imposteur* (1664) is also a satirical comedy and thus tends toward irony and tragic scapegoating rather than to the comic ending of marriage and dance. The exposure and punishment of Tartuffe, who is the center of attention, allows for the return to harmony in the marriage of Orgon and Elmire.[59] But the tricks and hypocrisy of Tartuffe become so dramatic and gather so much force of character that many in the audience cannot help but admire the daring scene or internal play that Tartuffe is directing. Even if Tartuffe is not morally admirable, he is one of Molière's most admirable creations. This ambivalence also occurs with Falstaff and Volpone. The centuries of controversy over the rejection of Falstaff demonstrate that the audience has a hard time to part with such an extraordinary comic character.[60] There is, then, a friction between characterological magnitude and the need to make an example of the great character. The blast of Juvenalian savage indignation and the frost of Horatian ironic satire try to contain the blaze of comic carnival. The tricks have to stop somewhere, and the hypocrite who doesn't play by the rules of conventional morality has to be scapegoated and punished. At the end of *2 Henry IV*, the Epilogue promises that Falstaff will reappear in a sequel, but when Shakespeare does write *Henry V*, he kills Falstaff early, offstage, and in a report, as if the appearance and speech of this white-bearded Satan of comedy would demand his return and his usurpation and rupture of the history play into a full comedy. Louis XIV himself asked that Moliere's Tartuffe and the eponymous comedy be resurrected. In the "Troisième Placet Présenté Au Roi Le Février 1669" (The Third Petition Presented to the King February 1669), Molière asks, "Would I dare ask again this grace of YOUR MAJESTY the same day of the great resurrection of Tartuffe, resuscitated by your bounty?" (vol. 1, 635).[61] As with all narrative and drama, the end can become the beginning again, even if the design of the work is not as self-conscious as that in *Finnegans Wake*.

In the preface to *Tartuffe*, a defense that Molière attached to the printed version in 1669, he says that those who were the objects of his comedy, from marquis to doctor, suffered mildly when they were represented and even pretended to be amused, with everyone else, by the portraits of them.[62] But not the hypocrites, Molière says, for they, being what they are, decided to hide behind a protest that alleged the impiety of the play rather than to look into their souls. He maintains that in this comedy he distinguished between the true devout and the hypocrite ("le vrai dévot" et "l'hypocrite") (vol. 1, 628–29). Tartuffe is a hypocrite who shows false religious devotion. Against those who assert that the theatre should not talk about religious matters, Molière points to the religious origins of comedy, which Jane Harrison (as well as Murray, Cornford, and Frye) would have insisted on.[63] Of his contemporary critics who say the drama should not discuss religion, Molière says,

> and, without a doubt, it would not be difficult to make them see that comedy, among the ancients, took its origin from religion, and was part of their mysteries; that the Spaniards, our neighbours, hardly celebrate feasts in which comedy is not mixed, and that similarly, among us, it owes its birth to the care of a brotherhood to which belongs again today l'hôtel de Bourgogne; that this is a place that was made for representing the most important mysteries of our faith; that one can still see comedies printed in Gothic letters, under the name of a doctor of the Sorbonne and, with looking so far that there have been played, in our time, the holy plays of Mister Corneille, who has had the admiration of all of France. (vol. 1, 629).[64]

Molière remembers the Théâtre de l'Hôtel de Bourgogne (or the Theatre of the Hotel of Burgundy), the first permanent theatre in Paris, which was a residence of the dukes of Burgundy that was used in 1548 by the Confraternity or Brotherhood of the Passion (les Confrères de la Passion), a group or guild of tradesmen who used it as a playhouse. Perhaps in his defense of comedy, Molière overemphasizes these religious origins, but it is sensible to stress the seriousness of comedy without making it solemn. He himself argues for something that supports my argument. He associates comedy with satire, which involves irony and a dark side, such as scapegoating, which makes the "happy" ending of comedy more complex: "If the work of comedy is to correct the vices of men, I do not see by what reason some would be privileged" (vol. 1, 629).[65] Molière says that virtuous theatre is founded on its ability to correct faults in people through satire because nothing achieves that correction more that a portrait of their vices. The reason he gives is that "One wishes well to be wicked; but one never wishes to be ridiculed" (vol. 1, 630).[66] The exposure of the ridiculous is the aim of comedy, at least Molière's satiric comedy, and the purging of sin is connected with the pleasures and successes of satire, that is, according to Molière and in accordance with my argument, satire is more powerful in achieving this end than are "the most handsome traits of a serious moral" (vol. 1, 630).[67] Even as some of Molière's opponents, those who occasioned the preface, howled and plotted as much as Tartuffe did, it may be, that in the long run, the very attractive repulsion or repulsive attraction of the character, Tartuffe, like Volpone before him, makes the audience see the glory of vice, in this case hypocrisy. The end of Tartuffe at the end of the comedy brings applause, and without his gargantuan vice, the play itself would not exist. The very pleasure the audience gains throughout the play and at its end is not simply one of a katascopic or god's-eye moral superiority as Molière suggests but also the dangerous pleasures of satiric comedy—that one is part of a grand ruse or game. The pleasures of dramatic irony, which is especially apparent in the gap between public virtue and private vice in hypocrites, have to end, but perhaps the audience is less glad at their conclusion.

The happy ending of comedy may be more mixed than Molière can admit publicly. He is like all of us who defend education and the arts publicly, in that we may be caught in our own rationalizations and hypocrisy. We have to put forward the ideal image of what we do and hope that society will leave us alone and think what we do beneficial, moral, and useful because the more we know our subject or job, the more doubts we have. And Molière, one of the greatest of satirists, would have been much aware of this delicate position and that all satire is a satire against ourselves, including the author. At some time or another, we all appear ridiculous. In a polemical battle, however, ambiguities and compromises are left beyond the margins. In the preface, Molière represents the objections of his detractors. Perhaps for the wrong reasons, they have hit on something when they concentrate on the character of Tartuffe. They are naive to equate his words with Molière's, and they have forced Molière on too narrow ground in wanting to say that the playwright has made Tartuffe's ideas dangerous by representing them in the theatre and impressing them on the souls of the audience (vol. 1, 630). There is some truth in this accusation if one sticks strictly to a moral argument, but the aesthetic dimension—the fact that this comedy is a fiction—complicates this matter. Molière is not Pascal or La Rochefoucauld writing *pensées* or maxims, but a playwright representing characters in a situation who speak of ideas in a kind of dramatic dialectic. The danger that Molière's opponents raise, however, is not easily dismissed even by those, like me, who admire his comedies.

For Molière, to condemn *Tartuffe* is to condemn all comedy. It is not really a matter of condemnation, but of understanding the stress between form and message at the end of the play. In the preface, Molière, like Corneille in the preface to *Théodore, vierge et martyre*, admits that some of the Church Fathers were not fond of drama: "it is that they took comedy differently, and that some considered it in its purity, when others regarded it in its corruption, and confounded with all these villainous spectacles that one had reason to call spectacles of turpitude" (vol. 1, 630).[68] Molière appeals to the important place that, Greece and Rome, at their height and not in their decline, accorded for comedy and the theatre (vol. 1, 630–31). Although he admits that comedy, like all things, has in some periods known corruption and its good has been turned to bad ends, he maintains that we must not confuse the kindness of things ("la bonté des choses") with the malice of its corrupters. If Rome banished medicine and Athens philosophy, it is not right to banish them in all times, and the same is true of comedy (vol. 1, 631). Molière will allow that comedy should be condemned for not regarding God directly, but only if all other such human activities are also condemned. He sees comedy as the most innocent diversion that people can have when they take a break from worship. Molière alludes to the Prince of Condé and reports the reply to the king's question about why Molière's comedy scandalizes people but not the comedy *Scaramouche*, in which a hermit dressed as a monk spends the night by the window of a married woman, saying from time to time, that his visits to the window are for mortifying his flesh (vol. 1, 921). The prince says that *Scaramouche* represents heaven and religion, which the scandalized people do not care about, but Molière's comedies represent these people, and that is what they cannot bear (vol. 1, 632). In outlining the ends of comedy, Molière calls upon the king and the prince as a means of invoking authority, to show how powerful his allies are, and to remind others that he has the king's favor, which they seek as the ultimate form of arbitration in the matter. It is easy to see why some critics want to emphasize the political nature of comedy.

In the preface Molière defends comedy by emphasizing its unequivocal nature and by appealing to the world of things, as distinct from the paradoxical realm of language: "And, in effect, when one must discover things and not words, and that most contraries come from not hearing and enveloping in the same word things that are opposed, to remove the veil of the equivoke (pun), and to regard what is comedy in itself, to see if it is condemnable" (vol. 1, 630).[69] Here, the playwright is defending the morality of comedy, not by stressing the anagogical or allegorical morals that it represents through story, but by talking about its essence and, by implication, rendering his "moralist opponents" Sophists, who accuse in a confusion of words. The ends of comedy are literal: Molière's defense would leave little, if any, room for interpretation. How much of this stance is a politics of necessary literalism, where the writer finds himself, yet again, in the position of saying—"I know what this work means because I made it, and it is clearly moral and will teach us all to be good"—remains to be seen. The preface is not the play, as the prefaces of Bernard Shaw illustrate. There may be a large gap between Molière's position (unless it is ironic or a courtesy to the king) and the post-Saussurian revolution in literary theory where many poststructuralists and postmodernists take an opposite and more rhetorical view of *mots et choses* ("words and things"). The ends of comedy are as much a matter of interpretative assumptions as of the words with which the playwright ends the play.

Molière's satirical comedy must show clearly the satirical targets, and it is true that satire is more pointed and apparently clear than many other literary forms. Nonetheless, the shifts in point of view, as we have seen in *Volpone*, complicate how satire is to be taken. Is the audience to be corrected or ridiculed as well? Are Volpone and Tartuffe so magnificent as characters that they are larger than life and therefore not ironic because the audience cannot look down upon them with a feeling of superiority? Are there substantial differences between Tartuffe and Volpone, explaining why the one is more resurrected than the other?

Molière begins the "First Petition Presented to the King on the Comedy of Tartuffe" ("Le Premier Placet Présenté au Roi Sur la comédie du Tartuffe") with "The duty of comedy being to correct men by entertaining them, I thought that, in the work in which I find myself, I had nothing better to do than to attack by ridiculous portraits the vices of my century" (vol. 1, 632).[70] The most dangerous vice, he continues, is hypocrisy, and he thought that he was doing a service to all the honest people in the kingdom (and thus to the king) to attack these hypocrites and to expose "all the studied grimaces of all these excessively good people, all the covert rogueries of these counterfeiters in devotion, who wish to trap men with a counterfeit zeal and a sophistical charity" (vol. 1, 632).[71] Molière claims to expose the sophistical words and feigning gestures of a hypocrite as a warning to the honest people of France. His equates comedy and satire, and this implicit move is not surprising considering the ritual satire of Aristophanic comedy. But, between correction and entertainment, the instruction and delight that Horace recommends, there lies an opening. Certainly, entertainment can make the instruction more palatable, but it can also divert the audience from the moral or make the duty of comedy seem less full and rich as the representation itself. *Tartuffe* is not a treatise on religious hypocrisy but a play.

Elsewhere, Molière makes this point that a comedy is not comic theory. He understands the complexity and difference of representation. Having discussed this matter elsewhere, I shall mention it only briefly here.[72] Even if Molière is less given to theory than Corneille is, he likes to state his views. In the preface to *Les Précieuses ridicules* (1659), Moliere sets out the ideas that he expresses throughout his career: comedy is a worthy genre; the public is the absolute judge of plays; the representation of the play is more important than learned, if not pedantic, criticism of drama (vol. 2, 193–94). He satirizes critics and criticism, as in the "Advertisement" ("Avertissement") to *Les Fâcheux* (1662); he claims not to care about the rules of laughter and says he may cite Aristotle and Horace if he publishes comments on his plays. In La Critique *de l'École des femmes* (1663), Dorante defends the playwright's work against Lysidas' claim that Aristotle and Horace would condemn Molière, however.[73] Amid the controversy between Molière and his opponents, he celebrates the comic spirit in *L'Impromptu de Versailles* (1663) and makes himself one of his characters in a royal performance for Louis XIV, who will empower and protect them. Particularly in the last speech of this comedy, the king becomes part of the story: here, Molière tells Béjart of the king's good grace toward them. This is a king blessing their comedic marriage and the end of their comedy. The distance between Louis XIV and the Molière as actors and as people is collapsed as much as possible. Here the playwright speaks to the godfather of his child as much as to his king.

As Molière represents Tartuffe to the king, it is a play that depends on his grace as much as the Tartuffe in the comedy and the Tartuffes of this world do. Despite the blessing of Louis XIV and that of his legate and prelates, a priest has written that Molière is a demon and a libertine. Molière puts himself in the hands of his king, who, like God, knows best, and he awaits his judgment (vol. 1, 633). The "Second Placet" or petition is also presented to Louis XIV, "In his camp before the city of Lille in Flanders" ("Dans son camp devant la ville de Lille en Flandre") in August 1667 (vol. 1, 634). *Tartuffe* placed Molière in a difficult situation, so that, at the end of the comedy, he wished for the grace of the monarch to set things right. Even as he wanted to distance himself from the equivocal fictionality of his play by stressing its clear relation to the world, his opponents showed how equivocal interpretation is by taking up the opposite side—that Molière's comedy was simply immoral and impious. Here are two ends to Tartuffe and the eponymous play, both insisting on the truth, plain and simple. The ends of comedy, then, have also to do with reception. When addressing the king, Molière takes his case to the battlefield—the literary war shifts to the site of an actual war: "It is a thing very foolhardy of me to come importuning a great monarch in the middle of his glorious conquests; but, in the state in which I see myself, or where else, SIRE, than at this place can I get protection? And who can I solicit against the authority of the power that overwhelms me, other than the source of the power and of the authority, the just dispenser of absolute orders, the sovereign judge and the master of all things?" (vol. 1, 634).[74] The playwright wants the king to become the ultimate arbiter of the play. Interpretation becomes a matter of patronage and authority. The king should have the final word.

This "Second Petition" shows the lengths to which Molière says he has gone to placate his critics. He tells the king that in vain he has produced the comedy under the title, *L'Imposteur* (*The Impostor*), disguised his character as a man of the world, and cut with care "all that I judged capable of furnishing the shadow of a pretext to the celebrated originals of the portrait I wished to make: all that served nothing" (vol. 1, 634).[75] Molière, who in his preface of 1664 had insisted on the clarity and morality of his play, has now succumbed to his critics' censorship. Even though he is now playing by their rules, he is not winning the game: "The cabal woke to simple conjectures that they could have of the thing" ("La cabale s'est réveillée aux simples conjectures qu'ils ont pu avoir de la chose") (vol. 1, 634). The thing ("la chose") is not as simple as Molière had said. There is more than one kind of politics of interpretation, even in comedy. Molière, like characters in Shakespeare's *The Tempest*, says he finds himself in a storm ("cette tempête"). This time the magician is caught in a tempest that is and is not of his own making. Owing to clerical pressure, he closed his theatre for seven weeks (vol. 1, 921). Now the playwright is confounded as to why he should ask his opponents' permission when the king had granted his: "Deign your bounty, SIRE, to give me your protection against their envenomed rage: and may I, after the return from such a glorious campaign, relax YOUR MAJESTY from the fatigue of his conquests, give him innocent pleasures after such noble works, and make laugh the monarch who makes all Europe tremble" (vol. 1, 635).[76] The place of comedy in the social sphere rests with the king's authority, his ability to direct a battle implicitly akin to his ability to direct the diversionary tactics of a play, or at least its reception. During Alexander the Great's eastward campaign, Alexander read Homer's epics, a copy of which Aristotle had apparently prepared for him.[77] Rather than epic inspiration, Molière offers Louis XIV comic relief from the campaign.

Molière's opponents took *Tartuffe* seriously, so that on February 5, 1669, he was again defending his comedy in a "Troisième Placet" or "Third Petition." With wit and satire, Molière seeks the king's grace to resurrect his comedy in order to be reconciled with the devout and with doctors, both of whom he has satirized (vol. 1, 635). The end of *Tartuffe* also exerts the king's authority, which through "The Officer of the Watch" ("L'Exempt"), descends *ex machina*. The Officer of the Watch comes to deliver Tartuffe to prison rather than to respond to his cries for deliverance. After the comic enormity of Tartuffe, such an order may seem like the appeal Edgar, Kent, and Albany make after the great gap of Lear's death (V.iii.313–27). Molière felt the public pressure of his opponents and owed a debt to the king for supporting public performances of *Tartuffe*, so that the reversal here has political dimensions. Like Volpone, Tartuffe must be imprisoned, but he, too, can be resurrected by the grace of the audience, in this case, of the very king whose authority must send him to prison.

Poetic justice is also served by the end of *Tartuffe*. After the Officer has emphasized and exercised the authority of the prince and after Dorine, Madame Pernelle, Elmire, Mariane, and Orgon have made their brief and approving exclamations about the king's power to punish Tartuffe, Cléante, and then Orgon provide amplification. The first expresses the hope that Tartuffe will return to virtue, correct his life while detesting his vice, and face the mild justice of the great prince, while the second seconds those words and celebrates hymen and love (V.vii.1897–1962). The stresses between Tartuffe's serial game of duping and the brief reversal that enforces moral order and closure express the ambivalence of comedy in which the holiday mood sweeps the audience away and the tricksters dazzle with traps and ploys, but in which the ethical anxieties of the world wait at the exit. It may also be that, for some, art is a supplement or world of wishes, where virtue is rewarded and vice is punished, precisely because in the world they live in, it is so often not the case.[78] *Tartuffe* is a satirical comedy, and while satire must punish the vicious and reward the virtuous, comedy is a festival that celebrates desires and dreams without end.

Ends and Transitions

The pastoral or romantic comedy tends to achieve order through marriage, whereas the satiric comedy through a pattern of poetic justice. These are different poles of comedy and often contain elements of the other but to varying degrees. Jaques and Malvolio bring in the satiric and tragic possibilities into pastoral and romantic worlds, whereas Volpone and Tartuffe need correction for the enormity of their tricks. The strength of these characters threatens to bend the comic logic of the plot out of shape. There are also thematic concerns, such as the role of women in the comic world, that make it even more difficult for a current audience to accept the structural movement toward harmony. Stresses occur, then, between the romantic and satirical aspects of comedy, what may be called the celebratory and cursing functions, between the form and the content.

These elements cannot be separated, and so feeling and thought meet, and modify the French proverb "Qui sent, pleurt; qui pense, rit" ("He who feels, cries; who thinks, laughs" [my translation]). Genres represent the range of human feeling and thought, and indeed, allow for a range of representation of the human. As Chremes says in Terence's *Heauton Timorumenos*: "Homo sum, humani nihil a me alienum puto," ("I am a man, I regard nothing human to be alien to me," [I.1. 25]).[79] Comedy needed its own advocates as Aristotle had not paid it as much heed as tragedy in *Poetics*. In *Arte nuevo de hacer comedias en este tiempo* (*The New Art of Writing Plays in This Age*, 1609), Lope de Vega, in speaking about the history of these genres, says, "Tragedy has as its argument history, and comedy fiction" (section 10) and, speaking of reception, notes: "Equivoke and the uncertainty arising from ambiguity have always held a large place among the crowd, for it thinks that it alone understands what the other one is saying" (section 24).[80] This suggests that language and structure, the ends of comic language and the plays themselves might well depend, however ironic Lope de Vega might be, on the knowing reception of the audience that, paradoxically, rests on ambiguity. The ends of comedy include thought and feeling both in the movement of comedy, which involves convention but with an infinite variety. In the very problems or tensions lie the energy of comedy, and so the generations return again and again to great comedies with different emphases on these tensions.

Comedy, romance, and history are mainstays of this book. They occur in dramatic and nondramatic texts. Prose tales and poems have dramatic moments, and drama often contains narrative. The ends and endings of works are part of the movement and motive of art. Having examined some comedies of the sixteenth and seventeenth centuries, I would like to discuss the relations among narrative, theory, and drama not just in a long view of the age of Shakespeare but how past and present meet. Each generation reinterprets the past, and both then and now keep moving in their mutual dance. Nothing is static and stays the same, not even the dead and their traces. Even as we circle back, the line of time keeps moving on.

CHAPTER 5

Narrative, Theory, Drama

The ambivalence of texts about expansion, the rhetoric of inside and outside, the sympathy, alienation, and supplement of romance, and the exploration of the ends of comedy all suggest the ways representation works. Prose texts and plays both show the intricacies of relations between form and content. Showing and telling can seem like separate arts between prose works and plays, but in drama, including comedy, characters and narrators tell stories while being part of the show. Narrative in drama deserves close attention in theory and practice. Once more, past and present meet, so that the theory and criticism of the era after the Second World War especially comes to terms with the estranged but generative world of the Renaissance. And the early modern period also included a double vision of ancients and moderns, so there is more than one movement of looking backward and forward.[1]

In a study of narrative in twentieth-century drama, one author claims that effective narrative in drama is a relatively new phenomenon, or that its psychological and dramatic importance is something that modern dramatists have seized on more than their predecessors.[2] The choric stage manager in Thornton Wilder's *Our Town* is a good example of the central use of narrative in a modern play. Wilder himself says that in the 1920s he began to resent the discrepancy between his belief in novels by Joyce, Proust, and Thomas Mann and the hundreds of plays he read and his disbelief in the "imaginative narration" of plays in performance.[3] Without denying the importance of narrative in modern drama, this chapter will suggest that playwrights have always valued and used narrative with dramatic results. Wilder's stage manager confronts the audience with its own self-conscious participation in the theatre just as the Chorus to Shakespeare's *Henry V* does. Shakespeare and Wilder play variations on the same convention. But too many critics have forgotten or neglected the importance of narrative in drama. Narrative is not a compact filler the dramatist uses when tired or suddenly aware that the play is getting too long. I seek to help redress this neglect as well as to explore other related aspects of narrative, drama, and genre during the Renaissance.

We should be able to observe relations between our times and the early modern period. This chapter will consider the classical, medieval, and modern contexts for the Renaissance, for the age of Shakespeare and his contemporaries. It will also suggest that narrative in drama possesses four primary functions: exposition, suggestion, compression, and address. Exposition consists of commentary and explanation, suggestion of description and reports of off-stage action, compression of action that would be protracted if represented, and speech of a chorus addressing the audience or another character or of a character telling a story to another character with that character in mind or being overheard by the audience or another character.

Narrative: Ancient and Modern

Even though no one agrees exactly on what constitutes narrative, here are a few basic definitions. Narrative, according to Gerald Prince, must represent events. Along with William Labov and Shlomith Rimmon-Kenan, he maintains that narrative should recount "at least two real or fictive events (or one situation and one event)."[4] Prince interprets events and makes sense of them, also illuminating "temporality and humans as temporal beings." A more elaborate definition occurs in Uri Margolin's discussion of what literary narrative is:

> It is a text, or verbal artefact, produced by an author in a particular situation of literary communication, utilizing and modifying elements from an available repertory of artistic procedures and textual models; it is one or more macro speech acts or utterances of the constative or representative type, produced by one or more posited textual speakers (narrators) and consisting of several propositions containing action descriptions and referring to one or more individuals (narrative agents) in some possible world(s).[5]

Margolin's emphasis is on the relation between authoring, narrating and the narrated from the point of view of the narrative act or utterance, which, as he defines it, is an act that involves at least a speaker, a proposition and a situation.

Situation is precisely where Ross Chambers picks up the debate on narrative.[6] He argues that with the waning of structuralism it has become apparent that meaning does not inhere in discourse and its structures but is contextual, and it derives from the function of the pragmatic situation where discourse occurs. Chambers argues that a story can have different points when it is told in different contexts. It is difficult to separate stories from their telling. He refers to Barbara Herrnstein Smith's observation that a story is someone relating something else to someone.[7] Literary theory and criticism should, Chambers implies, pay more attention to the performative function of storytelling rather than limit themselves, as they have done, to the study of narrative structure and the discourse of narration as if they were both a set of internal relations free of contexts. Consequently, Chambers argues, we possess a grammar of stories (Propp, Greimas,

Bremond, Todorov, Prince, and others) and a rhetoric of narration (Booth, Genette) but not a situational view of narrative. Narrative rhetoric explores the relation between story and discourse, and Seymour Chatman, as Chambers suggests, has synthesized and extended the grammar and rhetoric of narrative. Chambers calls for a shift in narrative and narrative theory that he wishes to help establish in *Story and Situation*:

> But what is lacking is recognition of the significance of situational phenomena—of the social fact that narrative mediates human relationships and derives its "meaning" from them; that, consequently, it depends on social agreements, implicit pacts or contracts, in order to produce exchanges that themselves are a function of desires, purposes, and constraints . . . the implications of the contextual nature of meaning for the analysis of *narrative texts themselves* remain to be explored; and the main title of this book, echoing Chatman's, is meant to focus attention onto the need, not simply to read texts in situation (which is inevitable) but also to read, in the texts, the situation that they *produce* as giving them their "point."[8]

Here, Chambers cites Othello's storytelling in the house of Brabantio as a *locus classicus* of a past literary creator realizing what contemporary critics have not, that storytelling has performative force by virtue of a presupposed situation and mobilized social relations.[9] For Chambers, Othello's speech performs social civility and courtship, and its retelling in the council chamber is a judicial defense that confirms Brabantio's accusation. The power of Othello's tale to seduce and of its retelling to exonerate gives his narrative a magical property, the ability to charm. But Chambers does not stop here. Unlike Gerald Prince, he takes the study of narrative beyond the prose tale and the novel to drama itself. Although Prince allows for many oral and written forms of narrative, he argues that a play on stage is not one of them: "a dramatic performance representing (many fascinating) events does not constitute a narrative either, since these events, rather than being recounted, occur directly on the stage."[10] Chambers, on the other hand, argues that the property of the theatre is that "'words' can never be proffered there independently of a represented context, so the audience of *Othello* sees the Moor working his verbal charms through the situational power of his noble presence, and they also undergo the seduction of his magnetic personality, much as the Duke does."[11] Drama then presents the "presence" of the character of the speaker. In the chamber scene, Shakespeare has, Chambers says, weighted the balance in favor of Othello by providing a political situation in which the Senate needs Othello, so that, without these contextual circumstances, Othello's tales would be less telling and his magical power less potent. Although Chambers and others have suggested the importance of narrative in the drama, more needs to be done and the division between drama and narration persists. Before exploring the relation between narrative and drama further, it would be helpful to look briefly at some of the background to this apparent opposition.

Narrative is as much a social as a formal act. The word "history" in Renaissance England meant a story about the past and a story. For the Romans, *historia* allowed for the possible narrative when facts were absent. Tacitus, like Herodotus and Thucydides, includes rhetorical speeches based on, in the absence of evidence, the premise—if that person were in that situation, what would he say? This practice is in keeping with the passage in Aristotle's *Poetics* where he discusses the probable and improbable in history.[12] Whereas Michael Grant argues that Tacitus was indebted to Greek historical writing, which "owed its very existence to Homer and the Greek epic poets" and also later came under the influence of Athenian tragedy, and whereas A. R. Burn says that "Herodotus . . . used literary sources when available," M. I. Findley argues that Thucydides learned from Herodotus that a historian could learn about politics and moral issues by studying events and not relying on the abstractions of philosophy and the myths of poetry. But Findley also admits that Thucydides often accepted the poets' "main narratives" as "historical fact," that he did not make the most of documentary evidence, that at Book I, chapter 22 of *The Peloponnesian War* he admits that because neither his informants nor he could remember the precise speeches, he made the speakers say what the situation warranted as in the famous Funeral Oration he gave to Pericles.[13] Traditionally, history, epic poetry, and drama shared narrative techniques and could not be readily separated. In Greece and Rome these narratives were often rhetorical.

Even though Plato distinguishes between diegesis and mimesis, between narrative and dialogue, not all modern critics agree with that distinction or with Prince that drama in performance cannot be narrative. In recent theoretical debates a division has continued between those like Gérard Genette who views narrative as being separate from drama and those like Thomas Pavel in "Narrative Tectonics" who consider the possibility of dramatic narrative.[14] Genette thinks that the distinction between telling and showing is misleading, and although he admits that fiction can be mimetic, he does not want to admit that drama can be diegetic.[15] He defines narrative as "*verbal* transmission" and thinks it is legitimate that those who study the mode of narrative rather than its content claim to be narratologists as opposed to those like Propp, Bremond, Greimas, the Todorov of the *Grammaire du Decameron* who examine content, and those like Barthes (1966), Chatman (1978), Prince (1982), and Shlomith Rimmon-Kenan (1983) who try to straddle content and mode.[16] This straddling of content and mode often means that the theorist considers narrative what Genette defines as extranarrative: drama, film, comic strip, *roman-photo*. According to Genette, there are no narrative contents. To substantiate that claim, he cites Aristotle's view that the story of Oedipus possesses the same tragic quality in narrative or dramatic form, so that this story is amenable to any kind of representation, and we call it narrative because we encounter it in a narrative mode.[17] Even though Genette criticizes Pavel for advocating dramatic narrative, Genette in his earlier work has discussed narrative in drama. He may have changed his mind, but some of his previous analyses of plays are helpful. Genette admits the importance of the opposition between "story time" or *erzählte Zeit* and "narrative time" or *Erzählzeit* as it relates to film and oral narrative. He cites as an example of the literary level of drama the narrative of Théramène, where he tells of Hippolytus' death, in Racine's *Phèdre*.[18] Some of the resistance to drama on the part of Genette and others occurs, as he implies, because of Aristotle's supremacy over Plato in making mimesis dominate diegesis. Genette reminds us that whereas Plato appealed for a purely narrative art, Aristotle upheld the superiority of the purely mimetic. Aristotle canonized tragedy as the supreme genre. His authority helped drama to exercise great influence over narrative to the extent, Genette argues, that the word "scene" is used to describe the basic form of narrative in the novel and that until the end of the nineteenth century that scene was a pale imitation of the dramatic scene.[19] Although Genette's subordination of drama or separation of narrative from the theatre is comprehensive and thoughtful, it reveals his self-consciousness about some of the motivations for such a move. He occasionally cites examples from drama to enhance an understanding of his point. Genette asserts that the curiosity of the intradiegetic listener, or the character hearing the tale within the text, is only a pretext to answer the reader's curiosity, a function similar to that of expository scenes in classical drama.[20] If Genette compares the oracle in Sophocles' *Oedipus Rex* to the narrative of love in Proust's *Un Amour de Swann* as narration as power, cunning, and destiny, he says that in Balzac, as in Molière, meaning rather than style determines verbal features of character.[21] Without belaboring the point, I want to demonstrate that even those who oppose drama and narrative admit some interplay and overlap. Genette's desire for division between narrative and drama, while claiming for narrative dramatic force, faces the implicit opposition of Chatman (1978), who places fiction and film side by side in the subtitle of his important study, and meets with the explicit difference of Derrida (1980), who cites Genette in his parody of genre study as the law and, more specifically, the code that genres shall not be mixed. The debates over genre that interpretations of Aristotle helped provoke in the Renaissance seem to be replayed in new configurations.[22]

It is, however, too narrow to assume that on one level drama is not narrative or that narrative is not an important part of plays. Dramatic texts are written and are read and heard. A. C. Bradley locates the theatre in the mind when he complains about the impossibility of playing *King Lear* and makes the written text performative in the reader's reception. Harley Granville-Barker attempts to combine his experience as playwright and critic in examining plays. Whereas New Critics like Robert Heilman concentrate on the play as poem or as written text, a director like John Barton emphasizes the acting of Shakespeare's text.[23] In connection with the semiotics of theatre, Keir Elam discusses the interplay of written or dramatic and theatrical or performance texts. Whether the two types of textual structure for plays belong to the same field of investigation is a concern for Elam, who observes that others like Gianfranco Bettetini, Marco De Marinis, and Franco Ruffini rule out the written or dramatic text. Elam reminds us that unlike the analyst of literature, myth, or the plastic arts, the critic or theorist of theatre must take into account two dissimilar, although related, texts, one composed for the theatre and the other produced in the theatre. He argues that plays involve fictional, logical, linguistic, structural, and communicational codes.[24] Semioticians of the theatre, like Elam, attempt in a different way to account for the whole, intricate production and consumption of theatrical texts.

To use a deconstructive argument, one might say that the Western tradition since Plato has given priority to the oral over the written, has been phonocentric, but that writing actually precedes the oral. Derrida criticizes the tradition that makes voice the source of the living, immediate and truthful as opposed to writing as the dead, distant and refractory. In a Derridean or grammatological analysis one might argue that the oral or performative text comes after the written text and relies on it or even that the oral text is written, whereas a traditionalist might say that performance is the only true way to experience a play because the actors present themselves immediately and give the audience an immediate connection between the intention and the meaning of language that is as "natural" as that link in conversation in everyday life. The Derridean interpretation of the play as text would dismantle the binary oppositions of oral and written and thus complicate our ideas of text and language. This view would mean that drama can use and be narrative as much as any other genre. Derrida deconstructs Artaud's theatre of cruelty with its desire to restore the existence of the flesh and the essence of being.[25] Using a method he describes as tectonics and which he says is a historical approach to narrative (which differs from new historicist and Marxist methodology), Thomas Pavel has tried to look briefly at the relation between narrative and drama in the sixteenth and seventeenth centuries. Pavel contrasts classical plays with Renaissance plays, especially those before 1630. Whereas, Pavel argues, Greek classical tragedy derives from Dionysian mysteries, whose liturgical structure displays long lyric sections and few episodes, European drama, during the Middle Ages and until the beginning of the seventeenth century, borrowed from narratives and organized its episodes like epic genres. The vernacular theatre treated many characters and lines of action, which, in Pavel's view, were often indistinguishable from narratives except for the dialogue form. Pavel maintains that singing a song or telling a story was a more important opposition during that time than the division between narrated and enacted stories. Classical French drama, Pavel argues, is an attempt to separate theatre from narrative, especially romance, by returning to the model of Greek tragedy, which did not seem to use narrative sources. Only Racine managed to avoid, and this only between 1667 and 1677, romance sources in favor of classical models. But then the novel, like Madame de Lafayette's *La Princesse de Cleves* (1678), began to use dramatic style.[26] Although not identical, drama and narrative interact: narrative can be dramatic and drama can be narrative. The question of genre also connects the narrative and the nonnarrative during the Renaissance.

Narrative, Drama, and Genre: The Renaissance

The Renaissance is not the period when drama and narrative first interact, but it is a time in which drama flourishes and has come to influence the making and study of subsequent literature. Although some historians and scholars in English studies often prefer the term "early modern period" to the Renaissance and comparativists often refer to seventeenth-century Baroque, I have most often chosen to continue with the general and recognizable word, "Renaissance."[27] As the vexed problem of periodization is not my primary concern here, I shall use the term "Renaissance" with a looseness akin to Shakespeare's use of "tragedy" and with a pragmatic and purposeful vagueness that allows for the differences in time of the rediscovery of the classics in Northern and Southern, Western and Eastern Europe and a period when Medieval, Renaissance, and Cartesian views and models coexist.[28] Given my emphasis, the blurriness is, I hope, enabling and heuristic and not simply negligent. The Renaissance is taken to mean a loose historical period that began in the late fourteenth century in Italy and continued into the second half of the seventeenth century in various parts of Europe. Although such a definition does not meet general agreement as it once might have, it is generous in recognizing the similar relations of native and vernacular to the classical in Italy, Spain, England, the Netherlands, France, and elsewhere with various emphases and at different times during this period.

Aristotle's *Poetics* is a familiar place to begin when discussing drama, narrative, and genre during the Renaissance.[29] Italian writers are the first to discuss systematically his views of literature. In *Librum Aristotelis de arte poetica explicationes* (1548) Francesco Robertello changes Aristotle's focus a little when he considers imitation in tragedy from the actor's and writer's points of view and in doing so concentrates on performance and the creation of the script.[30] Lodovico Castelvetro's *Poetica d'Aristotele vulgarizzata e sposta* (1570) also shifts Aristotle's emphasis on the text and its structure to the audience and insists that a performance of a play creates greater pleasure in the audience than reading it, whereas Aristotle equates the pleasures of performance and reading.[31] Castelvetro thinks that the scope of drama, as opposed to that of epic, is restricted and so militates against multiple actions although he acknowledges that the audience wants them. It is not surprising that Castelvetro prefers action to narration on the stage, but he does think that horrible and cruel actions should be narrated rather than staged not because of decorum but because they cannot be performed with verisimilitude. In the 1570s and 1580s respectively, Alessandro Piccolomini and Orazio Ariosto defend a new tragedy that can be freer in invention and plot but that should be based on known stories. Like Philip Sidney, Giordano Bruno argues that no rules govern poetry. The *farsa* and the tragicomic pastoral occasion a debate between innovators like Battista Guarini and classicists or traditionalists like Giasone Denores. Guarini's *Il pastor fido* (1590), a tragicomic pastoral, gained success in Italy and elsewhere. This new genre, which prospers from the 1580s onwards, upset Denores, who invokes Plato on the difficulty for one writer to succeed at tragedy and comedy, Aristotle on the purity of genres, and Cicero on the folly of mixed genres. Guarini redefines the classical idea of verisimilitude to argue for mixed genres as a more accurate imitation of reality. The critical debate is complex and persists into the battle between ancients and moderns that lasts to the mid-eighteenth century and that, in some form, never seems to go away.[32]

In Spain during the Renaissance, Italian ideas spread rapidly and, contrary to the distain that François Bertaut and some other Frenchmen of the mid-seventeenth century display in regard to Spain's dramatic accomplishment, the Spanish understand the relation of their own native tradition to the classics but often favor the former. In the preface to *Propaladia* (1517) Bartolomé de Torres Naharro redefines drama from the classic definitions of tragedy and comedy and shows independence from the ancients. Most European treatises on poetry in the Renaissance treat plays like poems. As early as in the time of Boethius, tragedy is considered as a narrative and not a dramatic genre. Alonso Lopez Pinciano's *Philosophia antigua poetica* (1596), however, discusses at length drama as performance. In the *siglo de oro*, according to Marvin Carlson, two groups—the moralists and classicists—beset the playwrights, the first because of the Spanish drama's corrupting influence, the second because of its putative disregard for the rules of ancient drama. Carlson also notes that one of the most famous attacks on the theatre, which occurs in Chapter 48 of the first part of Cervantes' *Don Quijote*, owes much to Pinciano (57–61).[33] Although Cervantes might share with the Canon or the Curate these deprecatory views of the native drama, for he gestures toward Spanish society by listing in this chapter plays by Lope de Vega, Cervantes, and other practicing playwrights, the author places these opinions in the mouths of characters, so that their opinions come to the reader through a specific story and situation that is fictional. This attack might contain as much irony as it does conviction. Cervantes might be satirizing these satirists of ecclesiastical and secular verse. Can clerics advise playwrights on playwriting? The answer in this narrative consideration of drama might be an ambivalent yes and no. Similarly, some critics sometimes forget that Hamlet, not Shakespeare, gives directions on drama to the players. It is the privilege of narrative and drama to claim to reflect the world or to disclaim any relation between word and world, but whatever the relation, it is refractory. Later, in the prologue to *Ocho comedias y ocho entremeses* (1615) and in one of his eight comedies *El rufián dichoso* Cervantes takes and represents respectively different views that are closer to Lope de Vega's. In the prologue to *El peregrino en su patria* (1604) and later in *Arte nuevo de hacer comedias en este tiempo* (1609), Lope—who is, in the traditional view, one of the butts of Cervantes' attack—says that the Spanish would never have accepted the classical rules for drama. The debate between *uso* and *arte*, custom and the classical rules, continues in the works of Barrada and Cascales among others. Important for our purposes is the work of the playwright Tirso de Molina, whose *Cigarrales de Toledo* (1621) responds to Cascales. Tirso's work is organized like Boccaccio's *Decameron*, as a group of stories and conversations among men and women who have left Toledo. Most importantly, Tirso wants the playwright to enjoy the same freedoms as the storyteller, especially the right to represent a unified action in as many locations or times as is necessary. Through the privilege of narrative, he argues for that privilege for drama.[34] Tirso also allows for the mixing of genres, and the mingling of comic and serious characters while asserting that verisimilitude does not have to follow history closely. Imagination is the poet's means of transforming history and nature, and Tirso also argues for historical context by saying that modern plays better suit modern audiences than classical plays do.[35] The power of the representations of Spanish drama weakens the effect of the arguments of the classicists: the native tradition prevails.

In England, Nicholas Grimald's preface to *Christus Redivivus* (1541) discusses the decorum of diction and justifies his variety of scenes in the practice of Plautus in the *Captivi* while Williame Bavande's *The Good Ordering of the Common Weal* (1559), a translation from the Latin of the Italian Montanus, recommends that classical stories must illustrate a moral lesson.[36] Jonas Barish has discussed at length the attacks on and defenses of the theatre in the course of Western history and includes a discussion of the works of those, like John Northbrooke and George Whetstone, who participate in the controversy in England. It does little good, then, to repeat Barish's work, except to say that the objections of Plato and the Church Fathers to mimesis are alive and well in the Renaissance. The battle between historical and fictional narration over the question of which is the more true and moral continues in George Puttenham's *Arte of English Poesie* (1589) and Sidney's *The Defence of Poesie* (1595). This last work is well enough known that it will suffice to mention that, for Sidney, poetry affirms nothing as it expresses imagination but, paradoxically, it is moral through its use of poetic justice. Sidney follows Aristotle in placing tragedy over epic but puts poetry above philosophy and history.[37] Ben Jonson in his various prefaces and inductions and in *Timber or Discoveries* defends his practice in light of the classics. Jonson, as is well-known, is ambivalent about Shakespeare's accomplishment because of his neglect of the classical rules of drama. Without diminishing Sidney or Jonson, Carlson correctly points out the former's debts to Aristotle, Plato, Horace, Scaliger, and Minturno and the latter's to Seneca, late classical theory, and to his erudite Dutch contemporary, Daniel Heinsius, whose words sometimes appear translated verbatim in *Timber*.[38] It is to the summation of classical rules in *Poeticarum institutionum libri tres* of the Dutch critic, Geraldus Vossius, that D'Aubignac and other French classicists turn when working out their classical ideas of drama.

Neoclassical ideas take a long time to dominate French literary theory and practice during the Renaissance. Nonetheless, they are always present. Regnaud Le Queux's *Instructif de la seconde rhétorique* (1501) argues for decorum in the miracle play or chronicle play while Charles Estienne's prefatory letter to his second edition of his translation of *Gl'ingannati—Les abusez* (1548)—says that the French should follow the Italians in using the classical rules. The Pléiade poets, led by Du Bellay, advocate classical models for French literature but in the French language as opposed to Latin.[39] In the 1550s Jacques Peletier du Mans recommends a characterization that would conform to character types: this decorum he calls *bienséances* (social properties), an idea that becomes central to French neoclassicists in the seventeenth century. During the 1560s Aristotle becomes important to French critics but neoclassicism does not take hold in France until well into the seventeenth century. Laudun's *L'Art poétique françois* (1598) takes, according to Carlson, a more flexible view of classical rules than Vauquelin's *L'Art poétique* (1605).[40] Alexandre Hardy and other playwrights continue to defy classical rules. In the preface to *Ligdamon et Lidias* (1631), Scudéry says that he has read all the authorities on drama but has ignored them in order to please his public.[41] The success of Corneille's *Le Cid* (1637) begins a famous controversy over the use of classical rules in French drama. In *Observations sur le Cid* (1637)

Scudéry anonymously attacks Corneille, who defends his practice. The anonymous *Traicté de la disposition du poeme dramatique* argues for freedom to imitate any action in any appropriate way to respond to the needs of a more complicated modern world. Although the *Sentimens de l'Académie françoise sur la tragi-comédie du Cid* (1637) does not agree with some of Scudéry's criticisms, it is harder on Corneille, especially in regard to how much action can be represented in a day and to the ethics of the play, and it maintains that drama should teach virtue through decorum, verisimilitude, propriety and poetic justice.[42] D'Aubignac furthers the neoclassical position and writes a practical guide to writing plays, *La pratique du théâtre* (1657). Even though d'Aubignac praises Corneille and cites his works as illustrations, Corneille writes three prefaces to the three-volume edition of his works (1660), in which he disagrees with much in French neoclassical theory. In the first essay Corneille still asserts that Aristotle is the central authority on drama but says that the primary objective of plays is pleasure and prefers the necessary to the probable in his discussion of verisimilitude. The second essay looks at catharsis and the third treats the unities, where he argues for flexibility about how many events can be represented, how many locations in a city are desirable and how a neutral room might permit private conversations.[43]

Molière is less given to theory than Corneille, although he is not adverse to stating his views. The preface to *Les Précieuses ridicules* (1659) is the first place where Molière mentions ideas that persist throughout his career: the public is the judge of plays; the representation of the play is more important criticism; comedy is a worthwhile genre.[44] In the "Avertissement" (Advertisement or Preface) to *Les Fâcheux* (1662) Molière says that he is not concerned with the rules of laughter but that he may one day publish his remarks on his plays in which he will cite Aristotle and Horace. For the moment, Molière, who may have only projected a critical document in order to satirize those like Corneille who think criticism important, will listen to his public: "In awaiting this examination, which perhaps will not come, I trust myself enough to the decisions of the multitude, and I hold it to be as difficult to fight a work of which the public approves as to defend one that it condemns."[45] Not surprisingly, Molière comes under attack for this anticritical position. In *La Critique de l'École des femmes* (1663) Molière has Dorante defend the playwright's work against Lysidas' view that Aristotle and Horace would condemn Molière. More specifically, Dorante defends Molière's characters as inconsistently consistent and says that dramatic action can involve monologues and narratives or *récits*.[46] In answer to the Marquis' challenge to respond to him, Dorante defends narrative in drama:

> First, it is not true to say that all the play is in narratives. We see many actions that take place on the stage, and the narratives themselves are actions, according to the constitution of the subject; all the more so since they are all made innocently, these narratives, to the interested person, who thereabouts enters, all the time, into a confusion to the greatest delight of the spectators, and takes, with each piece of news, all the measures that he can to counter the misfortune that he fears.[47]

This view holds that the narratives are action in drama and that they allow the audience to use them as a kind of comic catharsis. The debate soon dwindles to the Marquis singing a monosyllabic refrain of sounds rather than listen to Dorante and Uranie.

In *L'Impromptu de Versailles* (1663) Molière also celebrates the comic spirit, only this time he calls one of his characters Molière and makes his troupe the literal dramatis personae if not the protagonists of the piece (1.517). This play enters the controversy over Molière's plays directly yet through a fictional world. Molière makes himself part of the aesthetic controversy by participating in his practical aesthetic. Even though there is a gap between Molière the person and Molière the character, the playwright chooses the dramatic form to rupture or alter the means of controversy. He translates the pamphlet and essay of his opponents to a royal performance for Louis XIV, a means of empowerment and protection. The king becomes part of the story, particularly when in the last speech of the play Molière tells Béjart of the king's good grace toward them. This is a more indirect dramatic and narrative enclosure of involvement than the giving of the golden ball to Queen Elizabeth in George Peele's *Arraignment of Paris*, although that play is more mythological and the characters do not represent the actors who play them. In the preface to *Le Tartuffe ou l'Imposteur* (1669) Molière expresses outrage over the virulent attack on his play. He also wonders how people can create maxims to limit the subjects that comedy can represent, especially as comedy originated in the religion of the ancients and as Spanish festivals still mix comedy and religion, and so on.[48] In defending and exalting comedy, Molière says, "If the work of comedy is to correct the vices of men, I do not see by what reason some vices would be privileged." (1.629, see 628–32).[49] He tries to answer the charges against comedy—the Church Fathers condemned it—and the Platonic notion that representation—in this case comic mimesis—corrupts the soul. Molière relates a story of the king asking the prince why Molière's comedy offends people more than the irreligious Italian farce, *Scaramouche*. The prince replies that it is because, as opposed to that farce, which represents something these people never worry or preoccupy themselves about—heaven and religion—Molière's comedy portrays the people themselves and they cannot suffer that. This narrative once again appeals to the authority of Molière's royal supporters and protectors as a means, perhaps, of maintaining a space for his audience. The polemical and narrative preface helps to negotiate a place for the play in the world. After this point, Molière does not participate in the debate on drama.

Racine, Boileau, and others continue the discussion in the 1670s. Like Corneille and Molière, Racine suffers attacks and in prefaces to the plays defends himself and his dramatic practice. In the preface to *Mithridate* (1673) he is proud that most historians agree with his representation of Mithridate, but in the second preface to *Andromaque*, he says he has changed historical fact to conform with the modern view of Andromaque. The preface to *Bérénice* (1674) claims that only verisimilitude can move an audience in tragedy, but only once—in the preface to *Phèdre*—does he praise tragedy's moral purpose: "What I can ensure, is that I have not done anything in which the virtue is brought to light than in this case. The smallest faults are severely punished."[50] In the prefaces to *Alexandre* (1666) and *Britannicus* (1670) he defends his use of the unities of time and place because even at Racine, the neoclassical dramatist par excellence, some would throw the book: more often than not that book is Aristotle's *Poetics* or some strict neoclassical interpretation of it. Rapin's *Réflexions sur la poétique* (1674), Boileau's *Art poétique* (1674) and Saint-Evremond's "Sur nos comédies" (1677) and "De la comédie angloise" (1677) all contribute to the debate on classical rules in the drama and comment implicitly or explicitly on the role of narrative in plays. Rapin attacks Italian and Spanish writers for going beyond verisimilitude. He extends the idea of *bienséances*, which Peletier du Mans first discussed in the 1550s, to include social and moral as well as linguistic decorum. Like Aristotle, he favors tragedy over epic and comedy and prefers Greek to French tragedy because it is verisimilitudinous. Unlike Rapin, Boileau emphasizes pleasure over morality. He rejects the Spanish plays because they do not follow the unities and he places verisimilitude over historical truth. Although, as Carlson notes, Saint-Evremond concurs with the main assumptions of French neoclassicism, he also takes pleasure in the achievements of the Italian, Spanish and English drama.[51] If he admires Aristotle, he does not think that he can regulate theatre in all times and places. Saint-Evremond dislikes the practice of some of his contemporaries who substitute long discourse and tears for action.[52] It seems that he prefers mimesis to diegesis.

In Italy, Spain, England, the Netherlands, and France, playwrights and critics battle over the nature of the role of classicism in Renaissance culture. A significant part of that debate centers on Aristotle's *Poetics* and its implications for genre. Is tragedy greater than epic, drama better than narrative? What is the role of narrative in drama? Should genres be mixed? Should an author shape his stories according to the critics' rules and if so should they be ancient or modern critics? How moral should these stories be or should they give pleasure or can they do both? Some writers, like Sidney and Bruno, argue for poetic freedom and prefer poetic narrative to historical narrative. Molière defends narrative in drama, which was especially necessary to maintain the unities but which some neoclassical critics, like Saint-Evremond, criticize despite its use for unifying the place, time and action of the play. For the most part, those who write about drama, and many who discuss poetry generally, follow Aristotle in valuing tragedy above epic. This preference for drama over narrative is deeply embedded in the critical and theoretical heritage of many European countries, so that it is not surprising that it still appears late in the twentieth century in theoretical discussions.

The Function of Narrative in Drama

The question of narrative's function in the drama is not a new one. It has long been recognized that classical drama uses narrative extensively. The apparent development of Greek tragedy from one actor to two then three actors in addition to the Chorus implies that narrative was needed to enhance the scope of the play. The exposition, reports of offstage action, Chorus, parabasis, and other dramatic conventions all rely on narrative. Owing to the nature of the Greek theatre, which limited locale or setting, and owing to the general tendency in classical drama to represent actions in a sharply circumvented time, exposition in classical Greek plays tended to narrate in detail previous actions and the background for characters. The categories that this chapter examines—exposition, suggestion, compression and address—arise inductively from the use of narrative since classical times. They are cognitive and overlap, and are used for a more ready apprehension of narrative. Although each age has its own theatrical conditions, these categories of narrative function recur in recognizable forms.

Exposition

Exposition, which consists of commentary and explanation, may occur at the opening of a play, in choric speeches, in characters' dialogue or in various dispersed parts of the dramatic text. Narrative influences the reader and theatre audience in a similar way, except for the real and imagined differences between dramatic and nondramatic works. When narrative is dispersed in the text, it is like Osiris, until it can be pieced together in the imagination of the reader or audience. This is what I call the Osiris effect. In the satires of Rabelais and Swift, the essays of Montaigne, the novels of ideas of Dostoevsky and Thomas Mann and the drama of ideas like Shakespeare's *Hamlet, Troilus and Cressida*, and *Measure for Measure* and the *drame à thèse* of Ibsen and Shaw, the role of exposition as commentary and debate is the motivating force of, and not some impediment to, action. Some critics classified as problem plays or problem comedies some of Shakespeare's plays because their action did not resolve the questions raised in the characters' debates. T. S. Eliot thought that *Hamlet* failed because it lacked an objective correlative, which was a matter of decorum, for Eliot, as if the talk and the action of that play could be balanced in the same way he imagined classical plays to be.[53] Unlike these critics, I consider the friction between the spoken action of narrative and the physical action of events to be productive and to represent the frustration that often occurs when people compare their wishes and motivations with their actions. Exposition has a psychological dimension as well as a social and political one. Private desires and public necessities often conflict. Conflict, as the critical cliché goes, is necessary for successful drama. Rather than be extraneous, exposition, and the narrative of which it is a function, is dramatic and represents one of the techniques in the repertoire of playwrights.

Although the French have long discussed the importance of the *récit*, and hence of narrative, in Racine, critics in the English-speaking world have too often forgotten the crucial role of narrative in drama.[54] A generation or two ago the function of exposition in Greek drama was a commonplace. This function was not, however, always praised. In a handbook, *The Art of Drama* (1935), Fred Millett, who is coauthor with Gerald Eades Bentley, compares the expositions in Euripides' *Hippolytus* and Racine's *Phèdre*, both of which treat a similar story.[55] Despite Millett's knowledge of the subject, he displays, like Samuel Johnson, an impatience for direct narrative. This impatience characterizes many critics' attitude to narration. Millett says,

> The Greeks were sometimes content to open their dramas with a dramatic monologue. This at its worst was a perfunctory summary of the events preceding the first represented action with which it was necessary for the audience to be acquainted. At best it could indicate the nature of the drama that was to follow, establish the atmosphere, suggest the conflict out of which the plot was to rise, and the lines which the conflict was likely to take.[56]

Millett praises Aphrodite's opening soliloquy in Euripides' *Hippolytus* for specific applications of what he thinks best in the Greek use of exposition and contrasts it with Racine's more modern exposition in *Phèdre*, which raises three problems—is Theseus alive or dead? Hippolytus' love for her father's captive and enemy, Phèdre's enmity to Hippolytus—that are split and diffused structurally and resolve themselves at different points in the drama. Millett is not certain which of the dramatists' expositions is more effective, although his rhetoric seems to favor that of Euripides.[57] Similarly, Laurence Olivier thought that the narrative about the Salic Law at the beginning of *Henry V* was boring to a modern film audience and so used burlesque and clownish acting to save it from the tedium of an Elizabethan debate on succession and imperial designs.[58] The scene was good film, but this success probably tells us as much about the translation of Elizabethan into modern taste as it does about the translation of a play into film. The same translating occurs in Millett's evaluation of exposition in classical drama: the Greeks valued narrative in drama in various forms, including the monologue, whereas Millett thinks of narrative as serving drama.

Another point that Millett raises, and that narrative theory will later take up, is the dispersion of a narrative throughout the text. Millett's discussion demonstrates that it is difficult to generalize about any group of texts, for he discusses how sometimes Greek playwrights wanted to delay the disclosure of facts about the prehistory of the drama but had to reveal something of the situation at the beginning of, and at appropriate points in, the play. He thinks that such a delayed exposition in the play faces the danger of being vague and incomplete or risks boredom when the prehistory is at last revealed. The risk can be worth it because Millett cites Sophocles' *Oedipus Rex* as the supreme example of delayed exposition.[59]

The delayed and splintered story of the Ghost in *Hamlet* is also a wonderful example of exposition in a complex situation. Barnardo and Marcellus retell the story about the Ghost's appearance to Horatio, who is a skeptical narratee (I.i.).[60] The Ghost actually interrupts Barnardo's tale about the Ghost and serves as a dumb show that tests in dramatic fashion Horatio's very skepticism. The speech of the narration and of the characters' address to the Ghost contrasts with his silence and his motions, thereby making the scene more dramatic through this tension. Shakespeare chooses different ways—telling and showing—to demarcate the living and the dead. The Ghost will not heed Horatio's command to speak to him. Barnardo, Marcellus and Horatio provide commentary on the silence and the Ghost's thwarted speech, which never happens because the cock crows.

In the next scene Claudius addresses the court with an account of the mourning and marital and political consequences of the death of Hamlet Senior, whose Ghost occupied the stage and the narrative of the previous scene (I.ii.). This narrative is interrupted by Claudius' concern for Laertes, before the new king can return to Hamlet, the principal narratee of the scene, who shares with the audience his biting reception of Claudius' words, thereby making it another narratee. Gertrude and Hamlet quarrel over the proper way to interpret and react to Hamlet Senior's death. Claudius tries to mediate. Hamlet publicly makes up with his mother but, in a soliloquy, tells the story of his own doubt about his mother's hasty marriage after his father's death. Shakespeare interrupts this solitary narrative to the audience with the arrival of Horatio, Marcellus, and Barnardo, which, after pleasantries, leads back to the theme of the death of Hamlet Senior and to another narrative about the appearance of the Ghost, this time by the once-skeptical Horatio. This narrative is mainly for Hamlet's benefit, although it provides for the audience yet another description of, and point of view on, the Ghost and the death of Hamlet Senior. In the stichomythic exchange, in which Hamlet questions the three tellers about their polyphonous tale about the Ghost (Shakespeare splits it among them), the playwright buries a narrative that Hamlet will uncover here and for the rest of the play and will complicate as he becomes an active narratee who plays out the consequences of the dispersed story and becomes part of it. Hamlet becomes the subject of the exchanges between Polonius, Laertes, and Ophelia (I.iii). In the next scene Hamlet, Horatio, and Marcellus encounter the Ghost and enact a drama like that in the opening scene between speech and silence, until Hamlet follows the Ghost who has beckoned him (I.iv).

The Ghost's "narrative" continues in the next scene, when Hamlet refuses to go on until the Ghost speaks, which he does, as he tells his story. This tale includes the suggestion that he could tell a harrowing story, which is part of the tale he relates, a kind of *invitio* or *ennoia*, a type of *eclipsis* in which an attempt to withhold information implies it (I.v). The Ghost's horrible narrative affects the rest of the play and, subsequently, is never far out of mind. Like Hamlet, we remember the Ghost according to his command. Hamlet and the Ghost make Horatio and Marcellus swear not to tell the tale of what they have seen. As a result of the Ghost's narrative, Hamlet announces his strategy of putting on an antic disposition. The narrative dispersion is so complex as to exceed the space I have to consider it, but in one scene alone we can observe its operation in Hamlet's reading a book with the theme of death in mind and with his antic behavior in full display. The same can be observed in Hamlet's suggestion to the Players that they play *The Murder of Gonzago* with Hamlet's interpolation of 12 to 16 lines, and Hamlet's soliloquy, "O what a rogue and peasant slave am I!" which includes Hamlet's plot or story to have the players trap the king with a play "something like the murther of my father" (II.ii). Although other examples proliferate, the play-within-a-play, which includes Hamlet's narrative commentary, combines narration and dumb show in a manner that parallels and amplifies the two meetings with the Ghost (and the additional reported sighting) (III.ii). Shakespeare combines the dumb show, Hamlet's commentary, and a highly stylized play with narrative speeches, with the reactions of Claudius, Gertrude, and other characters as a means of showing the close relation and tension between showing and telling, the teller, tale and audience. There are two audiences, on the stage and within the theatre. The narrative is performed in word and deed and dispersed, so that the boundaries between the dramatic and the narrative are blurred. Each augments the other. The Ghost's appearance in Gertrude's chamber, where Hamlet is aware of his presence while his mother is not and where the prince kills Polonius, a player in his youth, by mistaking him for Claudius, begins another story one of revenge, which also picks up the revenge narratives of Laertes and Fortinbras (III.iv). It takes the rest of the play to play out the tale as well as the play.[61]

Suggestion

Narrative allusiveness and illusion of reference to a greater fictional world lies at the core of suggestion. These allusions can be a word or a phrase that refers to a person or a place in mythology or history or to other unrepresented times, places, words and actions in the "lives" of the characters. Suggestion is a form of compression but this is not its primary goal. Whereas compression hastens the action along instead of allowing the play to become bogged down with too much showing, suggestion is a world-building function that attempts to make the most of the limitations of a play, the enormous gap between word and world, what happens in nature and society and what can be said about it or in an adjacent symbolic verbal universe. The references to Antony's youth in Shakespeare's *Antony and Cleopatra* are primarily suggestive because they are more a means of building up Antony's heroism and honor (as opposed to showing them) than a way of avoiding scenes of, or a play on, the life of the young Antony. Shakespeare uses narrative to make the dramatic parts of Antony's life more dramatic. In *Julius Caesar* Antony is significant in his own right but is more important as a site of conflict between the worlds of Caesar and Brutus. Description or reports of off-stage action intensify the dramatic experience.

But descriptions of off-stage action may have social, political and religious motivations that vary from period to period. No violence occurs on stage in Greek tragedy, so that messengers report murders and other violent acts that happen off-stage. The *eccyclema*, one of the machines in the Greek theatre, revealed the dead bodies of the victims of this off-stage violence. In Greek tragedy narrative is indispensable and not a poor excuse for dramatic representation. The Greek Chorus has many functions. The members of the Chorus can be minor or major characters, or they can report events and comment on them as they do when they meet Prometheus in Aeschylus' *Prometheus Bound* and say that new rulers reign in heaven and with new customs Zeus rules (144–52).[62] Sometimes the Chorus speaks as one person, sometimes as a collective (180–88). It can be a collective narratee, characters to whom the tale is told, or an audience. The Chorus asks Prometheus to unfold the entire story, to tell them on what charge Zeus has taken and punished him, and to instruct them if no harm will come with the telling (196–99). Telling becomes dramatic: it creates as much tension as it does provide information. If this brief section of one Greek tragedy can suggest complex narrative functions for the Chorus, a study of the extant Attic tragedies would greatly complicate our notions of narrative in classical drama.

Medieval drama can also include the suggestion of biblical allusion, symbolism and typology. The following are primarily examples of suggestion but also include functions like address. *The Second Shepherds' Pageant* from the Wakefield Corpus Christi Cycle begins with a succession of three shepherds telling about the sorry state of the world and the oppression they face. Although only the first shepherd soliloquizes, the second and third speak as if they were alone and only when the first makes his presence known to the second and they together to the third, does the soliloquizer acknowledge that the audience is not simply overhearing him or that he is speaking directly to it. These tales of woe represent the atmosphere and the problem of the play. The weather is bad, the world is fallen. Like Mak, the shepherd who will steal their sheep, the world is in need of Christ's redemption. The shepherds must forgive Mak as Christ forgives them. Without the opening narrative, which enlarges the misery of the shepherds through allusion and natural tropes, the typology of the play's structure is much less effective. Narrative is also a guide, to shift metaphors, in the morality plays. In *The Castle of Perseverance* the suggestion of Christian theology is a primary narrative function but exposition and address also play important roles. The two Vexillators tell of the story of Mankind, who is born naked and will be naked at death, and of his relation to God, Mary and the Good and Bad Angels and how, with great difficulty, sinful Mankind will overcome the Castle of Perseverance with virtues. They also address the audience and speak directly to them as dear and faithful friends about the staging of the play and hope for God's grace and that Christ will keep actors and audience from the fiends. Besides telling the great Christian story, the two Vexillators announce that the play will be performed in a week's time at a certain location, so that the dramatic practice separates the Banns from the main body of action in time and place. When the play proper begins, Mundus then Belial then Caro then Humanum Genes then the Bonus Angelus and the Malus Angelus all speak at length in ways that introduce them to the audience (in talking stage directions), and tell their stories so as to characterize themselves and as a means of setting up the main conflict—the play—the fight between good and evil over humankind's soul. The story is about the temptations of this world and the necessity to overcome them to attain salvation in the next world.[63]

Renaissance playwrights draw on the convention of messengers' reports in classical drama and explore the role of narrative in their own works. In Ben Jonson's *News From the New World Discovered in the Moon*, a masque presented at court before James I in 1620, the two heralds dangle their news before three other characters interested in narratives or documents (in their case, written ones)—a printer, a chronicler and a factor. The narratees' very preoccupation with news—with narrative—becomes a premise and part of the plot because by expressing their interest they further and frustrate the heralds' narratives by suspending them. Narrative remains important for the visual show of a masque.

The narratives of Mithridate's final battle (lines 1558–1638) and of Hippolyte's death (V.vi), in Racine's *Mithridate* (1673) and *Phèdre* (1676) respectively, reveal how suggestive and detailed reports of offstage events can become.[64] Beyond messages, news and reports, other narrative devices are self-consciously narrative, such as the use of letters and comments about the narrative itself. Marlowe opens *Edward II* (ca. 1591–92) with Gaveston, the king's favorite, reading Edward's letter and providing the audience with commentary on it.[65] An example of meta-narrational awareness to which I return is Dorante's defense of narrative in the drama in *Critique de l'École des femmes* (1663) (scene vi). The act of narration in the play can call attention to the way a play is presented to the audience as well as to the role of narrative in our making sense. In particular, Jonson and Molière raise respectively the question of the dependence on news and the importance of storytelling in the drama.

Compression

Like an epic poet who begins his poem *in medias res*, the playwright often shortens the action of the play through narrative. This substitution of telling for showing (although all plays show their telling on stage and tell their showing in print) constitutes an effective means by which to give the play movement. In stories this movement is narrative drive. This compression differs only from suggestion in degree and emphasis. Paradoxically, this compression leaves to the imagination the supposition of fuller fictional worlds. In Jean Racine's theatre, *récits* are generally found in the first and fifth acts because classical conventions like decorum or *bienséances* and unity of time and place require exposition and denouement *récits*.[66] Similarly, compression can be a means of explanation. A narrative can tell about what happened, so that compression can also be expository, although its primary function is to abbreviate the action. Some expositions, as in the prince's soliloquies in *Hamlet* and the debate among the Greek generals in *Troilus and Cressida*, revel in their own verbal web and explore verbal action in opposition to physical action. In the Renaissance, where humanists like Erasmus, Colet and More celebrate an active life as opposed to a contemplative monastic life, tensions can occur between the desire to act and the contemplation of that desire or a repulsion against it. *Hamlet* is a textbook case.

A playwright uses compression more as a means of foreshortening action than as a way of contemplating something is happening. Seneca prefaces his *Hippolytus, or Phaedra* with an argument, which provides the background to the story, another narrative filter. This argument allows Hippolytus in the opening speech to assign the tasks of the day to his followers and thereby create an atmosphere for the play through evocative tropes describing nature in detail and to move the action forward through talk of future action. Nonetheless, as we can observe in Racine's case, the very compression can become an aesthetic with ontological, epistemological, and political implications. Are life and knowledge ordered, so that plays and other works of art should reflect that order, or are these aesthetic objects ways of wishing away, supplementing or answering disorder in the world?

Why is it better to leave violence off-stage? Does the playwright and his society want to dissuade people from violence by not showing it on stage or do they want to pretend it is remote and not central to life?

Address

Narrative in the drama also has the primary function of address. This address can be indirect, like Volpone's soliloquy in which he addresses directly the day briefly and then his gold at length and in doing so addresses his audience indirectly and by implication (I.i.1–33). The narrative function of address can also occur directly in dialogue but with an effect similar to a soliloquy, where the character ostensibly reviews his thoughts but speaks before an audience. In Sophocles' *Oedipus Rex* the king, the Messenger and the Herdsman discuss past events. When the king finds out from the reluctant Herdsman that he is the child of King Laius and therefore the son of his wife, Oedipus exclaims in an anagnorisis that all his terrible troubles will come clear now. This recognition he shares indirectly with the audience, for whom this tragic tale is ultimately uttered. The strophe and antistrophe of the Chorus comment on the events they have heard while they share the stage with Oedipus alone. They speak directly in their commentary to Oedipus but also for the benefit of the audience. Another example of an address that is direct but also indirect is Macbeth's response to Seyton's news about Lady Macbeth's death, which the audience overhears:

> Life's but a walking shadow, a poor player,
> That struts and frets his hour upon the stage,
> And then is heard no more. It is a tale
> Told by an idiot, full of sound and fury,
> Signifying nothing. (V.v.24–28)

This generalization about how life is a meaningless dramatic narrative is Macbeth speaking to himself in a private meditation meant for the public consumption of Seyton and the soldiers as well as the theatre audience. This speech reveals a self-conscious narrativity as much as a self-conscious theatricality.

But there is a narrative continuum between indirect and direct address. Perhaps one of the most direct forms of direct address is the *parabasis*. It is the best-known function of the Chorus in Old Comedy. After the agon, the two rival actors withdrew and the Chorus came forward to sing its *parabasis* or principal song in which the playwright often attacked members of the audience by name. In Aristophanes' *The Clouds* the leader of the Chorus addresses the audience and proceeds to boast of the playwright's talents and to curry favor with the audience. One of the boasts is that he only had to attack Cleon once to bring him low (500–600).[67]

The Prologue is another convention that can represent address, often a direct address to the audience, in concert with other functions. Plautus and Terence based their plots on those of the Greek New Comedy, and, like their Greek forerunners, they used conventions to advantage. The self-conscious theatricality of an appeal to the author is one of the conventions of dramatic narrative. When the Prologue to Plautus' *Menaechmi* introduces to the audience the playwright in person on the stage and not as he appears through the words in his books, he calls attention to the dual nature of a play. The Prologue then summarizes the plot but only does so after a seeming parody of such a convention because he says what comic poets often do and has fun with the vagaries of time and place. The locale is only somewhere when the action happens there onstage, in this case among Sicilian Greeks rather than the usual Athenians. After narrating the plot, the Prologue states the locale and mentions the different characters who can live in the house. Plautus represents the play through a narrative filter. In Terence's *Adelphoe* the Prologue defends the author against what the author considers to be the critics' unfair reception of his work. The Prologue provides a defense against the charges that Plautus and Terence plagiarized specific plays of New Comedy. This story of reception becomes a polemical filter through which we experience the play. In this defense the Prologue says how proud he is that Terence has won the praise of the nobles and the valiant Roman people as a whole. The Prologue also tells the audience not to expect the plot because the old men that first come on stage will disclose part of the story as they play their parts. Micio and Demea, the old men, tell that tale in Act One. With a wish that the goodwill of the audience will give the author energy to write, the Prologue ends his speech.

The direct address of Prologues and Epilogues in Renaissance drama can be used for nationalistic and political reasons. The case of the Chorus to Shakespeare's *Henry V* is well-known in this regard, and I have discussed it elsewhere.[68] Another fine example of this political myth making in narrative, which amplifies and points out the dramatic representation, occurs when the figure of Fame acts as an epilogue in Miguel de Cervantes' *El cerco de Numancia* (ca. 1585–87). After the Spanish boy, Bariatus, has vowed not to let the Romans conquer him, he jumps from the wall of the besieged Numantia for the love of his country. During the course of the play, Scipio, who had destroyed Carthage and thus won the name Africanus, now conquers Numantia, thereby gaining a second surname—Numantius. He is the last character to speak. He praises the boy for having so much valor in his breast and says that Spain has gained undying glory by such a heroic act, explicitly saying that the boy's suicide lays low all Scripio's victories and raises the youth to heaven in an apotheosis. This translation shows by implication a mere boy beating the Romans at their own game—suicide with honor—and reaching a Christian heaven. At the height of the Spanish empire, just before the defeat of the Armada, Cervantes has Scipio narrate a myth beloved to all European countries during the Renaissance (that that particular country is the true successor to Rome). The myths of Brute or Brutus after the fall of Troy founding a specific European country (and not just Britain) is a variation on this theme. Here, Spain will be greater than Rome. In case the audience misses the point, Cervantes adds a peroration to a peroration, the epilogic Fame to the eulogizing Scipio. Fame picks up where Virgil's Fama left off. Fame wants all nations to proclaim throughout the world Bariatus' great sacrifice for Spain, which is clearly proleptic. This deed foretells the valor of Spaniards in coming centuries.

Fame sings in immortal rhyme the example of an unconquered spirit in Numantia and remembers this bravest of unconquered nations. Fame also mentions that its speech is giving a sad story a happy ending, implying the comic ending of a new imperial power out of a denial of its earlier defeats. This is rewriting the colonial past for the imperial future. Fame's very narrative operation, however, can, by implication, be used in the future by other so-called unconquered nations to mythologize their defeat of the conqueror, Spain. Another Scipio will have to snatch defeat from the jaws of victory. Spain's victory will become like Rome's—a thing of the past. And so this kind of narrative address opens up the play to political meanings but even its explicit commentary cannot control the ambivalence toward its direct designs.

Narrative and drama often relate to each other in terms of genre. The conventions of telling and showing, no matter how distinct, overlap during the Renaissance. Narrative and drama relate in formal and historical ways and a study of their relation suggests exciting theoretical discussions and evocative interpretations of Renaissance texts and contexts in Italian, English, Spanish, French, and other languages. In the next chapter, I would like to continue discussing story in the context of plays and history, continuing the transition from the theoretical and critical to the close attention to the plays themselves.

CHAPTER 6

Story, Play, History

The more we explore the context of Shakespeare and his contemporaries, the more apparent it is that it expands to earlier and later periods. These Renaissance writers inherited traditions of poetics, rhetoric, drama, and narrative and translated them into new language and forms based on those traditions. The reception of Shakespeare and others of his age, in our own time, for instance, is part of the filter through which we interpret them.

Theory is a way of seeing but often theorizes what is practiced. Aristotle's *Poetics* is a good example of a theoretical or critical text that draws out its principles based on observations of actual plays and poems of his culture. Practice is theory in action. In the last chapter, I moved mainly from theory to practice in given works, and here I shall concentrate more on practical instances of narrative in texts but also in a context that includes play, irony, and historiography. Theory and practice read each other, and in some ways critical or theoretical views of literature fall short of literature; in a similar but less dramatic way, literature cannot represent the intricacy and vastness of the world. There are many slices of life that literature misses, and even realism is left with phantom slices that haunt the one represented. Representation presents again the absence as well as what was taken to be present. Story is one aspect of mimesis, as Aristotle so tellingly noted when he called tragedy the imitation of an action. A gap between word and world occurs in stories that are dramatic and nondramatic, historical and not. Here is one sliver to which I shall turn in this chapter, recognizing this one tranche is haunted by others not present in this analysis. Once more, Shakespeare and his contemporaries will find themselves in concentric contexts, a kind of still pool with various pebbles creating ripples that sometimes overlap.

The question of narrative is inseparable from the question of language. Language constitutes structure, which in turn determines the difference between events and their representation. How a tale is told or a play is presented often differs from the sequence of events. To restate this first principle of narrative in terms the Russian Formalists used and so many other narratologists recast: the story is not the plot. While I am not offering an analysis that is based on this formalism or on narratology, it is good to make this distinction, which Aristotle made in a sense in *Poetics* when he distinguished between history as following events as they happened and poetry as being able to tell the story in any order. The story is not the plot because it can present the sequence of events in a different order and shape. This is particularly important in discussions of narrative and drama, especially as they relate to the representation of history. Although it would be desirable to approach the topic in a linear fashion, it lends itself somewhat to *digressio* or *excursus* as a background, something that Cicero and Erasmus recommend.[1] I begin with the playful in narrative and drama and move to questions of irony in dramatic history.

The Ludic: Some Examples from Rabelais, Cervantes, and Shakespeare

During the Renaissance, writers played self-consciously with this narrative principle. Rabelais, Cervantes, and Shakespeare provide ample examples of this ludic attitude toward narrative. When Rabelais has Pantagruel and Panurge praise what kind of a fool Triboulett is, he does so with irony and soon has the two competing in parallel columns. This listing plays with the epistrophic "fol" at the end of each line in both columns and plays with blank spaces and the frustration of conventional grammar with its coherent sentences and the sense of a logical sequence of a tale long before Sterne did in *Tristram Shandy*.[2] The narrative embeds within itself a satire on pedantry and illustrates through this long and ludicrous list the *reductio ad absurdum* of listing. Rabelais also represents the trial of Juge Bridoye (Judge Bridlegoose), who views and reviews, reads and rereads, thumbs over, and peruses a myriad of texts, which the author lists at some length, but who decides the case by a throw of a dice.[3] Perhaps, Rabelais suggests, interpretation is as arbitrary as Bridoye's judgment. Reading is like casting the dice. This attack on logic is also summed up in Bridoye's declaration of a principle of canon law: "*Semper in obscuris quod minimum est sequimur*" (In obscure cases, we follow that which is least obscure").[4] The difficulty in finding a sequence to the inconsequential is a narrative problem. Pantagruel also satirizes the idea that names can be read for prophecy, as if temporal sequence can derive from the arbitrary relation between name and the person represented. Rabelais implies that the arbitrariness of naming is related to the arbitrariness of narrative. In fact, Pantagruel's account of Pythagoras' idea of naming reduces it to absurdity while enhancing Rabelais' narrative. The digressive language and the ironic gap between the logical precision of the style and the outlandishness of the content make the book more attractive and humorous:

> I am quite lost in my understanding when I reflect upon the admirable invention
> of Pythagoras, who by the number, either even or odd, of the syllables of every
> name, would tell you of what side a man was lame, hulch-backed, blind, gouty,
> troubled with the palsy, pleurisy, or any other distemper incident to human kind;
> allotting even numbers to the left, and odd ones to the right side of the body.[5]

Pythagoras' interpretation of nature becomes less the music of the spheres or the microcosm reflecting the macrocosm than a kind of quack narrative about quack medicine. Even as the report may be satirizing the long tradition of medical incompetence in which cause and effect were yoked accidentally and with dire consequences, it turns from nature and the world as the account becomes part of a large structure that compiles so many ludicrous instances that their sum is greater than their parts. Language and structure translate fact and observations of the world and shape them into great and improbable fictions.

Cervantes also uses narrative with canniness. One example cannot do justice to Cervantes' array of techniques, such as embedded novellas and references to print and books, but the episode of the curate and the barber in the library can call attention to the making of narrative. Besides a self-conscious satire on literary criticism and censorship at the beginning of a novel that transgresses many conventions and rules, the chapter calls attention to Cervantes' narrative technique. Near the end chapter and amid many other books, the author has the barber slip in a discussion of Cervantes' *La Galatea*. Like Chaucer in "The Tale of Sir Topas," Cervantes allows himself to be the butt of a joke, a humble author who has not quite mastered the art of narrative, a character whose apparently modest accomplishment only throws into relief—amid comic relief—the masterful artistry of the eponymous writer. In response to the barber, the curate criticizes this other work of Cervantes in the midst of his masterpiece.

> That Cervantes has been for many years a great friend of mine, and to my knowledge he has had more experience in reverses than in verses. His book has some good invention in it, it presents us with something but brings nothing to a conclusion: we must wait for the Second Part it promises: perhaps with amendment it may succeed in winning the full measure of grace that is now denied it; and in the mean time do you, señor gossip, keep it shut up in your own quarters.[6]

Possibly, Cervantes is complaining that his plots are misunderstood because they are not coherent Aristotelian actions but are episodic and go nowhere. Like Rabelais, Cervantes seems to be playing with the notion of the arbitrariness of narrative and interpretation. Narratives also create illusions that do not reflect the world but that translate it. In this chapter, the library contains Cervantes' book, but his book also contains a library. From the outset, Cervantes provides an inset. Through allusion, the narrative creates the illusion of alternate worlds, of books behind the titles. These books, which exist in the world, are represented and misrepresented in a precarious position between the library and the fire.

At the end of *Hamlet*, the dying prince asks Horatio to tell his story even though the audience has already witnessed it. This small incident says a great deal about the relation of narrative to drama. It calls attention to the difference between character and audience as the Danish people and Fortinbras do not, unlike the audience, know Hamlet's tale, so that Shakespeare emphasizes dramatic irony and the use of allusive narrative to create the illusion of a larger world in the play. The incident combines, while it distinguishes between, showing and telling, the dramatic and the narrative. It also makes us more aware of the importance of narrative in drama, which is too often forgotten in the theatre, where actors and directors distance themselves from readers and critics while acting on their readerly and critical acumen in creating interpretations of the play and its characters. In the study, a play can seem as narrative as a novel. A play is an oral and written text, for each aspect leaves its traces in the other. Drama is performative and narrative: it is a mistake, which has been made too often, to ignore the narrative nature of drama on and off the stage. Until recently, another neglected area has been the social and political dimension of narrative.[7]

Hamlet, Irony, and History

When Hamlet instructs Polonius to use the players well, "for they are the abstract and brief chronicles of the time," he is admitting the importance of the theatre for the remembrance of things past (II.ii.524–25). Hamlet does not leave the point ambiguous as he explains to Polonius what he means: "After your death you were better have a bad epitaph than their ill report while you live" (II.ii.511–14). Nor is Hamlet ambivalent about the players. His instructions show that he wants them to speak the words that he writes for them and that he is not sure about their imitation of emotions and not the emotions themselves, but then he tells Polonius to treat the players well because they are the cultural memory, to be more bountiful, the less they are deserving. Later, Hamlet uses "The Mousetrap" to test the king and places the theatre and its fictions at the very center of his life and of Danish history. Hamlet is Shakespeare's character and represents only one point of view, so that a simple identification between them, no matter how interested both are in the theatre and the past, would be naive. If literature is partly synecdoche or metonymy, a part representing a whole, so too is Hamlet synecdochic or metonymic of the play but not precisely of Shakespeare. The relation between any character and his or her author is complex and is one of the large and persistent problems of mimesis.

While I am going to concentrate most on Shakespeare's Second Tetralogy (*Richard II, 1* and *2 Henry IV, Henry V*), I think that Hamlet's comments on players and their role in representing the past are instructive for Shakespeare's representation of history and the views of history and the ideas of his contemporaries.[8] As Hamlet implies, the players are abstract and brief in their representation, but their plays serve as "exempla," as the memory of personalities from the past. They ensure fame or infamy in the future. Their brevity and abstraction make them difficult to understand. History abstracts from life and attempts briefly to represent the vast, confusing, and seemingly concrete events in life in which people participate. After defining "history," "history play," and "irony," I would like to look at the contribution Shakespeare's Second Tetralogy makes to history and the history play in the context of his contemporaries and of twentieth-century historiography and then discuss the plays themselves in light of the relation of irony to history. I shall argue that Shakespeare complicates historical drama and the Renaissance ideas of history through irony. With irony, he explores the limits of the genre, creates complex characters by identifying so much with each on he sides with none, represents through images and keywords the close and intricate relation between intention and profession, and examines the connection between theatre and world, which he places at the center of the second group of history plays. It is my contention that Shakespeare contributes so much to historiography in Renaissance England that, as interpretation involves the present engaging the past and moving into the future, modern historians and literary critics should not ignore Shakespeare's history plays. If literary criticism and historical interpretation are similar in the way I have just outlined, then in studying Renaissance historiography we by necessity measure Renaissance views of history against our own.

"History" is a difficult word to define and its definition must be provisional and help interpretation. The etymology of the term reveals that it originally meant inquiry, story, and story about the past. These meanings correspond respectively to science, literature, and history as we know them today. Traditionally, history was comprehensive, and it is this very comprehensiveness that created the conflict of various views of history in the late sixteenth and early seventeenth centuries. In the seventeenth-century writers like Francis Bacon and Thomas Sprat wanted history to be scientific and to rid itself of mythology, conjecture, and metaphorical language. From about 1594 to 1609, Samuel Daniel wrote his English historical epic, *The Civil Wars*, in verse but shifts to a less metaphorical prose in the period from 1608 to 1619, especially in *The Collection of the History of England*.[9] This split between scientific inquiry and telling stories about the past occurs at about the same time that Shakespeare's acting company shifted its emphasis from the public to the private theatre. In the public theatres the Lord Chamberlain (later called the King's Men after the ascension of James I and as an indication of his patronage) would have represented history plays in an audience that would range from pickpockets and whores to the nobility, in which the interests in historical topics would be representative of much of the society, whereas in the private theatres the audience would pay about five times as much and would be interested in heroic, noble, witty, or idyllic subjects played with pageantry and elaborate costuming, lighting, and sets in plays that are increasingly unhistorical and antihistorical.

In *Henry VIII* (ca. 1613) Shakespeare returns to the episodic plot of the so-called chronicle plays of the 1580s and 1590s, such as *The Famous Victories of Henry the Fifth* (ca. 1586–89), *The Troublesome Reign of John King of England* (1588–89), *The Raigne of King Edward the Third* (1590), Shakespeare's *Henry VI* plays (ca. 1590–92), and *Woodstock* (ca. 1591–94). As I assume that Shakespeare knew what he was doing when using old conventions, I think that *Henry VIII* questions the possibility of writing history, of taking a complex and troublesome reign and showing it as a triumphant concatenation of discreet episodes, as a pageant.[10] The friction between form and content produces a self-conscious awareness of the difficulty of avoiding the moralizing of nature and time. *Henry VIII* is history as romance in which poetic justice is willed as history consumes itself in a fairy tale that proclaims that all is true. The cognates of the word "truth" are repeated throughout the play, but the characters cannot agree on what truth is. The Prologue asks the audience to be part of historical interpretation by using their imaginations but will not abide the idea of the play as comedy. Nonetheless, despite the repetition of *de casibus* falls, which are tragic in that sense, the end attempts a comic celebration of community. This friction is a challenge to the audience and to history itself. Even though *Henry VIII* seems to be reminiscent of the chronicle plays, it is exploring history and historical drama in a new and exciting way. One of the problems is how much we desire or reason out patterns in history or whether the two are separable. The issue of how far one can stray from close mimesis in historical writing is addressed most vigorously in historical fiction.

To define the history play, which changes over time, is difficult. *Richard III*, *Richard II*, and *Henry VIII* are all history plays but differ significantly, the first tending toward melodrama, the second toward tragedy, and the third toward romance. I define the history play as any play that has as one of its central concerns what is thought at the time of writing or in later periods to represent history. When John Heminges and Henry Condell—fellow players and sharers in Shakespeare's company—gathered together *The First Folio* (1623), they considered as history plays only those that depicted English and not British or Roman history. Many today do not share this view of history as restricted to our national history, although many would admit that representations of our national pasts often have more immediacy and hold more interest for us. The history play is various. The difference between past and present historical and dramatic conventions creates interpretation while the similarities cause the initial interest to investigate. This section will implicitly and explicitly compare Elizabethan and twentieth-century views of history in a way that is meant to be suggestive and not exhaustive.

Irony is one connection between past and present and is something used in history and in literature, including in history plays. One of the grounds of similarity and difference is irony. Irony is as old as human culture, but its theory and classification long lagged behind its practice. The first appearance of the word "irony" in English occurred in *The Ordynary of Crystyanyte* in 1502 and meant a false pose of humility, which was to be avoided as much as excessive boasting. The author makes a Christian distinction between the moral or immoral posture of the person and the rhetorical device, but the trope resembles Quintilian's while retaining the moral disapproval that the term held with Aristotle and his predecessors. Often without this disapprobation, "irony" meant in the sixteenth century merely the verbal device or saying the opposite of what one means. Numerous rhetoricians echo this primary definition. A second and less popular definition is saying something "other" than one means and not the opposite. The third and least popular definition is, as John Marbeck wrote in 1581, "calling that foule which is faire, or that sweete which is sowre."[11] Until the Augustan age, most people view irony as a brief and taunting trope, although Thomas Wilson (1560) and Abraham Fraunce (1588) borrow Quintilian's figures, which extend irony through a whole speech or an entire life. By the end of this period, irony has not yet developed the philosophic or tragic connotations that it does in later criticism. Anticipating Connop Thirlwall's identification of Sophoclean or dramatic irony in 1833, however, both Thomas Nashe (1594) and Robert Burton (1621) in isolated passages happen on this kind of irony, and the recognition of Sophoclean irony marks the beginning of a broader and more speculative use of the term "irony."[12] In examining the relation between irony and history in Shakespeare's drama, we have to remember how irony has developed from a rhetorical trope to a philosophical stance. German Romantics like Friedrich Schlegel, August Wilhelm Schlegel, Adam Müller, Ludwig Tieck, Karl Solger, and others transformed the theory of irony. They were familiar with Socratic irony and with classical irony in general, the first important period in the development of ironic theory, so that their theoretical revolution in irony is partly grounded in a response to antiquity and classicism.[13] It is the German Romantics who achieve the second great period of innovation in ironic theory and who have influenced critics as different as I. A. Richards, William Empson, Northrop Frye, and Paul de Man.[14] Rather than meaning the opposite of, or something different from, what is said or done, it now means a godlike or bird's-eye view.

In the Renaissance, ironic practice was much more advanced than the theory. The Second Tetralogy represents dramatic irony, which is most like the traditional trope, but also a godlike sympathy and detachment. The Schlegels probably realized that Aristophanes used an irony that was godlike in its detachment and that their idea of detachment and the detached observer or overviewer, or "kataskopos," derived from classical times. Douglas Duncan reminds us that the "down-looker" or "overviewer" who belittles human concerns by observing them from on high was a commonplace of the Cynics and was associated with Menippius and Lucian.[15] "Kataskopos" was a commonplace in the Renaissance as Erasmus, More, Rabelais, and others were familiar with it, especially through Lucian, and they themselves were so influential that knowledge of the god's-eye view spread widely. Although speaking about the romances, Norman Rabkin calls attention to "the Renaissance commonplace that the artist is a second God creating a second nature," but in the second group of histories art and life exist in a fallen world in which, unlike the romances, they are at odds across a gap between word and world.[16] Art and life, history and the world can never be one, except metaphorically, as the gaps between them provide the grounds of representation. Historical drama exists in the world but is not the world. Shakespeare's histories explore that ironic gap but with more sympathy than Aristophanes or the katascopic observers have for human endeavors or for characters in their creation.

In the Second Tetralogy, Shakespeare uses multiplicity, a multiple irony, rather than a double view of irony. Multiplicity comprehends various aspects that work in concert but that, for the sake of clarity, will be examined separately in this study—irony of words, theatre, and structure. *Richard II, 1* and *2 Henry IV,* and *Henry V* all represent these constituent ironies. To summarize multiplicity, it occurs when the godlike but human playwright shares with his audience a sympathetic detachment from all characters, when he ironically juxtaposes the comic and the "serious"—when he balances multiple points of view, wanting the audience to understand the complexity of the play and of the world for which it is an analogue. Multiplicity can indicate multileveled effects, that is, not only does it juxtapose ironically many different events, characters, and situations, but it can also contrast ironically various levels of technique such as themes, "acting," words, images, and the arrangement of scenes. Multiplicity is Shakespeare's method of representing a postlapsarian world where questions must be asked, where answers must be tentative, where loose ends proliferate, and nothing is categorical, simple-minded, or dogmatic. The question becomes the answer, the method the meaning—this might be called the "epistemological view" of Shakespeare, the artist. Depicting human experience as Shakespeare does, means an interpenetration of such opposites as good and evil so that pure states break into many shades and characters become inscrutable to other characters. The use of multiplicity in the Second Tetralogy distinguishes Shakespeare from his contemporaries.

Shakespeare's History and Historiographers in Renaissance England

Shakespeare and his contemporaries were interested in the relation between history and poetry. Some of the most important statements on this subject may be found in Sidney, Hooker, Spenser, and Ralegh. We may only sample these writers here. Rather than looking for similarities between poets and historians, Philip Sidney, in "An Apology for Poetry" (ca. 1580, pub. 1595), prefers to find differences between them, primarily for the reasons Aristotle did in *Poetics*. Whereas the historian describes what actually happened and examines particular truths, the poet, according to both Aristotle and Sidney, writes about what might happen, what is probable and necessary. Both theorists prefer the truth of poetic fiction to that of historical fact. For Sidney, great poetry attempts to repair a fallen world by creating heroes and mythological beats not found in it, by making then a golden world. This is a very different realm from the Second Tetralogy. One of the best examples of the providential idea of history, John Hooker's dedication to Walter Ralegh in Holinshed's *Chronicles* (1587 edition) says that an important lesson that history teaches men is that God punishes rebels and traitors and protects the good. This is the poetic justice Sidney swears that history lacks. In a letter to Ralegh (1589), Edmund Spenser sees no contradiction in the phrase "historical fiction," for the poet can rearrange history as a story whereas the historian cannot. By now, it will be apparent that Ralegh is central to an understanding of the relation of poetry and history in the English Renaissance. In the Preface to *The History of the World* (ca. 1611, pub. 1614), Ralegh sets out his views of primary and secondary causes, which help illuminate Shakespeare's idea of history in the Second Tetralogy. If Raleigh saw the sacred history of the Bible as a manifestation of primary causes, or the direct participation of God in human events, he viewed profane history in classical times, and in any period not described in the Bible, as a world of secondary causes, that is, of human and merely natural causes. Historians, and indeed all men, cannot see the multiple shapes and ways of God in history, so that profane history is mostly a matter of conjecture, a flawed reconstruction in a ruined world using the faulty faculty of reason.[17] Without direct commentary, Shakespeare represents this world of secondary causes in the Second Tetralogy.

Elizabethan writers thought about various aspects of history: form and time, use and meaning, truth and fiction, its achievements and limits. On the whole, Philip Sidney's contemporaries valued history much more than he did. In dealing with a mind as uncommon as Shakespeare's, it is necessary to state briefly some of the shared wisdom of Elizabethan historians and historical poets. Historians, it was believed, were to seek truth—to record what actually happened in the past—and to show examples from the past in order to encourage virtue in the present. The use of history was to tell the truth and to instruct. History was also a refuge from "cormorant time," a favorite theme among Elizabethans. Time could be cyclical as many classical writers thought, or guided by God from creation to doom as earlier writers such as Augustine had said (so that human time could be contrasted with eternity). As an alternative to this apocalyptic view, history could be, as Herschel Baker says, a "cyclic alternation," which has an "alternative and antidote to the gloom of these apocalyptic schemes" yet something that still remained within the providential view.[18] Many historians and historical poets also accepted the doctrine of the fallen nature of humanity, and most chose to make history providential. In a time as diverse and full as the Elizabethan age, this generalization can only be taken so far.

Shakespeare and most of his contemporaries wrote within the rhetorical tradition of classical history, of what Aristotle described when discussing the universal truth of the poet, inventing speeches that did not occur but might have happened under similar circumstances. What happened or history is at least as possible as what might have happened or poetry, so that Aristotle's division between history and poetry actually allows for historical poetry or drama. Shakespeare creates a more complex view of history than his contemporaries. Few of Shakespeare's contemporaries shared with him a persistent concern with the structure of history—excepting Spenser, Daniel and, perhaps, Ralegh—being content, for the most part, to chronicle events or to place everything into the pattern of the fall of illustrious men or illustrations of a divine plan that is readily available to human interpretation. Perhaps above all his contemporaries, Shakespeare concerned himself with the form of history, differentiating each reign with a genre appropriate to the events of the time. Shakespeare shapes the second group of history plays through other genres—tragedy in *Richard II*, comedy in *1 Henry IV*, satire in *2 Henry IV*, and the problem play in *Henry V*. Self-conscious theatricality and the multileveled language ironically reflects the multiple structure, which, in turn, complicates the characters and creates a sense of multifold time.

Besides the kataskopic or Romantic irony of the godlike overviewer, Shakespeare also uses an irony similar to Kierkegaard's that limits, disciplines, and shapes itself. Through irony, Shakespeare represents the stability and instability in the genres of his plays and, by complex analogy, in the world. *Richard II* contains the tragic fall of Richard and of England and the comedy or tragicomedy of Aumerle, York, and the Duchess of York pleading for contrary ends before Bolingbroke. *1 Henry IV* includes the comic celebration of Hal and Falstaff and the victory of Henry IV but also the satiric isolation of Hal from his fellows and John of Lancaster's lies to achieve victory and a happy ending. *2 Henry IV* separates Hal and Falstaff and the different parts of England—court, tavern, rebel camp, and Gloucestershire—do not communicate in their satiric isolation, so much so that the prince ultimately rejects Falstaff. This rejection, one of the most controversial points in the response to Shakespeare's plays, is necessary for the public well-being of England but forces Hal, now Henry V, to suppress his private self. This is a crisis for history in which private and public selves coexist. The suppression of one by the other creates a problem. The problem play occurs when there is generic friction in a play, when it probes the boundary of the genre, in this case the history play. The rejection of Falstaff foreshadows the generic friction in *Henry V*. In the last play of the Second Tetralogy, tragedy, comedy, and satire rub together within the confines of the history play. *Henry V* is a play that questions itself. It almost calls into question the possibility of history as *Henry VIII* later does. For instance, the Chorus and the main action often contradict each other, and the sequence of choruses and events qualify each other so that there is no simple and heroic view of history. Even the Prologue will not allow a plain view of the past. The comic celebration of the engagement between Henry V and Katharine and the tragic epilogue, which announces that Henry V died young and Henry VI lost France, modify each other ironically. Shakespeare radically challenges the representation of time by trying to end the four history plays in one of the most temporally compressed poetic forms: the sonnet. It is as if Shakespeare is daring the audience to see that history cannot be ended, and this lack of an ending in the continuous flow of time is how Samuel Johnson defined a history play as opposed to a comedy or tragedy.[19] Shakespeare is playing with time because his audience, as the Epilogue reminds it, has already seen the story of Henry VI, which occurred later in the past. History is both past events and writing about the past. Shakespeare is exploring this relation, reversing time as Spenser's epic or historical poet might, but also following the chronicles as a historian might. By doing both, Shakespeare questions the relation between poetry and history and shows that the opposition is not so neat.

Paradoxically, on stage Shakespeare distills and condenses character and action to their essence, not cluttering his idea of history with extraneous or burdensome detail, but creates an image of history that is, in some ways, as complex as any yet conceived. Representing an array of intricate characters, Shakespeare balances their points of view and does not take a single view of the action or of history. There is no authorial dictation to a servile audience. Instead, Shakespeare asks the audience to collaborate imaginatively and to judge the world of characters that are "made flesh," given psychological depths and complexity rarely seen in any historical work before or after. By being so sympathetic to each character, Shakespeare does not choose sides and creates detachment. He asks the audience to participate in the interpretation of history, keeping the process alive with each generation by refusing to state causes but, rather, by "embedding" them in the action. A multiple irony creates a multiple view of the world full of conflicting and interpenetrating oppositions such as hope and despair, war and peace, truth and fiction. Shakespeare both distinguishes between periods and represents apparently universal elements in human action and character.

The idea of what constitutes history does change over time and has done so especially since the Renaissance. Some historians began to develop techniques of inquiry and to question literary and imaginative aspects of history. John Stow (ca. 1525–1605) has been properly praised for his use of public records and full notation. William Camden, the author of *Britannia* (1586) and the *Annals of Queen Elizabeth* (1615), used archives closely and was scrupulous in trying to discern between facts and myths in a highly political situation.[20] Some historians have neglected the contributions that Shakespeare and his more literary colleagues made to the study of history. F. J. Levy dismisses too easily the rhetorical tradition in history as "the superficial tricks of Tacitean history."[21] In the past generation or so, it has not been as easy for historians to limit the role of imagination and literary form in the writing of history. Hayden White has been instrumental in this debate over whether history is an objective representation of an objective past or a narrative choice in reconstructing a past that is as much a product of the historian's mind as of the traces or archetypes of past events.[22] Even in science we have come to learn of the interplay of observer and observed. If the past has vanished, its reconstruction cannot be attempted without reason, desire, and imagination. Fact itself is not history, and record itself is not truth. In our age, even in interpreting Shakespeare's view of history, let alone his specific representations of the past (free of all later critiques), it becomes difficult to avoid epistemological uncertainties as Shakespeare and the times he represents move further into the past as we further into the future.

As great as it is, Shakespeare's representation of history is limited. For instance, he does not illuminate the economic life of a medieval village. Nonetheless, two able historians praise Shakespeare's history. Pieter Geyl says that historical veracity cannot exist without spectacle, actions, life, "plastic capacity," and a concrete world. For Geyl, "history attempts to get to the truth of life in a way that cannot be simple, cannot be 'single' . . . And is it not so, indeed, that Shakespeare's drama owe their effectiveness as history largely to their not being 'single,' to their action being composite and varied?"[23] If Geyl appeals to Shakespeare's appeal to imagination in his histories, F. Smith Fussner says that "Shakespeare's history plays . . . are obviously central to any discussion of Tudor historical thought."[24] Fussner implies that even if a modern historian would not want to emulate Shakespeare's methods of invention, he or she might learn something from Shakespeare's subtle development of character and his use of irony. Irony, for Fussner, is more double than multiple.

Shakespeare's contribution to historiography has been and will be judged in light of the debate, since classical times at least, about what is truth in history and poetry and of the discussion, since the Renaissance, of the merits of historical poems, plays, or fiction. Many of the classical and humanist historians practiced a rhetorical and poetic craft, shaping their narratives, inventing speeches, and looking at the poetic "universal truths" in history, whereas chroniclers had, for the most part, merely agglomerated a compendium of fact and rumor. Shakespeare drew on both traditions. Fritz Stern and Hayden White realize the importance of literary art in history as well of science and philosophy. Stern argues for the "varieties of history" that would recognize within its achievement consummate historians such as Thucydides, de Toqueville, and Mommsen who balance the scientific and artistic sides of historical representation. White develops a whole theory of historiography on the relation between narrative choice and historical form. One of his three kinds of strategies in historiography is "explanation by emplotment" that includes the archetypes of romance, comedy, tragedy, and satire. He argues that the great historians of the nineteenth century and, indeed all historians, are literary and make a subconscious and poetic choice that affects the form each chooses for a particular history. According to White, verbal fictions relate closely to the structure of history as they do to literature. The ironic mode, White says, has been the predominant one since the nineteenth century, so that Shakespeare may be said to be "modern" in the self-critical language and form of his plays.

Shakespeare is unique in the range of the genres he uses to write history and he employs dramatic as well as literary conventions.[25] Whereas in the late sixteenth century and early seventeenth century history was shifting from rhetoric and poetry to science and inquiry, today the reverse is happening. I am not saying that the scientific claims of history have been overthrown but that it is not as possible to ignore the literary, rhetorical, and dramatic aspects of history. If R. G. Collingwood and Tom Driver have likened historical imagination to a dramatic reenactment in the mind, Shakespeare's dramatic history gains some of the importance that Hamlet claims for the theatre.[26] There is an art and craft to history, and history is also a rhetorical art as philosophy and literature are, so that to try to purge it of form and narrative for analysis and argument is difficult and improbable. The science and inquiry in history is positive, but they cannot escape the point of view of the writer or historian or the matter of style and form. Shakespeare's dramatic history, although not always accurate in today's terms or perhaps following the poet's needs for shape and literary success and lastingness, is memorable and a serious addressing of the past and the representation of the past—of history—and deserves more than dismissal or a one-eyed view by those who study and write history.

Theatre and World: Irony and History in the Second Tetralogy

Shakespeare's representation of history differs from Marlowe's and Ben Jonson's. Whereas Shakespeare represents English history in about ten plays and creates a close intertextuality among some of these plays, especially the First and Second Tetralogies, Marlowe writes only one English history play, *Edward II*, which resembles *Richard II* and may have influenced it or have been indebted to it. Like Shakespeare, Marlowe explores the relation between private and public, but Marlowe's play broaches the idea of homosexuality in an open manner. In *Dido Queen of Carthage* Marlowe rewrites the mythical story of Dido and Aeneas from *The Aeneid*. The two parts of *Tamburlaine* represent a Machiavellian and heroic protagonist trying to bend the world to his will, which raises significant questions about the relation between word and world and the role of mimesis in history. *The Massacre at Paris* is a Protestant polemic that may have influenced Shakespeare in *King John*. Apparently, although we are not sure of the dates, Marlowe moved from classical and foreign history to English history whereas Shakespeare began with English history moved on to British and Roman history and returned to English history with *Henry VIII*. Among the dramatists of Renaissance England, Jonson approaches most closely the humanist ideal of history. Jonson is more didactic in his tragic Roman histories or historical Roman tragedies, *Sejanus* and *Catiline* than the historical representations of Marlowe and Shakespeare. *Mortimer His Fall*, left unfinished at Jonson's death, is only one of three attempts at English history after *Henry VIII*.[27] In *Sejanus*, Jonson criticized censorship and was called before the Privy Council and was accused of "poperie and treason." Jonson places the trial of Cordus, the historian, at the center of the play. On the other hand, Jonson follows his sources, especially Tacitus, than Shakespeare does, although he is not adverse to the occasional compression of time and the use of anachronism. As Marlowe and Shakespeare represent the past to bear on the present, Jonson may have staged *Catiline* as an indirect commentary on the Gunpowder Plot of 1605, although the play achieves more than topical allusion. As a good humanist, Jonson uses classical Rome to teach Renaissance England. It is Shakespeare's use of irony to shape individual English history plays and a series of plays in the tetralogies that distinguish him from his contemporaries. In the Second Tetralogy Shakespeare balances points of view, explores the relation between generic shape and past events, intention and profession, and theatre and world.

The constituents of multiplicity—irony of structure, words and theatre—help complicate Shakespeare's representation of history in the Second Tetralogy. I will use a few examples to show how Shakespeare balances multiple points of view and encourages a contextualization of meaning. Multiplicity places meanings side by side in a series of qualifications and does not mean an undercutting. In the last section, we looked briefly at Shakespeare's use of generic experimentation in the second group of histories, so that I will concentrate here on other aspects of the irony of structure. An ironic reversal occurs in *Richard II*. At the beginning, Richard, who is implicated in the murder of his uncle Gloucester, judges the case of his cousin Bolingbroke and his friend Mowbray and banishes both and helps cause a rebellion by taking Bolingbroke's lands. By the end of the play, Bolingbroke exiles Isabel and Exton and causes a revolt by judging Richard, taking his kingdom and killing him, another member of the family. The structure seems to indicate that, although at first much seems to have changed in England, another look suggests another perspective, that little has changed except that yet another man suffers the grief and broils of kingship. The tragic fall is nearly as much of Bolingbroke as of Richard. All England suffers. Another example of ironic complication through structure will suffice. In *2 Henry IV* Shakespeare's irony of structure helps produce a complex satire as well as pushing satire into a realm where it mixes with comedy and tragedy and extends the bounds of the history play. Ironically, as a whole, the structure of *2 Henry IV* shows little development, representing the "movement that never moves" that often characterizes satire. Shakespeare juxtaposes the "tragic" fall of the rebels and the "comic" triumph of *Henry V* (celebrated in his coronation), and the audience is also faced with another problem: it must ask whether Falstaff is a comic or tragic scapegoat, whether he resembles Jaques or Malvolio or neither. Ultimately, the irony of the general structure in Part Two causes the audience to consider the relation among satire, comedy, tragedy, the problem play, and history.

In addition to these examples of aspects of irony of structure, two instances of irony of words will show, as Northrop Frye reminded us long ago, that we cannot take literary or dramatic language at face value.[28] Characters are unconscious of their desires or consciously repress them. Bolingbroke has been wronged, and Henry V is heroic, but their language qualifies their virtues. When Bolingbroke lands, he says that he only comes to reclaim his lands from Richard and not to take the crown, but his language shows the conflict within him. Ironically, in Act III, Scene iii, Richard talks in the same images that Bolingbroke has just used, warning the rebels that God is mustering in his "clouds" pestilence to curse their progeny for generations. The imagery of sun and weather appears to betray Bolingbroke, for it is warlike, stormy, sudden—all indicating sad consequences for Richard. The anticipation of Bolingbroke cornering himself substantiates this claim:

> Methinks King Richard and myself should meet
> With no less terror than the elements
> Of fire and water, when their thund'ring shock
> At meeting tears the cloudy cheeks of heaven.
> Be he the fire, I'll be the yielding water;
> The rage be his, whilst on the earth I rain
> My waters—on the earth, and not on him. (III.iii.54–60)

The images backfire. Water usually puts out fire. Bolingbroke will "rain" on Richard, will takes his "reins" and his "reign," a pun that supports the dramatic irony that alludes to images of weather, horses, and kingship, all of which are important in the play. Downward like Phaeton will Richard fall, unable to hold the reins of his horse. In what may be a Freudian slip, Bolingbroke catches himself when he says "on the earth, and not on him" (III.iii.60). The sun imagery also shows Bolingbroke's moral decline as well as Richard's fall, eclipse and loss of control. Controlling Bolingbroke, the new Apollo, now takes up the sun. By the end of the play, Bolingbroke, the king and so the sun, will put on the black of mourning and will banish Exton, the instrument with which he murders Richard, like Cain, "thorough shades of night," never showing his head "by day nor light" (V.vi.38–52).

The central speech that qualifies the gentleness of Henry V, in war at least, is his threat before Harfleur. Siege is an important verbal and stage image in *Henry V.* This imagery is sexual, the sack of the city being its rape. Shakespeare equates the city with virgins as Marlowe had in *Tamburlaine* and Homer identified the so-called rape of Helen with the siege of Troy. For example, Henry threatens, "If I begin the battery once again, / I will not leave the half-achieved Harfleur / Till in her ashes she lie buried" (III.iii.7–9). His soldiers will have a "conscience wide as hell," Henry says, and he characterizes "impious war" dressed in fire like Satan as if he himself has nothing to do with the war. The king emphasizes the rape of the young daughters of the citizens of Harfleur:

> What is't to me, when you yourselves are cause,
> If your pure maidens fall into the hand
> Of hot and forcing violation?
> What rein can hold licentious wickedness
> When down the hill he holds his fierce career? (III.iii.19–23)

Despite J. H. Walter's claim that contemporary writers often wrote about the sack of a city and its horrors and that Henry's procedure accords with contemporary military law, the king continues his penchant for making others responsible for his actions and his tendency to relish the thought of sexual violation, although it might be argued that he is merely using a rhetoric of terror to achieve a gentle peace.[29] As for the image of the uncontrollable horse of licentiousness, Henry can control his men if he chooses, for he rigorously keeps discipline when he sanctions the hanging of Nym and Bardolph and when he orders that no Englishman brag about the victory over the French (see IV.viii.115–18). It also seems odd that a king who claims the help of God would take up the role of Satan (see II.ii.184f.). Henry continues to associate himself with purity and heavenly grace, as if these violent images have pushed up from his unconscious mind or as if he has hidden his true intent from others. Shakespeare qualifies Henry's heroism.

As in *Hamlet*, in *1 Henry IV* Shakespeare places a play at the center of his play. The Boar's Head tavern acts as a theatre, as a dramatic school that Hal turns into training ground for his political acting. Early in the play, Hal uses the images of sun and cloud as his father had with Richard, to say that he will imitate the sun and hide behind the "base contagious clouds" of the taverners until he burns their vapor away and appears in his glory. He will reform when others least suspect it because of his dissembling in the tavern (I.ii.190f.). Hal consciously has been disguising his intentions, and he uses his tavern companions to learn vice to avoid it. Acting and action, theatre and world are closely related. It is appropriate that the tavern is the locale for one of Hal's most important acts, in the sense of action and disguise, his preparation for the rejection of Falstaff. Sir John suggests that he play Hal's father, so that the prince can explain to the king his wayward life. The theatre will be a school for life, but Hal and Falstaff do not agree on what kind of rules their theatre will use:

> *Falstaff.* This chair shall be my state, this dagger my sceptre,
> and this cushion my crown.

> *Prince.* Thy state is taken for a joint-stool, thy golden sceptre
> for a leaden dagger, and thy precious rich crown for
> a pitiful bald crown. (II.iv.373–77)

Falstaff makes the theatre more mimetic of the outside world, but Hal refuses these assumptions and names nature as he sees it. It is as if Sir John has read Aristotle and Hal, Brecht. According to Hal, Falstaff is a pitiful man playing as a player-king. The prince does and does not play a role. Soon, Hal grows tired of Falstaff's use of the role, no matter how comic he is, to promote his own interests. So they switch roles. Shakespeare gives us another point of view. This apparent improvisation is calculating and each character plays the same role differently as actors do in any theatre. Falstaff unabashedly turns the role of the prince, when speaking to the prince, to his own purposes. He would have Hal banish all their friends, their partners in riot, but him. In a consciously old-fashioned style, which Falstaff says he is borrowing from an old tragedy—*King Cambyses* (ca. 1561), Sir John ends his humorous, emotional bombast with the rhetorical "Banish plump Jack, and banish all the world!" There is a knock, an interruption, and Hal answers amid these distractions with cold but necessary words: "I do, I will" (II.iv.455–57, cf. 369). And the prince will do in the political world what he has rehearsed in the provisional theatre. He will banish plump Jack, and for some critics, he thereby banishes the world. For the public good, Hal must reject Falstaff but by doing so he suppresses his private life. He cannot win. Both Hal and Falstaff try to use acting in the theatre to affect action in the world.

The Chorus to *Henry V* especially explores the relation between theatre and world, drama and history. I will confine myself to a few comments about the Prologue. Through choric agency, the audience becomes involved with interpreting experience and history. Involving a muse, the Prologue conveys the theme of poetic aspiration to the audience. His muse of fire and his invention, his imagination and his discovery of topics, inhabit the "brightest heaven." The problem is whether historical poetry can represent historical events. The Prologue wishes for a kingdom in exchange for a theatre but implies that princes are actors and monarchs look at the world as a play divided into magnificent roles. In some ways, the stage is a kingdom and the kingdom, a stage. In addition, the Prologue contrasts the "unworthy scaffold," a small number of planks, with the "So great an object," a "cockpit" with the "vasty fields of France," wonders whether this "wooden O" can contain the military gear from the actual battle of Agincourt and asks whether the theatre can hold the world. Shakespeare is calling attention to the theatre but also to the machinery of the history play itself, a self-referentiality that is characteristic of the problem play.

The past also needs historical writings. By punning on "O," "cipher," and "accompt," the Prologue is pointing out that the theatre is both nothing and something, for the theatre is shaped like a zero, but a zero added to the right of a number adds value. The Prologue addresses the audience as nothings: "O pardon." The choric medication places the past in the realm of dramatic history. The fall back into history, into the already performed world of *Henry VI* on the English stage, is something the Epilogue returns to and takes with him the audience. The theatre of history returns to a representation of the world.

Past and Present

Aristotle and Philip Sidney may have differed on which ranked first, philosophy or poetry, but they both agreed that history came third of the three important elements of humane letters.[30] History was particular and not universal, for Aristotle and Sidney, and it was only a matter of which was the more universal, philosophy or poetry. Perhaps as a response to these earlier charges about the particularity, and therefore deficiency, of history, it is desirable to understand the underlying assumptions of history, historiography, and the philosophy of history developed as disciplines. But even before these developments in the discipline of history, which gathered strength over the past two centuries, three aspects of the writing of history had already developed traditions: biblical typology, rhetorical history, and the chronicles.

Biblical typology—in which, for instance, Adam is a type for Christ, Christ is an antitype for Adam, and more generally the Old Testament foreshadows the New Testament, which in turn fulfills it—flourished especially in the Middle Ages and has been revived in literary studies by Northrop Frye.[31] This tradition insists on a pattern in history and a teleology or end with meaning to it. Humankind fell but will be redeemed through Christ to gain a paradise happier still than the one lost. Rhetorical history reminds us that history was a branch of literature (at least that is the standard view in literary history). History and story are related, something the Elizabethans recognized in their interchangeable use of the word *history*. The narrative of history was, from Herodotus onwards, a narrative about what happened, but when what happened was unavailable to the historian what could have happened, the probable or possible world of literature, entered into the narrative. Thucydides, for example, was not there to record Pericles' oration and had to reconstruct it. Truth is an end in history, but there are also fictions of history. It is not probable that the particulars of history give an authentic and unmediated experience of history.

History is necessary for understanding culture and the world we inhabit. To confuse the experience of time in time for historical knowledge is errant. The very skepticism that new historicism uses in regard to history must also be used in regard to new historicism. Just as grand historical designs alone are not sufficient, so too are historical instances inadequate. We may experience time in examples, but we can only know the significance or the shape of those examples through a pattern derived from some process of generalization. Examples need schemes and schemes examples: they test each other. We cannot talk about history without generalization. Even if each of us says that his or her position is relative in a pluralistic field, we write from somewhere and are convinced that this somewhere matters. How many of us record random examples, or instances without implicit and explicit interpretation? History comes down to a knowledge of historical events and myths enacted and made by people: it is a matter of evidence and shaping that evidence. The evidence tests the shape, which tries to make sense of the evidence, in a kind of dialectic. Even more apparently than in literature, which has some kinds of "complete" texts, the study of history runs up against a receding and recalcitrant past, given to personification and other displacements.

Nonetheless, the historical record rears itself, even in a state of obscurity and decay, so that, with Aristotle, I still think the pamphlet is not a play and that history is, as much as it is possible, about what happened. What I am proposing, which is not novel, as one possible supplement or corrective in our ongoing search for history, is a history of genres, in both history and literature, so that we can understand each discipline better and their relation even more. We have to try to know where "here" is to know where "there" is: the same is true of "now" and "then."

Shakespeare: Reception, Representation, and Myth

In literary history there have been other ways of looking at Shakespeare, and there will be others to come.[32] All too briefly, I want to sketch out some of the methods used in the study of Shakespeare that will persist and transform themselves. Using earlier work and the historical record, it would be beneficial to compare anew the historical and the literary figure, Shakespeare. We have lost most of Shakespeare's other dimensions as a person, how his family and friends knew him. This is the biographical Shakespeare. What is more difficult is that the historical record began to translate Shakespeare very early. Even during his life Shakespeare was being translated into a figure with many cultural faces. We continue to translate him for various institutional purposes. Another term for translation might be appropriation, although they overlap and are not synonymous.

When Richard Quiney wrote to William Shakespeare on October 25, 1598, addressed him as his "Lovinge Contreyman" and asked him for the large sum of thirty pounds, he was addressing his neighbor and a businessman. In this only extant letter to Shakespeare, which was found among Quiney's own papers and so may never have been sent to Shakespeare, there is no reference to Shakespeare, the playwright. Quiney, who died in 1602, did not live to see his son, Thomas, marry Shakespeare's daughter, Judith, a few months before Shakespeare's death in 1616. The first child of that marriage, Shakespeare Quiney, died in childbirth in 1618. Shakespeare of Stratford, the entrepreneur that Edward Bond scrutinized in *Bingo*, is seldom the figure that literature and drama, criticism and theory explore. Shakespeare's contemporaries, in London at least, thought of him as a great poet and playwright.[33] With John Aubrey we find the first sketch Shakespeare's biography, the life of a man whom Heminges, Condell, and Jonson refer with such affection. In our time Samuel Schoenbaum has synthesized earlier biographies.

Another position, Shakespeare, the genius, is not a Romantic myth but an early modern enterprise. About the same time Richard Quiney was writing Shakespeare, others alluded to Shakespeare, the playwright. Between Christmas 1598 and 1601, the students of St. John's College, Cambridge, performed *The Return from Parnassus, Parts 1 and 2*. In the first part we hear Gullio praise Shakespeare in what were soon to become familiar terms, "O sweet Mr. Shakespeare, and to honoure him will lay his Venus, and Adonis vnder my pillowe, as we read of one (I do not remember his name) but I am sure he was a kinge, slept wth Homer vnder his beds heade" (IV.i.1198–1204). Two other characters, Will Kemp and Richard Burbage, the leading tragic and comic actors in Shakespeare's company, respectively, agree that Shakespeare "puts them all downe," that is the university wits and Ben Jonson, who smell too much of a received classicism (IV.iii.1766–74). Here is Shakespeare, the Bard, displacing Homer, the Bard of the classical past, and his Renaissance rivals. Whatever the nationalistic or other motives the students had, they were not in the business of canonizing, of creating the curriculum, and were not enshrining the classical and university training one might expect. In the tenth book of the *Republic* Socrates complains that Homer has dominated Greek education, and it was a while before Shakespeare did the same with English education. Bardology was an early response to Shakespeare that suffered through the vicissitudes of a neoclassical patronizing of Shakespeare's rude genius and, in the nineteenth century, became a cult after the Romantics put aside such qualms. This was the cult against which Bernard Shaw reacted. The positions are often mixed. For instance, in *Return from Parnassus*, Ingenioso invokes Shakespeare's name, and Iudico praises his verse on Adonis and Lucrece but wishes that Shakespeare could concentrate his gift on more serious subjects (I.ii.300–304). This comment begins the moral or serious position of which Samuel Johnson and F. R. Leavis are later representatives.

In *Pallis Tamia, Wits Treasury* (1598), Francis Meres is attempting to elevate English literature to the status of Greek, Latin, and Italian literature. This is the project of literary nationalism, for although Meres is evenhanded in his comparison of these literatures and the various authors who comprise them, he includes Shakespeare and highlights his accomplishments in the comparisons: "so the sweete wittie soule of *Ouid* hues in mellifluous & hony-tongu'd *Shakespeare*, witness his *Venus and Adonis*, his *Lucrece*, his sugred Sonnets among his priuate friends, &c." This position is a form of classicism used to validate the national literature in the vulgar tongue. Unlike Bardology, it admits the metempsychosis between classical past and vernacular present without elevating one over the other. In Meres there is not Gullio's forgetfulness about the transmitters of classical culture. Shakespeare is already becoming the national poet. This status is now undisputed: Terence Hawkes, for instance, explores the ideology behind the Englishness of Shakespeare.

Another related position is Shakespeare, the poet of Nature, which, in extant documents at least, begins with lines in Francis Beaumont's "To Mr. B.J." (ca. 1615), a poem addressed to Ben Jonson, in which he praises the clarity of Shakespeare's best lines (not all the lines—he is writing to Jonson), which are examples of how scholarship and learning can be an encumbrance. This view later recurs in Milton's early poem "What neede my Shakespeare," (1630) and Leonard Digges' "Poets are borne not made" (ca. 1640). Shakespeare is now the child of genius or nature. Digges raises Shakespeare above Jonson, so that critics and poets sometimes combine various positions in situating themselves in relation to Shakespeare.

Scaling down or demythologizing Shakespeare is another option. This view shows a skepticism about Shakespeare's genius because he does not always display learning or classical decorum. Robert Greene's allusion to Shakespeare in *Greenes,*

Groats-worth of witte, bought with a Million of Repentance (1592), which are the first comments we have on Shakespeare the professional, involves the envy of an accomplished and university-educated author for a more accomplished and less schooled author. The subposition might be called envying Shakespeare. Another subposition, "unclassical" and artless Shakespeare, is exemplified in Ben Jonson's comments in *Timber: or Discoveries; Made Upon Men and Matter* (1640), which supplement his eulogy or almost bardolatrous and nationalistic comments in "To the memory of my beloued, The Author, Mr. William Shakespeare: And what he left vs" (1623). Jonson criticizes Shakespeare's occasional lack of decorous diction, just as Voltaire and T. S. Eliot censure Shakespeare on other issues of decorum. Even these critics are ambivalent about Shakespeare and, perhaps because of their Englishness or admiration for things English, are less dismissive than Tolstoy is. Most of the critics and theorists of all ages who admire Shakespeare are still ambivalent about him.[34] They depend on him, as I do, but they sometimes feel uncomfortable and rebellious in their roles as attendant lords and ladies, sons and daughters. The anxiety of influence or the fear of obscurity is sometimes too much to bear for some members of what has come to be known as the Shakespeare industry. Classics, like Shakespeare's plays, are those works that subsequent generations cannot forget no matter how much they would like to bury or neglect them often because the burying and neglect make them look even larger and better.

Another position is Shakespeare as the object of close and extensive critical attention. This is a hybrid position, perhaps a superposition, if not a superimposition, that includes the positions and subpositions that I have just described. In *Sociable Letters* (1664) Margaret Cavendish is the first to give an extended general prose assessment of Shakespeare (see Letter 23). Before Cavendish, long dedicatory poems and eulogies and brief and almost incidental prose assessments of Shakespeare prevail. Cavendish speaks about the influence of Shakespeare on later writers and leaves "*Shakespeare's* Works to their own Defence, and his detractors to their Envy." She discusses Shakespeare, the dramatist (man of the theatre), another position, before Dryden does. Owing to his prestige, Dryden begins the commentary on Shakespeare in earnest. For the next three centuries or more, the editors take up the task of commentary to great effect.

Dryden, like Samuel Johnson, Bernard Shaw, and other great writer-critics, praises Shakespeare in one sentence only to qualify his accolade in the next only to qualify his qualification in the next. This is another position—the critic of Shakespeare as writer. This position involves a conflict of interest because the writer competes with Shakespeare for the reader's attention in English literature, literature in English, or world literature. A variation on this position is Tolstoy, who competes with Shakespeare on the international literary market, and whose national interests and nationalism may conflict with those of England or English-speaking countries, like the United States, that have made Shakespeare their cultural and economic business. Dryden praises Shakespeare as a poet of nature but one given too much to puns (an offence against classical decorum). He also undertakes to correct Shakespeare's plays and "translates" or adapts them for the stage. Nahum Tate, Shaw, Brecht, and others from 1660 onwards adapt Shakespeare, Milton, Dryden, Schiller, Wordsworth, Keats, Shelley, Tennyson, Shaw, Yeats, Eliot, and others all show his influence. It was understandable that Harold Bloom once exempted Shakespeare from the anxiety of influence, but Shakespeare could not escape the influences of the Bible, Ovid, and Christopher Marlowe. However, Shakespeare came early in the making of English literature and has influenced more English-speaking writers than they have him. This is another matter of history.

It is clear that most critics and writer-critics express many of the positions I have outlined in their baldest terms. Although I recognize the overlap, I also think that to call attention to some distinctions or strands should be helpful to work on a critical history of Shakespeare's reception in relation to a history of the genres in which he worked. Literature and criticism have their own histories that are part of a larger social, economic and political history but that are also distinct.

Positions are reiterated over time and in increasing detail. The "school" of character begins in earnest with Maurice Morgann's *An Essay on the Dramatic Character of Sir John Falstaff* (1777) and culminates, for the moment at least, in A. C. Bradley's *Shakespearean Tragedy* (2nd. ed. 1905). The German Romantic or ironic school, which influences "New Critics" like William Empson and Cleanth Brooks and a deconstructionist like Paul de Man, includes detailed work by Friedrich Schlegel, A. W. Schlegel, Adam Müller, Ludwig Tieck, Coleridge, Connop Thirlwall, and Kierkegaard. Here the paradoxically objective and subjective Shakespeare hovers katascopically above his creation in which he participates so fully.[35] Shakespeare as *the* artist begins as a product of England but, like the Industrial Revolution itself, is refined in Germany and sent to the United States for mass production. The Shakespeare myth as we know it in the academy is partly a German myth. The German Romantics and the German philologists made Shakespeare's text an object of close academic study. The philologists professionalized the editorial work of earlier English editors like Heminges and Condell, Rowe, Pope, Theobald, Johnson, and Steevens. Along with close editorial scholarship, increasingly, hermeneutics, the close reading that scholarly interpretation requires, changed the nature of Shakespeare as literature, drama, and cultural object.

One of the most powerful contributions that Shakespeare and his contemporaries made was in the history play. Dramatic history, rather than being some kind of work that slights the historical record, embodies history again and is one way to make it lively to people. The present represents the past in a dramatic fashion that lacks what some forms of history offer, but has something they lack. The very power of historical fictions on the stage and in poems, novels, and film can be of concern if they are fantastical and do not follow events, but the legendary and the historical record seem to persist in popular history as in a romance. The very popularity is threatening to historians who have worked in the name of accuracy, and the hybrid historical poet can sway between poetic invention and historical inquiry. Character can become as much a question as structure or style in the writing of history and historical fiction. The power of language that Shakespeare and his greatest contemporaries who wrote for the stage had made for a poetics and rhetoric of seduction where legend and myth and the poet's prerogative can come into friction with the historians. Even among historians there has sometimes been a conflict between popular and scholarly history, especially with the increased professionalization of history in the past century. So the poles of history and drama mean that a question of emphasis comes into play even within drama or history. In the next chapter, my interest continues in dramatic history, which is between poetics and historiography.

CHAPTER 7

Dramatic History

The drama of history can be found in dramatic history. Chronicle and history plays are important representations of the past even if they are more fictional than some might like in the pursuit of truth. What happened in the past has much to do with the question of who is interpreting the past and how. Historical representation and the interpretation of that representation are crucial and contested in the claim of history. Historical verisimilitude is as difficult as any verisimilitude. Time and space, the viewer and the viewed recede. The attempt at truth may well be asymptotic and is part of the drama of meaning. Mutability is part of the search for the immutable. Change is part of the desire to find something closer to the truth. All history seems revisionary. The dramatic history during the reigns of the Tudors and the Stuarts represents a past whose presence was immediate on the stage. Some of those plays we have in the traces of texts. Shakespeare is best known for the history play, but others produced chronicle and history plays that provide a drama of history.[1]

When first examining the representation of history in Shakespeare's Second Tetralogy (*Richard II*, *1* and *2 Henry IV*, and *Henry V*), I found the work on Shakespeare's First Tetralogy (*1*, *2*, and *3 Henry VI* and *Richard III*) to be helpful. However important Shakespeare's contribution to the history play, my emphasis in this chapter is on what others did to create dramatic history in England.[2] Any discussion of Shakespeare will occur in the context of his predecessors and contemporaries. As the relation of morality elements to Elizabethan drama has long been established, I shall mention in passing the morality aspects of humanist drama in regard to history plays but will take my discussion in other directions. In John Skelton's *Magnyficence* morality figures participate in an allegory of the secular struggle of politics, and later history plays begin to shed moral abstractions in their exploration of statecraft. In 1539, John Bale's *Kynge Johan* (ca. 1530–36) was performed at Thomas Cromwell's house during the Christmas holidays. Bale's case is not, however, so simple, because of revisions and as the play finds fault with many different parties, in England and Rome—past and present.[3] Bale's revision was played before Elizabeth at Ipswich in 1561 and drew on English chronicles.[4] The king is a protagonist of the Reformation and appears in a transitional play in which morality characters coexist with historical figures and represents a rewriting of history that attempts to affect ruler and ministers over three decades.

Norton's and Sackville's *Gorboduc* was written in the same year that *King Johan* was revised and played before the queen, and it was performed by the Inner Temple for Elizabeth on January 18, 1562, at Whitehall Palace. This play was the work of two counselors who were advising Elizabeth and differed from *Respublica*, which was performed by boys at court during the Christmas holidays of 1553 and paid heed more to the Catholicism of the newly crowned Queen Mary.[5] Both Norton and Sackville spell out the moral lessons of their tragic and historical play. Norton asserts that if the queen cannot settle on a successor, then parliament must decide on one to maintain order (V.ii).[6] As the argument on the back of the title page says, King Gorboduc's division of the kingdom in favor of his sons, Ferrex and Porrex, leads to dissension, murder, rebellion, uncertain succession, civil war, destruction of the royal family, and desolation of the kingdom. This plot is like *King Lear* and resembles the anxiety over civil war and succession that critics in the anxious times of just before and during Second World War especially emphasized in the Tudor myth.[7] I do not mean to suggest that the years 1561, 1605, and from 1935 to 1945 were the only times of anxiety about political stability and succession. If anything, this worry over instability and strife, divisiveness and violence and their actual occurrence happens as much in history as the contemplation and the unfolding of unity and peace. Although there may be critical times of extraordinary political and social strife, it appears that people are caught between war and peace and live in that tension. The unknown of the future seems to have been focused in religious and political tension surrounding the succession from the death of Henry VIII in 1547 until about 1570 and then in the late 1590s and early 1600s when Elizabeth was old or dying and when James had recently ascended the English throne. The execution of Mary, Queen of Scots, in 1587 and the threat of war with Spain and the battles with the Armada, particularly in 1588, show that political anxiety never left Elizabethan England. At the end of *Henry VIII*, Cranmer's retrospective prophecy, in the comfort of the future looking back, about the peace and plenty of the reign of Elizabeth is, from one vantage, a stirring speech in thanks for the relative quiet and prosperity under her rule.[8] Elizabeth's reaction to the playing of *Richard II* during the Essex Rebellion of 1601, while lenient, showed concern over order, so that the period was not as peaceful as experiencing it in retrospect, which is not surprising. The future confronts the present with the anxiety of the unknown that lies beyond individual human control.

Gorboduc is not full of moral abstractions but represents historical characters from the chronicles, perhaps directly from Grafton's *Chronicle* (1556) and indirectly from Geoffrey of Monmouth's *Historia Regnum Britanniae*.[9] These characters take their form from brief, almost schematic, plot sketches in the chronicles. Nonetheless, *Gorbuduc* contains the overt moralizing of the morality plays. Even the symbolism of the dumb shows before each act is explained in the headnotes as if to please the censor with clear distaste for rebellion and disorder. The explanations are not ambiguous and evasive as if confidently advising the young queen rather than circumventing her power to censure and censor. In the order and signification of the first dumb show, we may observe the narrowing of choice and the dictation of meaning:

> First the musicke of violenze began to play,
> during which came in upon the stage sixe wilde men
> clothed in leaves; all of whom the first bare in his
> necke a fagot of smalle stickes, which they all, both
> severally and together, assayed with all their strengthes
> to breake; but it could not be broken by them. At
> the length, one of them plucked out one of the stickes
> and brake it; and the rest plucking out all the other
> stickes one after an-other did easely breake them, the
> same being severed, which, being conioyned, they had
> before attempted in vaine. After they had this done,
> they departed the stage, and the musicke ceased.
> Hereby was signified that a state knit in unite doth
> continue strong against all force, but being divided
> is easely destroyed; as befell upon Duke Gorboduc
> dividing his his land to his two sonnes, which he
> before held in monarchie, and upon the discention
> of the brethern to whom it was divided.

This narrowing of interpretative response is the same kind of control propaganda, and more recently advertising, has tried to gain over its audience rather than the opening of possible response that poetry engenders. No writing is, however, entirely poetry or propaganda. Like the choruses in Shakespeare's *Henry V*, the notes, and the dumb shows they describe and explicate, may have an ironic relation to the action of the play. The conflict between or within the authors about the best way to govern a state and to ensure proper succession has long attracted critics. As didactic as the play tries to be, the entrance of history into the morality structure complicates the writing and response. The play may be grounded in medieval political theology, to use Ernst Kantorowicz's phrase, but its sources are chronicles that are supposed to report if not glorify the British kings from which the Tudors, including Elizabeth, were reputedly to have descended.[10] History charges the dramatic situation. Even if we take *Gorboduc* to be legendary or only faintly historical, many of the Elizabethans may not have. The Tudor claims of illustrious British ancestry would be enough to invest the analogy with larger meanings. The authors, Norton and Sackville, had a social station and political ambitions well beyond Shakespeare's, and they represented the ancient and powerful profession of the law rather than the upstart crowing of the players.[11]

The fifth and final act has no Chorus, which is displaced by two good "counsellors," Arostus and Eubulus. This displacement is no act of rebellion but invests these advisors with the structural and thematic momentum of the four previous

Choruses. Arostus and Eubulus end the play. In the penultimate speech, Arostus summarizes the mess everyone is in since the murder of the royal family, including Gorbuduc (V.115f.). He speaks about the waste of civil war, the uncertainty of succession, and prophesies that "climbing pride" will divide the kingdom into factions greedy for power and asks the lords to think of their ancient honor, present wealth and future of their children—past, present, and future—and pity the "torne estate." He focuses the image of bleeding England in slitting their mothers' throats. Rather than taking the crown by pretended right, they should call a parliament to decide the succession. Parliament, according to Arostus, will represent right, which will endure as wrong will not, and the people will grant the crown to someone born in Britain. The reference to "his or hers" is, perhaps, an acknowledgment, before Elizabeth, of the equal right of men and women to rule. As in *King Johan*, foreign rule is to be avoided. Eubulus laments "the end of Brutus royall line!" (V.180f.). He reiterates the ruin of the kingdom, the destruction of the royal family, the vacant throne, the image of "the proud and gredie mind" and "rising minds" that aspire to rule Britain, the likelihood of violence, the long civil war until someone can make a rightful claim to the throne. His prophecy to the lords is like Arostus'. His imagery is especially important because it is like Henry V's before Harfleur and so lends some credence to J. H. Walter's claim that violent language was used to deter actual violence:[12]

> The wives shall suffer rape, the maides defloured;
> And children fatherlesse shall weep and wail;
> With fire and sworde thy native folke shall perishe;
> . . . .
> Women shall and maides the cruell souldiers sword
> Shall perse to death; and sillie children, loe,
> That playing in the streetes and fieldes are found,
> By violent hand shall close their latter day!
> Whom shall the fierce and bloudy souldier
> Reserve to life? (V.209–11, 215–20)

The repetition may be stern and for emphasis, but, as in *Henry V*, it seems to show a fascination, if not delight in, the language of violence and possibly in the act of violence itself, though language and action are not so naively or directly connected. The relish or threat of the victimization of woman and children is particularly disturbing. Eubulus' prophecy also prefigures John of Gaunt's:

> And thou, O Brittaine, whilome in renowne,
> Whilome in wealth and fame, shalt thus be torne,
> Dismembred thus, and thus be rent in twaine,
> Thus wasted and defaced, spoyled and destroyed!
> These be the fruites your civil warres will bring. (V.229–32)

While the rhetoric here depends on amplification through synonyms, Gaunt's relies on apposition.[13] This prophecy of the future in the past is also one that in the present speaks to Elizabeth about the future of England, which is now our past. Point of view is as essential to history as it is to literature and drama.

Eubulus repeats the lessons of the Chorus and of Arostus. Violent civil war occurs, Eubulus asserts, when kings do not listen to "grave advise," when flattery prevails. He also describes the plague or curse that the gods bring in revenge when murder is the way to create new heirs and when rebels judge their own princes. There is no surprise. Parliament is the hope to settle on a rightful heir, which will bring obedience to the people. Apostrophizing the "happie man whom speedie death / Deprives of life," possibly Gorboduc himself, Eubulus summons the outside absence in, attempts to revive the death of the past in terms of his own present misery and to project the future through the desire and deflection of prophecy. (V: 272–73). And so he ends the play with an oft-repeated refrain: "Yet must God in fine restore / This noble crowne unto the lawfull heire; / For right will alwayes live and rise at length, / But wrong can never take deepe roote, to last" (V: 276–79). To the end, the authors of *Gorboduc* attempt to demonstrate their theme, that good counsel can save the Commonwealth from civil war and that history is a moral pattern that endures through examples. History is philosophy with examples. Poetic justice makes history tragic in the short term but comic at last. This play can teach us, and teaching is its principal aim, because it cherishes its plain and straight talk, its counsel, whereas Shakespeare's work in the Second Tetralogy is more polyphonous. *Gorboduc* is important for dramatic history.

Cambises (1569) and *Richardus Tertius* (1579–80) also bear on the questions of kingship. Shakespeare's *1 Henry IV* includes a parody of the rant in Thomas Preston's *Cambises*, a play that represents the divine punishment of a tyrant. Cambises rivals Herod in tyranny and madness but is less comic than the rendition of Herod in the Corpus Christi plays. Given the power of Elizabeth I and her government, Preston attempted to remove his play from the immediate historical context. Ambidexter, who is like the Vice of a morality play, is the comic and bawdy character. Preston's play is not so unmitigated in its high seriousness as *Gorboduc* is and in this regard resembles Shakespeare's *Henry IV* plays and, to some extent, *Henry V*. The title, which says the play is a lamentable tragedy mixed full of pleasant mirth, sounds as if the rude mechanicals in *A Midsummer Night's Dream* had devised it. Nevertheless, this mixed genre preoccupies Shakespeare in the Second Tetralogy. Although I am concentrating on English (and a little on British) history, it is also true that Egypt, Persia, Greece, and Rome in history plays always relate to the presence of Elizabethan England. Their distance in time and space makes them less sensitive even though biblical examples continued to be potent during the English Renaissance. History plays presented as well as represented. Although in Shakespeare's First Folio (1623) Heminge and Condell came to classify histories as plays about the English past, cosmographies, plays, and histories in Renaissance England often included images, maps, and representations of other states.

Like *Gorboduc*, *Cambises* is much concerned with good advice for princes, so much so that the first line of the Prologue broaches this subject. Preston's Prologue appeals to Agathon, Cicero, and Seneca for wise counsel for good governance. The Prologue appeals to the fall of Icarus and describes the transformation of Cambises into a tyrant (ll. 18–24).[14] Besides falling through pride, stubbornness and aspiration, Icarus ignored the counsel of Daedalus. To tell the moral before the representation, the Prologue gives a biblical tone to this classical story—measure for measure: "But, what mesure the king did meat, the same did Iove commence, / To bring to end with shame his race" (ll. 32–33). The Prologue's last words emphasize the brevity of Cambises' reign, which Preston has abbreviated by over two-thirds, and promises that the players will "make the matter plaine" and so win the patience of the audience (ll. 33–36). The matter is not entirely plain because, as Joseph Quincy Adams notes, the running title of the play is *A Comedie of King Cambises*, which does not take into account the tragic aspect of the title page, but then Elizabethan printers were not always precise. The end of the play tries to make the moral as unambiguous as possible. Cambises dies faster than Herodotus reports, and the First Lord declares, "A iust reward for his deeds the God above hath wrought, / For certainly the life he led was to be counted nought" (ll. 1193–94). The Second Lord says that Cambises should still receive a princely burial, and the Third Lord enjoins them to take up the body, and they all bear Cambises off the stage. With the Epilogue, Preston makes his point once more, hoping that the "tragicall history of this wicked king" has not offended anyone in the audience. The Epilogue also thanks the audience for its patience and ends with a prayer for Queen Elizabeth, which happens in the Epilogue in Shakespeare's *2 Henry IV*, except Preston's play ends with the prayer and Shakespeare's, at least in the state we have it, with Falstaff, and with the Epilogue probably kneeling when he bids the audience good night. The Epilogue to *Cambises* also prays for the counselors to Elizabeth to tell the truth, be just, defend the queen, maintain the word of God, and correct those who would abuse Elizabeth and her laws. In a final prayer, which sounds like part of "God Save the Queen," the Epilogue says, "Beseeching God over us she may raigne long, / To be guided by truth and defended from wrong" (ll. 21–22).

Thomas Legge's *Richardus Tertius* offered a transformation of Senecan tragedy on the subject of the fall of an English tyrant, Richard III. It is a three-part Latin play produced at St. John's College Cambridge in 1579–80.[15] Whereas Legge combined the Senecan tragedy and native chronicle tradition, Shakespeare paid close attention to the chronicles, like Hall and Holinshed, which incorporated Thomas More's portrait of Richard III as a tyrant in *The History of Richard III*. He also points the usual moral of the destruction of the tyrant. Shakespeare may have known the work, for it is mentioned in John Harrington's *Apologie for Poetrie* (1592), Thomas Nashe's *Have With You to Saffron Walden* (1596) and Francis Meres' *Pallis Tamia* (1598), all of which occur about the time of the writing of the First and Second Tetralogies.[16] The Senecan elements occurred in *Gorboduc* and *Richardus Tertius* and in English history plays like Shakespeare's *Richard III*. Another Senecan revenge tragedy that was influential, Thomas Kyd's *The*

Spanish Tragedy (ca. 1584–89), represents revenge that is private but has public effects because it involves the nobility, something that may have affected Shakespeare's histories and, probably more so, *Titus Andronicus* (ca. 1594), *Romeo and Juliet* (ca. 1595), and *Hamlet* (ca. 1600–1601). The Ghost of Andrea, a Spanish courtier, speaks about the separation from his beloved through his death in battle against Portugal. His speech is full of references to the classical afterlife, for as a lover and a warrior, Andea's fate in death was not certain. Would he walk among the "fields of love," as AEacus suggests, or among "the martial fields, / Where wounded Hector lives in lasting pain, / And Achilles' Myrmidons do scour the plain," as Rhadamanth says (Book I, Induction, 40–49)?[17] The play represents Andrea's revenge through Proserpine, and although the action concerns the nobility of Spain and Portugal, it concentrates on the code of military honor and the private lives of these public people rather than the close relation between private and public and the grave consequences to the countries involved.

Too often Shakespeare's ability blinds critics to the contributions of his predecessors.[18] These predecessors (and contemporaries as they wrote while he was young) gave him his first lessons, among others, in mixing genres, creating linked plays about the past, and using chronicles. Admittedly, sometimes these plays teach him what not to do, but to pretend that they had no affect on Shakespeare is to ignore context. Someone of Shakespeare's magnificent talent almost burns up history. Almost.

In examining some of the history or chronicle plays in the ten years prior to *Richard II*, and some of which seem to have overlapped in the time of writing with Shakespeare's First Tetralogy, I will concentrate on the relation between irony and history in five plays because irony is an important element in Shakespeare's history plays.[19] Oppositions of ideas recur in these plays, from *The Famous Victories of Henry the Fifth* (ca. 1586–88) to *Woodstock* (ca. 1591–94), for instance, heroism and cowardice, Englishness and Frenchness (or foreignness), ignorance and prophecy as well as kingship and rebellion. These oppositions do not differ significantly from those in the Second Tetralogy, but Shakespeare explores their interplay with greater intensity and duration. Still, these plays by contemporaries are groundbreaking and deserve close attention.

Famous Victories is at once both comic and serious, a play that shows both the jesting and chaotic aspects of peace and the heroic and cowardly sides to war. The anonymous playwright relates the main plot and the alternate plots, providing the beginnings of a multiple vision. Until the prince spurns the company of Ned, Tom, and Oldcastle, they are part of the alternate plot just as Derick and John Cobbler are throughout the play. The affairs of the prince and the king in England during the first half and the victories of Henry V in France during the second comprise the main plot. If the comic scenes are serious, they are not solemn. Their chaos is inversely related to the "order" of a kingdom ruled by a usurper, Henry IV, in the first part and to the cowardice of the common English characters in the second part, which complicates the heroic victory of Henry V. The apparently solemn scenes also contain humor.

Famous Victories displays some aspects of irony, though not the extensive multiplicity that occurs in the Second Tetralogy.

From the beginning of the play, the audience would know that the reprobate prince later becomes a victorious king. He begins with "Zounds" and ends the play with "God willing," moving from, "wounds" to will, gold to God, from vicious prince to brave king (i.16; xx.73).[20] Exeter and Oxford both know that the prince's villainy contains courage that will grow as he assumes responsibility, and they tell Henry IV so (scenes iii and viii). Knowing the story of Henry V or sensing these foreshadowings, the audience would have experienced Sophoclean (or dramatic) irony. Besides using irony of structure, the playwright enlists irony of words. The cognates of "brave" and "villain" run throughout the play, changing their meaning slightly as their context alters, complicating with shifting appearances and realities the nature of the history. When speaking to his friends, the prince asks, "Bravely spoken lads! But tell me, sirs, think you not that it was a villainous part of me to rob my father's receivers?" (i.8–10). The syntax is witty. Only "part of" the prince is villainous, implying that a part of him is not. He is also playing a part. As often is the case, the ironies of words and theatre play supporting roles. Ned replies that the robbery of four hundred pounds was "a trick of youth," which foreshadows Derick's cowardly tricks in scene 19, the ironic inversion of Henry V's victory, which is actually "brave" and not the parody of bravery as in the theft. Irony of structure, particularly in the reversal of the prince's fortunes when he becomes king, works together with Sophoclean, verbal, and theatrical ironies.

Transformation or sudden conversion is an essential part of this history play. In Scene iv, the prince begins by thinking that justice is hanging pick-purses, horse-stealers, and other villains while commending highwaymen. He says he would make Ned Lord Chief Justice so this kind of law could exist, but after his reform in the same scene, the prince tells his father, "and those vile and reprobate companions—I abandon and utterly abolish their company for ever!" (vi.20–37, 141–43). Later, not knowing that the prince has in his heart rejected their company, Ned claims that he shall be Lord Chief Justice and scorns the Thief as a "villain" who "stinks" and threatens to inform the king about him (ix.11–25).

Besides the repetition of key words, in which "brave" is used as praise and as sarcastic indictment, the repetition of the motif of Cockaigne, the promise of inverted or unjust justice, then the withdrawal of that promise, the return to everyday politics, gathers its own ironic momentum.[21] In the opening scene the prince says to Ned, Tom, and Oldcastle, "I tell you, sirs, if the King my father were dead, we would be all kings" (1.99–100). In scene six, just before conversion, the prince promises the same companions: "But I tell you, sirs, when I am King we will have no such things [punishments and hangings]. But, my lads, if the old King, my father, were dead, we would be all kings" (vi.14–17). The prince then reforms his villainous part and vindicates Oxford and Exeter. In scene nine, the rejection scene, Oldcastle and the others think that they will be kings, but the audience knows better because not only does the legend tell us of the prince's reform and rejection of his companions, but also the sixth and seventh scenes show his transformation. Here is the peak of dramatic irony (ix.8–12): Oldcastle, Tom, and Ned reject the thief as Henry V is to reject them immediately after, which heightens the irony.

At the end of Scene xviii, Henry woos Katherine, hoping to have as much success in love as in war. The humor of the scene and Henry's desire to marry Katherine demonstrates that the French are not monsters (at least when they accept English terms) but must heed the right of the English king to France (xviii.3). Katherine is of two minds, the official one that protests that she could not love someone who has been so hard on her father and France and the unofficial one, who, in an aside, counts herself the happiest in the world to be "beloved of the mighty King of England!" (xviii.71–78, 86–87). Before this play becomes unmoored on the high seas of patriotism and propaganda, John and Derick anchor it with comedy. John echoes Katherine's use of "hardly" in her protestation with Henry, and Derick characterizes himself as the architect of the "triumph" over the French (see viii.5–7, 78–80; xii.2–3; xv.11, 14). The cowards, John and Derick, modify the martial glory of the English. Like Falstaff after him, Derick plays heroic arithmetic (but was "four or five times killed") and made his nose bleed with straw to show his honor and to avoid fighting (xix.5–21). Derick's captain "bid me stand aside" and he did as Ned, Tom, and Oldcastle did when the king so bids them. The description that Derick provides reinterprets Henry's bloodthirsty cry for French blood (xv.1–4). Whereas the king can show an approach that can be both humorous and stern, these cowardly soldiers demonstrate a comic way that is humorous but has serious implications for the heroic code of war. Derick knows a trick to leave France without asking the king and shows that despite Henry V's famous victories, there are still unlawful tricks among the English.

Whereas Derick and the Frenchman were concerned with "crowns," Henry V and the King of France busy themselves with the right to the French "crown" (xvii, xx). Henry learned to reform and assumed the English crown and won the right to be heir in France, whereas Derick lost the Frenchman's crowns. The play ends with oaths of allegiance to Henry V and with the prospect of a marriage to Katherine, "God willing." Might and determination win and keep crowns as the father gained and guarded the crown "hardly" and as the son attested to Henry IV after his transformation into a potential heroic king (viii.67–81). Katherine uses the word "hardly" to describe Henry V (xviii.71–78). His right is one of force. Despite the heroic claims and celebration of Henry V in *Famous Victories*, the playwright also shows the underside of England and hints at the usurped right Henry has to the throne of England and to the "unreasonable demand" that the Archbishop Bourges and Katherine say that Henry has for the French crown (ix.119; xviii.53–54, 70). Whereas *Famous Victories* is more episodic and is a less complex play than *Henry V*, it is not as simple and crude as is often thought. The ironies of the earlier play also consist mainly in the echoing and recontextualization of images, the use of disguise, roles, and transformation literally and as metaphors, and the structural reversal and relations.

The Troublesome Raigne of King John (ca. 1588) reveals the strong influence of *Tamburlaine* on the Elizabethan stage. The address, "To Gentlemen Readers," appeals to those who have watched Marlowe's play and asks them to welcome "a warlike Christian and your Countryman," but rather than follow Tamburlaine from victory to victory, the audience observes that John goes from defeat to defeat. Like Shakespeare's Richard II, John makes bad decisions and falls. When he decides not to appoint Stephen Langdon and has Arthur's eyes put out, his misfortune begins in the face of Catholic power and the English nobles. The irony of structure and of the views of the Bastard, the citizens, and Lewes complicate the representation, so that *Troublesome Raigne* is not simply a play about a solitary tyrant but presents a troubled king who sometimes acts like a tyrant and who breaks oaths and dissembles among many other oath-breakers and dissemblers. In the last scene, now that John is dead, Lewes, at Pandulph's urging, gives up his claim to the crown. All sides have broken oaths (II.xx.1162–71).[22] Lewes says that treason can only win England for foreigners, perhaps an allusion to Spain and the execution of Mary Stuart as well as advice to Henry, who in the play will be crowned. The Bastard gives similar advice (II.ix.1196–97). Although this lesson comes in the final lines of the play, *Troublesome Raigne* is often ambivalent. Both France and England break oaths and follow policy in which they have their triumphs and setbacks. The papacy can help peace as well as make war, and the Bastard, the spirit of Richard the Lionheart, cannot be as heroic as his father could in a world where weeds grow on either side of the channel. If this play is not as complex as *King John* (ca. 1594–98) or the Second Tetralogy—for Shakespeare's mastery of theatre, structure, words, and characters is difficult to overreach—*Troublesome Raigne*, like most of the history plays in the 1580s and early 1590s, requires more attention than it has received.

The Raigne of King Edward the Third (ca. 1590) does not have an alternative plot or subplot that runs throughout the play as *Famous Victories* does. Like *Troublesome Raigne*, it makes oaths a central matter, and, like *Henry V*, it shows that the relation between public and private is important for kingship. Edward III learns private virtue to become a good public king. *Edward III* is not primarily an ironic play, but irony plays a role. Like *Famous Victories*, it represents rising and victorious action rather than the falling action of defeat that *Troublesome Raigne* depicts. In *Edward III* we find a heroic play in which there is no Ned and Derick and their respective if not respectable companions to play against and qualify the heroic king. Much of *Edward III* treats a lust or love interest from which Edward must learn, so that he is just enough for foreign war. The movement from domestic to foreign is like that in *Famous Victories* and *Henry V*. Whereas Edward's dissembling in love causes Sophoclean and theatrical ironies, his straightforward victories in France do not. After Act II, Edward III is loud on the trumpet with only a few ambivalences and ironies to keep the play from being too one-dimensionally heroic (see V.i.220–22).[23] No infamous English cowards qualify England's glory, but perhaps that complication would have worked against the heroic design.

Shakespeare learned irony early. Rather than discuss this extensive subject at length, I will look briefly at the end of *1 Henry VI* (ca. 1590), which is full of ironies. After a play full of falls, York laments, "Shall we at last conclude effeminate peace?" and complains that most of England's French towns were lost "by treason, falsehood, and by treachery" (V.iv.107, 109).[24] York's treachery, however, was one of the causes of Talbot's death. When Charles swears an oath, he is reluctant until his lords advise him on "policy," to swear only in name (V.iv.164). Even Henry VI breaks his first promise to marry against Gloucester's warnings. Gloucester and Suffolk have an altercation over the nature of the oath. Suffolk appeals to the injustice of forced marriages, which is partly ironic because Suffolk is so interested in Margaret himself that he is not terribly concerned for Henry's personal happiness. Henry falls in love with Suffolk's description and breaks his promise to the Earl of Armagnac's daughter, and Gloucester fears the consequences (V.v.79–102). The play ends with Suffolk depicting Margaret as Helen of Troy to his Paris, and although he says that he will "prosper better than the Trojan did," it is as if he is catching himself using a metaphor that works against his purpose and perhaps foreshadows something unfortunate for him. Where Joan Pucelle left off, Margaret will follow. Disorder is imminent. Suffolk speaks the last lines of the play: "Margaret shall now be Queen, and rule the king; / But I will rule her, the King, and the realm" (V.v.107–8). Shakespeare ironically contrasts the disaster of Henry V's funeral at the beginning of the play with the proposed and ill-boding marriage of Henry VI and Margaret. The prophecy in Henry V's time was right. The playwright also uses Sophoclean and structural irony to complicate the play. Only the figures of Henry V, Talbot, and John Talbot are honorable as Englishmen should be. Shakespeare complicates the view of the English by presenting the coward Falstaff and the kind and gentle Henry VI. Most of the English break oaths as easily as the French, but whereas the English are factitious, the French are not. Through irony, Shakespeare prevents the play from being too single and melodramatic. In a treacherous world, which is like that in *Troublesome Raigne*, heroic men like Talbot cannot survive.

Woodstock (ca. 1590–94) represents an ideal king against which the weak king can be ironically measured. For Richard II, this ideal is the Black Prince or Edward the Third. Richard is governed by flatterers. In Act Five, scene one the Ghost of the Black Prince states plainly what he would do if he were alive. He warns his brother of the rage of his wanton son and tries to wake Woodstock so he can fly from his murderers (V.i.67–76).[25] These speeches, which clearly condemn Richard, and the opening scene of the play provide an envelope for Woodstock's murder. They create Sophoclean irony when Richard appeals to the chronicles and boasts not to have the heroic nature of his great predecessors. The sharpest discrepancy between Richard and his father and his grandfather occurs when Richard commits his greatest wrong—the murder of Woodstock. A primary source of irony has been the contrast between Woodstock's plainness and the flatterers' fashioned outfits and elaborate speech, for the theatre relies on both speech and costume that are representative, symbolic and indirect. Woodstock dresses in plain black clothes and he and other characters constantly associate the word "plain" with him (I.i.97–102, 109f.). Like his brother, Woodstock thinks, in theory, that it is necessary to dissemble when there is good reason but, in practice, cannot (I.ii.181–83). Plain Thomas tells the truth at Richard's wedding, and the king calls the praise and criticism "double praise" (I.iii.18, 23, 35, 113). Richard and his followers mock Woodstock's dress and their speech is more elaborate than his (I.ii.70–120; iii.112–13). The playwright makes an emblem of actuality and appearance with this conflict. There is enmity in the jests, which the audience senses because it possesses more information than the characters. The anonymous author explores the conflict throughout the play. He also balances Richard's treachery with Lancaster's murder of a Carmelite, perhaps the same one at the beginning of the play, though Richard appears to be closer to tyranny than his uncles are (V.iii.68–82; I.i.23–24). Finally, when Greene is dead, the king realizes his error in killing Woodstock (V.iv.47–50; cf. 51–54). Nimble's final act of "conscience" is to betray his unconscientious master (V.v). Self-serving Nimble saves his own skin and gets his reward, and the text breaks off with Nimble telling Richard's uncle his causes for betraying Tresalian.

The irony takes on another dimension in the fall of Shakespeare's Richard II. Christ had two bodies—immortal and mortal—so in the Middle Ages, it is not surprising, as some kings and some theorists of kingship claimed, that kings were Christ's representatives, that there existed division between the king's two bodies: the divine and the human.[26] Such a division has important implications for the mature history plays of Shakespeare's Second Tetralogy or Lancastrian Tetralogy— *Richard II, 1* and *2 Henry IV*, and *Henry V*. The significance of these plays lies partly in the dynamic expression or representation of the tension in the king as a representative of human nature and the body politic. Those who witness the play are like the author and characters because they struggle to make sense of history, of human and divine authority, and they contend with the problem of interpretation. They grapple with problems such as where fact ends and interpretation begins, the relation between the word and the world, and language and power. Language expresses power so that ideology, or attitudes to power, take shape in rhetoric, which orders and systematizes language.[27] In the Second Tetralogy, the king himself cannot control his own power or his language about kingship no matter how much he tries. The society and the king create a fiction of the king's two bodies to accommodate their mutual power and vulnerability. In the reign of Elizabeth I, the king's two bodies implicitly became a question of the queen's two bodies or of the monarch's two bodies.[28]

In the Lancastrian Tetralogy, it is not in earth as in heaven. Here, the ideas of kingship and related problems of acting, lying, and incommunication suggest that allusion and reference are insecure and that, more generally, language is a means and block to action. These plays represent something akin to Raleigh's world of secondary causes.[29] From the opening of *Richard II*, uses of the words "God" and "king" and their cognates, as much as the occurrence of lies, ignorance, and obfuscation, throw into question the authority or divine right of kingship and, in the subsequent plays, the positions of the rebels. After the Fall, a secondary or fallen nature exists. It has implications for all human action, because it shows that people judge or interpret with a large degree of blindness, so that even as they appeal to God or nature or causes, they qualify their own ability to judge, to interpret. Like kings and authors, the audience is godlike and human, knowing and ignorant: its overview of and participation in temporal sequence interact. The condition of drama makes the position of the playwright more invisible, his or her voice more inaudible, than most writers of fiction or narrative historians. Through dramatic irony, the audience may be given greater knowledge than the characters, but it may still lack the information that narrators or narrative historians routinely give to their readers. If the audience shares the playwright's knowledge, it can also be as victimized as the characters. Perhaps members of the audience are caught between their two bodies, whether that is divine and human, corporate and individual, conscious and unconscious, thesis and antithesis. The fiction of the king's two bodies is peripheral to our society, but it is vital to us. We are estranged from it even as we must comprehend it to understand better the Lancastrian Tetralogy, Shakespeare's representation of history, and the nature of the fictions we use to justify our politics.

Language and time are fallen, and these represent the dilemmas so telescoped in kingship and the monarch's two bodies. Shakespeare represents characters who are caught in a temporal dilemma between overview and participation, synchrony and diachrony, eternity and now. Many of the characters, especially the kings, think that they can control time, but even the most successful in temporal power—Hal—comes to realize that, except for the occasional moment, they are time's subjects. The reaction to the rejection of Falstaff is not unanimous. Bates and Williams challenge Henry's view of responsibility in earth and heaven; Henry V dies at the height of his power; the fall of his son returns England to a state of chaos similar to that after Richard's fall. Hal may redeem time more than Richard, Bolingbroke, Hotspur, and Falstaff can, but, being human, he is fallen and cannot transcend language and time. The characters cannot have power over past, present and future, although at times their actions, interpretations of the past and prophecies lead us to expect such active and interpretative potency. The theatre, a temporal art, calls particular attention to the limits of time and the stage. In *Richard II* the garden scene is allegorical, and the Aumerle conspiracy or "the Beggar and the King" is tragicomic if not comic, so that it creates some generic friction in the play. The satiric and self-consciously theatrical nature of the tavern scenes as well as the nature of parody in the play also modifies the comic thrust of *1 Henry IV*. The Induction and Epilogue of *2 Henry IV* emphasize the theatrical nature of a satiric play and make us aware of the role of rumor and design in history. The rejection of Falstaff in Part Two also creates a crisis in the history play that is prolonged into *Henry V*, namely, that Henry's private and public selves are at odds and that the integrity of kingship is still in doubt when it is supposed to be most evident. By emphasizing the representation of history, the Chorus in *Henry V* helps broaden the focus of the play by introducing problem elements that later occur in the problem plays and questions of time, its shape and its interpretation, and the relation of author to audience. But the division between problems of theatre and problems of time is tenuous, and they become increasingly bound up in each other. The Lancastrian Tetralogy moves toward the problem play, questioning the genre of the history play, but not being able to resolve with satisfaction the problems and dilemmas *Henry V* and the other three plays raise, and unable to repair the ruins of fallen language and time.

Christopher Marlowe and Ben Jonson created intricate representations of history, so this brief discussion is meant to be suggestive but not exhaustive. Except in *Edward II*, Marlowe does not represent English history directly. From 1587 to 1593, Marlowe transformed the London stage. His characters' ideas of heroism, policy, and history challenged his audience and fellow playwrights. In *Dido Queen of Carthage* he explores the story of Dido and Aeneas differently from Virgil, representing especially the ambition and aspirations of the characters through apostrophe. They try to impose their will on the world, to summon the inside out, but without success, for Achates discovers that Hecuba is nothing, and Aeneas sees that he cannot raise Priam from the dead (II.i.12–14, 28).[30] Marlowe represents the frustrations of human desire before the limits of human nature and nature, so that his characters attempt to find an identity, a union of inside and outside—character and nature—but cannot because of the very language in which they express their desire is temporal and disjunctive. Dido, Iarbus, and Anna attempt unity through sacrifice, and the oppositions between inside and outside, word and world, are seemingly obliterated in sacrifice at the end of the play. In *Dido* Marlowe looks at the intersection between public myth and private desire and does not explore the intricacies of politics and secular struggles for power. *Tamburlaine* shows the power of strength, the rise of a shepherd in spite of class differences, a man, a hero and tyrant, who believes that might is right. Tamburlaine's "high astounding terms" are as powerful as his "conquering sword" (Prologue, 4–6). His early "will to power," his attempt to make the world conform to his desire, contravenes Christian idealism and morality. Like the rejection of Falstaff, the end of the second part of *Tamburlaine* is a crux because some critics think Tamburlaine is penitent or punished and others observe defiance in his death. In Part One he attempts to enclose Zenocrate with his language and reduces her to silence in the rape (I.ii.87–129). He makes his opponents into objects or kills them. Powerless to affect events directly, Zenocrate hopes Tamburlaine will pardon her father and fiancé, but Arabia is killed (V.ii.320f.). By the end of Part One Tamburlaine has it all his way, his beautiful words shaping an ugly and violent world. In Part Two he would go to war to avenge Zenocrate's death, so to "break the frame of heaven" (II.iv.104). Tamburlaine begins to discover the limits of his power, carting Zenocrate's corpse around in a parodic procession, and he devastates the city and kills Calyphas, the effeminate son whom Zenocrate had defended, in the middle of his dramatic speech (IV.ii.75–83). Like Othello after him, this teller will control his tale and break down the division of life and art, death and desire in narrative. He fears the breakdown of the division between male and female and associates the weak, beautiful, and cowardly with a woman and a womanly man. As Tamburlaine dies, he sees the world in terms of himself (V.iii.245–48). He does not wish for a monastery but tries to unite the world and himself in death as in life. Once again, Marlowe represents a story from history that had been transformed by legend. The source is a pretext for an exploration of ambition and power.

Although not strictly a history play, *The Jew of Malta* reveals the greed and callousness of Barabas and those who persecute him. Marlowe confronts the audience with a stage Machiavel, the Prologue, who taunts it with a paradox that may also apply to most of Marlowe's hero-villains; "Admired I am of those that hate me most" (Prol.9). The Governor of Malta, Ferneze, covets the wealth of the Jews but moralizes when Barabas defies his order to give up half his assets: "Excess of wealth is cause of covetousness, / And covetousness, O, 'tis a monstrous sin" (I.ii.124–25). Even if Barabas is overfond of money, his retort is just: "Ay, but theft is worse" (I.ii.26). As usual, Marlowe plays with taboos, for even if he ultimately punishes the Jew, he allows him to help expose Christian hypocrisy, the greed for worldly goods in the midst of otherworldly professions. Like Tamburlaine, Barabas dies unrepentant, attempting to make the facts of the world comply with his word. Before Jonson does in *Volpone*, Marlowe is representing the relation of gold and God. Like Barabas, Guise in *The Massacre at Paris* is a plotter and poisoner. He attempts to justify his own actions and says that he has subdued religion with policy (ii.34–36, 64–69). He is also aware that language is action. Guise, the Admiral, the Protestants, Ramus, Charles, Navarre, the Duchess, and Henry all apostrophize and dramatize themselves in order to try to identify themselves with the world, as if they can control it with speech, fit it into their story. They behave like Tamburlaine and display a like penchant for intertextuality, especially with classical poetry. Texts can become part of historical context. Guise, too, dies defiantly. Marlowe does not avoid exploring dissembling or the relation between religious and political crisis and controversy. If he examines the relation of gentile to Jew before *The Merchant of Venice,* he also experiments with polemic and propaganda before Shakespeare does in *King John.*

In *Edward II,* Marlowe represents more taboos: powerlust, greed, homosexuality, the abuse of knowledge, blasphemy. In this play, the king has a problem of identity. His father, the Mortimers say, made them swear that they would not let Gaveston return to England, but Edward cannot do without him (I.i.82–89). The king says, "Knowest thou not who I am? / Thy friend, thyself, another Gaveston!" (I.i.142–43). Isabella and England define themselves through the king but cannot do so as he is resisting custom and going outside the traditional definitions of husband, male and king. The queen and male "friend" are bound up in the king, who makes Isabella recognize the fact and tell Warwick (I.iv.218–19). The death of Gaveston throws the kingdom into disarray. Isabella and Mortimer kiss and conspire while the queen says God is on their side; Edward describes the burden of kingship as Shakespeare's Richard II, Henry IV, and Henry V will (IV.v.12–16, 25f., vi.9–62). Like Shakespeare, Marlowe represents the king's two bodies, how kingship is divided between heaven and earth, ideal and material. Edward says, "Two kings in heaven cannot reign at once" (V.i.58). Like Richard II after him, Edward wrestles with kingship and identity but does so mostly through apostrophe rather than metaphor. The end of *Richard II* seems to have borrowed much from the end of *Edward II.* Lightborn, the agent of Mortimer Junior, is like Exton, the agent of Bolingbroke. Even the Christ imagery in the plays is similar enough. Mortimer Junior sounds like the Machiavel at the beginning of *The Jew of Malta*: "Feared am I more than loved; let me be feared" (V.iv.52). Mortimer meets his end without penitence and Edward III apostrophizes the head of Mortimer and the corpse of his father's body to define his life through death, to begin his kingship. Although Marlowe did not explore English history in a systematic fashion, he brings a radical and experimental view of language, character, and history to the English stage. Shakespeare had already learned much from Marlowe when he beat his contemporary to the English history play.

Shakespeare shifted to Roman history from English in about 1599 or 1600 and only returned to English history in about 1612 with *Henry VIII*. Ben Jonson appears to have preferred Roman history to English. In the first decade of the seventeenth century, he wrote *Sejanus* and *Catiline*. At his death, his only English history play, *Mortimer, His Fall*, was incomplete. The only complete scene of *Mortimer* that may have been influenced by Marlowe's *Edward II* is Mortimer's Machiavellian speech. A pupil of Camden and a humanist, Jonson took his history seriously. He even annotated the 1605 edition of *Sejanus*.[31] Jonson thought highly of history and did not subordinate it to poetry as Philip Sidney did. When Jonson's library burnt in 1623, a nearly completed manuscript of the history of Henry V was said to be among the manuscripts lost. For Jonson, history meant truth and memory, a community that explores evidence and value.

Jonson also made the history play a more scholarly endeavor than Shakespeare did. Jonson, the poet, teaches his moral lesson by leaving out details of character, as in the representations of Sejanus and Tiberius. Jonson makes characters into types just as he did in his comedies of humor and in his satires. Perhaps ironically, Jonson places the trial of the historian, Cordus, at the center of Sejanus, right after the suicide of Silius. The playwright thereby telescopes Tacitus in order to show the violence to truth and virtue, to place before the audience the old notion of history as moral *exempla*.[32] Jonson may have wanted to use sources of antiquity as opposed to the popular chronicles that Shakespeare used. He stuck to the best historians and did not play with legends and invented characters. The end of Sejanus does not seem ironic. Terentius says, "Let this example move th' insolent man / Not to grow proud and careless of the gods. / . . . For whom the morning saw so great and high, / Thus low and little, 'fore the' even doth lie" (V.899–99, 902–3). The fall of pride and the wheel of Fortune point to the lesson. Jonson embraces and complicates the notion of the *de casibus* pattern and the moral fables of *The Mirror for Magistrates*. His history plays are more overtly moral than Shakespeare's, and Sejanus approaches *de casibus* tragedy more closely in its pattern than *Richard II* does. Like *Sejanus*, *Catiline* is a conspiracy play. It might also illuminate such contemporary conspiracies as the Essex Rebellion and, more especially, the Gunpowder Plot. *Cataline* calls attention to its moral tone and lesson.[33]

Jonsonian satire in his histories deals in types. The style of history that Jonson gives us has been at least as influential and important as Shakespeare's. Many professional historians might prefer Jonson as a historian to Shakespeare, but most "common" readers might well not. Shakespeare acted in Jonson's historical tragedy, a play that Jonson was proud of but one that was not popular at the Globe.[34]

Shakespeare's last foray into history is a romantic history, *Henry VIII*. Cranmer's paean to the Virgin Queen is the future reading itself back on the past. It provides a comic ending that is like the phoenix. Cranmer's description of Elizabeth finds joy arising from sorrow, good rising from the tragic falls of the illustrious. If Elizabeth, in Cranmer's words, shall be "a pattern to all princes living with her," the play urges itself as a pattern of virtue and happiness (V.iv.22).[35] But the Prologue did not want the play to be comic. More strife was to follow in the reign of Henry VIII. Moreover, truth and honor have been difficult and changeable words in the course of action. The structure of the play, which relied so long on Wolsey, who asked and received the greatest forgiveness, asks for charity. Once forgiven, Cranmer does not seem to bear grudges. Instead, he celebrates Elizabeth's birth with Henry. The Epilogue is about "naught," using wit to ask for happy applause. Like the epilogues to *As You Like It* and *2 Henry IV*, this one encourages but manipulates interpretation. Shakespeare returns to the old episodic chronicle play and supplements it with pageantry and masque. The influences of Beaumont, Fletcher, and Jonson may be apparent here. Perhaps with Fletcher's help, Shakespeare cuts the play loose from the closer mimesis of some of his earlier English histories, leaving his audience to follow the Chorus of *Henry V* in filling out the historical action with imagination.

The chronicle and history plays were something Shakespeare's predecessors, contemporaries, and successors devoted considerable energy. Plays about history were various and resilient, though their popularity waned between the domestic or romantic history of Thomas Dekker's *Shoemaker's Holiday* (ca. 1600) and John Ford's *Perkin Warbeck* (ca. 1632–34). An interesting development in the history play is Elizabeth Cary's historical plays, *Mariam* (1602–4) and *The History of Edward II* (1627). In the second play, a female playwright constructs historical characters of both genders in ways that embody and challenge the gender values of the age in which she wrote.[36] Historical drama has been alive and well enough to survive ever since.[37] Dramatic history might well eschew professional and scientific history as it particularly developed in the twentieth century, but as much as we interpret historical events in the writing and reading of history, we embody meaning and that a drama of meaning occurs in any interpretation between there and here, then and now. Plays about history are one of the many ways people wrestle with the representation and interpretation of historical events. The relation between past and present is so slippery that we need all the means possible to find some traction on the many paths we take. Dramatic history is itself exciting and precarious as it both represents the sequence of events that the historian need follow and the latitude to change that sequence that that poet is granted in the license to make myths and follow the imagination. The tension in a traditional meaning of word "history" as a story and a story about the past suggests the struggle of the writer as poet and historian. The historical poet may seem like an oxymoron to the modern reader, but the dramatist is both and suggests that historical drama gives us another way to think about the past and how we come to terms with it.

CHAPTER 8

Shakespeare's Romance

If playwrights can represent the events of history, they can also be poets of imagination and possibility and explore the what-if of comedy and romance. Genre allows for variety and explorations of actuality and its supplement. What is real and what is not can be examined from different angles, verisimilitude and the fantastic or improbable. Shakespeare has the ability to explore various forms in poetry and drama. His tragic, historical, and comic muses enabled him to sing an array of actions, characters and thoughts. In each work, Shakespeare brings something new: he is an innovator who draws on the stories and sources of others. He uses a measure of dramatic practice and of poetry to create powerful plays across the genres. What works on stage and on the page might sometimes be different, and it may be this tension that explains why some critics and playgoers have found some of Shakespeare's romances to be problematic. If we take into consideration the dream world of comedy and romance, the wish fulfillment, the dark sides, the rending and mending of nature as well as the complement of, but sometimes tension between, the play as theatre text and the play as reading text, then some of the gaps and apparent imperfections seem less pressing or dire.

The relation between showing and telling, theory and practice, past and present, which have been central concerns of this book, also becomes crucial in the debate over Shakespeare's art in his last plays. Romance itself deserves a careful and measured look, whether it is in regard to Greene's prose texts or Shakespeare's plays. What follows is a consideration of one way into two of Shakespeare's romances, a thread into the labyrinth, although there are others. To begin with, I examine one aspect of the reception of these plays.

Reception

For a long time, the dramaturgy, especially the endings, of *Cymbeline* (ca. 1609) and *The Winter's Tale* (ca. 1610) has sometimes puzzled audiences and critics alike. Both plays have been called improbable romances whose conclusions are contrived and unconvincing. Dr. Johnson's well-known remarks on *Cymbeline* dismiss it offhand:

> This play has many just sentiments, some natural dialogues, and some pleasing scenes, but they are obtained at the expense of much incongruity. To remark the folly of the fiction, the absurdity of the conduct, the confusion of the names, and manners of different times, and the impossibility of the events in any system of life, were to waste criticism upon unresisting imbecility, upon faults too evident for detection, and too gross for aggravation.[1]

Like Dr. Johnson, Bernard Shaw found *Cymbeline* so poorly wrought that it drove him to vitriolic reproofs. In 1896 Shaw said *Cymbeline* "is for the most part stagey trash of the lowest melodramatic order" and, except for Imogen, "would stand about as much chance of being revived now as *Titus Andronicus*."[2] Although prior to this review Shaw had disapproved of Henry Irving's cuts in his production of *Cymbeline*, 49 years later, Shaw himself rewrote the last act of the play in blank verse and called his creation *Cymbeline Refinished*. With irony, Shaw returned to the long tradition of rewriting Shakespeare's plays to improve them. In 1945 he said that "*Cymbeline*, though one of the finest of Shakespeare's later plays now on the stage, goes to pieces in the last act."[3] Nonetheless, as he himself saw, Shaw was caught up in his own joke, for he cut "the surprises that no longer surprise anybody," the "identification of Guiderius by the mole on his neck" and "infantile joys" such as "the revelation that Polydore and Cadwal are Imogen's long lost brothers and Cymbeline's long lost sons."[4] Beneath Shaw's contempt for Shakespeare's crude dramaturgy and lack of realism for an audience in the twentieth century lies a revaluation that reflects a shift from a negative view of *Cymbeline*, which was held at least as far back as Dr. Johnson, to a more positive assessment. Even though Shaw scorned Shakespeare's inability to unravel his plays, especially *The Two Gentlemen of Verona* and *Cymbeline*, in the last act, he scoffed at the theatres for not playing *Cymbeline verbatim*, for cutting the masque and comic jailor and for "mutilating the rest," offering the Shavian version only as a genius' cure for an ignorant public and indifferent critics. According to Shaw, it is one thing for the great to rewrite but for the dull and uninformed, Shakespeare is not, in Barthian terms, *scriptible*.[5]

The interest in *Cymbeline* and the other Shakespearean romances increased in the twentieth century, especially since the late 1930s. Although still a little apologetic for the play in general and the ending in particular, James Nosworthy, in his Introduction to the New Arden edition, credited Shakespeare with writing an "experimental romance." Judiana Lawrence has argued that the ending of *Cymbeline* reveals Shakespeare's sophisticated artistry, and others share this view enough that it no longer appears absurd, as it would to Dr. Johnson and the younger Shaw.[6]

As J. H. P. Pafford noted, even though *The Tempest* has always been popular, *Pericles, Cymbeline* and *The Winter's Tale* "have received much adverse comment."[7] Like *Cymbeline*, *The Winter's Tale* has suffered rewriting but has increasingly found, for the most part, sympathetic viewers and readers in the twentieth century. After

1634, when King Charles saw it, *The Winter's Tale* was not performed until 1741. When the play did appear on stage, it caused so much disenchantment in the audiences that in the next 15 years 3 adaptations were written. David Garrick's *Florizel and Perdita: A Dramatic Pastoral in Three Acts* (1758; facsimile edition, London: Cornmarket Press, 1969), the most successful of these rescriptings, replaced *The Winter's Tale* on the stage until the beginning of the nineteenth century. Maxwell has aptly described how David Garrick altered Shakespeare's play: in *Florizel and Perdita* the events of 16 years before are narrated by Camillo to a lord of Bohemia, where all the scenes are laid; there Paulina with the secreted Hermione had found refuge, and there Leontes, at last repentant, comes to ask forgiveness of Polixenes. By these changes Garrick sought to avoid the transfer of action from Sicilia to Bohemia and back to Sicilia the lapse of 16 years between Acts III and IV, and perhaps the absence from the stage for extended periods of certain principal characters.[8]

Although nineteenth-century critics such as Edward Dowden, Swinburne, and F. J. Furnivall treated *The Winter's Tale* as a reflection of the serenity of Shakespeare's retirement, others, like Barrett Wendell, thought the play exemplified Shakespeare's artistic decline. In 1904 Lytton Strachey denounced Dowden's view of *The Winter's Tale* and called this romance a reflection of the playwright's boredom. Twentieth-century criticism, however, more often looked at the romances as experiments of considerable success. The views of Arthur Quiller-Couch and J. M. Nosworthy are good examples of this trend.[9] In recent years many fine interpretations have attempted to show just what kind of an experiment *The Winter's Tale* is, although critics have not reached a consensus.[10]

So my interpretation is not the first to take these plays seriously or to observe their experimental nature.[11] I want to show another way of looking at *Cymbeline* and *The Winter's Tale*, one, but certainly not the only one, that might help illuminate Shakespeare's art in his last phase. By recapitulating at the end of *Cymbeline* or by making Time, the Chorus, tell the audience that he is sliding over 16 years at the beginning of Act Four of *The Winter's Tale* or by bringing Hermione to life at the end of the play, Shakespeare is not being realistic but is using a kind of Brechtian alienation effect *avant la lettre*. Just as Keats did not consider himself a Romantic poet, Shakespeare did not set out to use the alienation effect. Criticism often invents terms or uses old ones in new ways to describe the art of earlier ages. Because Shakespeare did not speak of the alienation effect does not mean that he did not "alienate" his audience any more than his failure to use the term "philosophical irony" prevented him from using an irony that reflected a view of the world and that did not restrict itself to the traditional trope. Neither a Marxist nor a structuralist, Shakespeare did not alienate his audience to enliven them to social criticism or to kick at the domination of the logocentric view, which, among other things, Bertolt Brecht and Roland Barthes have done. I contend that Shakespeare shares these estrangement effects with Brecht and Barthes but that his aims in *Cymbeline* and *The Winter's Tale* differ from theirs. Shakespeare's self-conscious technique underscores the miracle of theatre and the theatricality of miracle, a sense of wonder. These late plays succeed precisely because they are not realistic and are not trying to be so. Not all bourgeois art, and Shakespeare appears to have been bourgeois, is realistic, and realistic art is what Brecht and Barthes dread because it pretends it is natural and erases its own assumptions to assert the authority of the artistic, social and political status quo. But, as I hope to show, neither of these plays is realistic and both call attention to the illusion of the theatre, to the production of art. Shakespeare uses alienation with a difference, an unrealistic signification that semioticians, structuralists and poststructuralists such as Barthes and Jacques Derrida have developed in written texts rather than on the stage. Brecht's theatrical alienation differs from Shakespeare's in its interest or aim (assuming that authors can control their works to some degree, although they always had trouble doing so) but it is closely related.[12]

Brecht and Barthes

To argue my point, it is necessary to provide a brief background to the idea of Brecht's alienation effect and Barthes' double sign, so that it is possible to judge, however modestly, these Shakespearean plays in the light of some influential critical terms and vice versa. Brecht's alienation effect is a descendant, through Erwin Piscator and others, of the "estranged" language or defamiliarization of the Russian formalists and of Roman Jakobson's "poetic" word. Jakobson provides the link between the Russian formalists and the Czech structuralists, who inspire French structuralism and poststructuralism, theoretical movements to which Barthes contributed. In fact, Barthes was an early advocate of Brecht in France. Whereas Brecht was influenced by Bolshevik futurists and other Soviet artists of the avant-garde as well as the Soviet cultural revolutionists of the 1920s, Barthes' first major influence is Sartre's existentialism, although Barthes is sympathetic to socialism. In questioning the means of production in the theatre and by opposing realism for hiding those means, Brecht's alienation effect may have helped Barthes' idea of the "double" sign. For Barthes, the realistic sign pretends to represent nature and by erasing its own artificiality, its own mode of productivity, it creates the illusion that language represents the world rather than being the world. Barthes' double sign both gestures and means just as the alienation effect does.[13] Rather than chase poststructuralism in its pursuit of the disjunction between signifier and signified, it is more productive in this case to focus the discussion on the alienation effect and Barthes' view of it.

At the root of Brecht's alienation effect is an attack on Aristotelian theatre and capitalism. According to Brecht, Aristotelian dramatics require the audience to empathize with the actors, and he rejects Stanislavsky's method of acting because it promotes this illusion. For Brecht, theatrical and pictorial displays at old popular fairs, the Elder Brueghel's paintings, Chinese acting (which unlike European acting does not allow the audience to be an unseen spectator) all represent examples of a type of proto-"A-effect." In 1935 Brecht disagreed with the ideological aims of the schematized acting of the Chinese theatre, but he hoped to prise the technique loose from the politics and give it a social purpose. Brecht wanted to get away from the bourgeois theatre where the 'representation of people is bound by the alleged "eternally human"' and the plot reflects universal situations where capital M Man expresses himself.[14] Humankind is, in Brecht's view, historical and changes in time, so that drama must take man's environment seriously, must consider difference: "for the historicizing theatre everything is different. The theatre concentrates entirely on whatever in this perfectly everyday event is remarkable, particular and demanding inquiry."[15] Another important aspect of Brecht's alienation effect is the juxtaposition of incongruous elements. The Elder Brueghel's war painting, *Dulle Griet,* juxtaposes an Alpine peak with a Flemish landscape, old Asiatic costumes with modem European ones, its tragedy containing a comic aspect, its comedy a tragic one.[16] Shakespeare uses this technique throughout his canon, but, surprisingly, Brecht does not discuss this juxtaposition if he sees it. It is a commonplace that Hamlet's tragedy is comic and his comedy is tragic. The shifts in the language, tones and scenes as well as juxtaposition of disparate elements occur as much in *Cymbeline* and *The Winter's Tale* as in *Hamlet.* When discussing *King Lear,* and the alienation effect, Brecht is more preoccupied with the alienation of Lear's division of the kingdom. The actor pretends he is dispersing his own private property, so that "he throws some light on the basis of the feudal idea of the family."[17]

Nevertheless, Brecht does admit that the alienation effect can be alienated, which is what I propose to do in relation to *Cymbeline* and *The Winter's Tale.*[18] I am trying to make the estrangement effect strange because Shakespeare uses it in productive ways Brecht does not mention. Even if Shakespeare did not want to make his audience more critical of capitalism, which in Brechtian terms would be ahistorical, he is prodding his audience to be more critically aware of the medium of his art. Ultimately, Brecht forgets dramatic irony as a way to that criticism. In that old and basic form of irony, the playwright often shares with the audience knowledge that one or more of the characters lacks. Rather than identify with the ignorant character, the audience can scrutinize his motives and actions. In short, dramatic irony can alienate the audience from the character and, through this lack of empathy, from itself. Brecht, of course, is subtle and suggests an alienation of the actor from the character, for the person knows more than the personage and, rather than pretending he does not know the ending of the play, he should use his superior knowledge to show difference in time and place, "so as to make visible the knotting-together of the events."[19]

Lest I am doing violence to Brecht or am at least adapting him without just cause, I appeal to the experimental nature of *Cymbeline* and *The Winter's Tale.* In these plays Shakespeare makes his characters inconsistent and calls attention to their "experimental conditions," both important aspects of Brecht's alienation effect.[20] If Brecht is not an Aristotelian, Shakespeare of the romances is certainly not a strict Aristotelian. It was Francis Bacon's *Novum Organum* and not Aristotle's *Poetics* that partly inspired Brecht's "Short Organum."[21] If the Renaissance appears to influence Brecht's theory and practice, it is no surprise because it is a time in which the "alienation effect" is flourishing and one that is reconsidering Aristotle in a radical way both in science and art.

It is not necessary to elaborate at length Barthes' lucid account of Brecht's dramaturgy and theory. Barthes notes that Brecht's theatre is one that relies on a critical distance between the character and spectator, so that the drama encourages the spectator to develop a critical consciousness and the capacity to make history, to found revolutionary social and political action through a study of individual conduct, to investigate the changes of the here and now and not eternal man, to make people know that they need not be passive to the eternal essence of life and art because there is no such thing. According to Barthes, Brecht views humanity as historical and not "natural," sees nature as a construct with which the ruling classes oppress the people, suggests that nature is correctible, that a viscous art rather than Aristotelian empathy and transparency is the way to promoting revolutionary Marxism. Finally, Barthes himself sees the connection between semiology and Brechtian dramaturgy, which postulates that

> the responsibility of a dramatic art is not so much to express reality as to signify it. Hence there must be a certain distance between signified and signifier: revolutionary art must admit a certain arbitrary nature of signs, . . . Brecht's formalism is a radical protest against the confusions of the bourgeois and *petit-bourgeois* false Nature: in a still-alienated society, art must be critical, it must cut off all illusions, even that of 'Nature': the sign must be partially arbitrary, otherwise we fall back on an art of expression, an art of essentialist illusion.[22]

Without the same ideology, the dramaturgy of *Cymbeline* and *The Winter's Tale* shares some of the characteristics of the alienation effect and the "double" sign but with a difference. Shakespeare's critical estrangement calls attention to illusion, to the production of art, both for the sake of production and the sake of art. It is to a close examination of these plays that we now turn.

Cymbeline

The complexity of *Cymbeline* is no longer sure to evoke the disgust of critics. In 1976 Roger Warren could praise aspects of the play that in 1962 Gareth Lloyd Evans thought worthy of censure: "*Cymbeline* is not a lucid play, as the comedies are, but I think it is the very combination of the 'virtuoso' elements with a reworking of techniques from the comedies which gives it its particular power, enabling Shakespeare to emphasize, isolate, highlight such powerful emotions as Imogen's grief or joy, Posthumus's extravagance and jealous rashness, Iachimo's response to Imogen."[23] Warren makes an important point: Shakespeare's technical virtuosity and conscious reshaping of techniques from his comedies stress the emotions of the characters. The playwright draws the attention of the audience to the conventions of the play to remind it that *Cymbeline* is not a realistic play and that in romance or tragicomedy changes in character are swift and not always consistent. Like Judiana Lawrence, I think that *Cymbeline* is not Aristotelian because it eschews possibility and probability and uses visible signs and tokens as a means of discovery, which Aristotle condemns for lacking invention.[24] Lawrence says the ending of *Cymbeline* is not straight romance or parody of the genre but a complex "examination of the means and ends of fiction," and the concern of the audience is more with how Shakespeare is going to use the conventions of romance than with suspense about how the story will turn out.[25] This complex and conscious use of convention that Lawrence sees is one of the grounds for the alienation effect.

Although many aspects of the play such as the disparate juxtaposition of the tragic and comic styles of poetry and prose and Shakespeare's use of specific Elizabethan romances warrant discussion in relation to the alienation effect in *Cymbeline*, I shall limit my analysis to a couple of points—the play's conscious repetition and transformation of conventions of Elizabethan romance especially in its conclusion. Such an approach should reveal that, like *The Winter's Tale*, *Cymbeline* is both a tragicomedy and a romance. Perhaps J. H. P. Pafford describes Shakespeare's romances best:

> With the exception of *The Tempest* they are roomy plays in that they have scenes in many places and countries and they all show or recount events taking place over a lengthy period of time: they are often called romances and they are romantic in true Elizabethan senses of the word, dealing with love in people of high estate, events controlled by supernatural agency and by chance, and heroic adventure in both courtly and arcadian settings. They are written in similar style and have similar peculiarities of language and versification. Virtue, beauty, and happiness are in them all: but they contain evil, ugliness and misery too, and at times they all come near tragedy: yet they all end happily. Their story is of the evil caused by jealousy, hatred, or treachery and of the conquest of this evil in the course of time by integrity, constancy, and courageous love aided by good fortune.[26]

Although *Cymbeline* is less "roomy" than *The Winter's Tale*—for it represents 12 days on stage, but its plot covers 6 months, whereas *The Winter's Tale* shows 8 days on stage, and its story comprises 16 years, and the change of setting is less radical in *Cymbeline*—clearly both plays are not tight Aristotelian constructions.

But it is Shakespeare's echoing of his earlier plays that perhaps represents the most interesting use of self-conscious stagecraft. Shakespeare begins *Cymbeline* with a conventional situation commonly found in his comedies. As in *The Two Gentlemen of Verona* (ca. 1594), *A Midsummer Night's Dream* (ca. 1595), *As You Like It* (ca. 1598), in *Cymbeline* young lovers find a parental or an authoritarian block to their love. *Romeo and Juliet* (ca. 1596), which begins as a comedy and ends as a tragedy, also shows this pattern. A decade or so later Shakespeare's audience could see him setting up a similar comic pattern in Cymbeline's banishment of Imogen's husband, Posthumus (I.ii). And the playwright piles comic convention on comic convention from then on, so that the audience cannot help considering the conventions themselves. Although Imogen is a distinct character, she shows a like patience and virtue to earlier Shakespearean heroines or lesser female characters: Silvia in *The Two Gentlemen of Verona* and Isabella in *Measure for Measure* (ca. 1604), both of whom maintain their chastity before corrupt and persistent suitors, as well as Cordelia and Desdemona. Not only does Imogen suffer Cymbeline's disapproval for her marriage to Posthumus, but she also deflects Iachimo's advances and remains faithful to her husband (I. iii, vi). Imogen and Posthumus exchange rings as tokens of their faith in love. Shakespeare employs this device in *Two Gentlemen* when Proteus and Julia exchange rings for the same reason. Shakespeare also uses variations on the ring device in *Love's Labour's Lost* (ca. 1596), *The Merchant of Venice* (ca. 1597), *Twelfth Night* (ca. 1600) and *All's Well That Ends Well* (ca. 1603). Cymbeline is the tyrannical father or king who tries to block marriage in the younger generation as Egeus does in *A Midsummer Night's Dream* (ca. 1595) and Duke Frederick does in *As You Like It*. The audience has also witnessed unjust banishment in Duke Frederick's exile of Duke Senior and Rosalind before that of Belarius and Posthumus (also the Duke of Milan's banishment of Valentine), and the playgoer also sees the conventional contrast between the pastoral country (Belmont and the Forest of Arden) and the corrupt court or city in *Merchant* and *As You Like It* before it appears in *Cymbeline*.

The sheer number of conventions, especially comic ones, distinguishes *Cymbeline*. Not yet out of Act One, the audience also witnesses a stock villain and a poison motif. Although not identical, Oliver in *As You Like It* and Don John in *Much Ado About Nothing* (ca. 1599) act as comic villains as Cloten and Iachimo do in *Cymbeline*. Except that Iachimo confesses and repents, he is much like Iago and because he confesses and repents, he resembles Edmund. The use of poison as a device occurs in *Hamlet*, but the poison is only a drug that later has comic consequences for Imogen (I.iii, vi; cf. IV.iii) more like the effects of the juices of the flower in *A Midsummer Night's Dream* and the tragic results a similar drug has in *Romeo and Juliet*. Act One ends with a conscious repetition of the story of how Imogen's two brothers were stolen years ago and with Iachimo, a tragicomic villain, testing a heroine who is conventionally virtuous. (I.vii, cf. I. i.) By the end of the first act, the audience knows *Cymbeline* is thick with old conventions.

In the acts leading up to the final one, Shakespeare continues to make his audience conscious of his deliberate use of convention and also represents a self-conscious debate of the relation of art to life, a theme reminiscent of his early plays. Iachimo, a self-dramatized villain like Richard III and Iago, removes Imogen's bracelet and notes the mole on her left breast, so that he can convince Posthumus of Imogen's infidelity. The ring or jewel or some personal possession like the handkerchief in *Othello* appears especially in Shakespeare's comedies to identify characters, or to complicate and then resolve the plot, as in Act II, Scenes 2 and 3, and Act III, Scene 1. Posthumus thinks Iachimo has won the wager over Imogen's chastity, a recurrent theme in many of Shakespeare's comedies, tragedies and romances (III.i). Like Othello and the later Leontes, Posthumus grows jealous without cause. As in the Second Tetralogy, in *Cymbeline* the playwright consciously rubs together different types of generic matter—the tragic, comic and historical—and causes the audience to be aware of the problems of drama and particularly of romance.[27] For instance, Shakespeare juxtaposes the comic and the historic when in Act Three, scene one, Cloten's anger with Rome reflects his recent displeasure with Imogen. The incongruous, though common enough occurrence is that Cloten is an ass and a player in history. Bringing up a common theme of the histories and comedies, Imogen emphasizes her obedience when she tells Pisanio to kill her as his master, Posthumus, had ordered. Obedience is also the contention between Britain and Rome (III.iv). Pisanio cannot murder Imogen and says she must disguise herself as a man and serve Lucius, the Roman general.

Disguise and mistaken identity, especially of the androgynous women dressed as men, are common conventions of Shakespearean comedy. Julia, Portia, Rosalind, and Viola all disguise themselves as men. Shakespeare calls attention to disguise when Cloten says that he will dress in Posthumus' clothes because Imogen had said earlier that she loved Posthumus better than Cloten. In a perversion of disguise in the comedies, these clothes would allow Cloten to kill Posthumus and ravish Imogen (III.v). Ultimately, Cloten's disguise and ploy cause his death, and Shakespeare underscores disguise by making the clothes the man (IV.i.ii). This hollow man meets with hard measures: the playwright emphasizes the unreal aspect of the play by killing off a latter-day Parolles. The illusion of clothes and the convention of romance, where dying is like death in a fairy-tale, may trouble an audience who must also contend with the historical dispute. And to engage the audience's critical faculty even more, Shakespeare causes Guiderius to decapitate Cloten, so that Imogen, or Fidele, mistakes him for Posthumus. This mistaken identity is, of course, unrealistic if not as grotesque as the stuff of fairy-tales (IV.ii). Later in the same scene, the audience learns that Iachimo is leading a force from Italy to Britain, a detail that not only provides a link with the love plot but also contrasts the "realistic" plot with the fantastic events that center on the personal affairs of Cymbeline's family.

Three additional elements help prepare the audience for the concluding scene of *Cymbeline*: the conscious comparison of art and life, the use of dramatic irony and the masque or theophany of Jupiter. Like *A Midsummer Night's Dream*, *Cymbeline* wants to make the audience more aware of the complex relation between art and life, dream and waking. Although Imogen spurns Iachimo's advances, he notices, when she is asleep in her chamber, that "She hath been reading late, / The tale of Tereus, here the leafs turn'd down / Where Philomel gave up." (II.ii. 44–46.) So art is not life, although Iachimo will try to make Posthumus believe the artful delusion that Imogen "gave up." Shakespeare encourages the audience to examine this fiction within a fiction. He also uses song to show the seams or knots of his art. Cloten thinks that song will help "penetrate" Imogen, and the clod is only interested in the song if it succeeds. For Cloten, art is a tool to affect life (II.iii). In both the comedies and tragedies, some of Shakespeare's characters comment on songs, plays and riddles: the lovers in *A Midsummer Night's Dream* on a play (V.i), Orsino on music and Olivia on Feste's wit and song in *Twelfth Night* (I.i and v), Hamlet on the play and players (II.ii) and Lear on the Fool's wit (I. iv). Iachimo also takes his turn at the criticism of art: when he is trying to prove Imogen's unchastity to Posthumus, he describes, in poetry worthy of Enobarbus (*Antony and Cleopatra*, II.ii. 195–223), Cleopatra when she met Antony, noting the "workmanship and value" of an art true to life (II.iv. 68–78). If it is not Iachimo's realistic description that convinces Posthumus, it is his sense of denial that does. Posthumus believes him about the mole under her breast (II.iv. 134–36). Nonetheless, Iachimo's view of art will not serve, for Imogen is not Cleopatra, being neither lustful nor proud, and only Posthumus is fooled by his apparently realistic tale. Iachimo's detail can make a lie seem real. Only through his dream of his father, mother, two brothers and Jupiter can Posthumus see through appearance to actuality (V.iv.30–151).

Shakespeare's characters tell stories that serve dramatic irony. The playwright uses fiction within fiction to limit his characters and his own art, and once the audience understands these limitations, it can better comprehend the nature of art and life. Such stories are important in Shakespearean drama. In the opening scene of *The Comedy of Errors* (ca. 1590), Egeon relates his tale; Othello also tells his story early in the play; at the end of *Romeo and Juliet*, Friar Lawrence unfolds the story of the lovers; with irony, Shakespeare has Hamlet ask Horatio to tell his story when the play already has; in the last act, Marina relates her tale to Pericles. Similarly, Belarius had told Guiderius and Arviragus many tales, which he mentions often, but, as he tells the audience, he must conceal the true natures of the boys, so that the audience knows that they are the sons of Cymbeline (III.iii.l07). This dramatic irony not only helps prepare for the end of the play, where that irony abounds, but it also heightens the ironies along the way. For instance, Fidele, or Imogen, wishes Arviragus and Guiderius were her brothers, and the audience knows they are and can observe all three with detachment (III.vii.41–51).

Posthumus' dream or the masque of Jupiter also reveals dramatic irony. Neither the ghosts of the Leonati nor Jupiter himself tells the audience anything it does not know or cannot guess (V.iv.29–151). Perhaps Shakespeare is limiting the gods and the role of dream through dramatic irony, allowing the audience to be aware of the art of the scene and to question the nature of divinity and dream. The language—and probably the staging—of the masque is highly stylized and hardly realistic. This style contrasts most with that of the historical scenes. The masque informs Posthumus but not the audience just as the final scene does. Ultimately, the audience gains critical pleasure in this instance and in the recapitulation of the end.[28]

As in the masque of Jupiter and other scenes where dramatic irony prevails, the final scene of *Cymbeline* piques the audience: it knows the events and wants to see how Shakespeare will represent them. The alienation effect derives from the audience observing the characters learning the "facts" and not from its surprise. At the end of *The Comedy of Errors, The Two Gentlemen of Verona, A Midsummer Night's Dream, As You Like It, Twelfth Night* and *Measure for Measure*, Shakespeare concentrates his art on reconciliation, rediscovery, marriage and happiness. *Cymbeline* reveals increasingly a comic movement, which the audience can perceive in the repetitive variations on earlier conventions from the comedies. No play, perhaps, in the Shakespearean canon recapitulates so much at its conclusion as *Cymbeline*. Dramatic irony builds to a climax. Whereas the characters do not know much, the audience has only to learn how ignorant they were by watching them discover. Although masterfully done, Act V, scene five shows how unreal or theatrical or coincidental comedies and, more specifically, romances and their endings are by their very length and ingenuity. Not only has the audience witnessed the many forms of the unmasking of mistaken identity, the overcoming of parental or social barriers to marriage, the reunion of families long separated, the return from exile, the riddle solved, the letters reinterpreted, the restoration of peace, but each spectator also finds himself detached from the action through dramatic irony and the sheer artifice of this scene.[29]

In short, while the characters discover, the audience interprets. Shakespeare's conscious repetition burdens the expectations of "realistic" drama and questions the limitations of realism. The characters learn fast and thick: Cordelius reveals the death of the queen and her plan to poison Cymbeline and Imogen; Belarius thinks that Fidele was raised from the dead but soon learns otherwise; Pisanio apprehends Fidele's true identity; Iachimo confesses his abuse of Posthumus and Imogen; Imogen thinks Pisanio has poisoned her but Cornelius assures her that this is not the case; Cymbeline, Belarius, Guiderius, Arviragus and others learn that Fidele is Imogen; Pisanio uncovers Cloten's intent to kill Posthumus and to rape Imogen, and Guiderius, learning of Cloten's clothes, admits to killing him; Imogen discovers that Cloten, and not Posthumus, was the headless corpse; Belarius reveals his identity and that Arviragus and Guiderius are the king's lost sons and Imogen's brothers; Posthumus identifies himself as the courageous British peasant who fought so well against the Romans, and so on. Even though the audience will probably be wondering at the virtuosity, it will not put up with this recapitulation unless Shakespeare has good reasons for the repetition.

His rationale is ample. The playwright shows that no character escapes limitation, contrasts Iachimo's long speeches with the subsequent quick succession of discoveries, raises the question of why Cloten should die because of his clothes and language when other Shakespearean comic villains have been allowed to live. Shakespeare also makes the audience consider why, if Cloten wanted to rape and kill and fought a fair fight with Guiderius, Cymbeline would even condemn Guiderius to death and why the king pardons him when he finds out he is his own son, but the playwright still creates a sense of wonder in an audience that is aware of the artificiality of the play. Dramatic irony emphasizes the ignorant confusion of the characters. When Posthumus strikes the page, who is actually Imogen, Shakespeare is stressing Posthumus' cruelty and his bafflement before appearance. The repetition of this point, or a conscious knot, occurs in the dramatic irony of Pisanio's words: "O, my lord Posthumus! / You ne'er kill'd Imogen till now" (V.v.230–31). Like Iachimo, Belarius tells his tale. Shakespeare presents these fictions within fictions as if to say: let us consider these fantastic events. The old device of the birthmark as a means of identification, in this case the mole on Guiderius' neck (what about proof of Arviragus' identity?), reminds the audience that this is the stuff of romance, fairy tale, and epic (remember Odysseus' scar) and not of a "realistic" representation.

The end of *Cymbeline* asks the audience to be active in this interpretation. Shakespeare goads it with the limitations of the characters and by almost driving his dramatic irony too hard, a reason, perhaps, for the long-standing disaffection with the ending. In Act Three, scene seven, the audience experienced dramatic irony when Arviragus and Fidele wished that they were brothers (43–51). Imogen now says to Guiderius and Arviragus, "You call'd me brother / When I was but your sister: I you brothers, / When we were so indeed" (V.v. 377–79).

By watching Imogen wonder at the discovery, the audience derives pleasure and instruction from these lines. If the audience does not accept this artistic premise or think that Shakespeare is creating conscious knots for the audience to consider, I am afraid that for such critics, these lines, this scene, this play, and indeed of *The Winter's Tale* as well, is a failure and perhaps not even a failed experiment. For them, Shakespeare's alienation effect would be an excuse for discontinuities and flaws.[30] I prefer to give Shakespeare the benefit of the doubt, although I think bardolatry has its dangers. Even though Cymbeline wants to learn all about the strange events and about his sons whom he has not seen for some twenty years, all of which is understandable, his words, I think, are meant to be as humorous as they are wonderful. For instance, he says, "When shall I hear all through? This fierce abridgement / Hath to it circumstantial branches, which / Distinction should be rich in" (383–85). For Cymbeline, the telling is too short, but for the audience, it could not be much longer. Art is art because it is not life, an adage that applies to fictions within fictions. The needs of Cymbeline are related to but are not those of Shakespeare, the play, or the audience.

At the very end, Posthumus mentions his dream of Jupiter, which the audience witnessed in the previous scene, and says he cannot make sense of the scroll he found on his chest when he awoke (426f.). On Posthumus' request, the Soothsayer does interpret the riddle that the scroll contains. Like the riddle in *Macbeth*, it is ingenious, but, unlike *Macbeth*, this play explicates the riddle at length in elaborate and, perhaps, contrived ways rather than show the answer to the riddle with a few words of explanation. Shakespeare is calling attention to the medium and to his means of production and may be asking the audience to compare its interpretation with the Soothsayer's. The second explication concerns the public realm, the relations between Britain and Rome, and provides a link with the first, which deals with Posthumus and Imogen. The audience heard the Soothsayer say that his vision portended success to the Romans (IV.ii.346–52). Now he explains the new peace with Rome, yet another repetition, double vision and "double" sign. Just as *Cymbeline* invites the audience to interpret even its gods, so too does *The Winter's Tale*. The end of *Cymbeline*, in both senses, is the beginning of *The Winter's Tale*.

The Winter's Tale

Rather than recapitulate the techniques of alienation that these two romances share, I shall concentrate on how they differ. It is best, however, to show briefly their similarities. Like *Cymbeline*, *The Winter's Tale* has found critics who will defend its stagecraft. In 1958 Nevill Coghill argued with S.L. Bethell (1946) over how sophisticated Shakespeare's dramaturgical sophistication is in *The Winter's Tale*. Whereas Bethell advocated Shakespeare's deliberate "comic underlining of a deliberately crude technique," "a quite conscious return to naive and outmoded technique," Coghill, refuting these suggestions and others like them that the Cambridge editors have made, asserted that "Shakespeare's stage-craft in this play is . . . novel, subtle and revolutionary" and that he has found "a means of entry into the fabulous world of a life standing . . . in the level of dreams."[31] In turn, William Matchett (1969) wanted to build on Coghill's insights and go beyond them, but it seems that Matchett was not as far from Bethell as his conscious association with Coghill would suggest. Matchett's analysis of the bear points, I think, to my own method of looking at *Cymbeline* and *The Winter's Tale*:

> Shakespeare's bear—whether man or bear—is not a way of increasing the realistic effect; it is a way of making the audience aware of the medium, like Rodin's "Hand of God" emerging from the rock of which it is a part, so that one must experience not only the realized form but its relationship to the inchoate rock, or like those canvases of Van Gogh which remind us constantly that whatever has been achieved has been achieved with paint—not with magic but with material. The bear here inevitably reminds us of drama as pretence, insists that a tale is not life but an image of life.[32]

Nor is the debate on the dramaturgy of *The Winter's Tale* dead. In 1983 Andrew Gurr considered the stagecraft crafty: he called the bear and the moving statue "two such extraordinarily crude theatrical tricks," but ruses that make the audience do a double take, responding first in one way and then its opposite, so that the audience experiences what Barthes calls different levels of response.[33]

Like *Cymbeline*, *The Winter's Tale* echoes and transforms the conventions, especially the comic ones, of previous Shakespearean plays. At the same time, the play shares conventions with *Pericles* and *Cymbeline*, although many of these will be transformations of earlier conventions, their configuration makes them romances or tragicomedies. For instance, in *The Winter's Tale*, as in *Cymbeline*, a husband grows jealous and doubts the chastity of his virtuous wife, a servant disobeys an order to murder, a character dies a violent death, characters tell stories, lovers use disguises, oracles and the gods are very present, a parent "blocks" the marriage of his child, rings are used for identification, one or more lost children reappear, and the end is happy. Ultimately, *The Winter's Tale* distinguishes itself as a romance and as a play by the way it translates conventions and gives them a new context.

This play is like a reversal of *Romeo and Juliet*, for it begins as a tragedy and ends as a comedy whereas *Romeo and Juliet* shows the opposite pattern. Just as the stabbing of Mercutio is the fulcrum of *Romeo and Juliet*, so too is the death of Antigonus in *The Winter's Tale*. Both events are tragicomic. As Mercutio acts and jests so much, his friends do not know whether he is dying or playing at death. The turning point of the play occurs after the bear devours Antigonus and the Shepherd finds the infant, Perdita, and declares, "thou met'st with things dying, I with things new-born" (III.iii. 12–13). So the calm of the opening scene changes with Leontes' jealousy, a jealousy swifter than Othello's and with apparently similar results. Leontes has no Iago to goad or delude him. The king does not even have an Iachimo to bait him. Shakespeare calls attention to the shift from pastoral to tragedy through the irrational premise of, the seemingly motiveless change in, Leontes' character. Similarly, the playwright uses the bear and the statue to create conscious knots for the audience's inspection, the first to emphasize the turn from tragedy to comedy, the second to underscore a theatrical miracle or at least miraculous theatre—the awakening of Hermione—which is a variation on a comic ending. To alienate the audience into further thought, Shakespeare yokes narrative with represented scenes and causes some of his characters to refer to art and stories. The two most elaborate examples of this technique are Time, the Chorus, at the beginning of Act Four, scene one, and the long report of Act Five, scene two.

In the opening scene of *The Winter's Tale*, Leontes' jealousy, which through asides he makes known to the audience, begins to break the peace, but it is not until the beginning of Act Two that Hermione discovers what the playgoers already perceive. Through this dramatic irony, the audience considers her virtue and perplexity. Ironically, Leontes interrupts his son's sad tale of winter: Mamillius soon dies—a death that the king later blames on himself as Jupiter is angry with Leontes' jealousy—and his fiction gives way to a larger one (II.i. 21ff., cf. III.ii. 153ff.). Shakespeare also uses the oracle to emphasize the arbitrariness of the jealous king. Leontes looks rational when he wants to substantiate his suspicions of Hermione through Apollo's agency, but when the oracle of Delphos clears Hermione, Polixenes and Camillo, Leontes calls the counsel false and shows himself as stubborn as Lear. On closer inspection, even from the first mention of the oracle, the king reveals that the oracle is merely a tool to convince the credulous of Leontes' truth (II.i. 189–93, III.ii. 140ff.).

A drama of interruption and reversal, *The Winter's Tale* combines dramatic irony and surprise more than *Cymbeline* does. In addition to Leontes' interruption of Mamillius telling his mother a tale, to the king's disruption of his family, the 'deaths' of Mamillius and Hermione interrupt the king's jealousy; Time, the Chorus, halts the representational action with narrative and stands at the point of reversal where tragedy ceases and comedy begins, although a tragic residue colors the second half of the play. In this comic half Polixenes tries to stop the plan his son has to marry Perdita, and the king of Bohemia looks as if he will be as unreasonable as the king of Sicily was at the beginning of the first half (IV.iv. 418). Shakespeare uses repetition with a difference. Camillo resists both kings in their unreason: the parallelism is suggestive and represents another false start, for Autolychus' revelation that Perdita is Leontes' daughter quenches Polixenes' rage as much as the 'deaths' had Leontes'. The playwright asks the audience to consider the limitations of the characters by assessing these parallels. Just as Leontes' irrationality had wronged Polixenes, so too does the irrationality of Polixenes wrong Florizel, and just as one king repents, so too does the other.

The final interruption and reversal comes when Hermione, who was never dead, revives (a resurrection that art, but not life, can effect) and interrupts Leontes' sadness. This revival flaunts the artificiality of the play as well as playing with an irony the theatre affords: a person is playing a character who is supposed to be a statue but, even as Leontes notices, a statue that has trouble not breathing. He says, "Still methinks / There is an air comes from her. What fine chisel / Could ever yet cut breath?" (V.iii.77–79). Such a self-conscious allusion to the relation of art to life invites criticism from the audience, and shows the limitations of art. Only living creatures can breathe. The sculpture is not, though the Third

Gentleman says so, the creation of Julio Romano but the invention of Paulina (and ultimately of Shakespeare): it is art that is not art (V.ii.93–103; cf. V.v.). The audience experiences dramatic irony when the Third Gentleman praises the statue for its realism, for its "breath." Shakespeare questions realistic art as much in this play as in *Cymbeline*.

By yoking the representation of strange events with narration, the playwright achieves an alienation effect. Shakespeare creates conscious knots when the bear chases Antigonus and then the Chorus narrates the sliding of 16 years and when the gentlemen discuss the discovery of Perdita and the reunion of Leontes and Polixenes and then the statue comes to life. Whether the bear was originally a man or a tame animal from the baiting pit next door to the Globe or whether the bear is tragic or comic or tragicomic, it is curious on stage and may have been popular with the audience, for Pafford notes that whereas in the version of 1598 *Mucedorus* contained only a bear's head, in the version of 1610 it included a white bear. Similarly, in Jonson's *Masque of Oberon*, first performed in 1611, two white bears drew a chariot.[34] The audience, then, would be focusing on the bear on stage, would not forget the death of Antigonus and would be, through this device, increasingly aware of the shift in the play (III.iii. 58ff.). The words of the Shepherd about death and life and the speech of the Chorus follow within eighty lines and emphasize both the shift from tragedy to comedy and the strangeness of the events and the theatre that produces them.

Like the choruses in *Romeo and Juliet*, *Henry V*, *Troilus and Cressida*, and *Pericles*, the Chorus in *The Winter's Tale* shows the tension between showing and telling, between representation and narrative. Although these choruses share this tension, they differ in their purpose. In *Romeo and Juliet*, the Prologue is a sonnet that announces a love story; in *Troilus and Cressida* it is a prelude that sets the scene and announces the beginning of the action *in medias res*. Both *Henry V* and *Pericles* begin each act with a chorus and emphasize especially the discontinuities between narrative and representation, for the action of the plays qualifies what the choruses say. If the Chorus of *Henry V* asks, "Can this cockpit hold / The vasty fields of France?" (Prologue, 11–12), the Chorus in *The Winter's Tale*, appropriately called Time, has to announce the sliding of 16 years (IV.i.). Time self-consciously identifies himself. This Chorus says he tries all things, joy and terror, good and bad, and, in some ways, the whole play attempts the same thing. Both the Chorus and the play, in the words of Time itself, are able "To o'erthrow law, and in one self-born hour / To plant and o'erwhelm custom" (IV: Chorus: 8–9, see 7). Time speaks of the 16 years as that "wide gap," and Leontes, after discovering Hermione alive, says,

> Good Paulina,
> Lead us from hence, where we may leisurely
> Each one demand, and answer to his part
> Perform'd in this wide gap of time, since first
> We were dissever'd: hastily lead away. (V.iii.151–55)

Shakespeare yokes the Chorus with the end of the play and emphasizes the power and problems of art in time, thus enabling the audience to understand better this play and the drama in general.

So the bear, the Chorus, the narrative of the gentlemen, and the "enlivening" of the statue relate closely to one another. The playwright flaunts the conventions of his comedies: rather than show the reconciliation of parents and children as well as the joining of lovers, Shakespeare causes Autolychus and the three gentlemen to report these events (V.ii). Besides saving Shakespeare dramatic time and letting him concentrate on the "revival" of Hermione, this narrative has another purpose. The audience should compare the effects of the strange events reported and the strange event revealed and by doing so will discover the differences between the action and the means of production. Hermione's pretended death and resurrection have Shakespearean precedents: Hero is reported dead and revives at the end of *Much Ado About Nothing* when her honor is restored; in *All's Well That Ends Well* there are rumors of Helena's death and she finds a type of new life; Claudio, in *Measure for Measure,* is said to have died but, through Duke Vincentio's agency, reveals himself to be alive in the final scene. These deaths and "rebirths" do, however, involve disguises whereas Hermione's resurrection involves art. She is and is not a statue. Her acting requires a different technique from those characters who conceal their identities behind clothes. Shakespeare hopes to break the laws of life in his art and, like Time, to overthrow human law and custom. Hermione's revival shows the wonder of art by revealing the art itself, the primary objective of the alienation effect in *The Winter's Tale.*

Transitions and Conclusions

Cymbeline and *The Winter's Tale* both use the alienation effect to show the miracle of theatre and the theatricality of miracle, but although they share the uses of alienation, they also employ these effects with a difference. Both plays use their dramaturgy to make the audience critical of the relation between art and life and of the theatre itself, and both employ dramatic irony to alienate the audience. Through experiment, these plays give an alternative to realistic art. Neither do they merely echo the comedies: their wonder is not the wonder of *Much Ado About Nothing* and *Twelfth Night* that Dolora Cunningham has described.[35] The endings of these two romances differ from each other. Whereas *Cymbeline* uses the dramatic irony of recapitulation, *The Winter's Tale* uses the surprise of unlikely revival. These plays are not Aristotelian, but this discovery is not as surprising as Brecht and Barthes might find it, for in *The Defence of Poesie* Philip Sidney turns Aristotle on his ear, placing poets above philosophers. Sidney also defends the golden world of the imagination and says that art can improve on nature. Even though the author of *The Arcadia* did not think highly of the drama of his day, had he lived to see *Cymbeline* and *The Winter's Tale* he would, I think, have approved precisely because they do what nature cannot, because they are not realistic.

As England expanded tentatively in the shadow of the power of Spain, its writers were able to create a dynamic literature, as, by the way, the Spaniards were also doing. It is not easy to say why, but by examining closely the language of theory, criticism and literature and its contexts, I hope to have shown the richness of Marlowe, Greene, and others and of works that do not always receive the same attention. Greene's *Pandosto* is a case in point. Shakespeare and his contemporaries were not always concerned to be realistic in the sense of what some in the late nineteenth and first half of the twentieth century might have thought appropriate. When Shakespearean criticism professionalized, naturalism and realism were in their ascendency. Thus, with the growth of professional Shakespearean and Renaissance critics and editors inside the universities, there were discussions, among others, about Shakespeare's problem comedies or problem plays and there was a sense among some critics that his later plays were a dissipation of his tragic and comic energies into tragicomedy. Marlowe's overreaching, Greene's turn to romance, the ends of Renaissance comedy in England and on the Continent, the relation between theory and practice, the connection between narrative and drama, the link between story and history, and the way drama represents history all suggest that representations of the world are not in a thin band but draw on multifold poetics and rhetoric and an array of genres. There is not one way to show and tell about the world, and I have attempted to unfold some of the richness and the variety. Shakespeare and his contemporaries drew on the ancients and their predecessors in Renaissance Europe and on themselves and they had a great effect on their successors. One of the themes of some of the chapters, especially of the ends of Renaissance comedy and this chapter, is about ends, the motives and endings of comic plays, some of which we now call romances or tragicomedies. This subsequent reception of Shakespeare in context is something I return to in the Conclusion.

Conclusion

In his Introduction, Edmund Gosse describes Algernon Swinburne's devotion to the Elizabethan and Jacobean writers and how he came to put together a posthumous volume of Swinburne's on the topic.[1] Swinburne himself speaks highly of Christopher Marlowe: "The father of English tragedy and the creator of English blank verse was therefore also the teacher and the guide of Shakespeare."[2] Swinburne combines an appreciation of Marlowe with an offering to Shakespeare: "It has not always been duly remarked, it is not now always duly remembered, by students of the age of Shakespeare that Marlowe is the one and only precursor of that veritable king of kings and lord of lords among all writers and all thinkers of all time."[3] This is an Arnoldian displacement of religion to poetry and echo of the Chorus in Part 2 of the libretto to Handel's *Messiah* (itself an echo of Revelation 19:16). Here, Christ becomes Shakespeare or Shakespeare becomes Christ. Although Swinburne thinks Lily, Greene, Peele, Nashe, and Lodge to be "true though not great poets, who blundered into playwrighting"; he has a high opinion of the prose style of Robert Greene and his contemporaries: "Lily, Nash, and Greene, were writers of prose which it would be difficult to overpraise if we had here to consider the finest work of Greene in romantic fiction, of Nash and Lily in controversial satire."[4] Swinburne ranges from these writers through detailed accounts of George Chapman, Beaumont, and Fletcher (their early plays) to discussions of later writers like Philip Massinger, John Day, Robert Davenport, Thomas Nabbes, Richard Brome, and James Shirley. My own account differs from the one Gosse helped to assemble after Swinburne's death as I have integrated Shakespeare into the discussion and context and I have also placed him in a wider European literary and historical context that puts England within Europe and the world. I have also expanded Shakespeare's contexts and "contemporaries" backward and forward beyond what Gosse did with Swinburne, and I did all this oblivious, until the end of my writing, of Swinburne's collection. When I came across it, I had long changed my book's title from *Shakespeare and Company* for obvious reasons, and not simply because of Sylvia Beach's famous bookshop in Paris and its connection with the printing of James Joyce's *Ulysses*. My new title, I had discovered, and this is something that happens to anyone writing on Shakespeare, had been used in a similar form before by Gosse.

But my book is Shakespeare *and* his contemporaries, so there is some difference. My tone may be a little less of a votary and a late Romantic, although I admire Shakespeare and the writers of his time and I have my share of idealism in the broken wheel of the world. But Swinburne is dramatic and flowery, as sometimes was his age, and so historical difference shows once more that the subsequent reception of Shakespeare's contemporaries has also something to do with the interpretations that I and others now offer.

For a moment, I shall back up from Swinburne's time. In England during the eighteenth century, ambivalence marks many responses to Shakespeare. John Dennis declares, "If *Shakeſprear* had theſe great Qualities by Nature, what would he not have been, if he had join'd ſo happy a Genius Learning and the Poetical Art."[5] A little beforehand, Dennis had praised Shakespeare's natural discretion and strong and penetrating judgment and explains his ignorance of the "Rules" as owing to lack of "Time and Leiſure for Thought."[6] Lewis Theobald, signing his preface in March 1725, writes in his Introduction about his wish for a genius to befriend the memory of Shakespeare, the immortal poet, "and contribute to the Pleaſure of the preſent and of future Times, in retrieving, as far as poſſible, the *original Purity* of his *Text*, and rooting out that vaſt Crop of *Errors*, which has almoſt choak'd up his *Beauties*."[7] This quest for the original text has been a long labor of Shakespearean scholarship, one that has in recent decades been called into question. The debate between Alexander Pope and Theobald over whether to emend or not is still with us. In this controversy of the early eighteenth century, Shakespeare is a genius with flaws left for the world to see or a genius who can be improved in search of a more sensible or comprehensible poet. At the opening of his study of Shakespeare, John Upton, in 1746, puts it well in the spirit of the general truths that are so eloquently stated in that age: "'Tis a common obſervation, and therefore perhaps not altogether untrue, that critics generally ſet out with theſe two maxims; the one, that the author muſt always dictate what is *beſt*; the other, that the critic is to determine what that *beſt* is."[8] Upton answers those, like Theobald, who consider Shakespeare's learning to be deficient: "I HAVE often wonder'd with what kind of reaſoning any one could be ſo far impoſed on, as to imagine that Shakeſpeare had no learning; when it muſt at the ſame time be acknowledged, that without learning, he cannot be red with any degree of underſtanding, or taſt."[9] Shakespeare's learning in relation to the taste of a later age is a concern of many eighteenth-century commentators on him. In 1749, Elizabeth Montagu defends Shakespeare from Voltaire's charges of barbarism and wonders how Corneille and French romances can be exempt from a similar criticism. She also dismisses the Aristotelian unities as a mark of good drama, takes into account cultural and historical differences, praises Shakespeare above all others for his "giving an air of reality to every thing" by rising above the ignorance and barbarism of his time, admits the superiority of the culture and theatre audience of the Athens of Sophocles and Euripides, and appeals to nature and sentiment in seeing Shakespeare's genius while appealing to judgment and taste to admit his faults.[10] Later, in 1777, Joseph Baretti, a secretary for foreign correspondence of the British Royal Society, calls into question Voltaire's knowledge of English and his authorship of his work on Shakespeare.[11] Shakespeare in a European context becomes complicated. In 1765, Samuel Johnson talks about comparison, something that a book on Shakespeare and his contemporaries must address implicitly and explicitly, and shows that Shakespeare compares favorably and thus endures, becoming, like Euripides and Homer, ancients who have established their worth through the comparisons others have made to them over time. For Johnson, "Shakeſpeare is above all writers, at leaſt above all modern writers, the poet of nature; the poet that holds up to his readers a faithful mirror of manners and of life."[12] Hamlet himself uses this image of the mirror for the poet, and Beaumont, Milton and others from 1615 to the 1670s and beyond, call Shakespeare a poet of nature before Johnson does. Richard Farmer (third edition, 1789) defends Shakespeare from those critics who would pick up on Ben Jonson's comments in the First Folio (1623) on Shakespeare's knowledge of Greek and Latin that would make him one of the illiterate or, in Cervantes' terms, the braying faction.[13] On March 10, 1790, Edmund Malone writes to John Jordan, a poet, about the life and documents of Shakespeare and his family, which shows a keen interest in the biography of the playwright.[14]

In the nineteenth century, the attitude to Shakespeare often became more unambiguously positive and even laudatory. In "A Course of Lectures," Samuel Taylor Coleridge writes about the importance of literary topics for "higher and middle classes of English society."[15] For Coleridge, England must be seen in the context of Europe and that is how he organizes his course of lectures. Although Coleridge begins his 14 lectures with the classical past and the Middle Ages in northern Europe and Gothic literature and art, as he calls it, he discusses the troubadours, Boccaccio, Petrarch, Pulci, Chaucer, and Spenser. Coleridge then examines Ben Jonson, Beaumont and Fletcher, and Massinger, praising, for instance, the originality of Jonson as being untouched by Shakespeare, whom he calls "our great master in every thing."[16] Coleridge has the happy view of English literature being a European literature and assumes that the English should be exposed to Continental works as well. This is the spirit in which I wrote *Shakespeare and His Contemporaries*. Shakespeare is of England, Europe and the wider world. Coleridge discusses Cervantes' *Don Quixote* and then the humor of Rabelais, Swift and Sterne; the poetry of Donne, Dante, and Milton; Asian and Greek mythologies, Robinson Crusoe and the imagination in education; dreams, apparitions, and alchemists; and on style. This is the comparative method that Samuel Johnson talked about. Still, in *Literary Remains*, put together by his nephew, Coleridge uses a different model than I do because he writes most about Shakespeare separately, in the extensive "Shakspeare, with Introductory Matter on Poetry, the Drama, and the Stage," which appears side by side with fairly long distinct notes on the works of Jonson and of Beaumont and Fletcher.[17] The Romantic language of Coleridge's high praise joins some of the great but ambivalent laudation by eighteenth-century writers: "Clothed in radiant armour, and authorized by titles sure and manifold, as a poet, Shakspeare came forward to demand the throne of fame, as the dramatic poet of England. His excellencies compelled even his contemporaries to seat him on that throne, although there were giants in those days contending for the same honor."[18] Toward the end of the nineteenth century this Romantic vision of Shakespeare could sometimes yield to something more demythologized, for instance, in the work of Henry Lee. In his preface to his biography of 1898, Lee writes, "Æsthetic studies of Shakespeare abound, and to increase their number is a work of supererogation. But Shakespearean literature, as far as it is known to me, still lacks a book that shall supply within a brief compass an exhaustive and well-arranged statement of the facts of Shakespeare's career, achievement, and reputation, that shall reduce conjecture to the smallest dimensions consistent with coherence, and shall give verifiable references to all original sources of information."[19] Replacing conjecture with scholarship is an aim of Shakespearean studies, and might well have been influenced not just by the editing of plays but by German scholarship and changes within the universities toward professionalization. This changing context seems also to have percolated into the community of writers working outside the universities in Britain and North America. The age of scholarship was upon us. The twentieth century, even more than the late nineteenth century, produced an array of studies, biographies, and editions of Shakespeare and his contemporaries.

Interest in Shakespeare, as well as his contemporaries, spread beyond England early. The great American fascination with Shakespeare and the Renaissance had material consequences that gathered momentum first with James Lenox (1800–1880) of New York, whom Sidney Lee saw as a pioneer in the westward movement of book collecting.[20] In 1850, Ralph Waldo Emerson's *Representative Men*, including Plato, Swedenborg, Montaigne, Shakespeare, Napoleon, and Goethe, was published. For Emerson, Shakespeare was the representative poet as Goethe was the representative writer. According to Emerson, who thinks that originality, the spinning of something from oneself, is overrated in the estimation of the great: "Shakspeare knew that tradition supplies a better fable than any invention can."[21] His view is that innovation through a use of the past is the way of Shakespeare. In a manuscript of his book, *Shakespeare on the Continent*, Justin Winsor, a historian who trained at Harvard and studied at Paris and Heidelberg and was later the librarian at Harvard College from 1877, had an outward view of Shakespeare, including German contributions to Shakespearean criticism: "Shakespeare's native land hardly possesses a more learned commentator than Ludwig Tieck, and none has proclaimed so startling a discovery, as he did, when he announced that Shakespeare's plays were known and even played in Germany during the dramatist's life-time."[22] Shakespeare was becoming a more and more major figure on the Continent and across the Atlantic. Like Swinburne, Joseph Howe, in Halifax in British North America, for the three-hundredth anniversary of the birth of Shakespeare in 1864, begins his speech with the birth of Jesus of Nazareth, moves to the birth of Robert Burns and then to Shakespeare, to show that the humble have left more and are more remembered than most kings and emperors. Howe sees Shakespeare as the genius of England, a greater writer than the ancients and modern dramatists of Europe, and something of pride for the British Empire and all British peoples, including those in Boston and the United States generally.[23] The greatest period of Anglo-American expansion was occurring, and Shakespeare works, *Pilgrim's Progress*, and the Bible were all part of that expansion in the hands, pockets, and bags of the migrants. At the end of the 1800s, on July 13, 1899, Monsieur Jules Claretie, an academician, delivered a lecture at the Lyceum Theatre in London, entitled *Shakspere and Molière*. Claretie describes his stroll to the Comédie Française morning after morning where he passes by a statue of Shakespeare and another of Molière, "of the Great Tragedian and the Great Comedian."[24] This *A et B* or A-and-B comparison became a landmark of comparative literature in French. Whether one can discount the comic abilities of Shakespeare or the darker side of Molière is beside the point, it is the contextual and comparative spirit of studying Shakespeare and his contemporaries that is impressive.

It is in this vein that I wrote my book, and while others have approached this task with great effect, they have, by necessity, taken their own approach and made their own parameters. I have sought to place England in context as a more vulnerable state than the triumphant one of the victors over the Spanish Armada, have decentered Shakespeare in Europe and the wider world, not because, he lacks greatness and talent, but partly because he becomes a poet of the English tongue and of Europe as it expanded into the world. By now people of all religions and backgrounds, secular or not, have a chance to read or hear Shakespeare in the original or translation, or to see his plays on film, and so Shakespeare is of England and beyond. He also had dynamic contemporaries like Marlowe, Greene, Jonson, and others, who in their own right contributed to the language, literature, and culture of England and elsewhere. In some ways, the ancients and moderns were Shakespeare's teachers, and others just after him and then in subsequent ages become his contemporaries and not. We are, in Jan Kott's sense, Shakespeare's contemporaries and not. He and we live in a world of language, of writing and reading, and a drama of meaning or asymptotic semantics that ever approach and never arrive, and in narrative and drama, theory and practice, we experience word and world. Rhetoric, poetics, and genre have a history and also communicate across time, and as past and present meet, we all come together and contend as individuals and groups in a search for knowledge and pleasure so often located in the tension between other and I and expressed through action, character, and thought. And in this change each seeks to change and sometimes would wish to change change itself.

Notes

Introduction

1. Jan Kott, *Shakespeare, Our Contemporary*, trans. Boleslaw Taborski (Garden City, NY: Doubleday, 1964).
2. For more on the Cambridge of Greene and Marlowe and beyond, see the most recent history of the university, G. R. Evans, *The University of Cambridge: A New History* (London: I. B. Tauris, 2009). For a more detailed analysis of Renaissance Cambridge, see *A History of the University of Cambridge. Vol. I The University to 1546*, gen. ed. C. N. L. Brooke and ed. Damian Riehl Leader (Cambridge: Cambridge University Press, 1988), and *A History of the University of Cambridge, Vol. II. 1546–1750*, ed. Victor Morgan (Cambridge: Cambridge University Press, 2004). For Oxford, see Charles Mallet, *A History of the University of Oxford*, 3 vols. (London: Methuen, 1924–27), and *The Illustrated History of Oxford University*, ed. John Prest (Oxford: Oxford University Press, 1993). An important examination of both universities during this period is M. H. Curtis, *Oxford and Cambridge in Transition, 1558–1642* (Oxford: Clarendon, 1959).
3. For perceptive discussions of gender and empire and in a comparative western European context, including a discussion of Elizabeth Cary, see Margaret W. Ferguson, *Dido's Daughters: Literacy, Gender, and Empire in Early Modern England and France* (Chicago: University of Chicago Press, 2004).
4. On empire, see, for instance, Anthony Pagden, *Peoples and Empires: Europeans and the Rest of the World, from Antiquity to the Present* (London: Weidenfeld & Nicholson, 2001), and Jonathan Hart, *Empires and Colonies* (Cambridge: Polity Press, 2008).
5. Rhetoric is a key to western education, and this is true from the Middle Ages to the Enlightenment. See, for instance, *Renaissance Rhetoric Short-Title Catalogue 1460–1700*, 2nd ed., ed. Lawrence D. Green and James J. Murphy (Aldershot, UK: Ashgate, 2006).
6. See Aristotle, *Aristotle: Poetics and Longinus*, ed. and trans. W. Hamilton Fyfe, and *Demetrius on Style*, ed. and trans. W. Rhys Roberts [1927] (London: Heinemann, 1932, rpt. 1946).
7. For historians who use story in history brilliantly, see Natalie Zemon Davis, Carlo Ginzburg, and Robert Darnton.
8. See Jacques Derrida, *L'Écriture et la différence* (Paris: Seuil, 1967), and Gérard Genette, *Narrative Discourse Revisited*, trans. J. E. Lewin (Ithaca, NY: Cornell University

Press, 1988). See also Thomas G. Pavel, *Fictional Worlds* (Cambridge, MA: Harvard University Press, 1986), and his "Narrative Tectonics," *Poetics* 11 (1990): 349–64.

9. My fullest and most accessible argument for irony in the Second Tetralogy is in *Theater and World: The Problematics of Shakespeare's History* (Boston: Northeastern University Press, 1992).

10. William Shakespeare, *Mr. William Shakespeares Comedies, Histories & Tragedies, Publiſhed according to the True Originall Copies* (London: Printed by Iſaac Jaggard and Ed. Blount, 1623), A6r.

11. Harry Levin was apt in entitling his study *The Overreacher: A Study of Christopher Marlowe* (Cambridge, MA: Harvard University Press, 1952).

Chapter 1

1. Thanks to my graduate class in Shakespeare and Empire at the University of Alberta for helping to explore themes in this field.

2. Another angle for the importance of Spain can be seen in Albert Loomeie, *The Spanish Elizabethan: English Exiles at the Court of Philip II* (London: Burns & Oates, 1963). See also Peter Holmes, *Resistance and Compromise: The Political Thought of Elizabethan Catholics* (Cambridge: Cambridge University Press, 1982), and Antonia Fraser, *The Gunpowder Plot: Treason and Faith in 1605* (London: Weidenfeld & Nicolson, 1996).

3. For recent work on comparative studies of empire or of global empire, see Michael Hardt and Antonio Negri, *Empire* (Cambridge, MA: Harvard University Press, 2000); Anthony Pagden, *Peoples and Empires: Europeans and the Rest of the World, from Antiquity to the Present* (London: Weidenfeld & Nicholson, 2001); and Jonathan Hart, *Empires and Colonies* (Cambridge: Polity Press, 2008). For more specific recent works on European expansion and empire in this period, see Peter C. Herman, "'We All Smoke Here': Behn's *The Widdow Ranter* and the Invention of American Identity," *Envisioning an English Empire: Jamestown and the Making of the North Atlantic World*, ed. Robert Appelbaum and John Wood Sweet (Philadelphia, PA; University of Pennsylvania Press, 2005), 254–74; Stewart Mottram, "'An Empire of Itself': Arthur as Icon of an English Empire, 1509–1547," *Arthurian Literature* 25 (2008): 153–73.

4. This section has some overlap with chapter 4 of my *Comparing Empires: European Colonialism from Portuguese Expansion to the Spanish-American War* (New York: Palgrave Macmillan, 2003).

5. See Anthony Farrington, *Trading Places: The East India Company and Asia 1600–1834* (London: The British Library, 2002), 10–19.

6. Farrington, *Trading Places*, 17–22, 34–39. See Richard Hakluyt, *Discourse of Western Planting*, ed. David B. Quinn and Alison M. Quinn (London: Hakluyt Society, 1993), 28, 31.

7. Farrington, *Trading Places*, 41–47.

8. Ibid., 48.

9. Ibid., 48–53.

10. Thanks to the students in my class in slavery at the University of Alberta. This brief section overlaps with some material in chapter 5 of *Contesting Empires: Opposition, Promotion, and Slavery* (New York: Palgrave Macmillan, 2005).

11. Jean Alfonse, *Les voyages avantureux,* quoted in Jean-Paul Duviols, *L'Amérique espagnole vue et rêvée. Les livres de voyages de Christophe Colomb à Bougainville* (Paris: Promodis, 1985), 183, note 23; my translation. For Duviols' view, see ibid.

12. André Thevet, *La Cosmographie vniverselle d'André Thevet cosmographe dv roy* (Paris, Chez P. L'Huilier, 1575), vol. 2, bk. 1, ch. 11, fol. 498, verso; see A. C. de C. M. Saunders, *A Social History of Black Slaves and Freedmen in Portugal 1441–1555* (Cambridge: Cambridge University Press, 1982), 11–12, 33.

13. Jean de Léry, *History of a Voyage to the Land of Brazil*, trans. and introduction by Janet Whatley (Berkeley: University of California Press, 1990), 9, see 4.

14. C. R. Boxer, *The Dutch in Brazil, 1624–1654* (Oxford: Clarendon Press, 1957), 106–10.

15. Patricia Seed, *Ceremonies of Possession* (Cambridge: Cambridge University Press, 1995). For a discussion of the *Requerimento*, and the *encomiendas*, which were not feudatories like the lands granted in the French colonies other quasi-independent occupation in English America, see Anthony Pagden, *Lords of all the World: Ideologies of Empire in Spain, Britain, and France c. 1500–c.1800* (New Haven, CT: Yale University Press, 1995), 91.

16. There is a brief overlap here with chapter 3 of my book, *Shakespeare, Columbus, and the Interpretation of the New World* (New York: Palgrave Macmillan, 2003).

17. Hugh Honour, *The New Golden Land: European Images of America from the Discoveries to the present Time* (1975; London: Allen Lane, 1976), 22–24; see Hugh Honour, *The European Vision of America* (Cleveland: Cleveland Museum of Art, 1975), 30–32. For an extended discussion, see James Snyder, "Jan Mostaert's West Indies Landscape," in *First Images of America: The Impact of the New World on the Old*, ed. Fredi Chiapelli, Michael J. B. Allen, and Robert L. Benson (Berkeley: University of California Press, 1976), vol. 1, 495–502. Snyder favors Coronado's expedition of 1540 as the subject of Mostaert's painting. For this theme in literature, see Arthur Lovejoy and George Boas, *Primitivism and Related Ideas in Antiquity* (Baltimore, MD: Johns Hopkins University Press, 1935), and Harry Levin, *The Myth of the Golden Age in the Renaissance* (Bloomington: University of Indiana Press, 1969).

18. Honour, *The New Golden Land*, 52–53. This map is in the collection of the British Library, Department of Manuscripts.

19. For an accessible image and description, see *Encountering the New World, 1493–1800*. Catalogue of an exhibition by Susan Danforth; introductory essay by William H. McNeill (Providence, RI: John Carter Brown Library, 1991), 18.

20. John Parker, *Books to Build an Empire: A Bibliographical History of English Overseas Interests to 1620* (Amsterdam, 1965), 21–23. For *Of the new landes . . .*, see Edward Arber, ed. *The first Three English books on America [?1511]–1555 A.D. . . .* (Westminster: A. Constable and Co., 1895), xxiii–xxxvi.

21. Ibid., C1r.

22. On Belleforest and Thevet, see Olive P. Dickason, "Thevet and Belleforest: Two Sixteenth-Century Frenchmen and New World Colonialism," *Proceedings of the Annual Meeting of the French Colonial Society* 16 (1992): 1–11.

23. Thevet uses the phrase "cruels jusques au bout;" André Thevet, *La Cosmographie Vniverselle D'André Thevet Cosmographe dv Roy . . . Tome Second* (Paris, Chez P. L'Huilier 1575), in *Les Français en Amérique pendant la deuxième moitié du XVIe Siècle: Le Brésil et les Brésiliens*, ed. Charles-André Julien, notes by Suzanne Lussagnet, 2 vols. (Paris: P. U. F., 1958), vol. II, 29.

24. Francisco López de Gómara, *Histoire Generalle des Indes Occidentales et Terres Nevves, qui iusques à present ont estre descouuertes. Traduite en françois par M. Fumee Sieur de Marly le Chatel* (Paris: M. Sonnius, 1578), A4v; my translation.

25. Urbain Chauveton, "Sommaire," *Histoire Novvelle dv Novveav Monde, Contenant en somme ce que les Hespagnols ont fait iusqu'à present aux Indes Occidentales, & le rude traitement qu'ils ont fait à ces poures peuples-la* (Geneva: Par Evstace Vignon,

1579), [no signature] 1v. *Brief Discours* and *Requeste au roy* are numbered together and continuously after Benzoni's work, which was first published in Italian in 1565. For a discussion of Chauveton, see Benjamin Keen, "The Vision of America in the Writings of Urbain Chauveton," in *First Images of America: The Impact of the New World on the Old*, ed. Fredi Chiapelli, et al. 2 vols. (Berkeley : University of California Press, 1976), vol. I, 107–20.

26. Urbain Chauveton, "Sommaire," *Brief Discours et histoire d'vn voyage de qvelqves François en Floride . . .* (Paris: Vignon, 1579), [no signature] 1v. My translation of Chauveton here.

27. Richard Hakluyt, *The Principall Navigations . . .* (London: George Bishop, 1589); the actual Latin inscription is "AMERICA SIVE IN DIA NOVA Ao 1492 a Christophoro Colombo nomine regis Castelle primum detecta." "Noua Francia" appears to the east.

28. John Smith, *New Englands Trials . . .*, 2nd ed. (London: William Iones, 1622), in *Tracts and Other Papers, Origin, Settlement, and Progress of the Colonies in North America, from the Discovery of the Country to the Year 1776*, collected by Peter Force, 4 vols. (Washington: P. Force, 1836–46), vol. II, 23.

29. Ibid., vol. II, 809.

30. Walter Ralegh, *The Discoverie of the Large, Rich, and Bevvtifvl Empyre of Gviana, with a Relation of the Great and Golden Citie of Manoa (which the Spanyards call El Dorado . . .)* (London: Robert Robinson, 1596), 99. Copy available at Princeton.

31. See Jonathan Hart, *Representing the New World* (New York: Palgrave 2001).

32. For a discussion of this point, see chapter 4 of my *Comparing Empires* (2003).

33. See Jonathan Hart, *Shakespeare: Poetry, History, and Culture* (New York: Palgrave Macmillan, 2009). For interesting groundbreaking work in the field of gender and poetics, see Annette Kolodny, *The Lay of the Land* (Chapel Hill: University of North Carolina Press, 1975); Nancy Vickers, "Diana Described: Scattered Woman and Scattered Rhyme," *Critical Inquiry* 8 (1981): 265–79; Patricia Parker, *Literary Fat Ladies: Rhetoric, Gender, Property* (London: Methuen, 1987).

34. See chapter 4 of my *Shakespeare, Columbus, and the Interpretation of the New World* (New York: Palgrave, 2003). There is some overlap here (in much briefer form) with that chapter.

35. See Jean-Paul Duviols, *L'Amérique espagnole vue et rêvée. Les livres de voyages de Christophe Colomb à Bougainville* (Paris: Promodis, 1985), 43–44. He mentions a few classical examples.

36. Antonio de Herrera, "The Voyage of Francisco de Orellana down the River of the Amazons," from the sixth decade of his "General History of the West Indies," Book IX, in *Expeditions into the Valley of the Amazons*, trans. and ed. Clements R. Markham (London: Hakluyt Society, 1859).

37. Ibid., 122.

38. Ibid., 126.

39. Ibid. This collection also contains an extract from the second part of Garcilaso de la Vega's *Royal Commentaries*, but it has no references to women and Amazons.

40. Title page of Abraham Ortelius' *Theatrum Orbis Terrarum* (Antwerp, 1570). Bibliothèque Nationale. The first painting of America as woman is in a fresco at the palace at Caprarola, near Rome, built for Cardinal Alessandro Farnese (1574). Engraving by Etienne Delaune, of the Fontainebleu School (1575). Bibliothèque Nationale. Illus. in Honour, no. 76. Jost Amman (Swiss). Prints of the 4 continents as landscapes with figures (1577). Bibliothèque Nationale. Philippe Galle (Flemish); a print (1581). Bibliothèque Nationale. Illus. in Honour, no.77.[Works by Philippe

Galle also in Lynn Glaser, *America on Paper*, Philadelphia: Associated Antiquaries, 1989, pp. 136 and 165].

41. No 86, "Vespucci Discovering America." Jan van der Street, called Stradamus. Pen and ink, 1589. NY Metropolitan Museum of Art. Other less highly finished drawings in the Biblioteca Laurenziana, Florence (cod. pal. 75). No. 87. Plaquette: "America." Germany 1580–1590. Lead with gilt. NY Metropolitan Museum of Art.; no. 92. "America." Marcus Gheerarts. Engraving ca. 1590–1600, NY Metropolitan Museum of Art, no. 93. One of 11 playing cards representing parts of America. Stefano de Bella. Etchings, 1644. NY Metropolitan Museum of Art.; NY Metropolitan Museum of Art. - 95. "America." Nicolaes (or Claes) Berchem. Black chalk and ink, 1640–50. NY Metropolitan Museum of Art. This book has many eighteenth-century representations of America as a woman.

42. Title page of Abraham Ortelius' *Theatrum Orbis Terrarum* (Antwerp, 1570). Bibliothèque Nationale. Finally, Honour gives information on the representation of America as a woman in royal festivals and spectacles. He expands on the fact that many of these images had wide diffusion in books, or transposed onto tiles or tankards. He also cites many eighteenth-century representations of America as a woman.

43. See Julián Juderías, *La Leyenda Negra* (Madrid: San Lorenzo de El Escorial, 1914); Rómulo D. Carbia, *Historia de la Leyenda Negra Hispano-Americana* (Buenos Aires: Ediciones Orientación Española, 1943); Manuel Cardenal, "La Leyenda Negra," *Diccionario de Historia de España*, 2 vols. (Madrid: Revista de Occidente, 1952), vol. II, 231; Ignacio Escobar López, *La Leyenda Blanca* (Madrid: Ediciones Cultura Hispánica, 1953). The discussion on Spain below overlaps briefly with material from my *Representing the New World: French and English Uses of the Example of Spain* (New York: Palgrave, 2001). For other discussions of this topic, see Benjamin Keen, "The Black Legend Revisited: Assumptions and Realities," *Hispanic American Historical Review* 49 (1969): 703–19; William S. Maltby, *The Black Legend in England: The Development of Anti-Spanish Sentiment, 1558–1660* (Durham, NC: Duke University Press, 1971); Roberto Fernandez Retamar, "Against the Black Legend," *Ideologies and Literature: A Journal of Hispanic and Luso-Brazilian Studies* 2 (1979): 16–35; Gordon A. Kinder, "Creation of the Black Legend: Literary Contributions of Spanish Protestant Exiles," *Mediterranean Studies* 9 (1996): 67–78; Chris Schmidt-Nowara, "'This Rotting Corpse': Spain between the Black Atlantic and the Black Legend," *Arizona Journal of Hispanic Cultural Studies* 5 (2001): 149–60; J. H. Forse, "How 'Black' Was the 'Black Legend' in Elizabethan England?" *SRASP* 25 (2002): 13–33; Maria DeGuzman, *Spain's Long Shadow: the Black Legend, Off-Whiteness, and Anglo-American Empire* (Minneapolis: University of Minnesota Press, 2005); Samuel Amago, "Why Spaniards Make Good Bad Guys: Sergi Lopez and the Persistence of the Black Legend in Contemporary European Cinema," *Film Criticism* 30 (2005): 41–63; Elizabeth Heale, "The *De Navigatione* of Stephen Parmenius of Buda, Old World Barbarism and the Spanish 'Black Legend,'" in *Writing the Other: Humanism versus Barbarism in Tudor England*, ed. Zsolt Almasi and Mike Pincombe (Newcastle upon Tyne, UK: Cambridge Scholars, 2008), 136–58; Linda Bradley Salamon, "Gascoigne's Globe: The Spoyle of Antwerpe and the Black Legend of Spain," *Early Modern Literary Studies: A Journal of Sixteenth- and Seventeenth-Century English Literature* 14 (2008), electronic edition; and Eric Griffin, "Nationalism, the Black Legend, and the Revised Spanish Tragedy," *English Literary Renaissance* 39 (2009): 336–70.

44. In Sverker Arnoldsson, *La Leyenda Negra: Estudios Sobra sus Orígenes* (Göteburg: Almqvist & Wiksell, 1960), 8.

45. Lewis Hanke, *Bartolomé de Las Casas: An Interpretation of his Life and Writings* (The Hague: Nijhoff, 1951), 1, 43–44, 55.
46. Philippe Du Plessis-Mornay, "Discours au roy Henri III sur les moyens de diminuer l'Espagnol" (1584), in *Mémoire et correspondence*, 12 vols. (Paris: Treuttel et Wurtz, 1824–25), vol. II, 590. For a discussion of Du Plessis-Mornay in the context of "Protestant geopolitics," see Frank Lestringant, *Le Huguenot et le sauvage* (Paris: Aux Amateurs de livres: Diffusion, Klincksieck, 1990), 123–24, see 125–26.
47. John Florio, "To the Curteous Reader," *Montaigne's Essays: John Florio's Translation*, ed. J. I. M. Stewart, 2 vols. (London: Nonesuch Press, 1931), vol. I, xxi. The quotations are from the first edition of 1603.
48. Peter Burke, *Montaigne* (Oxford: Oxford University Press, 1981). See also Tzvetan Todorov, "L'Etre et l'Autre: Montaigne," in *Montaigne: Essays in Reading*, ed. Gérard Defaux (New Haven, CT: Yale University Press, 1983), 118–19, see 120–44, and David Quint, "A Reconsideration of Montaigne's *Des cannibales*," in *America in European Consciousness, 1493–1750*, ed. Karen Ordahl Kupperman (Chapel Hill: University of North Carolina Press, 1995), 166–91.
49. See Warren Boutcher, "Florio's Montaigne: Translation and Pragmatic Humanism in the Sixteenth Century" (unpublished PhD dissertation, University of Cambridge, 1991), introduction, ch. 1–2.
50. See *Les Français en Amérique pendant la deuxième moitié du XVIe Siècle: Les Français en Floride*, ed. Charles-André Julien (Paris: Presses universitaires de France, 1958), vol. II. See Cornelius Jaenen, "France's America and Amerindians: Image and Reality," *History of European Ideas* 6 (1985): 405–20.
51. Julien, "Introduction," *Les Français* (1958), vol. II, v, see vi–viii. On Spain and France in Florida, see Les Français en Amérique pendant la première moitié du XVIe siècle, ed. Charles-André Julien (Paris, Presses universitaires de France, 1946), vol. 1: 336; Carl Ortwin Sauer, *Sixteenth-Century North America: The Land and the People as Seen by Europeans* (Berkeley: University of California Press, 1971), 189–227.
52. On Gouges, see Lestringant, *Le Huguenot*, 156–64, 174–75.
53. Julien, ed. *Les Français* (1958), vol. II, viii.
54. For a discussion of Le Challeux, see Lestringant, *Le Huguenot*, 113–15, 152–55.
55. Le Challeux's original reads: *Discours de l'histoire de la Floride, contenant la trahison des Espagnols, contre les subiets du Roy, en l'an mil cinq cens soixante cinq. Redigé au vray par ceux qui en sont restez, Chose autant lamentable à oüir, qu'elle a esté produitoirement & cruellement executee par les dits Espagnols: Contre l'autorité su Roy nostre Sire, à la perte & dommage de tout ce Royaume* (Dieppe, 1566). This is the edition I am using (from the Houghton Library, Harvard University), except I am drawing on one of the two editions that do not specify a place of publication and that scholars think was printed in Paris. Another edition appeared in Lyons during the same year. The translation of the title and Le Challeux's text are mine here and below.
56. Ibid., 3. Little is written on Le Challeux; see Lestringant, *Huguenot*, 105. Urbain Chauveton used Le Challeux's text against Spanish Catholics; see *Brief Discours et histoire d'vn voyage de qvelqves François en Floride* . . . (Paris: [E. Vignon], 1579). On bibliographical information on Le Challeux's account, see Jean-Paul Duviols, *L'Amérique*, 363–64.
57. Le Challeux, *Discours*, 6–7.
58. The phrases are "Qui veut aller à la Floride" and "je meurs de fain."
59. John Parker, *Books to Build an Empire*, 57–59.
60. Nicolas Le Challeux, "The Epistle," *A true and perfect description*, A4v. I am using the British Library copy of Hacket's translation and have consulted original French versions in the Houghton at Harvard as well as Gravier's edition of 1872 and the one

in *Les Français* (1958), ed. Julien, vol. II, 201–38. Gravier and Julien both include the verse epistle and the "Reqveste." See Le Challeux, *A true and perfect description*, E4v.

61. See ibid., 22–23.

62. For a discussion of Thevet regarding this voyage, see Gilmore, "New World," 520–21, and Lestringant, *Le Huguenot*, 13–14.

63. William Camden, *Annales Rerum Angliae* (1717), vol. II, 259–60, in L. C. Green and Olive Dickason, *The Law of Nations and the New World* (Edmonton, AB: University of Alberta Press, 1989), 11.

64. R. B. Wernham, *After the Armada: Elizabethan England and the Struggle for Western Europe 1588–1595* (Oxford:Clarendon Press, 1984), vii.

65. See Carlos Gómez-Centurión Jiménez, "The New Crusade: Ideology and Religion in the Anglo-Spanish Conflict," in *England, Spain and the Gran Armada 1585–1604: Essays from the Anglo-Spanish Conferences London and Madrid 1988*, ed. M. J. Rodríguez-Salgado and Simon Adams (Edinburgh: Donald, 1991), 264–67.

66. Wernham, *After the Armada*, vii–ix.

67. See, for instance, David B. Quinn and A. N. Ryan, *England's Sea Empire, 1550–1642* (London: Allen & Unwin, 1983).

68. Quinn and Ryan, 232–4, 75, 78, 112–19, 122.

69. Parker, *Books to Build an Empire*, 61. See James A. Williamson, *Hawkins of Plymouth* (London: Black, 1949), 132–46.

70. John Hawkins, *A True Declaration of the Troublesome Voyadge . . . to the Parties of Guynea and the West Indies* (London: Thomas Purfoote for Lucas Harrison, 1569), B7v.

71. Dominique de Gourgues, *Histoire memorable de la reprinse de L'Isle de la Floride* (1568), in *Les Français en Amérique pendant la deuxième moitié du XVIe Siècle: Les Français en Floride*, ed. Charles-André Julien, 2 vols. (Paris, 1958), vol. II, 241–42.

72. Parker, *Books to Build an Empire*, 65–66. See Nicholas Canny's work on the English in Ireland, *The Elizabethan Conquest of Ireland: A Pattern Established 1565–76* (Hassocks, Sussex: Harvester Press, 1976); "The Permissive Frontier: Social Control in English Settlements in Ireland and Virginia, 1550–1650," in *The Westward Enterprise: English Activities in Ireland, the Atlantic, and America 1480–1650*, ed. K. R. Andrews, N. P. Canny, and P. E. H. Hair (Liverpool: Liverpool University Press, 1978), 17–44; "Identity Formation in Ireland: The Emergence of the Anglo-Irish" in *Colonial Identity in the Atlantic World, 1500–1800*, ed. Nicholas Canny and Anthony Pagden (Princeton: Princeton University Press, 1987), 159–212; *Kingdom and Colony: Ireland in the Atlantic World 1560–1800* (Baltimore: The Johns Hopkins University Press, 1988).

73. See Parker, *Books to Build an Empire*, 65–66, and also Canny, *Elizabethan Conquest*, 54, 133–34. For another discussion of the connection between Ireland and the New World, see David B. Quinn, *Ireland and America: Their Early Associations, 1500–1640* (Liverpool: Liverpool University Press, 1991). Quinn discusses the Irish and Spanish America; ibid., 11–16.

74. Humphrey Gilbert, *Discourse of a Discoverie for a New Passage to Cataia* (London: H. Middleton for R. Jhones, 1576), J2r–J2v. George Gasgoigne, "A Prophetical Sonnet of the Same George Gascoine, Vpon the Commendable Trauaile Disclosed in this Worke," in Gilbert, qqq.i.

75. Gilbert, *Discourse of a Discoverie*, B2r.

76. Anonymous, "A Discovery of Lands Beyond the Equinoctial," in *The Three Voyages of Martin Frobisher*, ed. Richard Collinson (London: Hakluyt Society, 1867), 4.

77. Ibid., 5.

78. The phrase is John Parker's in his *Books to Build an Empire*, 70, see 69.

79. Abraham Fleming, ". . . Capteine Forbisher," in Dionyse Settle, *True Reporte of the Laste Voyage into the West and Northwest Regions* (London: Henrie Middleton, 1577), A1v.

80. Dionyse Settle, *True Reporte*, A4r. See J. Parker, *Books*, 70–71. See also Louis B. Wright, *Religion and Empire* (Chapel Hill, NC: The University of North Carolina Press, 1943).

81. George Beste, "The Epistle Dedicatory" to "A True Discourse of the Late Voyages of Discoverie for Finding of a Passage to Cathaya, by the North-weast, under the Conduct of *Martin Frobisher* General . . ." in *Three Voyages*, 17–18.

82. Parker, *Books to Build an Empire*, 72, 104–8. John Parker observes that it is curious that no book is extant describing Drake's preeminent Elizabethan voyage (107). See Augustín de Zárate, *The Strange and Delectable History of the Discouerie and Conquest of the Prouinces of Peru* (London: Richard Ihones, 1581), J4v. In an account printed almost 50 years later, Drake's chaplain, Francis Fletcher, described the Spanish as thinking they do favors in whipping and torturing the Natives. See Francis Fletcher, *The World Encompassed by Sir Francis Drake* (London: N. Bovrne, 1628), 104.

83. For my most concentrated discussion of this context, see Jonathan Hart, "Las Casas in French and Other Languages," *Approaches to Teaching the Writings of Bartolomé de Las Casas*, ed. Santa Arias and Eyda M. Merediz (New York: Modern Language Association of America, 2008), 224–34.

84. M. M. S., *Spanish colonie* (London: [Thomas Dawson] for William Broome, 1583), sigs q2 recto–qq recto.

85. For a sound bibliographical account of early French editions of Las Casas, see André Saint-Lu, *Las Casas Indigeniste: études sur la vie et l'œuvre du défenseur des Indiens* (Paris: L'Harmattan, 1982), 159–70.

86. Herbert Ingram Priestley, "Introduction" in *The Conquest of the Weast India (1578) by Francisco López de Gómara*. Facsimile of the copy in the New York Public Library of *The Pleasant Historie of the Conquest of the VVeast India, now called new Spayne, Atchiued by the vvorthy Prince Hernando Cortes Marque of the valley of Huaxacac, most delectable to Reade: Translated out of the Spanishe tongue, by T. N.* (London: Henry Bynneman, 1578), iii–xxi, esp. xvii.

87. For an examination of Walsingham's patronage in Ireland (1574–80), his embassy to the Netherlands in 1578 (with the backing of Leicester and Hatton at court), and his promulgation of the marriage between Elizabeth I and the duke of Anjou (1579–81), see Mitchell MacDonald Leimon, "Sir Francis Walsingham and the Anjou Marriage Plan, 1574–1581" (unpublished PhD dissertation, University of Cambridge, 1989), esp. ch. 3, 5, 6, 8.

88. Ibid., 28, 34, 185, 216.

89. Thomas Nicholas, *The Pleasant Historie of the Conquest of the VVeast India, now called new Spayne, Atchieued by the vvorthy Prince Hernando Cortes Marques of the valley of Huaxacac, most delectable to Reade: Translated out of the Spanish tongue, by T. N.* (London: Henry Bynneman, 1578), A4r.

90. *Histoire Novvelle dv Novveav Monde, Contenant en somme ce que les Hespagnols ont fait iusqu'à present aux Indes Occidentales, & le rude traitement qu'ils ont fait à ces poures peuples-la. Extraite de l'italien de M. Hierosme Benzoni Milanois, qui ha voyagé xiiii ans en ce pays-la: & enrichie de plusieurs Discours & choses dignes de memoire. Par M. Vrbain Chavveton. Ensemble, Vne petite Histoire d'vn Massacre commis par les Hespagnols sur quelques François en la Floride. Auec un Indice des choses plus remarkable* (Geneva : Eustace Vignon, 1579); my translation.

91. Bartolomé de Las Casas, *Tyrannies et crvavtez des Espagnols, perpetrees és Indes Occidentales, qu'on dit le nouueau monde: brieuement descrites en langue Castillane, par*

l'Euesque Don Frere Bartelemy de las Casas ou Casavs, Espagnol de l'ordre Sainct Domi-nique, fidelement traduites par Iaques de Miggrode (Paris: Guillaume Iulien, 1582); my translation here and below. In Geneva in the same year G. Cartier brought out the same translation under the equally sensational title, *Histoire admirable des horribles insolences, cruautez, & tyrannies exercees par les Espagnols es Indes Occidentales* . . . For an argument that Miggrode was Flemish but chose French because of its literary quality and its ability to reach a large audience in Europe, see Saint-Lu, *Las Casas*, 161.

92. M. M. S., Foreword. The identity of the translator does not seem to be known. On the translations and text, see Nigel Griffin, "A Note on Editions and on this Translation" in Bartolomé de Las Casas, *A Short Account of the Destruction of the Indies*, ed. and trans. Nigel Griffin and introduction by Anthony Pagden (Harmondsworth, UK: Penguin, 1992), xlii–xliii.

93. Owing to the Wars of Religion, this book was not published until 1578. As is common practice, the edition I am using here is the corrected and augmented 1580 edition, which, in the matter I treat does not differ, except in the corrections, from the 1578 edition. There is no augmentation. Jean de Léry, *Histoire d'vn voyage faict en la terre dv Bresil, avtrement dite Amerique* . . . (Geneva: Antoine Chuppin, 1580). For the difficult circumstances of the writing and publication of this text, see Paul Gaffarel, "Préface de l'éditeur" in Jean de Léry, *Histoire d'un voyage faict en la terre du Brésil, nouvelle édition avec une introduction & des notes par Paul Gaffarel* (Paris: A. Lemerre, 1880), vol. I, vi–xii. On pages vii and viii, Gaffarel cites an unidentified but poignant contemporary account of the mutual cruelty of the Protestants and Catholics in Midi. Léry, whose parents were reformers in Burgundy, became one of Calvin's missionaries to the New World in the colony of Durand de Villegagnon, one of Calvin's fellow students at University of Paris. See Gaffarel, "Préface de l'éditeur," i–v; Lestringant, *Le Huguenot*, 79–119; Stephen Greenblatt, *Marvelous Possessions: The Wonder of the New World* (Chicago: University of Chicago Press, 1991), 14–22.

94. See Janet Whatley, "Introduction," Jean de Léry, *History of a Voyage to the Land of Brazil*, trans. and introduction by Janet Whatley (Berkeley: University of California Press, 1990), xx. Jean de Léry, *Histoire d'vn voyage faict en la terre du Bresil, autrement dite Amerique.* (Geneva: Pour Antoine Chuppin., 1580), Aij recto.

95. See Whatley, "Editions and Reception of Léry," in Léry, *History of a Voyage*, 221.

96. Janet Whatley, "Introduction," Léry, *History of a Voyage*, xvii.

97. Janet Whatley, "Editions and Reception of Léry," Léry, *History of a Voyage*, 246, note 14.

98. Jean de Léry, *History of a Voyage to the Land of Brazil*, trans. Janet Whatley (Berkeley: University of California Press, 1990), 131–32.

99. Ibid., 132.

100. Lancelot Voisin, sieur de La Popelinière, "Av Roy," *L'Histoire de France* . . . (n.p. [La Rochelle], 1581), vol. I, a. and b. ij recto.

101. Martin Basanier's *Histoire notable de la Floride* . . . (Paris: guill. Auvray, 1586). Réne Laudonnière in Basanier, ed., *Histoire notable*, [no signature] 64r. For another account of this mutiny and other events on this expedition to Florida, see Jacques Le Moyne, *Brevis narratio eorum quae in Florida Americae provincia Gallis acciderunt, secunda in illam Navigatione, duce Renato de Laudonniere classis Praefecto*, ed. Théodore de Bry (Frankfurt-am-Main: Th. De Bry, 1591), 10–13. For a discussion of the relation among Basanier, Hakluyt, and Ralegh, see Lestringant, *Le Huguenot*, 163, 170–71, 180. Richard Hakluyt, *Divers Voyages Touching the Discoverie of America, and the Islands Adjacent unto the Same* . . . (London: [By Thomas Dawson]

for Thomas VVoodcocke, 1582). For a brief analysis, see Parker, *Books to Build an Empire*, 109–11

102. Richard Hakluyt, *Divers Voyages Touching the Discoverie of America, and the Islands Adjacent unto the Same . . .* (London: [By Thomas Dawson] for Thomas VVoodcocke, 1582). For a brief analysis, see J. Parker, *Books*, 109–11.

103. Hakluyt, *Divers Voyages*, ¶ recto.

104. For a brief discussion of Hakluyt's "Discourse," especially how it relates to labor, see Mary C. Fuller, *Voyages in Print: English Travel to America, 1576–1624* (Cambridge: Cambridge University Press, 1995), 27–29.

105. The phrase is Jack Beeching's; see his "Introduction" in Richard Hakluyt, *Voyages and Discoveries: The Principal Navigations Voyages, Traffiques and Discoveries of the English Nation*, ed. Jack Beeching (1972; Harmondsworth, UK: Penguin Books, 1985), 18. For Beeching's comments on "Discourse," see ibid., 16–18. Lestringant leaves out a discussion of "Discourse" in his section on Hakluyt in Paris, which might be because Hakluyt's role in the disappearance of French manuscripts could be of more interest to the French reader than a secret document to the English crown; see Lestringant, *Le Huguenot*, 213–18. Both aspects of Hakluyt's work in Paris were, however, complementary and should be seen together. David Armitage discusses Hakluyt in terms of the relation between his humanism and ideology; see Armitage, "The New World and British Historical Thought From Richard Hakluyt to William Robertson" in *America in European Consciousness, 1493–1750*, ed. Karen Ordahl Kupperman (Chapel Hill: University of North Carolina Press, 1995), 52–59.

106. For an informative examination of the context of this state paper (one that informs my account), see David B. Quinn and Alison M. Quinn, "Introduction," Richard Hakluyt, *Discourse of Western Planting* (London: Hakluyt Society, 1993), xv–xxxi, esp. xv.

107. For a reconstruction of Hakluyt's reading, particularly of works pertaining to Spanish colonies in the New World, see ibid., xviii–xx.

108. The Quinns seem certain that Hakluyt knew this work; ibid., xvii. See Philippe Duplessis-Mornay, "Discours au roy Henri III, sur les moyens de diminuer l'Espagnol" in *Mémoire et correspondence*, ed. Auguis et La Fontenelle de Vaudoré (Paris: Treuttel et Würtz, 1824–25), II, 580–93. For a discussion of Duplessis-Mornay, see Lestringant, *Le Huguenot*, 119–26.

109. Quinn and Quinn, "Introduction," *Discourse*, xx–xxi.

110. The Quinns provide a good summary of the *Discourse*; ibid., xxii–xxx.

111. Parker, *Books to Build an Empire*, 121.

112. There are various discussions of rhetoric in the field. Andrew Fitzmaurice asserts the differences in the use of rhetoric by the English and Spanish (the one is promotional and the other Aristotelian and Thomist, although Fitzmaurice admits to Hakluyt and others using Aristotle and Aquinas); see Fitzmaurice, "Classical Rhetoric and the Literature of Discovery 1570–1630" (unpublished PhD dissertation, University of Cambridge, 1995), 73, 133–35, 171–79, 189. Elsewhere, I have argued for Thevet's and Hakluyt's imitation, rhetorical and otherwise, of Oviedo; see Jonathan Hart, "Strategies of Promotion in Oviedo and Thevet and Hakluyt," *Imagining Culture: Essays in Early Modern History and Literature*, ed. Jonathan Hart (New York: Garland, 1996), 73–92.

113. On the collapse, see Huguette and Pierre Chanu, *Séville et l'Atlantique, 1504–1650* (8 vols., Paris: A. Colin [puis] S.E.V.P.E.N., 1955–59), vol. VIII, ii.ii, ii, cinquième partie, and J. H. Elliott, *The Old World and the New 1492–1650* (1970; Cambridge: Cambridge University Press, 1992), 97–104.

114. See Rómulo D. Carbia, *Historia de la Leyenda Negra Hispanoamericana* (Madrid: Consejo de la Hispanidad, 1944), and Pierre Chaunu, "La Légende Noire Antihispanique," *Revue de Psychologie des Peuples* (Caen, 1964), 188–223.

115. On this rivalry, see Lestringant's account of Hakluyt's use or acquisition of Thevet's French manuscripts (Laudonnière and others) during his mission in Paris from 1583 to 1588; Frank Lestringant, *Le Huguenot et le Sauvage* (Paris: Aux Amateurs de livres: Diffusion, Klincksieck, 1990), 213–18. Lestringant observes that in *Divers Voyages* (1582) Hakluyt mentioned Thevet with approval and Hacket translated *Singularitez* in 1568, whereas in France and Germany, those with knowledge of the sea and travel had condemned Thevet for a long time: Hakluyt's stay in France would have made him aware of the critiques of Thevet. This cosmographer, in La Popelinière's view, was given to fantasy, a mythical geography rather than a geography of the imagination. He wrote that those who knew the particulars of the world would not believe "how much Belleforest and Thevet have prejudiced the youth and, consequently, the State. Interpreting so badly, and often all against the good, infinite passages: corrupting and falsifying the materials"; Lancelot Voisin de La Popelinière, *L'Histoire des histoires. Avec l'idée de l'histoire accomplie . . .* (Paris: Jean Houzé, 1599), 457–58; my translation. Thevet's *Le Grand Insulaire . . .*, which is in manuscript at la Bibliothèque Nationale and appears in part in English translation in *André Thevet's North America*, ed. Roger Schlesinger and Arthur P. Stabler (Kingston: McGill-Queen's University Press, 1986), discussed the commodities found in Canada in contrast with the silver of Potosí and denounced the "marvellous gulf of avarice and ambition" that Spain opposed to France and England; see Thevet's *Le Grand Insulaire*, vol. I, folio 150 verso, quoted in Lestringant, *Le Huguenot*, 218; my translation. Despite Hakluyt's newfound differences with Thevet, he shared this anti-Spanish sentiment, which Thevet seemed to developed more in his later work.

116. Loren E. Pennington, "The Amerindian in Promotional Literature, 1575–1625" in *The Western Enterprise*, eds. K. R. Andrews, N. P. Canny, and P. E. H. Hair (Liverpool: Liverpool University Press, 1978), 175–94, 179.

117. Robert Payne, *A Briefe Description of Ireland: Made in this yeare, 1589 . . .* (London: Thomas Dawson, 1589). I have checked copies at Houghton Library, Harvard; the University Library, Cambridge; and the British Library against the copy in the Bodleian at Oxford, Shelfmark: Mal. 551. See *The English Experience*, 548, for a modern reprint.

118. Ibid., A3r–A4v.

119. Ibid., A4v.

120. Ibid., A4v–A4r.

121. Ibid., A4r.

122. Hakluyt, *Principal Navigations . . .*, in *Voyages* (1907; London: Dent, 1967), vol. I, 1.

123. Ibid., 2.

124. Pennington, "The Amerindian," 180–83.

125. Richard Hakluyt, *Virginia Richly Valued*, facsimile of 1609 edition (Ann Arbor: University Microfilms, 1966); see Anonymous foreword, *Virginia Richly Valued*, March of America Facsimile Series, No. 12 (Ann Arbor, MI: University Microfilms, 1966). I discuss this work at more length in chapter 2 of *Comparing Empires* (New York: Palgrave Macmillan, 2003).

126. Walter Ralegh, *A Report of the Trvth of the fight about the Isles of Açores, this last Sommer. Betwixt The Reuenge, one of her Maiesties Shippes, And an Armada of the King of Spaine* (London: Printed [by John Windet] for William Ponsonbie, 1591), A3r.

127. Ibid., D recto.

128. Ibid. D recto–D verso. The title was *The Spanish Colonie*, but in other languages the titles sometimes did include the Spanish cruelties.

129. Walter Ralegh, *The Discouerie of the Large, Rich, and Bewtiful Empyre of Guiana, with a Relation of the Great and Golden Citie of Manoa (which the Spanyards call El Dorado . . .)* (London: Robert Robinson, 1596), L2v–L4r.

130. Ibid., A3v.

131. Ibid., q3v.

132. Ibid., C recto.

133. Ibid., D4v.

134. Ibid.

135. Ralegh, *Discouerie,* vol. I, A recto and verso; vol. II, 367.

136. See R. M., *Nevves of Sr Walter Rauleigh. With a True Description of Gviana* (London: Printed [by George Eld] for H. G[osson], 1618), in *Tracts and Other Papers, Origin, Settlement, and Progress of the Colonies in North America, from the Discovery of the Country to the Year 1776,* collected by Peter Force (4 vols., Washington: P. Force, 1836–46), vol. III, 11.

137. *De Nouo Orbe, Or The Historie of the west Indies, Contayning the actes and aduentures of the Spanyardes, whuch haue conquered and peopled those Countries, inriched with varietie of plesant re-lation of the manners, Ceremonies, Lawes, Gouernments, and Warres of the Indians* (London: Thomas Adams, 1612).

138. Ibid., B verso.

139. Ibid., B verso.

140. For an account of Acadia, see Marcel Trudel, *Histoire de la Nouvelle-France,* vol. 1, *Les vaines tentatives, 1524–1603* (Montréal: Fides, 1963). On New France, see W. J. Eccles, *France in America* (1972; Vancouver: Fitzhenry and Whiteside, 1973), 12–15. Concerning internal divisions in Spain, see John Lynch, *Spain Under the Hapsburgs* (2 vols., Oxford: Blackwell, 1964–69), vol. II, 1–13. See also Marcel Trudel, *Histoire de la Nouvelle-France,* vol. 2, *Le Comptoir, 1604–1627* (Montréal: Fides, 1966), 9–15, and Eccles, *France,* 14–15.

141. All the editions of Lescarbot's *Histoire de la Nouvelle France* (1609, 1611–12, 1617–18) included an appendix consisting of a short collection of poems, *Les Muses de la Nouvelle France.* The last two editions involved a reshaping and a completion of the account of New France until the date of composition.

142. See Anthony Pagden, *Spanish Imperialism and the Political Imagination, Studies in European and Spanish-American Social and Political Theory 1513–1830* (New Haven, CT: Yale University Press, 1990), 4.

143. Thus far, no copy of the contemporary biography of Lescarbot by the poet, Guillaume Colletet, has been found. See René Baudry, "Lescarbot, Marc," 469–71, in *Dictionary of Canadian Biography,* gen. ed. George W. Brown, vol. 1, 1000–1700 (Toronto and Québec, 1966).

    W. L. Grant, the translator of Lescarbot, writes of him: "Lescarbot, like Herodotus, whom he so much resembles, should be read in the original"; see Grant, "Translator's Preface," in Marc Lescarbot, *The History of New France,* trans. W. L. Grant and introduction by H. P. Biggar (3 vols., Toronto: The Champlain Society, 1907–14) vol. I, vii.

144. Marc Lescarbot, *Histoire de la Novvelle-France . . .* (Paris: Chez Iean Milot, 1609), ã ij recto, ã iiij recto and verso, ã iiij recto; my translations here and below.

145. Ibid., b iiij recto.

146. See Frank Lestringant, *Le Huguenot et le Sauvage* (Paris: Aux Amateurs de livres: Diffusion, Klincksieck, 1990), 266–70.

147. Pierre d'Avity, sieur de Montmartin, described America in his *Les Estats, empires et principavtez dv monde* . . . (Paris, 1613), 133–34.

Chapter 2

1. Since this work was completed, some relevant works on Marlowe have appeared. See *"A Poet and filthy Play-maker," New Essays on Christopher Marlowe*, ed. Kenneth Friedenreich, Roma Gill, Constance B. Kuriyama (New York: AMS Press, 1988); John S. Mebane, *Renaissance Magic and the Return of the Golden Age: The Occult Tradition and Marlowe, Jonson, and Shakespeare* (Lincoln: University of Nebraska Press, 1989); Thomas Cartelli, *Marlowe, Shakespeare, and the Economy of Theatrical Experience* (Philadelphia: University of Pennsylvania Press, 1991); Jean Dubu, "Rhétoriques de la déchéance royale chez Marlowe et Shakespeare," *Shakespeare: Rhétoriques du texte et du spectacle*, ed. Marie-Thérèse Jones-Davies (Paris: Belles Lettres, 1992), 79–89; Katherine A. Sirluck, "Marlowe's Edward II and the Pleasure of Outrage," *Modern Language Studies* 22 (1992): 15–24; Emily Bartels, *Spectacles of Strangeness: Imperialism, Alienation and Marlowe* (Philadelphia: University of Pennsylvania Press, 1993). See the new preface to the second edition of Harold Bloom, *The Anxiety of Influence* (New York: Oxford University Press, 1997). See also José Manuel González Fernández de Sevilla, *El teatro de Christopher Marlowe* (Zaragoza: SEDERI, 1998); *Marlowe's Empery: Expanding His Critical Contexts*, ed. Sara Munson Deats and Robert A. Logan (Newark: University of Delaware Press, 2002); *The Cambridge Companion to Christopher Marlowe*, ed. Patrick Cheney (Cambridge: Cambridge University Press, 2004); Park Honan, *Christopher Marlowe, Poet and Spy* (Oxford: Oxford University Press, 2005); Garrett A. Sullivan, Jr., *Memory and Forgetting in English Renaissance Drama: Shakespeare, Marlowe, Webster* (Cambridge: Cambridge University Press, 2005). On contemporary actors and playwrights, see Stanley Wells, *Shakespeare and Co.: Christopher Marlowe, Thomas Dekker, Ben Jonson, Thomas Middleton, John Fletcher, and the Other Players in His Story* (London: Lane, 2006). On religion, see Thomas Healy, "Shakespeare and Marlowe," *Oxford Handbook of English Literature and Theology*, ed. Andrew Hass, David Jasper and Elisabeth Jay (Oxford: Oxford University Press, 2007), 382–97. See also Robert A. Logan, *Shakespeare's Marlowe: The Influence of Christopher Marlowe on Shakespeare's Artistry* (Aldershot, UK: Ashgate, 2008). For a collection of essays, see *Placing the Plays of Christopher Marlowe: Fresh Cultural Contexts*, ed. Sara Munson Deats and Robert A. Logan (Aldershot, UK: Ashgate, 2008); Robert Sawyer, "Shakespeare and Marlowe: Re-Writing the Relationship," *Critical Survey* 21 (2009): 41–58.

2. Jonathan Culler, "Apostrophe," *The Pursuit of Signs: Semiotics, Literature, Deconstruction* (Ithaca, NY: Cornell University Press, 1981), 135–55. This was true at the time of writing. I would like to thank the Marlowe Society of America for having me give a paper on this topic at the meetings of the Modern Language Association of America in New York in 1986. My thanks also to the editors of *Language and Style* for permission to reprint a different and revised version of the article in this chapter.

3. Elizabeth Wright, *Psychoanalytic Criticism: Theory in Practice* (London: Methuen, 1984), 1–2. See Barbara Johnson, "Apostrophe, Animation, and Abortion" *Diacritics* 16 (1986): 29–49. Her article is perceptive, although I cannot agree with de Man, Culler, and her that apostrophe or the figure of address is special to the lyric, for the drama also makes great use of it. See Paul de Man, "Lyric Voice in Contemporary Theory, "*Lyric Poetry: Beyond New Criticism*, eds. C. Hosek and P. Parker (Ithaca, NY: Cornell University Press, 1985). Marjorie Garber, Thomas Greene, G. B. Evans, and Harry Levin kindly read an earlier version and gave

their encouragement and suggestions. I thank Marjorie and remember with thanks Harry, Gwynne, and Thomas.

4. Jacques Lacan, *Ecrits: A Selection* (London: Tavistock, 1977), 1–7, see Sigmund Freud, "On Narcissism," XIV, *The Standard Edition of the Complete Psychological Works,* 24 vols (London: Hogarth Press and the Institute of Psychoanalysis, 1940–68); Stanley A. Leavy, "The Image and the Word: Further Reflections on Jacques Lacan," *Interpreting Lacan,* ed. Joseph H. Smith and William Kerrigan (New Haven: Yale University Press, 1983), 10; Wright, 108–9.

5. Jacques Lacan, "Seminar of 21st January 1975," *Feminine Sexuality: Jacques Lacan and the école freudienne,* ed. Juliet Mitchell and Jacqueline Rose (London: Macmillan, 1975), 165; Lacan, *Ecrit* 196–200.

6. Aristotle, *The "Art" of Rhetoric,* trans. J. H. Freeze (1926; Cambridge, MA: Harvard University Press, 1959) 1:3.3–6, 3:10.6–11, 4; Quintilian, *The Institutio of Quintilian,* trans. H. E. Butler, 4 vols. (1922; Cambridge, MA: Harvard University Press, 1936), (for courtroom use) 2.4.Prol.3–7, (for literary use) 3:9.2.38–40, 3.23–28, see 4:1.1, 5, 10–16, 28–9, 58–72; Culler 135–36; Miriam Joseph, *Shakespeare's Use of the Arts of Language* (New York: Columbia University Press, 1947), 390; Edward P. J. Corbett, *Classical Rhetoric for the Modern Student,* 2nd ed. (1965; New York: Oxford University Press, 1971), 460; Laurence Perrine, "Apostrophe," *Princeton Encyclopedia of Poetry and Poetics: Enlarged Edition,* ed. Alex Preminger (1965; Princeton University Press, 1974), 42.

7. Quintilian, vol. 2, 4. Prol., 3–7.

8. Quintilian, vol. 2, 4.1.58–61; vol.3, 9.2.38–40, 9.3.23–28; Culler 135–36.

9. For a position that emphasizes the courtroom and that seems indebted to Quintilian, see John Hoskyns, "Directions for Speech and Style," Louise Brown Osborn, *The Life, Letters and Writings of John Hoskyns, 1566–1638* (New Haven, CT: Yale University Press, 1937), 162–3. See also Johnson, "Apostrophe, Animation, and Abortion," 390.

10. George Puttenham, *The Arte of English Poesie,* eds. Gladys D. Willcock and Alice Walker (1936; Cambridge University Press, 1970), 237–39.

11. Paul de Man, "Semiology and Rhetoric," *Allegories of Reading* (New Haven: Yale University Press, 1979), 3–4; Jacques Derrida, *Of Grammatology,* trans. Gayatri C. Spivak (1967; Baltimore: Johns Hopkins University Press, 1976), 3–4, 30, 34–51, 59–65; Wayne C. Booth, "Intrinsic/Extrinsic Repudiated," *Critical Understanding: The Powers and Limits of Pluralism* (Chicago: University of Chicago Press, 1979), 237–44.

12. Harry Levin, *The Overreacher: A Study of Christopher Marlowe* (Cambridge, MA: Harvard University Press, 1952), esp. 24, 41, 48, 56–60, 114–16; Eugene M. Waith, *The Herculean Hero in Marlowe, Chapman, Shakespeare and Dryden* (London: Chatto & Windus, 1962).

13. For Baudelaire and apostrophe, see Culler 144–45.

14. For general studies of Marlowe's language, see Tucker Brooke, "Marlowe's Versification and Style," *Studies in Philology* 19 (1922); 186–205; Marion Bodwell Smith, *Marlowe's Imagery and the Marlowe Canon* (Philadelphia, PA: Lippincott, 1940); Clifford Leech, *Christopher Marlowe: Poet for the Stage,* ed. Anne Lancashire (New York: AMS Press, 1986); J. R. Mulryne and Stephen Fender, "Marlowe and the 'Comic Distance,'" ed. Brian Morris (London: Ernest Benn, 1968), 47–64; Christopher Fanta, *Marlowe's Agonists: An Approach to the Ambiguity of His Plays* (Cambridge, MA: Harvard University Press, 1971); Judith Weil, "Christopher Marlowe's Prophetic Style," *Christopher Marlowe: Merlin's Prophet* (Cambridge: Cambridge University Press, 1977), 7–22. Brooke, for example, argues that, at Zenocrate's

death bed, Tamburlaine uses more rhetorical devices than Edward II does in his last lamentation (204–205). If, however, this claim is in some measure true, it is also interesting that Tamburaline is allusive and metafictional whereas in his apostrophe Edward addresses his own body as it feels more and more absent as his mind grows increasingly confused. The work of Garber (1977) and C. Davidson (1985) bears more on structure and genre in Marlowe's plays. See Marjorie Garber, "'Infinite Riches in a Little Room': Closure and Enclosure in Marlowe," *Two Renaissance Mythmakers: Christopher Marlowe and Ben Jonson*, ed. Alvin Kernan (Baltimore, MD: Johns Hopkins University Press, 1977), 3–22; Clifford Davidson, "Renaissance Dramatic Forms, Cosmic Perspective ands Alienation," *Cahiers Elisabethains* 27 (1985): 1–16. Although all these works are provocative and fruitful, none examines the implications of apostrophe or the relation of direct address and apostrophe in the Marlovian canon. See Audrey Davidson and Clifford Davidson for a brief discussion of apostrophe in the context of the relation of music and rhetoric; Audrey and Clifford Davidson, "The Function of Rhetoric, Marlowe's Tamburlaine, and Reciprocal Illumination," *Ball State University Forum* 22 (1981): 27–28.

15. Keir Elam, *The Semiotics of Theatre and Drama* (London: Methuen, 1980), 2–3.

16. The Gorgian conception of rhetoric is also important for our discussion; see Brian Vickers, "Territorial Disputes: Philosophy versus Rhetoric," *Rhetoric Revalued: Papers from the International Society for the History of Rhetoric*, ed. B. Vickers (Binghampton, NY: Medieval & Early Renaissance Studies, 1982), 249–50. Gorgias examines the "magical violence" that speech possesses, and his idea of rhetoric is that humans are "forever cut off from the knowledge of being, forever locked in the partial, the contradictory, and the irrational"—Stephen Greenblatt, "Marlowe and the Will to Absolute Play," *Renaissance Self-Fashioning: From More to Shakespeare* (Chicago: University of Chicago Press, 1980), 215. See Dodds on the Greeks and the irrational, especially on ate (infatuation) (1–27) and the relation of inward monition and power, as well as the transposing of an event from the interior to the exterior world (14–15); E. R. Dodds, *The Greeks and the Irrational* (Berkeley: University of California Press, 1963).

See also de Romilly for an examination of the relation between rhetoric and poetry and, more specifically, pre-Gorgian poets and Gorgian rhetoric; Jacqueline de Romilly, "Gorgias et le Pouvoir de la Poesie," *Journal of Hellenic Studies* 93 (1973): 155–62. For Gorgias in the Renaissance, see William J. Kennedy, *Rhetorical Norms in Renaissance Literature* (New Haven: Yale University Press, 1978), 1; and, for a more general view of sixteenth-century rhetoric, see Lee A. Sonnino, *A Handbook to Sixteenth-century Rhetoric* (New York: Barnes and Noble, 1968), esp. 1–14. Clemen's discussion of Kyd's rhetoric provides a good comparison to Marlowe's use of language. See Wolfgang Clemen, "The Uses of Rhetoric," *Shakespeare's Contemporaries*, ed. Max Bluestone and Norman Rabkin (Englewood Cliffs, NJ: Prentice-Hall, 1961), 36–45. Sackton discusses hyperbole and rhetorical structure in Marlowe; see Alexander H. Sackton, *Rhetoric as a Dramatic Language in Ben Jonson* (New York: Columbia University Press, 1948), 117–24.

17. See Christopher Marlowe, *The Complete Plays of Christopher Marlowe*, ed. Irving Ribner (New York: Odyssey Press, 1963). All quotations from, and citations to, Marlowe's plays are from this edition.

18. Palmer and Barber look at magic in *Doctor Faustus*. Palmer reminds us that poetry for the Elizabethans was supposed to move, persuade and convince whereas rhetoric should document the means of swaying those addressed. The "transforming spell" of Marlowe's rhetoric is, according to Palmer, never complete because tragedy reveals that Faustus' magic is "a cheat"—D. J. Palmer, "Magic and Poetry in Doctor Faustus,"

Critical Quarterly 6 (1964): 60. Barber argues that the "omnipotence" in the opening scenes of the play is more overtly magical than that in *Tamburlaine*. For Barber, Faustus' motives and subservience to his pact with the devil, which is for magic and power, demonstrates Marlowe's understanding of Protestant theology and worship; see C. L. Barber, *Creating Elizabethan Tragedy: The Theater of Marlowe and Kyd*, ed. Richard P. Wheeler (Chicago: University of Chicago Press, 1988), 87–95. Mahood notes that in the opening scene Faustus turns away from the study of divinity; see Molly Mahood, "The Tragedy of Renaissance *Humanism*," *Shakespeare's Contemporaries*, ed. Max Bluestone and Norman Rabkin (Englewood Cliffs, NJ: Prentice-Hall, 1961), 110–11. Frey emphasizes antithesis and balance in Doctor Faustus that also have implications for the structure; see Leonard Frey, "Antithetical Balance in the Opening and Close of Doctor Faustus," *Modern Language Quarterly* 24 (1963): 350–53. On the illusory see A. Bartlett Giamatti, "Marlowe: The Arts of Illusion," *Yale Review* 61 (1972): 530–43.

19. See Plato's *Cratylus*. Cratylus argues against the magical nature of language but uses language magically. He observes that names and things are connected. Conversely, Hermogenes sees no logic in names or a correspondence of word and world. Socrates is to resolve the conflict between Cratylus and Hermogenes but complicates it by refuting both; *The Dialogues of Plato*, trans. B. Jowett, vol. 1. (1892; New York: Random House, 1937), esp. 228–29. For a discussion of the relation between analogy and identity and a placement of the debate in the Renaissance about words and things in its context, including Plato's *Cratylus*, see Brian Vickers, "Analogy versus identity: the rejection of occult symbolism, 1580–1680," *Occult and Scientific Mentalities in the Renaissance* (Cambridge: Cambridge University Press, 1984), 95–101. I would also like to remember with thanks Thomas Greene, who shared his learning in the area of language and magic. At the time of the writing of the longer revised version of original article, Thomas M. Greene's article was forthcoming; see his "Ritual and Text in the Renaissance," *Canadian Review of Comparative Literature/Revue Canadienne de Littérature Comparée* 18 (2–3) (June–Sept.1991): 179–97. Waswo aptly observes that ideas of semantic reference occurred in "symbiotic confusion" with our view of the logos' magical power, so that reference requires magic. If, as Waswo says, magic is the "felt correspondence of word and thing," then criticism and theory, like poetry and incantation, are magical. In Waswo's view, "naive magic" does not divide words and world but seeks to exercise power of the former over the later, whereas "sophisticated magic" attempts to exorcise it by dividing them and then being magical in "backhanded ways" to overcome the division of words and world; see Richard Waswo, *Language and Meaning in the Renaissance* (Princeton, NJ: Princeton University Press, 1987), 28–29. I argue that Marlowe gives his characters a language that is magical and antimagical, full of wishes for identity of word and world but also aware of the distinction between them. Apostrophe shows us that the characters want magic: they both wish for it and lack it. The audience, too, through interpretation (which is akin to criticism and theory), is full of magic while trying to empty themselves of it and, perhaps, also lacking magic while attempting to fulfil themselves in it.

20. Virgil, *The Aeneid of Virgil*, ed. T. E. Page, 2 vols. (London: Macmillan, 1964), Book IV, 584–620.

21. For a discussion of writing and unwriting in Marlowe, see Garber; she makes an interesting point: "Patterns of intertextual reference, texts 'deconstructing' or undoing other texts, and authors asserting competing authority recur throughout Marlowe's plays"—Marjorie Garber, "'Here's Nothing Writ': Scribe, Script, and Circumscription in Marlowe's Plays," *Theatre Journal* 36 (1984): 301. She discusses

Tamburlaine, Faustus, and Edward as writers. For a more general study of Marlowe's rhetoric of love, see George S. Rousseau, "Marlowe's Dido and a Rhetoric of Love," *English Miscellany* 19 (1968): 25–49.

22. In Tamburlaine, Greenblatt says, Marlowe insists on the meaninglessness and vacancy of theatrical space, represents in his plays the voices of characters that express conquest, unfinished wants and "transcendental homelessness" and creates a sense of place open to "radical questioning" (195–96). Most pertinent in relation to my argument is Greenblatt's observation on space and time in Marlowe's plays: "That man is homeless, that all places are alike, is linked to man's inner state, to the uncircumscribed hell he carries within him" (197). By looking at direct address and apostrophe in Marlowe, I am attempting to examine the characters' projection of their wishes on the world and their confusion of absence and presence, inside and outside. These wishes and conflations often reveal disturbing attitudes toward military, political, and sexual power as well as the wistful powerlessness of others. In fact, characters like Tamburlaine and Faustus display violent projections on the world and their personal limitations in death.

23. Irving Ribner, "Marlowe's 'Edward II' and the Tudor History Play," *Shakespeare's Contemporaries*, ed. Max Bluestone and Norman Rabkin (Englewood Cliffs, NJ: Prentice-Hall, 1961), 152.

24. For a more general view of rhetoric in *Tamburlaine*, see Donald Peet, "The Rhetoric of Tamburlaine," *English Literary History* 26 (1959): 137–55; Davidson and Davidson; Richard A. Martin, "Marlowe's Tamburlaine and the Language of Romance," *Publications of the Modern Language Association of America* 93 (1978): 248–64. Martin, for example, argues that "the tonal irregularities in *Tamburlaine* result from Marlowe's manipulation of the conventions of romance." (248). Using Northrop Frye's notion of romance in the secular scripture, Martin asserts that *Tamburlaine* is more romance than tragedy, for it tends toward imagination and dream without the consequences of reality. Although Martin says that in Zenocrate's speech over the bodies of Bajazeth and Zabina, we "consider the tragic implications of conquest only to reject them," he thinks Tamburlaine a Herculean hero (as Waith had asserted) and this warrior's aspirations become that of all romantic idealism, its obliviousness to natural restraints (248, 250, 263). Even though Martin (and the other critics I have listed) does not discuss apostrophe and celebrates imagination and romance with less equivocation than I do, his general views support the observation that apostrophe reveals Tamburlaine's aspiring reach and his natural limits. How much the "overreach" is a good thing depends, in part, on the reception of the reader or audience.

25. Unlike Tillyard and F. P. Wilson but like Kocher, Ribner considers *Edward II* a history play with political concerns and argues that Edward shows deficiencies in public virtue and Mortimer, in private virtue; Ribner, "Marlowe's 'Edward II' and the Tudor History Play," 143–47; see E. M. W. Tillyard, *Shakespeare's History Plays* (London: Chatto & Windus, 1944); F. P. Wilson, *Marlowe and the Early Shakespeare* (Oxford: Clarendon Press, 1954); Paul H. Kocher, *Christopher Marlowe: A Study of his Thought, Learning and Character* (Chapel Hill: University of North Carolina Press, 1946).

26. Mulryne and Fender regard this episode with the stone "a paradigm because it is only one of the instances in Marlowe in which contradictory views of experience are brought together and left unresolved: the ideal and the common sense; the hint of a comprehensive order and the rejection of all order; the socially concerned and the individualist; the moral and the libertine; metaphor and fact" (50). Whereas Mulryne and Fender emphasize ambivalence, the distancing of the emblem, and the

absurd (in Camus' terms) primarily in *Tamburlaine* and *Edward II*, I am stressing presence and absence, inside and outside throughout the plays.

27. Steane cites a number of examples in *Massacre*, which happen to be direct addresses and apostrophes, but does not mention this fact or extrapolate from it; see J. B. Steane, *Marlowe: A Critical Study* (Cambridge: Cambridge University Press, 1964), 240–42.

28. Brown looks generally at the rhetoric of Tamburlaine's address to Zenocrate on her death-bed; see John Russell Brown, "Marlowe and the Actors," *Tulane Drama Review* 8 (1964): 157–58.

29. Marlowe, ed. Ribner, 103.

30. From a Freudian point of view, Barber makes some perceptive observations about the death of Zenocrate, especially about "the troubling fusion of symbolic life and literal death" and necrophilia (68–71). Lacan illuminates our discussion of apostrophe. According to Muller, in Lacan's view, for the psychotic, "The real has no gaps or lacks, and this absence of lack (if this can be conceived) is the inverse of what goes on in signification. Lacan tells us the word is 'a presence made of absence.'" John P. Muller, "Language, Psychosis, and the Subject in Lacan," *Interpreting Lacan*, ed. Joseph H. Smith and William Kerrigan (New Haven, CT: Yale University Press, 1983), 28. Muller also describes Lacan's view of the psychotic as the relation between madness and freedom (21). Tamburlaine does not accept separation and absence (which Lacan and others relate to the infant's attachment to the mother), attempts to make present the absent (Zenocrate's soul in her corpse) and tries to control the future after his death, so that his use of address and apostrophe at her death and his vacillates between madness and freedom. Muller's discussion of Lacan's views applies to Tamburlaine's dilemma: "To be finitely human means to live as decentered subjects, split and barred from unconscious desire, forced to channel our wants through the narrow defiles of the signifier, which offers a limited satisfaction by affording us symbolic presences. The alternative is either death or psychosis, where there is neither presence nor absence and no speaking subject." (31). Winnicott explores a third area between "inner reality" and "external life" that acts as "a resting-place for the individual engaged in the perpetual human task of keeping inner and outer reality separate yet interrelated." D. W. Winnicott, *Playing and Reality* (London: Tavistock, 1971), 2. It is not certain that Tamburlaine is always aware of the difference of inside from outside and he sometimes yearns for omnipotence. Gardner views the representation of Tamburlaine's death as medieval, for it shows how inevitable it is and how it is the "final check to Tamburlaine's fantasies of omnipotence." Helen Gardner, "The Second Part of 'Tamburlaine the Great,'" *Shakespeare's Contemporaries*, ed. Max Bluestone and Norman Rabkin (Englewood Cliffs, NJ: Prentice-Hall, 1961), 83. For an interesting and related discussion of the relation between representational order and sexual order, and the partial and costly "directing of desire on its appropriate objects" in *Hamlet* and *Measure for Measure*, see Jacqueline Rose, "Sexuality in the Reading of Shakespeare: *Hamlet* and *Measure for Measure*," *Alternative Shakespeares*, ed. John Drakakis. (London: Methuen, 1985), esp. 98–99.

31. See Greenblatt, 215–21 on self-naming.

32. E. R. Dodds, *The Greeks and the Irrational* (Berkeley: University of California Press, 1962).

33. Bevington observes that in *The Jew of Malta*, as in *Tamburlaine*, we find in the combination of secular material and moral structure a key to the play's characteristic ambiguity." David M. Bevington, "The Jew of Malta," *Marlowe: A Collection of Critical Essays*, ed. Clifford Leech (Englewood Cliffs, NJ: Prentice-Hall, 1964), 158. This observation is perceptive, and although I agree with it, I am focussing on

the complexities of invocation and projection, indeterminacy, and situational and hermeneutic division through rhetoric and notions of the self.

34. Birringer (1984) and Barber discuss Faustus' address to his body. Birringer emphasizes the "physicality" of the language, the relation "between word sound cadence and body gesture space time." Johannes H. Birringer, "Between Body and Language: 'Writing the damnation of Faust,'" *Theatre Journal* 36 (1984): 349–50. From the point of view of acting, he also discusses the last soliloquy in terms of the shifts and breaks between two "internal" impulses, the "'fleeing' self" and the "'realistic' self" (353). Birringer (1982) includes a more general discussion of Faustus' dilemma. See Johannes H. Birringer, "The Daemonic Flight of Dr. Faustus: Hope and/or Escape?" *Massachusetts Studies in English* 8 (1982):17–26 See Keefer for a discussion of Faustus and magic; see Michael H. Keefer, "Verbal Magic and the Problem of the A and B Texts of Doctor Faustus," *Journal of English and German Philology* 82 (1983): 324–46. More generally, Crewe notes a dissolving "interiority" in the "theatre of monstrous idols" with which Rankin and Marlowe are concerned; Jonathan V. Crewe, "The Theatre of the Idols: Marlowe, Rankins, and Theatrical Images," *Theatre Journal* 36 (1984): 333.

Chapter 3

1. Robert Greene, *Greenes, groats-vvorth of witte, bought with a million of repentance Describing the follie of youth, the falshoode of makeshifte flatterers, the miserie of the negligent, and mischiefes of deceiuing courtezans. Written before his death, and published at his dyeing request* (London: Imprinted for William Wright, 1592), f verso.

2. At the time of final revisions for this book, another study of authorship will soon appear in April 2010. See James Shapiro, *Contested Will: Who Wrote Shakespeare?* (New York: Simon & Shuster, 2010). This chapter was written as an essay in the 1980s and was left unpublished as part of a larger study. Since then some important work on Greene and or related in some way to him has appeared. It is not surprising that Shakespeare and Greene are sometimes discussed together. Here is a selection. See Katherine Duncan-Jones, "Shakespeare, the Motley Player," *Review of English Studies* 60 (2009): 723–43 for a discussion of Greene's comments on Shakespeare, who might have been more of a leading actor than what was commonly thought; Steve Mentz, "Forming Greene: Theorizing the Early Modern Author in the *Groatsworth of Wit." Writing Robert Greene: Essays on England's First Notorious Professional Writer,* ed. Kirk Melnikoff and Edward Gieskes (Aldershot, UK: Ashgate, 2008), 115–31, for an analysis of Greene in terms of Shakespeare and of the writer as literary critic and dramatist; John Rumrich, "The Literary Friendship of Robert Greene and William Shakespeare," *Reconciliation in Selected Shakespearean Dramas,* ed. Beatrice Batson (Newcastle: Cambridge Scholars Publishing, 2008), 175–89, for an examination of humanist friendship and rejection; David Margolies, "Shakespeare and Elizabethan Popular Fiction," *Shakespeare and Elizabethan Popular Culture,* ed. Stuart Gillespie and Neil Rhodes (London: Arden Shakespeare, 2006), 112–35, for an interpretation of character and plot and the use of sources; Lori H. Newcomb, *Reading Popular Romance in Early Modern England* (New York: Columbia University Press, 2002), which includes a discussion of relation of *Pandosto* to Shakespeare's *The Winter's Tale;* Helen Hackett, *Women and Romance Fiction in the English Renaissance* (Cambridge: Cambridge University Press, 2000), for an analysis that includes, among its topics, cross-dressing and romance as a genre about gender; Claudia Corti, "Quando dire è fare: Da *Pandosto* a *The Winter's Tale."* *Rivista di letterature moderne e comparate* 44 (1991): 19–44, for an interpretation of

Greene's *Pandosto* as a source for this Shakespearan romance; Inga-Stina Ewbank, "From Narrative to Dramatic Language: *The Winter's Tale* and Its Source," *Shakespeare and the Sense of Performance: Essays in the Tradition of Performance Criticism in Honor of Bernard Beckerman*, ed. Marvin Thompson and Ruth Thompson (Newark: University of Delaware Press, 1989), 29–47, for a discussion of style in prose romance and its dramatic counterpart.

3. *The nevv inne. Or, The light Heart A comoedy. As it was neuer acted, but moſt negligently play'd, by ſome, the Kings Seruants. And more ſqueamiſhly beheld, and cenſured by others, the Kings Subiects. 1629. Now, at last, ſet at liberty to the Readers, his Maties Seruants, and Subiects, to be iudg'd. 1631. By the Author,* B. Ionson (London: Printed by Thomas Harper, for Thomas Alchorne, and are to be ſold at his ſhop in Pauls Church-yeard, at the ſigne of the greene Dragon, MDCXXXI [1631]), H recto.

4. Ben Jonson, "The Indvction on the Stage," *Bartholmew fayre: a comedie, acted in the yeare, 1614 by the Lady Elizabeths Seruants, and then dedicated to King Iames, of most blessed memorie* (London: Printed by I.B. for Robert Allot, and are to be ſold at the ſigne of the Beare, in Pauls Church-yard, 1631), B1r.

5. Jared Sparks, letter to John G. Palfrey, February 7, 1812, "Letters to John Gorham Palfrey," Box 17, bMS Am 1704 (862), Houghton Library, Harvard University, 1.

6. Ibid., 1.

7. Ibid., 6.

8. For works that treat romance seriously but not solemnly, see Northrop Frye, *Anatomy of Criticism: Four Essays* (Princeton: Princeton University Press, 1957), esp. 186–206; *A Natural Perspective: The Development of Shakespearean Comedy and Romance* (New York: Harcourt, Brace & World, 1965); *The Secular Scripture: A Study of the Structure of Romance* (Cambridge, MA: Harvard University Press, 1976); Harry Levin, *The Myth of the Golden Age in the Renaissance* (Bloomington: University of Indiana Press, 1969), esp. pp. 84–111; Howard Felperin, *Shakespearean Romance* (Princeton: Princeton University Press, 1972), esp. pp. 3–57, 211–46; Patricia Parker, *Inescapable Romance: Studies in the Poetics of a Mode* (Princeton: Princeton University Press, 1979), esp. pp. 3–16, 219–45; A.C. Hamilton, "Elizabethan Romance: The Example of Prose Fiction," *Journal of English Literary History*, 49 (1982): 287–299; and "Elizabethan Prose Fiction and Some Trends in Recent Criticism," *Renaissance Quarterly*, 37 (1984): 21–33. This chapter, from this point on, is based on an unpublished essay written in the 1980s.

9. For various views of this paradox, Frye, *Secular Scripture*, esp. 3–31; Parker, *Inescapable Romance*, 3–16, 219–45; Felperin, *Shakespearean Romance*, 3–54, 242–45.

10. Richard Hurd, quoted in Felperin, *Shakespearean Romance*, 287; see also Hurd in Parker, *Inescapable Romance*, 1.

11. *The Republic of Plato*, trans. Allan Bloom (New York: Basic Books, 1968), 595A–609A. Aristotle, "The Poetics," in *Literary Criticism: Plato to Dryden*, ed. Allan H. Gilbert (Detroit, MI: Wayne State University Press, 1962), 71–82.

12. See Hamilton, "Elizabethan Romance," 290.

13. Philip Sidney, "The Defense of Poesie" (1583), in *Literary Criticism: Plato to Dryden*, ed. Allan H. Gilbert (Detroit: Wayne State University Press, 1961), 414; Tasso, in Gilbert, *Literary Criticism: Plato to Dryden*, 481, see 480.

14. Boccaccio, in Gilbert, *Literary Criticism: Plato to Dryden*, 210. Whenever possible, to make reference easier for the reader, I have tried to use Gilbert's *Literary Criticism* for well-known critical works.

15. Sidney, in Gilbert, *Literary Criticism: Plato to Dryden*, 413–14, 417; Tasso, in Gilbert, *Literary Criticism: Plato to Dryden*, 476, see 480–81. See John Milton, *Of Education*, in *Complete Poems and Major Prose*, ed. Merritt Y. Hughes (1957; Indianapolis, IN:

Odyssey Press, 1977), 631, for a view of education similar to Sidney's. Here, Hughes cites a like position in "Of the Interpretation of Nature," in *The Works of Francis Bacon*, ed. Spedding and Ellis, III, 219.

16. Boccaccio, *Life of Dante*, in Gilbert, 209, see chs. 21–22, 208–12. Sidney, *Defense*, 412–13, 417–18, 424–25.

17. Thomas Elyot, *The Governor* (1530), 240–41; Giraldi Cinthio, *On the Composition of Comedies and Tragedies* (1543), 252; Cinthio, *On the Composition of Romances* (1549), 271–72; Jacapo Mazzoni, *On the Defense of the Comedy* (1587), 379–80; Sidney, *Defense* (1583), 425–26; Torquato Tasso, *Discourses on the Heroic Poem* (1594), 468–69; for a view that poetry is not primarily moral, see Lodovico Castelvetro, *The Poetics of Aristotle Translated and Annotated* (1571), 317, all in Gilbert, *Literary Criticism*. Many of these critics and poets also argue for delight in poetry as they keep in mind Horace's dictum in *The Art of Poetry* that "The poet's aim is either to profit or to please, or to blend in one the delightful and the useful" (in Gilbert, ll. 133–34, 139).

18. Cinthio, *On the Composition of Romances*, 269–90. For modifications of Aristotle, see, in Gilbert, Cinthio, *Romances*, 263; Antonio Miturno, *L'Arte Poetica* (1564), 287; Castelvetro, *On the Poetics*, 342–43; Mazzoni, *Discourse in Defense of the Comedy* (1572), 359; Mazzoni, *On the Defense of the Comedy*, 391; Sidney, *Defense*, 422–31; Giambattista Guarini, *The Compendium of Tragicomic Poetry* (1599), 527; for discussions of the marvelous, which has its beginnings in Aristotle's *Poetics*, chap. 24, 60a26, but which is extended to include romance, see Cinthio, *Romances*, 270; Minturno, *L'Arte*, 291; Castelvetro, *On the Poetics*, 322, 328, 338–44; Mazzoni, *On the Defense of the Comedy*, 370–71, 388; Tasso, 479–81, 492; for comments on romance, Cinthio, 267–71; Minturno, 277–82, 288; Tasso, 475, 485, 498–501; for tragicomedy, which is closely related to romance, see Giangiorgio Tissino, *Poetica* (1529), 225; Sidney, 430, 451; Guarini, 504–33; for a questioning of the classification of Shakespeare's "last plays" as romances, see D. T. Childress, "Are Shakespeare's Late Plays Really Romances?" in *Shakespeare's Late Plays: Essays in Honor of Charles Crow*, eds. Richard C. Tobias and P. G. Zolbrod (Athens: Ohio University Press, 1974), 44–55.

19. Sidney, 412–413, 425.

20. Edmund Spenser, "To the Right noble, and Valorous, Sir Walter raleigh knight . . ." (1589) in *The Faerie Qveene*, ed. A. C. Hamilton (London: Longman, 1977), 737.

21. All quotations and citations from *Pandosto* and *The Winter's Tale* will come from *The Winter's Tale*, ed. J. H. P. Pafford (1963; London: Methuen, 1982). Pafford uses the 1595 text of Pandosto and collates it with the editions of 1588 and 1592. For the reader's convenience and to keep consistent modernized spelling, I have used this version instead of the one in *The Life and Complete Works in Prose and Verse of Robert Greene, M.A.*, ed. Alexander B. Grosart (New York: Russell & Russell, 1964), vol. 4.

22. *The Metamorphoses of Ovid*, trans. Mary M. Innes (1955; Harmondsworth, UK: Penguin, 1976), 77–80.

Chapter 4

1. See Northrop Frye, "The Argument of Comedy." *Shakespeare: Modern Essays in Criticism*, revised edition, ed. Leonard F. Dean (1957, rev. 1967; London: Oxford University Press, 1975), 79–89; Z. J. Jagendorf, *The Happy End of Comedy: Shakespeare, Jonson, Molière* (Newark: University of Delaware Press, 1984). For some work that appeared since an earlier version of this chapter, see *Contexts of Renaissance Comedy*, ed. Janet Clare and Roy Eriksen (Oslo: Novus, 1997). For some other earlier studies, see *Comparative Critical Approaches to Renaissance Comedy*, ed. Donald Beecher

and Massimo Ciavolella (Ottawa, ON: Dovehouse, 1986). On recent work on Shakespearean comedy that is relevant to this chapter, see Jennifer Drouin, "Cross-Dressing, Drag, and Passing: Slippages in Shakespearean Comedy," *Shakespeare Re-Dressed: Cross-Gender Casting in Contemporary Performance*, ed. James C. Bulma (Madison, NJ: Fairleigh Dickinson University Press, 2008), 23–56; *The Cambridge Companion to Shakespearean Comedy*, ed. Alexander Leggatt (Cambridge: Cambridge University Press, 2002).

2. See Catherine Belsey, "Disrupting Sexual Difference: Meaning and Gender in the Comedies," *Alternative Shakespeares*, ed. John Drakakis (London: Methuen, 1985), 166–90.

3. In a chapter on comic theory I argue for a recognition of recognition. Comic recognition, or *agnitio* or *cognitio*, became equivalents for Aristotle's *anagnorisis*, or discovery. Recognition is a central part of comic structure. Although I do not have space here, I think it is important to make this point. Aristotle speaks about anagnorisis in tragedy, but not, in the extant version of *Poetics*, of comic discovery or recognition. Menander is credited with refitting the recognition plot to comedy, and Plautus and Terence provide examples of the use of comic recognition. Like Terence Cave, I am interested in the ways recognition unsettles the boundaries of genre that poetics sets out; see Terence Cave, *Recognitions: A Study in Poetics* (Oxford: Clarendon Press, 1988), 50–54. The recognition most often occurs toward the end of comedies and has tragic origins or at least analogues, so that it complicates the ends of comedy. Donatus, Franciscus Robortellus, Cinthio, Guarini, and Ben Jonson all comment on discovery and peripeteia (reversal), which bring about catastrophe; see Marvin T. Herrick, *Comic Theory in the Sixteenth Century* (Urbana: University of Illinois Press, 1964, 106–26). Like Guarini, Northrop Frye tries to defend tragicomedy, and especially romance. He does so by making recognition (sometimes as vision and epiphany) the center of his defense of romance and, perhaps even, of literature and culture. See Northrop Frye, *Anatomy of Criticism: Four Essays* (1957; Princeton: Princeton University Press, 1973); Northrop Frye, *The Secular Scripture: A Study of the Structure of Romance* (Cambridge, MA: Harvard University Press, 1976); Jonathan Hart, *Theater and World: The Problematics of Shakespeare's History* (Boston: Northeastern University Press, 1992); Jonathan Hart, *Northrop Frye: The Theoretical Imagination* (London: Routledge, 1994); Cave, *Recognitions* 190–99. Before Frye's return to recognition, ritual, and order in comedy and romance, Cambridge anthropologists and theorists like Francis Cornford had discussed these matters. A subtext of my chapter is the shared ritual origins of tragedy and comedy and the implication that this common provenance is one reason comic ends can be at least partly tragic. Cornford's predecessors and contemporaries often emphasized the asymmetrical and exceptional elements of the end of Old Comedy. Horace emphasizes how in the Old Comedy personal freedom degenerated into excess until a law was passed that silenced the Chorus: "successit vetus hic comoedia, non sine multa / laude; sed in vitium libertas excidit et vim / dignam lege regi: lex est accepta chorusque / turpiter obsticuit sublato jure nocendi"—"To these succeeded Old Comedy, and won no little credit, but its freedom sank into excess and a violence deserving to be checked by law. The law was obeyed, and the chorus to its shame became mute, its right to injure being withdrawn," *Ars Poetica*, 281–84; see Horace, *Satires, Epistles, Ars Poetica*, trans. H. Rushton Fairclough (1926; London: William Heinnemann Ltd, 1942). The Latin and English are from this Loeb Classic edition. The stresses that satire causes between social order and criticism is evident in the controversy surrounding *Tartuffe*, which this chapter later discusses. In *De Comaedia et Tragaedia*,

Donatus draws on the Ciceronian view that comedy is an imitation of life, a mirror of custom, and a reflection of truth, and discusses the ritual origins of comedy and cites Horace on Old Comedy. The *parabasis*, especially as it appears in Aristophanes, provides interesting contrasts with the structure of Renaissance comedy. See Zielinski, *Gliederung d. altattischen Komödie* (Leipzig, 1886), qtd. in Francis Cornford, *The Origins of Attic Comedy* (1914; Cambridge: Cambridge University Press, 1934), 2, 5. On the structure of Greek comedy, including *parabasis*, see Cornford vii–viii, 1–3; Cornford also credits Jane Harrison as an influence. See Jane Harrison, *Themis* (Cambridge: Cambridge University Press, 1912). The Middle Comedy gave up the *parabasis* and what Horace calls the *ius nocendi* or right of injury, such as Aristophanes' taunting of Cleon. See Harry Levin, *Playboys and Killjoys: An Essay on the Theory and Practice of Comedy* (Oxford: Oxford University Press, 1987), 30–31.

4. Levin, *Playboys and Killjoys*, 131.

5. I want to thank students in my graduate seminar in Renaissance comedy in the Department of Comparative Literature at University of Alberta for their discussions of genre in a comparative European context. The reason for my comments on the metaphysical *La vida es sueño* (Hart, "Narrative," 16), which some may not think of as a comedy, is that it shows structural affinity to romantic comedy and romance. For that reason, it also appeared in my course. See Jonathan Hart, "Introduction: Narrative, Narrative Theory, Drama: The Renaissance," *Renaissance Narrative and Drama / Récit et Théâtre à la Renaissance*, ed. Jonathan Hart. Special issue of *Canadian Review of Comparative Literature / Revue Canadienne de Littérature Comparée* 18, no. 2–3 (1991): 117–65. My thanks to this journal, the Canadian Comparative Literature Association, and to Taylor Francis for granting the reprinting of this revision of these earlier versions. See Jonathan Hart, "The Ends of Renaissance Comedy," *Reading the Renaissance*, ed. J. Hart (New York: Garland, 1996), 91–127.

6. Northrop Frye, *Anatomy of Criticism: Four Essays* (1957; Princeton: Princeton University Press, 1973), 182–83. Frye contrasts the green world of the forest or wild setting with the city world.

7. See "Introduction." in Pedro Calderón de la Barca's *No hay burlas con el amor [Love is No Laughing Matter]*, trans. Don Cruickshank ad Sean Page (Warminster: Aris & Phillips, 1986), xiv.

8. Louise George Chubb mentions the fashion for Sophoclean irony in *Pastor fido*, see her "Introduction," *Italian Plays (1500–1700) in the Folger Library* (Firenze: Leo S. Olschki Editore, 1968), xxxiv.

9. The original reads: "Tu dunque in altro albergo, /Dorinda, poserai che'n quel di Silvio?/Certo ne le mie case, /o viva o morta,/oggi sarai mia sposa; /e teco sarà Silvio, o viva o morto" (IV.ix.318). Battista Guarini, *Il Pastor Fido [The Faithful Shepherd]*, trans. Richard Fanshawe (1647) and ed. and intro by J. H. Whitfield (Edinburgh: Edinburgh University Press, 1976).

10. Guarini. *Il Pastor Fido*: the original reads: "E come a tempo . . ." (IV.ix318f.).

11. Guarini's original reads: "Assai lieta son io / del perdon recevuto e del cor sano" (V.x.408).

12. Whitfield, Introduction, *Il Pastor Fido*, 23.

13. Ibid. He gives the original Italian: "a me pare che'l Pastorfido n'habbia gran parte, essendosi in lui, con tanta esquisitezza osservato il precetto dell'unita, che c'insegna il grande Aristotile" (Whitfield, 40).

14. For the Italian original in Guarini, see "Oh fortunata coppia" (v.x.410).

15. Anne Barton, "Introduction: *As You Like It*," *The Riverside Shakespeare*, ed. G. Blakemore Evans. (Boston: Houghton Mifflin, 1974), 368.

16. For discussions on cross-dressing, see Jean Howard, "Cross-Dressing, the Theatre and Gender Struggle in Early Modern England," *Shakespeare Quarterly* 39 (1988): 418–40, and Marjorie Garber, *Vested Interests: Cross-Dressing and Cultural Anxiety* (New York: Routledge, 1992).

17. In an epilogue to a comedy in 1564, Ronsard uses the trope that Jaques employs as a context ("All the world's a stage"): "Le monde est un théâtre, et les hommes les acteurs" ("The world is a theatre, and men actors," my translation). See Ernst Curtius, *European Literature and the Latin Middle Ages*, trans. Willard R. Trask (Bern, 1948; New York: Harper and Row, 1963), 138, 133–44; Hart, *Theater and World*, 151, 231–32.

18. See Hart, *Theater and World*, esp. ch. 4.

19. It has been years since I began discussing sexual ambiguity in *As You Like It* with my classes. Two instances, however, stand out and may reflect the importance of an understanding of the conventions in experience and literature in the response to this aspect of the comedy. In 1985–86, I lectured on the topic to first year students at Trent University and later discussed it in a seminar with them. Most of them seemed quite uncomfortable with the topic. At Alberta, a few years later, I approached the same topic with a graduate class on Renaissance comedy, and there appeared to be more interest in sexual ambiguity in *As You Like It* and more tolerance for it. Since then, there has been more interest in, and understanding, of the subject.

20. See Katy Emck, "Female Transvestism and Male Self-Fashioning in *As You Like It* and *La vida es sueño*," *Reading the Renaissance*, ed. Jonathan Hart (New York: Garland, 1996), 75–88; Natalie Zemon Davis, "Women on Top: Symbolic Sexual Inversion and Political Disorder in Early Modern Europe," *The Reversible World: Symbolic Inversion in Art and Society*, ed. Barbara Babcock (Ithaca, NY: Cornell University Press, 1978), 147–90.

21. See Jackson I. Cope, *The Theater and the Dream: From Metaphor to Form in Renaissance Drama* (Baltimore, MD: Johns Hopkins University Press, 1973).

22. Cruickshank and Page, xvi.

23. Cruickshank and Page, xvi–xvii.

24. Calderón, 125. For the Castilian or Spanish original, see ("¡Oh, nunca hubiera inventado . . ." 1957–60).

25. Calderón's original: "aunque miento en esta parte, / puesto que yo no los traigo: / ellos vienen a buscar me / dentro de mi casa" (2992–95).

26. The original in Caldero: "pues por ti Don Luis hace / desprecios de ella, y de mi" (3006–7).

27. Calderón's original reads:

> *Moscatel.* En fin, el hombre mas libre,
> de las burlas de amor sale
> herido, cojo y casado,
> que es el mayor de sus males.
> *Inés.* En fin, la mujer más loca,
> más vana y más arrogante,
> de las burlas del amor.
> contra gusto suyo, sale
> enamorada y casada.
> que es lo peor (3103–12).

28. The original in Calderón reads: "todos del amor se guarden" (3118).

29. Calderón's original: "Eso no, / que tener no puedo yo / hermana libidinosa" (619–20).

30. Calderón's original reads; "no habla palabra jamas / sin frases y sin rodeos; / tanto, que ninguno puede / entenderla sin comento" (305–8).
31. The original in Calderón: "si en ella veo / virtud, hacienda y noblessa, / gran beldad y gran ingenio?" (462–64).
32. Calderón's original reads: "Sepa una mujer hilar, / coser y echar un remiendo, / que no ha menester saber / gramatica, ni hacer versos." (471–74).
33. The original in Calderón reads: "Vamos, pues" (486).
34. Calderón's original reads: "Deténte; / no te apropincues a mí" (603–16).
35. Calderón's original: "Verdad es que, en mi concepto, / todas, por qué quererlas, / y todas, por que dejarlas" (1065–66, see 1059–88; see Levin).
36. The original in Calderón: "Dile a tu amo, villano" (1257–66).
37. Calderón's original reads: "biene verse puede, / si a hablar asi te acomadas, / que qui en no habla como todas, / como todas no procede" (1440–42).
38. Calderón's original: "unas *Horas* de romance / le bastan a una mujer. / Bordar, labrar y coser / sepa sólo; deje al hombre / el estudio" (1456–60).
39. The original in Calderón reads:

> *Don Pedro.* ¡Perdiendo, Beatriz, el vicio,
> bien enmendada te veo!
> *Beatriz.* Por tu anticipata . . .
> *Don Pedro.* Creo
> que hoy me has de quitar el juicio (1474–77).

40. Calderón's original: Eso a reyes de comedia / no hay condesa que no diga / de Malfi, Mantua o Milán, / mas no las de Picardía" (1486–89).
41. Cruickshank and Page, 96.
42. Calderón's original reads: "¡Válgate el diablo, picaña!" (1496).
43. The original in Calderón: "Mi firmeza me destruye" (1510).
44. Calderón's original reads: "que, como es niño" (1559).
45. Calderón's original: "¡Vive Dios, que antes me deje / morir, que a una mujer siga" (1627–28, see 1595–1642).
46. The original in Calderón: "que voto a Dios que primero / con diez hombres legos riña / que con una mujer culta" (1651–53).
47. Calderón's original reads:

> *Don Juan.* Yo no quiero que tu amor
> sea, sino que lo finjas,
> que esto todo ha de ser burla.
> *Don Alonso.* Mucho el ser fingido obliga,
> y hacer burla de una loca
> tan vana y tan presumida . . .
> *Moscatel [ap.].* ¡Qué presto hizo la razón
> a la ocasión que le brinda!
> Tan loco nos venga el año.
> *Don Alonso.* Cuanto sea engaño y mentira,
> vaya; mas pensar que tengo
> de obligarla ni sufrirla,
> es pensar un imposible.
> *Don Juan.* Ni nadie a aqueso os obliga. (1665–78)

48. See Cruickshank and Page, 114–17.
49. Calderón's original: "Atención, señoras mías: / entre mentir o querer, / ¿cuál será lo verdadero, / si esto lo fingido es?" (1833–36).

50. The original in Calderón: "En fin, no hay cosa más fácil / que engañar una mujer" (1873–74).
51. Calderón's original reads: "en fin, en fin, ha de ser / mujer cualquiera mujer" (2184–85).
52. Calderón's original: "y fuera historia muy mala/haberme llevado a ser / el burlado yo" (2322–24).
53. The original in Calderón: "Novedad se me hace extraña" (2449)
54. Calderón's original: "A mí no, porque en sabiendo / que era tu voluntad falsa, / supe que sería dichosa; / que por no acertar en nada, / más con nosotras merece / quien finge, que no quien ama" (2450–55).
55. See Cruickshank and Page, xix–xxiii.
56. On satire, see Hart, *Theater and World* 165–69.
57. Ben Jonson, *Timber* (2648–50, 52–53, 589). For quotations and citations from Jonson, see *Ben Jonson*, ed. Ian Donaldson (Oxford: Oxford University Press, 1985).
58. See Whitfield, 31. For a perceptive discussion of Jonson as classicist and of the denouement, see the Introduction to the Revels Plays edition: Ben Jonson, *Volpone*, ed. R. B. Parker (Manchester: Manchester University Press, 1983), 12–14, 43–44; and see the Introduction to the Revels Student Edition of *Volpone*, ed. Brian Parker and David Bevington (Manchester: Manchester University Press, 1999), 1–3, 22–23.
59. Henry Peyre notes: "A few cantankerous or supercilious critics, reading the play in their studies and scrutinizing every detail, have taken issue with the relief provided by this dénouement. On the stage, the illogic is readily accepted and the happy ending in no way detracts from the audience's pleasure." See Peyre, "Introduction," Molière, *Tartuffe & The Would-Be Gentleman*, trans. H. Baker and J. Miller and illustrations by Serge Ivanoff (New York: The Limited Editions Club, 1963), xi [Houghton, Harvard copy]. As Peyre says, Tartuffe was performed in its revised version on February 5, 1669 (vii). Louis XIV was the godfather to Molière's son, Louis, and in 1664, as part of festivities at court, three acts of *Tartuffe* were performed and well received. After, the archbishop of Paris banned the play, but the king intervened and *Tartuffe* played to packed houses. Although clerics and their party attacked Molière and his young wife, he stood his ground (ix). The structure and the ending of the plays, as much as its content, contributed to this censorship and contest of the various authorities. The hypocrisy of holy men and the bourgeois world are concerns of the play. Molière himself played Orgon, the hapless and foolish husband, who tries to control his wife and family through Tartuffe, and Molière's wife played Orgon's wife, Elmire (xi). Peyre speculates on a comparison of the religious views of Shakespeare, author of *Twelfth Night* and *Measure for Measure*, with Molière, whom Peyre also discusses in terms of what Malraux so tellingly called "the aftermath of the absolute" (xiii). Goethe, W. G. Moore and others have been great admirers of Molière's comic talent (xiii). Peyre and I differ because I think there is sympathy for Tartuffe in Molière's portrayal (xiv–xv). Donald Frame also mentions the difficulties Molière had with the reception and staging of *Tartuffe* and he also discusses the nature of and history of translating Molière, including Richard Wilbur's great translations; see Donald M. Frame, Introduction, *Tartuffe and Other Plays by Molière*, trans. Donald M. Frame, Signet edition (New York: North American Library, 1967), xi, xii–xv. Wilbur's translation is excellent, and the bilingual edition is especially useful. "A Note to the Bilingual Edition," "Introduction," and "A Note to the Harvest edition (1963)," are brief but helpful; see Molière, *Tartuffe: A Comedy in Five Acts*, bilingual edition, trans. Richard Wilbur (New York: Harcourt Brace & Company, 1997), v–xii. The revised Penguin translation is also good, based on a translation of 1959. On the troubles of reception and staging of *Tartuffe*, see

David Coward, "Introduction to Molière," *The Misanthrope and Other Plays*, trans. John Wood and David Coward with an introduction and notes by David Coward (London: Penguin Books, 2000), xiii. Although I have had to use editions from the original languages in this chapter, I have tried to provide bilingual editions for the reader when possible. Unfortunately, in all the English translations of Molière I have consulted since the 1670s, none seems to translate the prose that accompanies the poems, and I have had to translate this for this chapter. My original essay only used the original languages without translation, which was the convention of the publisher, field, and time.

60. See Hart, *Theater and World*, esp. 125–26.

61. All references to Molière are to Jean-Baptiste Molière, *Théâtre Complet*, 2 vols, ed. Robert Jouanny (Paris: Garnier, 1962). All translations of Moliére in the text are mine. My thanks to Nicole Mallet, who graciously read my translations and made suggestions for improvement. I include the original French in this and following notes. The original reads: "Oserais-je demander encore cette grâce à VOTRE MAJESTÉ le propre jour de la grande résurrection de *Tartuffe*, ressuscité par vos bontés?"

62. Molière's translator, Medbourne, puts the world "Puritan" on the title page and gives it another title, *Tartuffe or the French Zealot*, at the head of the first scene (B). In the dedication "The Right Honourable Henry Lord Howard of Norfolk, Baron of Casterising," Medbourne opens with a great claim: "Here Preſent your Honour with the Master-Piece of MOLIERE'S Productions, or rather of all *French* Comedy" (A3). See *Tartuffe: Or The French Puritan. A Comedy, Lately Acted at the Theatre Royal. Written in French by MOLIERE and rendered into Engliſh with much Addition and Advantage, By M. MEDBOURNE, Servant to His Royal Highneſſ* (London: Printed by H. L and R. B. for *James Magnus*, 1670). Copy, Houghton Library, Harvard. Another translation came out of Molière; see *The Works of Moliere. In Six Volumes. A New Translation* (Berwick: Printed for R. Taylor, 1771). A copy is found in Houghton, and volume 3 is the volume in which *Tartuffe* is found. The Restoration and eighteenth-century translations at their best show the importance of rhythm in Molière's language.

63. See Jane Harrison, Francis Cornford, and Northrop Frye as well as Timothy Murray, *Theatrical Legitimization: Allegories of Genius in Seventeenth-Century England and France* (New York: Oxford University Press, 1987).

64. The original in Molière reads: "et, sans doute, il ne serait pas difficile de leur faire voir que la comédie, chez les anciens, a pris son origine de la religion, et faisait partie de leurs mystères; que les Espagnols, nos voisins, ne célèbrent guère de fêtes où la comédie ne soit mêlée, et que même, parmi nous, elle doit sa naissance aux soins d'une confrérie à qui appartient encore aujourd'hui l'hôtel de Bourgogne; que c'est un lieu qui fut donné pour y représenter les plus importantes mystères de notre foi; qu'on en voit encore des comédies imprimées en lettres gothiques, sous le nom d'un docteur de Sorbonne et, sans aller chercher si loin que l'on a joué, de notre temps, des pièces saintes de M. de Corneille, qui ont été l'admiration de toute la France."

65. The original reads: "Si l'emploi de la comédie est de corriger les vices des hommes, je ne vois pas par quelle raison il y en aura de privilégiés."

66. The original says: "On veut bien être méchant; mais on ne veut point être ridicule."

67. The original reads: "Les plus beaux traits d'une sérieuse morale."

68. The original says: "c'est qu'ils ont pris la comédie différemment, et que les uns l'ont considerée dans sa pureté, lorsque les autres l'ont regardée dans sa corruption, et confondue avec tous ces vilains spectacles qu'on a eu raison de nommer des spectacles de turpitude." See Jonas Barish, *The Antitheatrical Prejudice* (Berkeley: University of California Press, 1981).

69. The original in Molière: "Et, en effet, puisqu'on doit discourir des choses et non pas des mots, et que la plupart des contrariétés viennent de ne pas entendre et d'envelopper dans un même mot des choses opposées, il ne faut qu'ôter le voile de l'équivoque, et regarder ce qu'est la comédie en soi, pour voir si elle est condamnable."

70. The original reads; "Le devoir de la comédie étant de corriger les hommes en les divertissant, j'ai cru que, dans l'emploi où je me trouve, je n'avais rien de mieux à faire que d'attaquer par des peintures ridicules les vices de mon siècle."

71. The original says: "toutes les grimaces étudiées de ces gens de bien à outrance, toutes des friponneries couvertes de ces faux monnayeurs en dévotion, qui veulent attraper les hommes avec un zèle contrefait et une charité sophistique."

72. See Hart, "Narrative, Narrative Theory, and Drama: The Renaissance," *Canadian Review of Comparative Literature/Revue Canadienne de la Littérature Comparée* (*CRCL/RCLC*) 18 no. 2/3 (1991): 149–51.

73. See Molière, vol. 2.

74. The original reads: "C'est une chose bien téméraire à moi que de venir importuner un grand monarque au milieu de ses glorieuses conquêtes; mais, dans l'état où je me vois, où trouver, SIRE, une protection qu'au lieu où je la viens chercher? et qui puis-je solliciter contre l'autorité de la puissance qui m'accable, que la source de la puissance et de l'autorité, que le juste dispensateur des ordres absolus, que le souverain juge et le maître de toutes choses?"

75. Here is the original: "tout ce que j'ai jugé capable de fournir l'ombre d'un prétexte aux célèbres originaux du portrait que je voulais faire: tout cela n'a de rien servi."

76. The original says: "Daignent vos bontés, SIRE, me donner une protection contre leur rage envenimée: et puissé-je, au retour d'une campagne si glorieuse, délasser VOTRE MAJESTÉ des fatigues de ses conquêtes, lui donner d'innocents plaisirs après de si nobles travaux, et faire rire le monarche qui fait trembler toute Europe!"

77. Ernst Breisach, *Historiography: Ancient, Medieval, & Modern* (Chicago: University of Chicago Press, 1983), 28.

78. Some critics might not find the ends of *Volpone* and *Tartuffe* to be intricate and problematic. In discussing Molière's *Dom Juan* and Shakespeare's *Troilus and Cressida* as two plays in search of an audience, Nicholas Grene says that the figure of le Ciel in *Dom Juan*, who is a menace who wreaks vengeance on the sinner, presents "a much more serious difficulty than that with *Tartuffe* or *Volpone*, where the arbitrariness of the denouement could be reconciled with the satiric viewpoint of the whole play." See Nicholas Grene, *Shakespeare, Jonson, Molière: The Comic Contrast* (London: Macmillan, 1980), 182.

79. Terenti Afri (Terence), *TIMORVMENOS*, Text, with Stage Directions by John C. Rolfe (Boston: Ginn & Company, 1900), 10; my translation.

80. Félix Lope de Vega Carpio, *Arte nuevo de hacer comedias en este tiempo [The New Art of Writing Plays in This Age],1609*, in *European Theories of Drama*, ed. Barrett H. Clark, rev. Henry Popkin (1918; New York: Crown, 1947, rev. 1965), 63–67. The original translation is by William T. Brewster, *Papers on Play-Making I*, intro. by Brander Matthews (New York: Dramatic Museum of Columbia University, 1914).

Chapter 5

1. This chapter appeared in an earlier form as part of "Narrative, Narrative Theory, and Drama: The Renaissance," *Canadian Review of Comparative Literature/Revue Canadienne de la Littérature Comparée* (*CRCL/RCLC*) 18 no. 2/3 (1991): 117–65. This was a special issue, "Renaissance Narrative and Drama," which I edited. My thanks

to the editors of *CRCL/RCLC* on behalf of the Canadian Comparative Literature Association for permission to reprint. Beyond that contribution, I have discussed narrative and drama in Jonathan Hart, "Alienation, Double Signs with a Difference: Conscious Knots in *Cymbeline* and *The Winter's Tale*," *CIEFL Bulletin* (New Series) 1 (1989): 58–78. Since that time, some interesting works on narrative have appeared, especially as they relate to Shakespeare. My colleague Rawdon (Robert R.) Wilson produced an important full-length study of the problem of innovation in terms of a range of problems in narrative conventions; see his *Shakespearean Narrative* (Newark: University of Delaware Press, 1995). Although he and I have taken a different tact (my interest has been more in terms of poetics and rhetoric as in Shakespeare's narrative poems in other of my works), Wilson's exploration of narratology and adjacent theoretical frameworks has always instructed me. Another scholar who has made a book-length contribution to the field is Barbara Hardy; see her *Shakespeare's Storytellers: Dramatic Narration* (London: Peter Owen, 1997). Hardy concentrates on narrative constructions (for instance, self-conscious narrative), themes (like memory and gender), and narrative in *Hamlet, King Lear*, and *Macbeth*. Wilson details earlier work in the field of narrative and Shakespeare and narrative; Hardy provides few notes. More recently, Richard Meek has produced a book in a related field; see his *Narrating the Visual in Shakespeare* (Farnham: Ashgate, 2009). Meek concentrates on the plays as debates over the nature of text and performance and examines this concern in *Venus and Adonis, The Rape of Lucrece, Hamlet, King Lear*, and *The Winter's Tale*. For work that is adjacent to Shakespeare and narrative but not directly related, see Leonard Barkan, "Making Pictures Speak: Renaissance Art, Elizabethan Literature, Modern Scholarship," *Renaissance Quarterly* 48 (1995): 326–51; Pauline Kiernan, *Shakespeare's Theory of Drama* (Cambridge: Cambridge University Press, 1996); Alison Thorne, *Vision and Rhetoric in Shakespeare* (Basingstoke: Palgrave Macmillan, 2000); essays in *Shakespeare Survey* 53 (2000) on "Shakespeare and Narrative;" Russ McDonald, *Shakespeare and the Arts of Language* (Oxford: Oxford University Press, 2001); Peter Mack, *Elizabethan Rhetoric: Theory and Practice* (Cambridge: Cambridge University Press, 2002); Alastair Fowler, *Renaissance Realism: Narrative Images in Literature and Art* (Oxford: Oxford University Press, 2003). In classical rhetoric, *diegesis* or *narratio*, that is narration in a speech, was important. For a general sense of the history of rhetoric, see Thomas M. Conley, *Rhetoric in the European Tradition* (New York: Longman, 1990).

2. Kristin Morrison, *Canters and Chroniclers: The Use of Narrative in the Plays of Samuel Beckett and Harold Pinter* (Chicago: University of Chicago Press, 1983), 3–4; see Joan Rees, *Shakespeare and the Story: Aspects of Creation* (London: Athlone Press, 1978); Marcello Pagnini, *Shakespeare e il paradigma della specularita. Lettura di due Campioni: 'King Lear' a 'A Midsummer Night's Dream'* (Pisa: Pacini, 1976); Cesare Segre, "Narratology and Theater," *Poetics Today* 2 (1981): 95–104; Karellynne Wertheimer Watkins, "The Use of Narrative in Shakespeare's Drama," *Dissertation Abstracts International* 42 (1982): 5133A.

3. Thornton Wilder, *Three Plays: Our Town, The Skin of Our Teeth, The Matchmaker* (1957; New York: Avon Books, 1976), viii, 5–7, 29–31, 49–52, 64.

4. Shlomith Rimmon-Kenan, *Narrative Fiction: Contemporary Poetics* (London: Methuen, 1983), 1–5; William Labov, *Language in the Inner City* (Philadelphia: University of Pennsylvania Press, 1972). See Jean-Michel Adam *Le Récit* (Paris: Presses Universitaires de Paris, 1984), 3–38, and Steven Cohan and Linda M. Shires, *Telling Stories: A Theoretical Analysis of Narrative Fiction* (New York: Routledge, 1988), 1–20, esp. 1. For recent work on narrative theory, see Gerald Prince, "Gérard Genette and the Pleasures of Poetics," *Narrative* 18 (2010): 3–7. For a discussion of why philosophers are becom-

ing more interested in narrative (in the wake of Arthur C. Danto, Hannah Arendt and Paul Ricoeur), see Noël Carroll, "Introduction," *Journal of Aesthetics and Art Criticism* (*JAAC*) 67 (2009): 1–3 and this special issue on narrative. See also *Handbook of Narratology*, ed. Peter Hühn, John Pier, Wolf Schmid, and Jörg Schönert (Berlin: de Gruyter, 2009). For a discussion of narrative in terms of cultural poetics and cultural negotiation, drawing on Stephen Greenblatt's views, see Luc Herman and Bart Vervaeck, "Narrative Interest as Cultural Negotiation," *Narrative* 17 (2009): 111–29. See also *Narratology in the Age of Cross-Disciplinary Narrative Research*, ed. Sandra Heinen and Roy Sommer (Berlin, Germany: de Gruyter, 2009); Monika Fludernik, *An Introduction to Narratology* (London: Routledge, 2009). On grammar, logic, and rhetoric (the *trivium*) and their relation to the nature of narrative, see John Rodden, "How Do Stories Convince Us? Notes towards a Rhetoric of Narrative," *College Literature* 35 (2008): 148–73. For a helpful and wide-ranging review article, see Sabine Gross, "Surveying Narratology," *Monatshefte für Deutschsprachige Literatur und Kultur* 100 (2008): 534–59. For a recent discussion of narrative and drama that supplements the special issue I edited in 1991, see Monika Fludernik, "Narrative and Drama," *Theorizing Narrativity*, ed. John Pier, García Landa, and José Angel (Berlin, Germany; de Gruyter, 2008), 355–83. For a study that combines drama and theory well but that is outside the time period of my book, see Peter Buse, *Drama + Theory: Critical Approaches to Modern British Drama* (Manchester: Manchester University Press, 2001).

5. Uri Margolin, "Narrative and Indexicality: A Tentative Framework," *Journal of Literary Semantics* 13 (1984): 181. On possible and fictional worlds, see Jerome Bruner, *Actual Minds/Possible Worlds* (Cambridge, MA: Harvard University Press, 1986); Thomas G. Pavel, *Fictional Worlds* (Cambridge, MA: Harvard University Press, 1986), and Jonathan Hart, "A Comparative Pluralism: The Heterogeneity of Methods and the Case of Possible Worlds," *Canadian Review of Comparative Literature/Revue Canadienne de Littérature Comparée* 15 (1988): 320–45.

6. Ross Chambers, *Story and Situation: Narrative Seduction and the Power of Fiction*. Minneapolis: University of Minnesota Press, 1984), 3–4.

7. Ibid., 213–36.

8. Ibid., 4. Thomas Pavel does not argue for a contextual study of narratives, which he says has been successfully made before, but seeks to defend some aspects of formalism and narratology, which are closely related, because of contextualist and historicist critiques. He offers, instead, what he calls "a historical approach to narrative." Thomas Pavel, "Narrative Tectonics," *Poetics* 11 (1990): 354, see 349–64.

9. Chambers, *Story and Situation*, 5–6.

10. Gerald Prince, *A Dictionary of Narratology* (Lincoln: University of Nebraska Press, 1987), 58–60.

11. Chambers, *Story and Situation*, 5.

12. See Aristotle, *Aristotle: Poetics and Longinus*, ed. and trans. W. Hamilton Fyfe, and *Demetrius on Style*, ed. and trans. W. Rhys Roberts [1927] (London: Heinemann, 1932, rpt. 1946).

13. Michael Grant, "Introduction," *Tacitus: The Annals of Imperial Rome*, trans. M. Grant, rev. ed. (1971; Harmondsworth, UK: Penguin, 1983), 10; A. R. Burn, "Introduction," *Herodotus: The Histories*, ed. Aubrey de Selincourt, trans. A. R. Burn, rev. ed. (1972; Harmondsworth, UK: Penguin, 1976), 26; M. L. Findley, "Introduction," *Thucydides: History of the Peloponnesian War*, trans. Rex Warner, ed. M.L. Findley, rev. ed. (Harmondsworth, UK: Penguin, 1972), 15–32.

14. See Gérard Genette, *Figures III* (Paris: Seuil, 1972) and his *Nouveau discours du récit*. Paris: Seuil, 1983, and, in translation, his *Narrative Discourse*, trans. J. E. Lewin (Ithaca, NY: Cornell University Press, 1980) and *Narrative Discourse Revisited*, trans.

J. E. Lewin (Ithaca, NY: Cornell University Press, 1990). See Thomas Pavel, *La Syntaxe narrative des tragedies de Corneille: Recherches et propositions* (Ottawa, ON: Presses Universitaires d'Ottawa, 1976), and his "Narrative Tectonics" (1990). See also Antonio Gómez-Moriana, *La Subversion du discours rituel* (Québec, QC: Préambule, 1985); Wallace Martin, *Recent Theories of Narrative* (Ithaca, NY: Cornell University Press, 1986); Peter J. Rabinowitz, *Before Reading: Narrative Conventions and the Politics of Interpretation* (Ithaca, NY: Cornell University Press, 1987); Richard Waswo, *Language and Meaning in the Renaissance* (Princeton: Princeton University Press, 1987).

15. See also Mieke Bal, *De theorie van vertellen en verhalen* (Muiderberg: Coutinho, 1980), and her *Narratology: Introduction to the Theory of Narrative*, trans. Christine van Boheemen (Toronto: University of Toronto Press, 1985).

16. See, for instance, Roland Barthes, *Sur Racine* (Paris: Seuil, 1963); Seymour Chatman, *Story and Discourse* (Ithaca, NY: Cornell University Press, 1978); Gerald Prince, *Narratology* (Berlin: Mouton, 1982); Shlomith Rimmon-Kenan, *Narrative Fiction: Contemporary Poetics* (London: Methuen, 1983).

17. Genette, *Narrative Discourse Revisited* (1990), 16–17, 44–45.

18. Cf. Genette, *Narrative Discourse* (1980), 33, and Nina C. Ekstein, *Dramatic Narrative: Racine's Récits* (New York: Peter Lang, 1986), 111–21. See Jean Racine, *Phèdre*, ed. Michel Autrand (Paris: Librairie Larousse, 1971) and Jean Racine, *Oeuvres completes*, ed. Pierre Clarac (Paris: Seuil, 1962).

19. Genette, *Narrative Discourse* (1980), 173.

20. Ibid., 232.

21. Genette, *Narrative Discourse* (1980), 183, 243. See Sophocles, *Sophocles*, ed. and trans. F. Storr, 2 vols. (London: Heinemann, 1912).

22. Seymour Chatman, *Story and Discourse* (Ithaca, NY: Cornell University Press, 1978); Jacques Derrida, "La Loi du genre/The Law of Genre," trans. Avital Ronnell, *Glyph: Textual Studies* 7 (1980): 176–232.

23. A great work in the tradition of Shakespearean criticism that discusses the nature of plays and the text and the connection between particulars and universals is Samuel Johnson, *Johnson on Shakespeare*, ed. Arthur Sherbo, vols. 7 and 8 of *The Yale Edition of the Works of Samuel Johnson* (New Haven, CT: Yale University Press, 1968).

24. Keir Elam, *The Semiotics of Theatre and Drama* (London: Methuen, 1980), 3; see *Shakespeare's Universe of Discourse: Language Games in the Comedies* (Cambridge: Cambridge University Press, 1984).

25. Jacques Derrida, *Of Grammatology*, trans. Gayatri Chakravorty Spivak (Baltimore, MD: Johns Hopkins University Press, 1976), 43; the original appeared as *De la grammatologie* (Paris: Minuit, 1967); Jacques Derrida, *L'Écriture et la différence* (Paris: Seuil, 1967), 343–68.

26. Pavel, "Narrative Tectonics" (1990), 355–58. On romance, see *Unfolded Tales: Essays on Renaissance Romance*, ed. and intro. George M. Logan and Gordon Teskey, foreword by Northrop Frye (Ithaca, NY: Cornell University Press, 1989).

27. Margaret W. Ferguson with Maureen Quilligan and Nancy J. Vickers, "Introduction," *Rewriting the Renaissance: The Discourses of Sexual Difference in Early Modern Europe*, ed. M. W. Ferguson, M. Quilligan, and N. J. Vickers (Chicago: University of Chicago Press, 1986), xvi–xvii.

28. There is also the influence of Seneca; see Seneca, *Seneca: Tragedies*, ed. and trans. Frank Justus Miller, 2 vols. (London: Heinemann, 1917).

29. Marvin Carlson, *Theories of the Theatre: A Historical and Critical Survey, from the Greeks to the Present* (Ithaca, NY: Cornell University Press, 1984), 37–111.

30. Ibid., 39.

31. Ibid., 48. See also Thomas M. Greene, *The Light in Troy: Imitation and Discovery in Renaissance Poetry* (New Haven, CT: Yale University Press, 1982), 171–96.

32. Carlson, *Theories of the Theatre*, 49–55.

33. Miguel de Cervantes, *Obras Completas*, ed. Angel Valbuera Prat, 6 vols. (Madrid: Aguilar, 1917).

34. On Spanish views of theatre, see H. J. Chaytor, *Dramatic Theory in Spain* (Cambridge: Cambridge University Press, 1925). Pavel mentions the close relation between prose narrative and drama in French plays of the sixteenth and seventeenth centuries. See his "Narrative Tectonics" (1990).

35. Carlson, *Theories of the Theatre*, 62–65.

36. Ibid., 77–79.

37. Jonas Barish, *The Antitheatrical Prejudice* (Berkeley: University of California Press, 1981); Margaret W. Ferguson, *Trials of Desire: Renaissance Defenses of Poetry* (New Haven, CT: Yale University Press, 1983), 137–62; Philip Sidney, "An Apology for Poetry," *English Critical Texts*, ed. D. J. Enright and Ernst de Chickera (1962; London: Oxford University Press, 1975), 3–49; George Puttenham, *The Arte of English Poesie*, ed. Gladys D. Willcock and Alice Walker (Cambridge: Cambridge University Press, 1970).

38. See Ben Jonson, *Ben Jonson*, ed. C. H. Herford and Percy and Evelyn Simpson, 11 vols. (Oxford: Clarendon Press, 1925–52). Carlson, 82, 86–87.

39. See Ferguson, *Trials* (1983), 18–53. See Gisèle Mathieu-Castellani, "Le Contrat et le sacrifice dans la poétique de d'Aubigne," *Renaissance and Reformation* 23 (1987): 77–87.

40. Carlson, *Theories of the Theatre*, 67–74.

41. Ibid., 90, 93.

42. Ibid., 94–96.

43. Ibid., 98–103.

44. Molière, *Oeuvres completes*, ed. Robert Jouanny (Paris: Garnier Freres, 1962), 193–94. All quotations in the notes below are from this edition and my translations in the main text are based on it.

45. All translations are my own. Once more, my thanks to Nicole Mallet, who kindly read my translations and suggested ways to improve them. Molière's original is as follows: "En attendant cet examen, qui peut-être ne viendra point, je m'en remets assez aux décisions de la multitude, et je tiens aussi difficile de combattre un ouvrage que le public approve, que d'en défendre un qu'il condamne" (1.365).

46. On *Récits*, see Gerard Genette, *Nouveau discours du récit* (Paris: Seuil, 1983); Jean-Michel Adam *Le Récit* (Paris: Presses Universitaires de Paris, 1984).

47. My translation; the original in Molière reads: "Premièrement, il n'est pas vrai de dire que toute la pièce n'est qu'en récits. On y voit beaucoup d'actions qui se passent sur la scène, et les récits eux-mêmes y sont des actions, suivant la constitution du sujet; d'autant qu'ils sont tous faits innocemment, ces récits, à la personne intéressée, qui par là entre, à tous coups, dans une confusion à réjouir les spectateurs, et prend, à chaque nouvelle, toutes les mesures qu'il peut pour se parer du malheur qu'il craint" (vi.1. 509).

48. See Harry Levin, *Playboys and Killjoys: An Essay on the Theory and Practice of Comedy* (Oxford: Oxford University Press, 1987). For New Comedy, see Plautus, *Plautus*, ed. and trans. Paul Nixon, 5 vols. (London: Heinemann, 1916) and Terence, *Terence, ed. and trans.* John Sargeaunt, 2 vols. (London: Heinemann, 1912).

49. My translation; and the original in Molière is as follows: "Si l'emploi de la comédie est de corriger les vices des hommes, je ne vois pas par quelle raison il y en aura de priviliégés."

50. Racine, preface to *Phèdre* 31; my translation. The original reads: "Ce que je puis assurer, c'est que je n'en ai point fait où la vertu soit plus mise en jour que dans celle-ci. Les moindres fautes y sont sévèrement punies."

51. Carlson, *Theories of the Theatre*, 109.

52. Cf. Carlson, *Theories of the Theatre*, 99–111, and Nina C. Ekstein, *Dramatic Narrative: Racine's Récits* (New York: Peter Lang, 1986), 1–10, 83.

53. See Frederick S. Boas, *Shakspeare and His Predecessors* (New York: Scribner's, 1896); T. S. Eliot, "Hamlet" (1919), *Selected Essays* (1932; London: Faber and Faber, 1976), 141–46; W. W. Lawrence, *Shakespeare's Problem Comedies* (New York: Macmillan, 1931).

54. See Ekstein, *Dramatic Narrative*.

55. Fred B. Millet and Gerald Eades Bentley, *The Art of the Drama* (New York: Appleton-Century-Crofts, 1935), 182–83.

56. Ibid., 182.

57. Ibid.

58. *The Chronicle History of King Henry the Fift with His Battell Fought at Agincourt in France*, film, directed by Laurence Olivier (United Kingdom: Eagle-Lion Distributors Limited, 1944), 137 minutes.

59. Millet and Bentley, *The Art of the Drama*, 183. Millet and Bentley write different sections of the book.

60. All references are to William Shakespeare, *The Riverside Shakespeare*, ed. G. Blakemore Evans (Boston: Houghton Mifflin, 1974).

61. See Robert R. Wilson, "Narratives and Narrators in *Hamlet*," *Hamlet Studies* 6 (1984): 30–40.

62. Aeschylus, *Aeschylus*, ed. and trans. Herbert Weir Smith, 2 vols. (1926; London: Heinemann, 1952).

63. The four narrative functions—exposition, suggestion, compression, and address—work in concert. The openings of *Mankind* and *Everyman* illustrate the interplay of the four categories. When in *Mankind* Mercy opens the play by telling about God's sacrifice of Christ, by exhorting the audience to rectify their conditions with humility and reverence and to incline themselves to Christ, by introducing himself as Mercy and by explaining his role in their salvation through Christ from the temptations of this world, Mischeffe interrupts and challenges him by belittling his preaching and his language and by using parodic verse and doggerel Latin. The conflict begins between good and evil and after about 140 lines Mankind enters with his spade, kneels at the feet of Mercy but soon suffers an onslaught from the figures of temptation. *Everyman* opens with a messenger who acts as a Prologue. He addresses the audience, points a moral lesson with a warning to Man, and asks them to listen to what God, who is calling Everyman to a general reckoning, will say. God's narrative is an amplification of the Messenger's. After he speaks of his own suffering on the cross and of human disobedience, of his hope for his people and the mercy he offers them, he summons death. The human and divine narratives introduce the conflict that humans can live through God's mercy or die in unrepentant sin. See David Bevington, *Medieval Drama* (Boston: Houghton Mifflin, 1975).

64. Ekstein, *Dramatic Narrative*, 16.

65. All references in this chapter are to Marlowe's text are to Christopher Marlowe, *The Works of Christopher Marlowe*, ed. C. F. Tucker Brooke (1910; Oxford: Clarendon Press, 1946).

66. Ekstein, *Dramatic Narrative*, 4.

67. Aristophanes, *Aristophanes*, ed. and trans. Benjamin Bickley Rogers, 3 vols. (London: Heinemann, 1924). I am not arguing that these four functions occur separately. The

categories reflect the emphasis that is put on each function. Other functions occur in the passage noted in *The Clouds.* In Aeschylus' *Agamemnon* the dialogue between the Chorus and the Herald about the fall of Troy reports offstage action and leads the Chorus to say that the Herald's tale shows that he himself was wrong. Part of Clytaemnestra's response to the Herald's long speech is to ask why she should listen to him rather than to Agamemnon. After the Herald praises Clytaemnestra's vaunt of loyalty to her husband, the Chorus wants to hear about the story of Menelaus. The Herald is self-consciously rhetorical about his method of mixing good news of the Greek victory with the terrible news of the subsequent storm. Nevertheless, he represents the storm by telling about it. The Chorus then comments on the fall of Troy and engages Agamemnon on his version of events. Clytaemnestra then steps forward and tells her story of suffering and loneliness and says that part of her pain derived from false stories or rumors about Agamemnon's fate. (This narrative of pain is uttered with some dark irony considering her plans for the imminent murder of her husband.) She, along with Agamemnon, help to create in their exchange a triumphant return full of splendor that the conventions of the Attic theatre would not allow to be represented on stage.

68. See Jonathan Hart, "Temporality and Theatricality in Shakespeare's Lancastrian Tetralogy," *Studia Neophilogica* 63 (1991): 69–88, and Hart, *Theater and World: The Problematics of Shakespeare's History* (Boston: Northeastern University Press, 1992).

Chapter 6

1. This chapter is a revised version of part of my Introduction to a special issue I edited, "Renaissance Narrative and Drama," for *CRCL/RCLC*; see "Narrative, Narrative Theory, and Drama: The Renaissance," *Canadian Review of Comparative Literature/Revue Canadienne de la Littérature Comparée* 18, no. 2/3 (1991): 117–65. My thanks to the editors for their permission on behalf of the Canadian Comparative Literature Association to publish this. For some relevant works since the writing of the original version of this chapter (which discusses Shakespeare or refers to work in the field in various contexts), see Frank Kermode, *Poetry, Narrative, History* (Oxford: Blackwell, 1990); Earl Miner, *Comparative Poetics: An Intercultural Essay on Theories of Literature* (Princeton: Princeton University Press, 1990), esp. 143–45; Barbara Hodgdon, *The End Crowns All: Closure and Contradiction in Shakespeare's History* (Princeton: Princeton University Press, 1991); Howard Marchitello, *Narrative and Meaning in Early Modern England: Browne's Skull and Other Histories* (Cambridge: Cambridge University Press, 1997); Nicholas Grene, *Shakespeare's Serial History Plays* (Cambridge: Cambridge University Press, 2002); Alastair Fowler, *Renaissance Realism: Narrative Images in Literature and Art* (Oxford: Oxford University Press, 2003); Dominque Goy-Blanquet, *Shakespeare's Early History Plays: From Chronicle to Stage* (Oxford: Oxford University Press, 2003); Jane Kingsley-Smith, *Shakespeare's Drama of Exile* (New York: Palgrave Macmillan, 2003); Emma Kafalenos, *Narrative Causalities* (Columbus: Ohio State University Press, 2006); Jonathan Hart, *Shakespeare: Poetry, History, and Culture* (New York: Palgrave Macmillan, 2009); and Richard Meek, "Shakespeare and Narrative," *Literature Compass* 6 (2009): 482–98.

2. François Rabelais, *Oeuvres completes*, ed. Jacques Boulenger et Lucien Scheler (Paris: Gallimard, 1955), bk. 3, ch. 38, 464.

3. Ibid., bk. 3, ch. 40, 471–74.

4. Ibid., bk. 3, ch. 39, 470. This is my English translation of the Latin.

5. François Rabelais, *Gargantua and Pantagruel,* "Chapter 4.XXXVII.—How Pantagruel sent for Colonel Maulchitterling and Colonel Cut-pudding; with a discourse well worth your hearing about the names of places and persons," in *The Works of Rabelais Faithfully Translated From the French with Variorum Notes, and Numerous Illustrations by Gustave Doré* (London: Chatto & Windus, n.d.), 476. For the electronic version, which is the Derby edition of the Moray Press of 1894, the translation, is by Sir Thomas Urquhart of Cromarty and Peter Antony Motteux. In that text, the editor notes: "(Motteux reads—'even numbers to the Right, and odd ones to the Left.')". The Project Gutenberg version on the Internet contains the following note: "The text of the first Two Books of Rabelais has been reprinted from the first edition (1653) of Urquhart's translation. Footnotes initialled 'M.' are drawn from the Maitland Club edition (1838); other footnotes are by the translator. Urquhart's translation of Book III. appeared posthumously in 1693, with a new edition of Books I. and II., under Motteux's editorship. Motteux's rendering of Books IV. and V. followed in 1708. Occasionally (as the footnotes indicate) passages omitted by Motteux have been restored from the 1738 copy edited by Ozell." The French original reads: "Je suys tout confus en mon entendement quand je pense en l'invention admirable de Pythagoras, lequel par le nombre *par* ou *impar* des syllabes d'un chascun nom propre, exposoit de quel cousté estoient les humains boyteulx, bossus, borgnes, gouteux, paralytiques, pleuritiques et aultres telz maléfices en nature: sçavoir est assignant le nombre *par* au cousté guausche du corps, le *impar* au dextre" (Rabelais, *Oeuvres completes,* bk. 4, ch. 37, 640).

6. For the print version of this translation, see chapter 6 of Part I, in Miguel de Cervantes Saavedra, *The Ingenious Gentleman Don Quixote of La Mancha,* trans. John Ormsby (London: Smith, Elder & Co., 1885), 161–62. "CHAPTER VI. OF THE DIVERTING AND IMPORTANT SCRUTINY WHICH THE CURATE AND THE BARBER MADE IN THE LIBRARY OF OUR INGENIOUS GENTLEMAN," in the electronic book on Project Gutenburg, produced by David Widger. The original reads: "Muchos años ha que es grande amigo mío ese Cervantes, ye sé que es más versado en desdichas que en versos. Su libro tiene algo de buena invención; propone algo, y no concluye nada: es menester esperar la segunda parte que promete, quizá con la emienda alcanzará del todo la misericordia que ahora se le niega; y entre tanto que esto se ve, tenedle recluso en vuestra posada, señor compadre," Cervantes, part 1, ch. 6, 127.

7. All references to *Hamlet* are from William Shakespeare, *The Riverside Shakespeare,* ed. G. Blakemore Evans (Boston: Houghton Mifflin, 1974). The narrative issues that the characters in Rabelais, Cervantes, and Shakespeare discuss relate closely to those issues that preoccupied writers during the Renaissance. How language means, how tales unfold and how drama relates to the society that produces it are the subjects that Richard Waswo, Walter Cohen, the contributors to Logan's and Teskey's volume, and Nina Ekstein explore. Their work is especially germane here in terms of the relation of language to narrative, narrative to society, nondramatic to dramatic literature, and dramatic narrative. See Richard Waswo, *Language and Meaning in the Renaissance* (Princeton: Princeton University Press, 1987); Walter Cohen, *Drama of a Nation: Public Theater in Renaissance England and Spain* (Ithaca NY: Cornell University Press, 1985); George M. Logan and Gordon Teskey, eds., *Unfolded Tales: Essays on Renaissance Romance* (Ithaca, NY: Cornell University Press, 1989); Nina C. Ekstein, *Dramatic Narrative: Racine's Récits* (New York: Peter Lang, 1986). I discuss these studies in "The Crisis in Narrative: Language, Tale and Drama in the Renaissance," *CRCL/RCLC* 18, no. 2/3 (1991): 365–92.

8. From the late 1970s to the early 1990s, I discussed Shakespeare's representation of history and especially on the connections among the history play, genre, and irony. The last extended treatment of this question with a focus on the Second Tetralogy, see *Theater and World: The Problematics of Shakespeare's History* (Boston: Northeastern University Press, 1992). Here, I have telescoped my analysis for the purposes of the argument of this chapter and of this book. This book is out-of-print, and I own the copyright and so give myself permission to reprint and rework.

9. For Francis Bacon's view of intellectual history and the three great revolutions in knowledge in ancient Greece, Rome and Western Europe, see *The Works of Francis Bacon*, ed. James Spedding, R. L. Ellis, and D. D. Heath, 15 vols. (London: Longman's & Co., 1857–74), iv, 74–77. In the address to the reader in *Britannia*, Camden explains his research skills and regimen to "search" and "truth": "subsidio mihi antiquissimae linguae Britannicae et Anglo-Saxonicae notitiam qualemcunque comparavi. Angliam fere omnem peragravi. Versatissimum et peritissimum quemque in sua regione consuli. Scriptores patrios, Graecos, Latinos qui vel semel Britanniae meminerunt studiose evolvi. Publica regni commentaria, sacra scrinia et archiva, bibliothecas plures, urbium et ecclesiarum tabularia, monumenta et veteres schedas excussi, eaque quasi testimonia de coelo omni exceptione maiora advocavi, et certe ipsissimis quibus loquuntur verbis, licet barbarie infuscatis, ut veritati suus integer constet honos, in medium, cum res postulare videretur, produxi." Philemon Holland translates the passage thus in his translation of 1607: "I have attained to some skill of the most ancient British and English-Saxon tongues: I have travailed over all England for the most part; I have conferred with most skillfull observers in each county, I have studiously read over our owne countrie writers, old and new, all Greeke and Latine authors which have once made mention of Britaine. I have had conference with learned men in other parts of Christendome: I have beene diligent in the Records of this Realme. I have looked into most Libraries, Registers, and memorials of Churches, Cities, and Corporations. I have poored upon many an old Rowle, and Evidence: and produced their testimonie (as beyond all exception) when the cause required, in their owne words (although barbarous they be) that the honor of veritie might in no wise be impeached." For an electronic text, see the hypertext critical edition by Dana F. Sutton, University of California, Irvine, posted June 14, 2004. In "In Certaine Aduertiſements to the Reader," Samuel Daniel writes: "For the Worke it ſelfe I can chalenge nothing therein but only the ſowing it together, and the obſeruation of thoſe neceſſary circumſtances, and inferences which the Hiſtory naturally miniſters: deſirous to deliuer things done, in as euen, and quiet an order, as ſuch a heape will permit, without quarrelling with the *Beliefe* of Antiquity, deprauing the actions of other Nations to aduance our owne, or keeping backe those Reaſons of State they had, for what they did in thoſe times: holding it fitteſt and beſt agreeing with integritie (the chiefeſt duty of a Writer) to leaue things to their owne Fame, and the Cenſure thereof to the Reader, as being his part rather then mine, who am onely to recite things done, not to rule them" (see S[amuel] D[aniel], *The Collection of the historie of England* (London: Nicolas Oakes, [1618], A3 recto-A4 verso). In "An Advertisement to the Reader," Sprat allows for the nature of a history as a defense, in this case of a great society of natural philosophers: "The Style perhaps in which it is written, is larger and more contentious than becomes that purity and ſhortneſ which are the chief beauties of Hiſtorical Writings: But the blame of this ought not so much to be laid upon me, as upon the Detractors of ſo noble an Institution: For their Objections and Cavils againſt it, did make it neceſſary for me to write of it, not altogether in the way of a *plain Hiſtory*, but ſomtimes of an *Apology*," see Tho[mas] Sprat, *The History of the Royal-Society of London, For the Improving of Natural Knowledge* (London: T. R. for

J. Martyn, 1667). Since the first writing of this work, other books have appeared on Renaissance historiography, which I include in the following selected list of works that illuminate the field. Besides the other work in the area that I have cited in other notes, see Jacob Burckhardt, *Civilization of the Renaissance in Italy*, trans. S. G. C. Middlemore, 8th edition (1861; London: George Allen & Unwin, 1921); Wallace Ferguson, *The Renaissance in Historical Thought: Five Centuries of Interpretation* (Boston: Houghton Mifflin Co., [1948]); E. B. Fryde, *Humanism and Renaissance Historiography* (London: London: Hambledon, 1983). William Kerrigan and Gordon Braden, *The Idea of the Renaissance* (Baltimore: Johns Hopkins University Press, 1989); D. R. Woolf, *The Idea of History in Early Stuart England: Erudition, Ideology, and the 'Light of Truth' from the Accession of James I to the Civil War* (Toronto: University of Toronto Press, 1990); *Palgrave Advances in Renaissance Historiography*, ed. Jonathan Woolfson (Basingstoke: Palgrave Macmillan, 2005). For a study of history on the stage, see Michael Neill, *Putting History to the Question: Power, Politics, and Society in English Renaissance Drama* (New York: Columbia University Press, 2000).

10. I make this case more fully in "Henry VIII: The Play as History and Anti-History," *AEVUM* 3 (1991): 561–70, and in revised form in *Shakespeare: Poetry, History and Culture* (New York: Palgrave Macmillan, 2009), esp. ch. 9.

11. Anonymous, *Here followeth . . . Ordynarye of Chrystyanyte . . .* (London: Wynken de Worde, 1502), Part IV, sect. xxii. For the first definition, see, for example, Thomas More, *Works* (London, 1557), ch. 5, 939, and Henry Peacham, *The Garden of Eloquence . . . Corrected and augmented by the first Author* (London, 1593), 35–36. For the second definition, see, for instance, see Miles Coverdale, "A confutation . . ." (1540) in *Remains . . .*, ed. G. Pearson (Cambridge, 1846), part II, 333, and Richard Sherry, *A Treatise of the figures of Grammer and Rhetorike* (London, 1555), folio 23, xxvi. For the third definition, see John Marbeck, *Notes and Commonplaces . . .* (London, 1581), 560, cited in Norman Knox, *The Word Irony and Its Context, 1500–1755* (Durham, NC: Duke University Press, 1961), 33.

12. For a discussion of irony, in relation to Thomas Nashe, especially, *The Unfortunate Traveller* (1594), and Robert Burton, *The Anatomy of Melancholy* (1621), see Knox, 7–8, 22, 24, 59, 93–94, 141. Bishop Connop Thirlwall was the first to name this kind of irony "dramatic irony" in his essay "On the Irony of Sophocles," *Remains Literary and Theological of Connop Thirlwall*, ed. J. J. Stewart Perowne (London: Daldy, Isbidster, 1878). vol. 3, 1 57; originally published in *Philological Museum* in 1833.

13. Friedrich Schlegel, "Notebooks," fragment 1, no. 1144, 1204; see 1208, *Lectures on the History of Literature Ancient and Modern* (London: H. G. Bohn, 1859), 274–75; originally published in German in 1815. A. W. Schlegel, *Lectures on Dramatic Art and Literature*, trans. John Black, 2nd. ed., rev. (London: George Bell and Sons, 1900), 368–72. Adam Müller, "Fragmente über William Shakespeare," *Ueber die dramatische Kunst* (1806), 153–63, in *Shakespeare in Germany, 1740–1815*, ed. Roy Pascal (Cambridge: Cambridge University Press, 1937), 55–71; see also Pascal's Introduction, 10, 30–33. Ludwig Tieck, *Tony—A Drama in Three Acts by Th. Korner*, trans. Mark Ogden," and Karl Solger, *Erwin; or, Four Dialogues on Beauty and Art* (1816), in *German Aesthetic and Criticism: The Romantic Ironists and Goethe*, ed. Kathleen Wheeler (Cambridge: Cambridge University Press, 1984).

14. See I. A. Richards, *Principles of Literary Criticism* (1925; London: Routledge, 1949); William Empson, *Some Versions of Pastoral* (London: Chatto & Windus, 1935); Northrop Frye, *Anatomy of Criticism* (1957; Princeton: Princeton University Press, 1973), esp. 236–37, and Paul de Man, *Blindness and Insight: Essays in the Rhetoric of Contemporary Criticism* (1971; Minneapolis: University of Minnesota Press, 1983).

15. See Douglas Duncan, *Ben Jonson and the Lucianic Tradition* (Cambridge: Cambridge University Press, 1979).

16. Norman Rabkin, *Shakespeare and the Problem of Meaning* (Chicago: University of Chicago Press, 1981), 139.

17. Philip Sidney, "An Apology for Poetry," *English Critical Texts: 16th to 20th Century*, ed. D. J. Enright and Ernst de Chickera (1962; London: Oxford University Press, 1975), 17, 20–22, 34; Aristotle, "On the Art of Poetry," *Classical Literary Criticism*, ed. T. S. Dorsch (1965; Harmondsworth, UK: Penguin, 1975), 43–44; John Hooker, "The Epistle Dedicatorie " (to Sir Walter Raleigh), *Holinshed's Chronicles of England, Scotland and Ireland: Volume 6: Ireland* (London: Printed for J. Johnson et al, 1808; rpt. New York: AMS Press, 1954), 102; Edmund Spenser, "A Letter of the Authors . . . To . . . Sir Walter Raleigh etc.," in *The Fairie Queene: Book One in Works (Variorum)*, ed. Edwin Greenlaw et al. (Baltimore, MD: The Johns Hopkins University Press, 1932), I: 168–69; see also 167, 170; and Sir Walter Ralegh, Preface, *The History of the World*, in *Selections: From his Writings and Letters*, ed. G. E. Hadlow (Oxford: Clarendon Press, 1917), 40–57.

18. Herschel Baker, *The Race of Time: Three Lectures on Renaissance Historiography* (Toronto: University of Toronto Press, 1967), 16–18, 45–46, 52–59.

19. Dr. Johnson, "Preface to Edition of Shakespeare: 1765," *Johnson on Shakespeare*, ed. A. Sherbo, Yale ed. of the *Works*, vol. 7 (New Haven, CT: Yale University Press, 1968), 68.

20. William Camden, Preface, *Annals*, quoted in Peter Burke, *The Renaissance Sense of the Past* (London: Edward Arnold, 1969), 127–28; see Burke, 134; F. J. Levy, *Historical Thought* (San Marino, CA: Huntington Library, 1967), 280–85; F. Smith Fussner, *The Historical Revolution: English Historical Writing and Thought, 1580–1640* (London: Routledge and Kegan Paul, 1962), 281–82.

21. F. J. Levy, *Historical Thought*, 285–87.

22. See Hayden White, *Metahistory: The Historical Imagination in Nineteenth-Century Europe* (Baltimore, MD: Johns Hopkins University Press, 1973).

23. Pieter Geyl, "Shakespeare as Historian: A Fragment," *Encounters in History* (1947; Cleveland: The World Publishing Co., 1961); 60, see 4–50, 54–56.

24. F. Smith Fussner, *Tudor History*, 33, 229–31.

25. See White, *Metahistory*, and Fritz Stern, "Introduction," *The Varieties of History: From Voltaire to the Present*, ed. Fritz Stern (New York: Meridian Books, 1956), 24–27, 30.

26. R. G. Collingwood, *The Idea of History*, ed. T. M. Knox (1946; Oxford: Clarendon Press, 1948), 214–15 and Tom F. Driver, *The Sense of History in Greek and Shakespearean Drama* (1960; New York: Columbia University Press, 1967), 5–17.

27. Matthew Wikander, *The Play of Truth and State: Historical Drama from Shakespeare to Brecht* (Baltimore: Johns Hopkins University Press, 1986), 50.

28. Frye, *Anatomy of Criticism*, 73–86.

29. I refer here to Walter's note; see William Shakespeare, *King Henry V*, ed. J. H. Walter, Arden. ed. (1954; London: Methuen, 1977). See Hart, *Theater and World: The Problematics of Shakespeare's History* (Boston: Northeastern University Press, 1992), 52.

30. Aristotle, "On the Art of Poetry," *Classical Literary Criticism*, ed. T. S. Dorsch (1965; Harmondsworth, UK: Penguin, 1975), 33–75; Philip Sidney, "An Apology for Poetry," *English Critical Texts: 16th Century to 20th Century*, ed. D. J. Enright and Ernst de Chickera (1962; London: Oxford University Press, 1975), 3–49.

31. *The Great Code: The Bible and Literature* (New York: Harcourt Brace Jovanovich, 1982). See Jonathan Hart, "Stephen Greenblatt, *Shakespearean Negotiations: The Circulation of*

Social Energy in Renaissance England," *Textual Practice* 5 (1991): 429–48, for a further elaboration of this point and a detailed discussion of analogy.

32. Some of what follows is revised from a part of Jonathan Hart, "New Historical Shakespeare: Reading as Political Ventriloquy," *English* 42 (1993): 193–219. My thanks to the editor and to the English Association for permission to use this material.

33. The following primary texts are not always readily available. Excerpts from these texts may be found in *The Riverside Shakespeare,* ed. G. Blakemore Evans (Boston: Riverside, 1974), so that for the sake of space and accessibility this will be the only version I quote from and cite.

34. See, for instance, Gary Taylor, *Reinventing Shakespeare: A Cultural History From the Restoration to the Present* (1989; New York: Oxford University Press, 1991). In a lively argument, especially in the chapter on singularity, Taylor combines many attitudes to Shakespeare and concludes that critics cannot make a difference in what he calls "Shakesperotics" because Shakespeare has become a black hole where he was once a star. Ultimately, Taylor argues against sychophancy in Shakespearean criticism, which is a wise warning, to which I might add, "Shakespearenvy" (411). Somewhere between might lie a better critical place. To borrow Emerson's image of Shakespeare as a horizon that Taylor invokes, I see Shakespeare as calling us beyond ourselves (which includes the distance Taylor and I both ask for [Taylor, 404]) and as opening up to possibilities, but not as a pretext for worshipping Shakespeare as a god at dawn or twilight or as a demon whose beyondness goads us into blindness and carping. Shakespeare deserves criticism, not idolatry or denunciation. See Taylor, 395–411.

35. My study, *Theater and World,* belongs, in part, to this tradition.

Chapter 7

1. Thanks to Anne Lancashire for her seminar on drama of the 1580s in 1979–80 when my first work on historical drama of the 1580s began. Here I shall note some relevant material that has appeared on the histories after I completed the original work contained in this chapter. See Richard Helgerson, "Murder in Faversham: Holinshed's Impertinent History," *The Historical Imagination in Early Modern Britain,* ed. Donald R. Kelley and David Harris Sacks (Cambridge: Cambridge University Press, 1997), 93–105; Paul Budra, *A Mirror for Magistrates and the De Casibus Tradition* (Toronto: University of Toronto Press, 2000); Graham Holderness, *The Histories* (Basingstoke: Palgrave Macmillan, 2000); Derek Cohen, *Searching Shakespeare: Studies in Culture and Authority* (Toronto: University of Toronto Press, 2003); Richard Helgerson, "Shakespeare and Contemporary Dramatists of History," in *A Companion to Shakespeare's Works, Volume II: The Histories,* ed. Richard Dutton and Jean E. Howard (Oxford: Blackwell, 2003); the essays in *Shakespeare's Histories and Counter-histories,* ed. Dermot Cavanagh, Stuart Hampton-Reeves, and Stephen Longstaffe (Manchester: Manchester University Press, 2006) (most especially for my purposes, Stephen Longstaffe's "The Commons will Revolt: *Woodstock* after the Peasants' Revolt," 135–51). On theatre, see Andrew Gurr, *The Shakespeare Company, 1594–1642* (Cambridge: Cambridge University Press, 2004). On politics, see Andy Wood, *Riot, Rebellion and Popular Politics in Early Modern England* (London: Palgrave, 2002).

2. See, for instance, Don Ricks, *Shakespeare's Emergent Form: A Study of the Structures of the "Henry VI" Plays* (Logan: Utah State University Press, 1968); David Riggs, *Shakespeare's Heroical Histories: "Henry VI" and Its Literary Tradition* (Cambridge, MA: Harvard University Press, 1971); Paul Bacquet, Les pièces historiques de

Shakespeare: La première tétralogie et "Le roi Jean" vol. 1 (Paris: Presses Universitaires de France, 1978). For an earlier work, see Richard Simpson, "The Politics of Shakespeare's Historical Plays," *The New Shakespeare' Society's Transactions* (1874), 402–5. On past and present, including the jumble of legend and history in the popular mind, see Keith Thomas, *The Perception of the Past in Early Modern England* (London: Weidenfeld & Nicolson, 1984). A draft of this chapter was written and completed by 1991 based on material I worked on from 1978 to 1983. Some related material to this chapter occurs in Jonathan Hart, "Afterword," *Theater and World: The Problematics of Shakespeare's History* (Boston: Northeastern University Press, 1992), 242–50.

3. *The Dramatic Writings of John Bale*, ed. John S. Farmer (London, 1907); see David Bevington, *Tudor Drama and Politics: A Critical Approach to Topical Meaning* (Cambridge, MA: Harvard University Press, 1962), 97–105.

4. Honor McCuskor, *John Bale, Dramatist and Antiquary* (Bryn Mawr, PA, 1942), 32–47, cited in Irving Ribner, *The English History Play in the Age of Shakespeare* (1957; New York: Barnes and Noble, 1965), 34; see also Ribner, 33–39.

5. For a discussion of *Respublica* and the unwelcome advice on the succession that Gorboduc gives, see Bevington, *Tudor Drama*, 112–19, 141–47, and Ribner, *The English History Play*, 36–49.

6. "Gorboduc; or Ferrex and Porrex," in *Chief Pre-Shakespearean Dramas: A Selection of Plays Illustrating the History of the English Drama from Its Origin Down to Shakespeare*, ed. Joseph Quincy Adams (Boston: Houghton Mifflin, 1924), 530–35.

7. This is an instance of why E. M. W. Tillyard and others seized on the Tudor myth and why it can be complicated but not discounted or undercut. E. W. Talbert, Henry A. Kelly, Moody Prior, John Wilders, and others have complicated the interpretation of the Second Tetralogy by looking at other myths such as those of the Houses of Lancaster and York.

8. For a more detailed discussion of this and other aspects of this play, see Jonathan Hart, "Henry VIII: the Play as History and Anti-History," *Aevum: Rassegna di Scienze Storiche-Linguistiche e Filologiche* 3 (1991): 561–70 (which was forthcoming at the time of writing), and for a revised version as chapter 8 in *Shakespeare: Poetry, History, and Culture* (New York: Palgrave Macmillan, 2009).

9. "Thomas Norton and Thomas Sackville," in *Elizabethan and Stuart Plays*, eds. Charles Read Baskervill, et al. (New York: Henry Holt, 1934), 77. See the section on *Gorbuduc* in Geoffrey of Monmouth, *History of the Kings of Britain*, trans. Sebastian Evans, rev. Charles W. Dunn (New York: E. P. Dutton, 1958), 43–44.

10. Ernst Kantorowicz, *The King's Two Bodies: A Study in Mediaeval Political Theology* (Princeton: Princeton University Press, 1957).

11. I have examined the relation between all the dumb shows and the Chorus but, for the sake of space, I leave that for another study. To relay what such a discussion would partly entail, I will give one example. The Chorus warns in the last two lines of the first act: "A Myrrour shall become to princes all / To learne to shunne the cause of such a fall." A *de casibus* motif is never too far from the surface of *Gorbuduc*. At the end of the second act, the Chorus proclaims that youth without guidance—apparently without the advice of counselors like those in the play and of Sackville and Norton—will bring the state and all else "downe with headlong fall." Once more, the Chorus warns of pride (Phaeton was young and proud; perhaps Elizabeth was, too, at 28) and of "the climbing minde," an idea that Marlowe later explores. This peril can hardly be "represt," the Chorus adds, and when kings avoid advice and yield to "pleasing tales," or fictions and flatteries, they will learn too late the troubles of a "misguided state." Woe to the prince, the Chorus bewails, who "yeldes his mind to poysonous tales that

floweth / From flattering mouth!" This warning will be important for Richard II and his relation to Gaunt, York, and Bolingbroke on the one hand and Bushy, Greene, and Bagot on the other. See Ernst H. Kantorowicz, *The King's Two Bodies: A Study in Mediaeval Political Theology* (Princeton: Princeton University Press, 1957), 7–41.

12. In John Pickering's *Horestes* (1567), the eponymous character's threats and offers at the gate are like those Henry utters before Harfleur (ll. 810–55); see Bevington, *Tudor Drama*, 152. J. H. Walter ed., William Shakespeare, *King Henry V*, Arden ed. (1954; London: Methuen, 1977).

13. I have discussed of Gaunt and *Richard II* in various places including *Theater and World* and in *Shakespeare*. Ribner has pointed out that the end of *King Johan*—beginning "For the love of God, look to the state of England" (Farmer, ed., 197)—also foreshadows Gaunt's speech (36).

14. Thomas Preston, "A Lamentable Tragedie Mixed Full of Plesant Mirth, Containing the Life of Cambises, King of Percia . . .," in *Chief Pre-Shakespearean Dramas*, ed. Adams, 638f. For a discussion of *Cambises*, see Ribner, *History Play*, 50–56, and Bevington, *Tudor Drama*, 156–60.

15. For the text, see W. C. Hazlitt, *Shakespeare's Library*, V, 135–220, which Ribner also uses. See Ribner, *History Play*, 65–68.

16. See Ribner, *History Play*, 67.

17. Thomas Kyd, "The Spanish Tragedy," in *Elizabethan and Stuart Plays*, eds. Charles Read Baskervill et al. (New York: Henry Holt, 1934), 424.

18. See F. P. Wilson, *Marlowe and Early Shakespeare* (Oxford: Clarendon Press, 1953), 106, and Robert Ornstein, *A Kingdom for a Stage: The Achievement of Shakespeare's History Plays* (Cambridge: Harvard University Press, 1972), 2–6.

19. I argue that irony is a key to Shakespeare's histories in several places in the 1980s and early 1990s, culminating in *Theater and World* (1992).

20. Anonymous, "The Famous Victories of Henry the Fifth," in William Shakespeare, *The History of Henry IV* (Part One), ed. Maynard Mack (Signet) (New York: New American Library, 1965).

21. For the use of "brave," see especially xx:16–22, 34–39; xvi:1–14.

22. Anonymous, "The Troublesome Raigne of King John," in *Narrative and Dramatic Sources of Shakespeare*, ed. Geoffrey Bullough, vol. 4 (London: Routledge & Kegan Paul, 1962), 72f.

23. Anonymous, "The Reign of King Edward the Third," *Three Elizabethan Plays*, ed. James Winny (London: Chatto & Windus, 1959).

24. William Shakespeare, *The First Part of Henry VI*, ed. Andrew S. Cairncross (London: Methuen, 1962).

25. Anonymous, *Woodstock: A Moral History*, ed. A. P. Rossiter (London: Chatto and Windus, 1946).

26. Ernst H. Kantorowicz, *The King's Two Bodies: A Study in Medieval Political Theology* (Princeton: Princeton University Press, 1957), esp. 7–41.

27. Umberto Eco, "Language, Power, Force," *Travels in Hyperreality*, trans. William Weaver (1986; London: Pan, 1987), 239–55; see also Roland Barthes, "Inaugural Lecture," *The Barthes Reader*, ed. Susan Sontag (New York: Hill and Wang, 1982), and Michel Foucault, *Discipline and Punish*, trans. Alan Sheridan (New York: Random House, 1979), 16–17, and his *The History of Sexuality: An Introduction*, trans. Robert Hurley (New York: Pantheon, 1978), I: 92–94. Rather than rely on a pun to establish, as Barthes and others do, the writer as *auctor* and political *auctoritas*, I suggest the analogy between king and author, subjects and audience as an imaginative force and not as an irrefutable connection in the world. Like Aristotle's audience in *Poetics*, the audience sympathizes with the characters, but, like Brecht's audience, it

also experiences an alienation effect and realizes that differences exist between king and subjects, playwright and spectators. In the very language and conventions of the drama, the audience, is reminded at times that the theatre is not the world. Possibly, the audience's experience of empathy and distancing culminates in an Aristotelian catharsis. The audience, like subjects, can sometimes relate to the playwright's god-like and human attributes. If by analogy, the king has lost his right to rule and control meaning in history, perhaps the author has forfeited the sway of his intended meaning over reader and audience in the history plays. Paradoxically, however, subjects and audience seem to want to return to order, meaning and an authority even as they are caught up in a fallen world or hermeneutical uncertainty. They want to limit the authority they have given to the playwright but recognize that to take that authority back is to call into question the possibility of a stable power. In other words, by analyzing the word "king" in these plays, I am assuming, at least in part, that Shakespeare and his text have some stability and meaning even in am saying that at the same time the term is questioning the possibility of stability and meaning. Questioning the author's authority and the rights of readers—which Roland Barthes, Michel Foucault, Wolfgang Iser and others have advocated—may suggest why the fight over kingship has not died down in Renaissance and Shakespearean studies even all these years after E. M. W. Tillyard's book and Arthur Lovejoy's work on the Great Chain of Being. How free is the reader or audience and how absolute or relative is meaning are questions that are as political as they are interpretative. The critical and theoretical debate in Shakespearean studies centers on the nature of kingship and authority and is related to the authority of the playwright over his audience. The playwright is both theatrical presenter and author and so, like the king, has two bodies just as the person who receives a play is both a member of the audience and a reader. See Roland Barthes, "The Death of the Author," in *The Discontinuous Universe*, trans. Richard Howard (New York: Basic Books, 1972), 7–13; Michel Foucault, "What is an Author?" in *Language, Counter-Memory, Practice: Selected Essays and Interviews*, ed. Donald Bouchard (Ithaca, NY: Cornell University Press, 1977), 113–39; Wolfgang Iser, *The Implied Reader* (Baltimore: Johns Hopkins University Press, 1974); Umberto Eco, *The Role of the Reader* (Bloomington: Indiana University Press, 1979); Stanley Fish, *Is There a Text in this Class: The Authority of Interpretive Communities* (Cambridge, MA: Harvard University Press, 1980), esp. 1–17, 303–21; Keir Elam, *The Semiotics of Theatre and Drama* (London: Methuen, 1980), esp.87–97, 135–38, 208–10. See Arthur Lovejoy, *The Great Chain of Being: A Study of the History of An Idea* (Cambridge, MA: Harvard University Press, 1936).

28. See Marie Axton, *The Queen's Two Bodies: Drama and the Elizabethan Succession* (London: Royal Historical Society, 1977).

29. Walter Ralegh, Preface to *The History of the World*, in *Selections: From his Writings and Letters*, ed. G. E. Hadlow (Oxford: Clarendon, 1917), 42, see 40–45. For another view of fallenness and deception in Shakespeare's histories, see John Wilders, *The Lost Garden: A View of Shakespeare's English and Roman History* (London: Macmillan Press, 1978); Paul Bacquet, *Les pièces historiques de Shakespeare: La deuxième tetralogie et 'Henri VIII'*, vol. 2 (Paris: Presses Universitaires de France, 1979). This paragraph is indebted to one that appears in my "Temporality and Theatricality in Shakespeare's Lancastrian Tetralogy," *Studia Neophilologica* 63 (1991): 69–88, a longer version of which is contained in chapter 3 of my *Theater and World*. The paragraph before and after is based on two paragraphs in my "The Body Divided: Kingship in Shakespeare's Lancastrian Tetralogy," *CIEFL Bulletin* (Hyderabad) (New Series) 2, no. 2 (1990): 24–52, parts of which appear in chapter 2 and the Afterword to my *Theater and World*. Both journals granted permission to reprint, and I own the copyright to

Theater and *World*, which is out of print. My thanks to the then editors for publishing my work and for granting permission for reprinting.

30. All quotations and citations from Marlowe's plays will be from *The Complete Works of Christopher Marlowe*, ed. I. Ribner (New York: Odyssey Press, 1963). For other views of Marlowe's history, see "The Idea of History in Marlowe's Tamburlaine," *English Literary History* 20 (1953): 251–66; Stephen Greenblatt, "Marlowe and the Will to Absolute Play," in *Renaissance Self-Fashioning*, 193–221; Clifford Leech, *Christopher Marlowe: Poet for the Stage*, ed. Anne Lancashire (New York: AMS Press, 1986).

31. Ben Jonson, *Sejanus*, ed. Jonas A. Barish (New Haven: Yale University Press, 1965). See Barish's Introduction, 1–24; Ribner, *History Play*, 290–99; Matthew H. Wikander, *The Play of Truth & State: Historical Drama From Shakespeare To Brecht* (Baltimore: Johns Hopkins University Press, 1986); 50–57, 62–64; Herbert Lindenberger, *Historical Drama: The Relation of Literature to Drama* (Chicago: University of Chicago Pres, 1975), esp. 3–5, 30–32.

32. Barish, 10–18; Wikander, 52–54.

33. Wikander, 62.

34. For a perceptive and elegant discussion of the play and its use of history and Tacitus' *Annals*, see Anne Barton, *Ben Jonson, Dramatist* (Cambridge: Cambridge University Press, 1984), 92–108.

35. William Shakespeare, *King Henry VIII*, ed. R. A. Foakes (1957; London: Methuen, 1968). For an illuminating view of *Henry VIII*, see Wikander, pp. 36–49, for an interesting but almost opposite view, see Alexander Leggatt, "*Henry VIII* and the Ideal England," *Shakespeare Survey*, 38 (1985): 131–43.

36. I would like to thank Margaret Ferguson for discussing Cary with me, for sharing some of her course materials on Cary and for making me aware of the work of Tina Krontiris' on *Edward II*.

37. Not only does Herbert Lindenberger's study show the importance of Shakespeare in the shaping of the history play, but it also demonstrates the transnational and transtemporal nature of this kind of play. According to Lindenberger, the history play is far from dead. See also Wikander, *The Play of Truth & State* (1986).

Chapter 8

1. Samuel Johnson, *General Observations on the Plays of Shakespeare* (1756), quoted in James Nosworthy, ed., *Cymbeline* (1955; London: Methuen, 1966), xl. This paper was originally delivered as the University of Calgary Exchange Lecture in 1985, and thanks to my hosts there. My thanks to the editor for permission to reprint a revised version of "Alienation, Double Signs with a Difference: Conscious Knots in *Cymbeline* and *The Winter's Tale*," *CIEFL Bulletin* (New Series) 1 (1989): 58–78. Since this paper and article in their earlier forms, other relevant work has appeared. See, for instance, Maurice Hunt, *Shakespeare's Romance of the Word* (Lewisburg, PA: Bucknell University Press, 1990); Richard Hillman, *Intertextuality and Romance in Renaissance Drama: The Staging of Nostalgia* (New York: St. Martin's Press, 1992); Marco Mincoff, *Things Supernatural and Causeless: Shakespearean Romance.* (Newark: University of Delaware Press, 1992); T. G. Bishop, *Shakespeare and the Theatre of Wonder* (Cambridge: Cambridge University Press, 1996); Simon Palfrey, *Late Shakespeare: A New World of Words* (Oxford: Clarendon Press, 1997); Walter S. H. Lim, *The Arts of Empire: The Poetics of Colonialism from Ralegh to Milton* (Newark: University of Delaware Press, 1998), esp. 18–23; Joan Pong Linton, *The Romance of the New World: Gender and the Literary Formations of English Colonialism* (Cambridge: Cambridge University Press, 1998); Thomas Rist, *Shakespeare's Romances*

and the Politics of Counter-Reformation (Lewiston, NY: Mellen, 1999); Helen Hackett, *Women and Romance Fiction in the English Renaissance* (Cambridge: Cambridge University Press, 2000); Michael D. Friedman, *"The world must be peopled": Shakespeare's Comedies of Forgiveness* (Madison, NJ: Fairleigh Dickinson University Press, 2002); Lori H. Newcomb, *Reading Popular Romance in Early Modern England* (New York: Columbia University Press, 2002); Alex Davis, *Chivalry and Romance in the English Renaissance* (Cambridge: Brewer, 2003); Helen Cooper, *The English Romance in Time: Transforming Motifs from Geoffrey of Monmouth to the Death of Shakespeare* (Oxford: Oxford University Press, 2004); Christopher J. Cobb, *The Staging of Romance in Later Shakespeare: Text and Theatrical Technique* (Newark: University of Delaware Press, 2007); Benedict S. Robinson, *Islam and Early Modern English Literature: The Politics of Romance from Spenser to Milton* (New York and Basingstoke, UK: Palgrave Macmillan, 2007).

2. Edwin Wilson, ed., *Shaw on Shakespeare: An Anthology of Bernard Shaw's Writings or Plays and Production of Shakespeare* (New York: E. P. Dutton, 1961), 54, 56. Subsequent references to this volume will be indicated under "Shaw."

3. Ibid., 62.

4. Ibid., 64.

5. Ibid., 67. See John Sturrock, ed., *Structuralism and Since: From Levi Strauss to Derrida* (Oxford University Press, 1979), 71; Roland Barthes, *A Lover's Discourse: Fragments*, trans. Richard Howard (New York: Hill and Wang, 1979), *passim*; Terry Eagleton, *Literary Theory: An Introduction* (Oxford: Basil Blackwell, 1983), 137.

6. Judiana Lawrence, "Natural Bonds and Artistic Coherence in the Ending of *Cymbeline*," *Shakespeare Quarterly* 35 (1984): 440–60.

7. J. H. P. Pafford, ed., *The Winter's Tale* (London: Methuen, 1963), xxxviii. All citations and quotations from *Cymbeline* and *The Winter's Tale* will be from the Arden editions cited above. References to other Shakespearean plays will be from William Shakespeare, *The Complete Works*, ed. Alfred Harbage (1969; New York: Viking, 1977).

8. Baldwin Maxwell, "Introduction," *The Winter's Tale* in *Pelican Shakespeare*, 1335; see also 1334.

9. Edward Dowden, *Shakespeare* (1877), 60; Barrett Wendell, *William Shakespeare* (1894); Lytton Strachey, "Shakespeare's Final Period," *Independent Review* 3 (August, 1904): 405–18; Arthur Quiller-Couch, *Shakespeare's Workmanship* (1918) and *Studies in Literature*, 3rd series (1929), 114–15; J. M. Nosworthy, *Cymbeline*, esp. xlviii–lxii. Cited in J. H. P. Pafford, "Introduction," xxxix–xl.

10. Many books and articles have attempted to define *Cymbeline* and *The Winter's Tale*. Here, in chronological order, is a list of some of these works: Richard C. Tobias and P. G. Zolbrod, eds., *Shakespeare's Late Plays: Essays in Honor of Charles Crow* (Athens: Ohio Univ. Press, 1974), esp. 44–56 and 131–42; Northrop Frye, *The Secular Scripture: A Study of the Structure of Romance* (Cambridge, MA: Harvard University Press, 1976), 51, 107–8, 122, and 155; Barbara A. Mowat, *The Dramaturgy of Shakespeare's Romances* (Athens: University of Georgia Press, 1976), *passim*; Richard Proudfoot, "Verbal Reminiscence and the Two-Part Structure of 'The Winter's Tale,'" *Shakespeare Survey* 29 (1976): 67–78; Carol M. Kay and H. E. Jacobs, eds., *Shakespeare's Romances Reconsidered* (Lincoln: University of Nebraska Press, 1978), esp. 1–11, 31–39, 91–104, and 134–49; Charles Frey, *Shakespeare's Vast Romance: A Study of 'The Winter's Tale'* (Columbia: University of Missouri Press, 1980), 57–78, 128–38, and 143–62; Robert W. Uphaus, *Beyond Tragedy: Structure & Experience in Shakespeare's Romances* (Lexington: University of Kentucky Press, 1981), esp. 49–92; for other more recent secondary sources, see some of the references, especially note 1.

11. The romances have been taken seriously enough that *Shakespeare Survey* has devoted most of volume 11 (1958) and volume 29 (1976) to these plays; the former volume includes Philip Edwards, "Shakespeare's Romances: 1900–1957," 1–19, the latter, F. David Hoeniger, "Shakespeare's Romances since 1958: A Retrospect," I–II. Mowat (1976) has briefly discussed Brechtian elements in the romances but not systematically.

12. Jacques Derrida, *Positions*, trans. Alan Bass (Chicago: University of Chicago Press, 1981), *passim*; Keir Elam, *The Semiotics of Theatre and Drama* (London: Methuen, 1980), 19–20; Jonathan Culler, "Jacques Derrida," in Sturrock, 165, 169–70; John Sturrock, "Roland Barthes," in Sturrock, 61.

13. Eagleton, *Literary Theory*, 136–37; Elam, *The Semiotics of Theatre*, 16–20; Bertolt Brecht, "The Street Scene: A Basic Model for an Epic Theatre," in *Brecht on Theatre: The Development of an Aesthetic*, trans. John Willett (London: Methuen, 1964, rpt. 1965), 121, 125. (Subsequent references to the last volume will be made under "Brecht.")

14. Brecht, 91–97, 136, 157.

15. Ibid., 97.

16. Ibid., 157; see also 101–02.

17. Ibid., 143.

18. Ibid., 145.

19. Ibid, 194, see also 193.

20. Ibid., 194–96.

21. John Willett notes: "if the 'Messingkauf' was derived from Galileo, the new work seems to relate both formally and stylistically to the *Novum Organum* of Francis Bacon, the other great Renaissance scientist whose name occurs a number of times in Brecht's writings. (On this point, see Dr. Reinhold Grimm's essay in the symposium *Das Argernis Brecht*, Basilius Presse, Basle 1961, where he suggests that Bacon's book attracted Brecht because it was directed against the *Organum* of Aristotle, Aristotle being of course not only the implied enemy of the non-Aristotelian drama but also the ideological villain of Galileo.)" Note in Brecht, 205.

22. Roland Barthes, "The Tasks of Brechtian Criticism," 74–75, see also 71–73, 76; "Mother Courage Blind" (1955), 33–36; 'The Brechtian Revolution' (1955), 37–39; all in Roland Barthes, *Critical Essays*, trans. Richard Howard (Evanston, IL: Northwestern University Press, 1972).

23. Roger Warren, "Virtuosity and Complexity in 'Cymbeline,'" *Shakespeare Survey* 29 (1976), 48; Gareth Lloyd Evans in *The Guardian*, July 18, 1962, cited in Warren, 48.

24. Lawrence, "Natural Bonds and Artistic Coherence," 441; Aristotle, "On the Art of Poetry," in *Classical Literary Criticism*, trans. T. S. Dorsch (Harmondsworth, UK: Penguin, 1965), 53; cited in Lawrence, 41.

25. Lawrence, "Natural Bonds and Artistic Coherence," 442–43, 457.

26. Pafford, xxxviii; E.C. Pettet, *Shakespeare and the Romance Tradition* (1949), 174ff, cited in Nosworthy, xlvii. Nosworthy also notes the time schemes in the romances.

27. See my unpublished dissertation, "Irony in Shakespeare's 'Second Tetralogy'" (University of Toronto, 1983), *passim*, for a discussion of the rubbing together of genres in *Richard II, 1* and *2 Henry IV*, and *Henry V.*

28. See Kenneth Muir, "Theophanies in the Last Plays," in Tobias, 32–44; Richard Paul Knowles, "'The More Delay'd, Delighted:' Theophanies in the Last Plays," *Shakespeare Studies* 15 (1982): 269–81.

29. For another view of comic endings, see Stanley Wells, "Happy Endings in Shakespeare," *Shakespeare-Jahrbuch* (Heidelberg, 1966), 103–23

30. See Kristian Smidt, *Unconformities in Shakespeare's History Plays* (London: Macmillan, 1982), 1, 12–15.

31. Nevill Coghill, "Six Points of Stage-Craft in *The Winter's Tale,*" *Shakespeare Survey* 11 (1958), 31; S. L. Bethell, *The Winter's Tale, A Study* (1946), 47, quoted in Coghill, 31; Arthur Quiller-Couch and John Dover Wilson, *The Winter's Tale* (1931; Cambridge 1931, 1950), xvi, cited in Coghill, 31.

32. William Matchett, "Dramatic Techniques in "The Winter's Tale,'" *Shakespeare Survey* 22 (1969) 99; see also 93.

33. Andrew Gurr, "The Bear, the Statue and Hysteria in *The Winter's Tale,*" *Shakespeare Quarterly* 34 (1983): 420, 422–23. See also H. Carrington Lancaster, "Hermione's Statue," *Studies in Philology* 29 (1932): 233–38; Adrien Bonjour, "The Final Scene of *The Winter's Tale,*" *English Studies* 33 (Amsterdam: 1952): 193–208; Kenneth Muir, "The Conclusion of *The Winter's Tale,*" in *The Morality of Art: Essays presented to G. Wilson Knight by His Colleagues and Friends* (London: Routledge, 1969); Dennis Biggins, "'Exit Pursued by a Beare': A Problem in *The Winter's Tale,*" *Shakespeare Quarterly* 13 (1962): 3–13; Louise George Clubb, "The Tragicomic Bear," *Comparative Literature Studies* 9 (1972): 17–30.

34. Pafford, 69n.

35. Dolora Cunningham, "Wonder and Love in the Romantic Comedies," *Shakespeare Quarterly* 35 (1984): 262–63, 266.

Conclusion

1. Edmund Gosse, "Introduction," Algernon Charles Swinburne, *Contemporaries of Shakespeare*, ed. Edmund Gosse and Thomas James Wise (London: William Heinemann, 1919), vii–xii. The books and manuscripts used in this conclusion are all originals in Houghton Library, Harvard.

2. Algernon Charles Swinburne, *Contemporaries of Shakespeare*, ed. Edmund Gosse and Thomas James Wise (London: William Heinemann, 1919), 3.

3. Ibid., 3.

4. Ibid., 4.

5. John Dennis, *An Essay On The Genius and Writings of Shakespear: With Some Letters of Criticism to the Spectator* (London: Printed for Bernard Lintott, 1712), 3–4.

6. Ibid., 2.

7. Lewis Theobald, *Shakespeare reſtored: Or, A Specimen Of The Many Errors As Well Committed, as Unamended, by Mr. Pope In his Late Edition of the Poet* (London: Printed for R. Francklin [etc.], 1726), i.

8. John Upton, *Critical Observations on Shakespeare* (London: Printed for G. Hawkins, 1746), 1.

9. Ibid., 11.

10. Elizabeth Montagu, *An Essay on the Writings and genius of Shakespear, Compared with the Greek and French Dramatic Poets, with Some Remarks upon the Misrepresentations of Monſ. de Voltaire* (London: Printed for J. Dodsley [etc.], 1749), 1–21, esp. 20 for the quotation.

11. Joseph Baretti, *Discours sur Shakespeare et sur Monsieur de Voltaire par Joseph Baretti* (London: Chez J. Nourse et Paris chez Durand neveu, 1777), 1–20.

12. Samuel Johnson, *Mr. Johnson's Preface To his Edition of Shakeſpear's Plays* (London: J. and R. Tonson [etc.], 1765), viii, see vi.

13. Richard Farmer, *An Essay on the Learning of Shakespeare: Addressed to Joseph Craddock, Eſq; The Third Edition* (London: T. Longman, 1789), 2–3.

14. Edmund Malone, *Original Letters from Edmund Malone, the Editor of Shakespeare, John Jordan, the Poet, Now Printed from the Autograph Manuscripts Preserved at Stratford-upon-Avon*, ed. J. O. Halliwell (London: Thomas Richards, 1864), 7.

15. Samuel Taylor Coleridge, *The Literary Remains of Samuel Taylor Coleridge*, ed. Henry Nelson Coleridge, 4 vols. (London: William Pickering, 1836–39), vol. I, 61.

16. Ibid., vol. I, 99.

17. Ibid., vol. II, 7–267 (drama and Shakespeare); vol. II, 268–88 (Jonson), vol. II, 289–322 (Beaumont and Fletcher).

18. Ibid., vol. II, 53.

19. Henry James' copy in the Houghton Library of Sidney Lee, *A Life of William Shakespeare*, 2nd ed. (London: Smith, Elder, & Co., 1898), vi.

20. Robert M. Smith, "The Formation of Shakespeare Libraries in America," *The Shakespeare Association Bulletin* 4 (1929), 66.

21. R. W. Emerson, *Representative Men: Seven Lectures* (Boston: Philips, Sampson and Company, 1850), 194.

22. Justin Winsor, "*Shakspeare=Firstlings in Germany*," *Shakespeare on the continent: manuscript, 1857*, folder 1, page 1, Houghton fMS Am 2582. On Windsor's life (1831–1897), *Dictionary of American Biography*, ed. Dumas Malone (New York: Charles Scribner's Sons, 1936), see 403–4. For references to his report for the college library (1894), introduction of a classification system for the library and his death as librarian at Harvard College, see William Bentinck-Smith, *Building a Great Library: The Coolidge Years at Harvard* (Cambridge, MA: Harvard University Library, 1976), 10, 12, 38. Winsor was interested in Shakespeare's library and other things Shakespearean, such as early editions of Shakespeare's poems; see Justin Winsor, "Notes on Shakespeare; manuscript [not after 1874], folder 1, Houghton fMS Am 2583 c. 1 of 2.

23. Joseph Howe, *Shakespeare* (Halifax, NS: Citizen Printing and Publishing Office, 1864), 1–25, esp. 17.

24. Jules Claretie, *Shakspere and Molière* (London: Office of Publication, 1899), 3.

Index

CPSIA information can be obtained at www.ICGtesting.com
Printed in the USA
LVOW102126301012

305169LV00006B/17/P